Capital Flight and Capital Controls in Developing Countries

To My Graduate Students:
Past, Present And Future

Capital Flight and Capital Controls in Developing Countries

Edited by

Gerald A. Epstein

Professor of Economics and Co-Director of the Political Economy Research Institute (PERI), University of Massachusetts, Amherst, USA.

Edward Elgar
Cheltenham, UK • Northampton, MA, USA

Published by
Edward Elgar Publishing Limited
Glensanda House
Montpellier Parade
Cheltenham
Glos GL50 1UA
UK

Edward Elgar Publishing, Inc.
136 West Street
Suite 202
Northampton
Massachusetts 01060
USA

A catalogue record for this book
is available from the British Library

ISBN 1 84376 931 X (Cased)
Printed and bound in Great Britain by MPG Books Ltd, Bodmin, Cornwall

Contents

PART THREE   POLICY ISSUES

Figures

Tables

Contributors

Abdullah Almounsor works for the Research Department at the Saudi Arabia Monetary Agency (SAMA) and is currently a graduate student in Economics at the University of Massachusetts, Amherst.

Edsel L. Beja, Jr. is a graduate student in Economics at the University of Massachusetts, Amherst.

Burak Bener is a graduate student in Economics at the University of Massachusetts, Amherst.

James Boyce is Professor of Economics and Director of the Program on Development, Peace Building and the Environment, Political Economy Research Institute (PERI), University of Massachusetts, Amherst.

Mathieu Dufour is a graduate student in Economics at the University of Massachusetts, Amherst.

Anil Duman is a graduate student in Economics at the University of Massachusetts, Amherst.

Gerald Epstein is Professor of Economics and Co-Director, Political Economy Research Institute (PERI), University of Massachusetts, Amherst.

Hakki C. Erkin is a graduate student in Economics at the University of Massachusetts, Amherst.

Deger Eryar is a graduate student in Economics at the University of Massachusetts, Amherst.

Kade Finnoff is a graduate student in Economics at the University of Massachusetts, Amherst.

Ilene Grabel is Associate Professor of International Finance, Graduate School of International Studies, University of Denver.

Eric Helleiner is Professor of Political Science, Trent University.

Arjun Jayadev is a graduate student in Economics at the University of Massachusetts, Amherst.

Sundaram Kwame Jomo is Professor in the Applied Economics Department, Faculty of Economics and Administration, University of Malaya.

Pokpong Junvith is a graduate student in Economics at the University of Massachusetts, Amherst.

Kang-kook Lee is Associate Professor of Economics at Ritsumeikan University in Japan.

Chunxiang Li is a graduate student in Resource Economics at the University of Massachusetts, Amherst.

Seeraj Mohammed is a graduate student in Economics at the University of Massachusetts, Amherst.

Léonce Ndikumana is Associate Professor of Economics, University of Massachusetts, Amherst.

Jared Ragusett is a graduate student in Economics at the University of Massachusetts, Amherst.

Fatma Gül Unal is a graduate student in Economics at the University of Massachusetts, Amherst.

Andong Zhu is a graduate student in Economics at the University of Massachusetts, Amherst.

Preface and Acknowledgments

This book started off as an in-class project in my PhD level graduate course in International Finance at the University of Massachusetts, Amherst. For a long time I had been mulling over the idea of doing a book project with my students, but had not identified the right topic to make it work. Then I had a serendipitous conversation with my good friend and colleague Jim Boyce, who, for a number of years, had pioneered research on capital flight from developing countries and who was currently doing research on capital flight in sub-Saharan Africa with our colleague Leonce Ndikumana. In speaking to Jim I realized that capital flight would be a great topic for an in-class, group project, and even possibly a book.

I assigned the students the task of forming groups, choosing a country and researching capital flight using the 'Boyce–Ndikumana' method as we called it. Léonce was very generous with his time, instructing the students in the arcane ways of capital flight estimation. Edsel Beja, Jr., one of the students and contributors to this book, who, coincidentally, is writing his dissertation on capital flight, became everyone's 'junior' teacher on the subject. Without their efforts, this book could never have been completed.

More generally, though, this book would never have been written except for the hard work, persistence, and group spirit of the graduate students themselves. Each paper went through more drafts than any of us can now count; at each stage, students helped each other decipher the IMF statistics, analyze the data and interpret the meaning of capital flight. It has been an inspiring experience for me to see the hard work, dedication and professional work accomplished by these economists.

I also thank the other authors who contributed to this book, including several graduate students who were not part of the original group, and other colleagues who were willing to contribute their work to this collection.

Alan Sturmer at Edward Elgar Publishing has been a fabulous editor: patient, encouraging and timely, always on top of things. Sue Holmberg and Lynda Pickbourn have done a marvelous job with editorial assistance, including turning the manuscript into camera-ready copy.

Finally, I thank the Political Economy Research Institute (PERI) for crucial financial assistance, my friend and co-director, Robert Pollin, for his support and PERI's Administrative Manager, Judy Fogg, without whose assistance this book could not have been completed.

PART ONE

Setting the Stage

1. Capital Flight and Capital Controls in Developing Countries: an Introduction

Gerald Epstein

WHY CAPITAL FLIGHT?

This book concerns capital flight in developing countries: How big is it? What causes it? How are we to interpret it? What are its effects? What can be done about it? The core of the book consists of seven case studies of capital flight from developing countries (Brazil, Chile, China, South Africa, Thailand, Turkey and a set of Middle Eastern and North African countries) connected by a common methodology used to estimate capital flight. These case studies are sandwiched between several chapters, including one debunking the myth that capital account liberalization is necessarily good for economic growth and income distribution, and several chapters at the end that offer some solutions to the problem of capital flight that affects so much of the developing world. This chapter briefly introduces the book.

First, however, is the matter of definition. When people hear the term 'capital flight' they think of money running away from one country to a money 'haven' abroad, in the process doing harm to the home economy and society. People probably have the idea that money runs away for any of a number of reasons: to avoid taxation; to avoid confiscation; in search of better treatment, or of higher returns somewhere else. In any event, people have a sense that capital flight is in someway illicit, in someway bad for the home country, unless, of course, capital is fleeing unfair discrimination, as in the case of the Nazi persecution. These commonsense ideas are also roughly what we mean by capital flight. It turns out, however, that it is quite difficult to transform this commonsense meaning into rigorous, economic definitions, data and analysis. (See Beja, Chapter 3, for an extensive discussion of this issue.)

There will be much discussion in what follows about the proper definition of capital flight, and, indeed, whether the term can be usefully defined at all. For now, though, we will define capital flight this way:[1] capital flight is the transfer of assets abroad in order to reduce loss of principal, loss of return, or loss of control over one's financial wealth due to government-sanctioned activities. Fears of wealth confiscation, increases in taxes on wealth or the imposition of regulations that limit the prerogatives of wealth holders are examples of the types of government activities we have in mind. Hence, capital flight consists of international capital flows that are trying to escape government controls or the consequences of government policies. From this perspective one can immediately see an important theme running throughout this book: capital flight is an inherently political phenomenon involving the role of the government and the prerogatives of those – usually the wealthy – with access to foreign exchange. As a result, the issue of capital flight necessarily involves the political economy of class power, conflict and the state.

This definition, however, immediately raises a fundamental problem: since the definition involves the motives for capital outflows, it is inherently difficult, if not impossible, to measure accurately, given the obvious difficulty economists have in identifying actors' reasons for engaging in certain activities. For that reason, we have to use a proxy for capital flight, an imperfect measure that captures as much as possible the phenomenon we are trying to understand. Indeed, one of the unique contributions of this book, described in more detail below, is that the case studies develop a common measure of capital flight across a number of countries, facilitating comparisons across time and space.

The measure we will use – the residual measure – tries to calculate unrecorded net outflows of capital from developing countries.[2] The use of unrecorded flows captures the notion that, by our definition, capital flight involves the attempt by wealth holders to avoid government policies. Apart from purely technical or logistical issues of data collection, if the wealth holders were not trying to avoid government policies, then presumably they would not engage in capital flows that would be unrecorded. Of course, there might also be cases where wealth holders are motivated by the desire to avoid the effects of government-sanctioned policies and send funds through recorded channels. So, in some cases, capital flight will consist of recorded and unrecorded outflows. We, however, calculate capital flight using only unrecorded outflows. Therefore, it is important to understand that our measure, based on unrecorded flows, is a minimum estimate of capital flight. It is a floor on the likely degree of capital flight occurring in the episodes we study.

In some cases, the difference between our minimum estimates and the likely actual amount of capital flight might be substantial. For example, if one is evaluating an episode in which capital flees abroad because the central bank is trying to lower interest rates to generate more employment, and there are no or very laxly-enforced capital controls, then virtually all net capital outflows, measured or not, constitute capital flight by our conception. Where capital controls are tight, then the unmeasured flows will capture the bulk of the capital flight. In short, in some cases, all capital outflows are capital flight. In others, unrecorded outflows are the best measure.

This suggests that the correct measure of capital flight is likely to vary by episode and raises the question as to whether it is really meaningful to adopt one approach to measuring capital flight for a broad range of countries as we have done here. Of course, there are trade-offs associated with any decision about uniformity in order to enable comparisons across countries, versus idiosyncratic measurement, which makes it difficult to make comparisons but delivers more precise measures for each country. We have chosen the uniformity approach in this book under the hypothesis that much can be learned from these comparisons. (See also Schneider 2003.)

Why Study Capital Flight?

The question remains, why should we study capital flight? We argue in this book that capital flight is important because it can have significant social costs; it is also a barometer of the sovereignty of government policy versus that of class privilege and it relates to the impacts of important economic policies such as financial liberalization. We address all these issues, in different ways and to different degrees, in the chapters that follow.

Social Costs

Capital flight has been both sizeable and costly in many developing countries in recent decades. The estimates in our case studies suggest that capital flight has ranged from less than 1 percent of GDP in Iran to over 60 percent GDP in Kuwait, for example. Capital flight can be costly where capital or foreign exchange is scarce, as is often the case in developing countries. The loss of scarce capital and foreign exchange potentially leads to a loss of investment in countries that are in great need of more infrastructure, plant and equipment, and human capital. Since capital is likely to be more scarce in developing countries than in developed ones, social returns to investment in many developing countries are likely to be higher at home than abroad.

In poor countries, the marginal social benefits of investment are likely to be considerably higher than the private benefits, at least in those cases where the economy functions reasonably well. On the other hand, if wealth holders take capital abroad, then presumably they have calculated that the private returns are higher abroad. This divergence between social and private returns will be especially significant where capital flight accompanies increases in foreign borrowing. In that case the society is incurring foreign debt not to increase domestic investment which could create jobs and raise productivity at home, but, rather, to enrich people abroad. As Boyce and Ndikumana show (see Chapter 13) in these cases, and often at the behest of the IMF, paying foreign debt service will likely involve cuts in social spending or increases in taxes on the poor to make up for the scarce foreign exchange that is fleeing through capital flight. This can have serious social costs in terms of forgone consumption, and social investment by those who are most needy or most productive.

As this last example suggests, the efficiency costs of capital flight are likely to be accompanied by other costs. As our definition of capital flight suggests, capital flight is often fleeing perceived increases in taxation, or increased control over private wealth. Thus, capital flight is likely to have negative impacts on equality, with wealthy citizens escaping higher taxation, or lower after tax returns at home, while poorer citizens face higher taxation and cuts in social services. In addition, if capital flight contributes to financial crises, it can impose further costs in the form of unemployment and slower economic growth. Like the costs of capital flight itself, these crises often impose disproportionately high costs on the poorer members of society. With capital flight induced financial crises, then, capital flight imposes a double whammy on the poor (Jayadev and Lee, Chapter 2). Moreover, among the poor, it is often the most vulnerable – often women and children – who bear the greatest burden.

'Capital Strike' and the Prerogatives of Wealth

These economic costs of capital flight provide sufficient reason to study the subject. Still, they do not exhaust the rationale for this book. For as I said earlier, capital flight is an inherently political phenomenon replete with issues related to the state, class and conflict. This becomes clearest when one considers that capital flight can be a powerful political weapon against government policies that threaten the wealth or the prerogatives of the rich. In this role, capital flight has sometimes been called 'capital strike' evoking the idea that capital as a class goes on strike against undesired taxation or regulatory policies (Crotty 1993; Crotty and Epstein 1996). In this regard, capital flight raises large and important issues of political economy. When does the sovereignty of capital undermine the sovereignty of the state? To what extent has financial 'globalization' undermined the ability of governments to implement economic policies that wealth holders oppose? What are the political, economic and distributional implications of this exertion of 'one dollar, one vote' as opposed to 'one citizen, one vote'?

From this perspective, capital flight and policies to reduce them raise profound political questions. For libertarians, there can be no such thing as capital flight: private control of capital, as private property, is an inalienable right, and any movement of it, no matter what the purpose, is legitimate. For most others, however, the right of states to regulate private property for the common good is clear, and the real debate concerns matters of degree and circumstance. Within this latter framework, the differences, nonetheless, remain significant. What some may see as capital flight undermining the sovereignty of governments to tax for legitimate and desirable social purposes, others may see as wealth holders teaching the government a useful lesson about the limits of government policy (see Lessard and Williamson 1987).

This issue arises in ways that are invisible to many: what if the government simply wants to lower interest rates to achieve full employment and wealth holders flee? Is that capital flight or a harmless portfolio decision? What impact will such 'capital movements' have on the ability of governments to make economic policy? From our perspective, such movements of capital do represent 'capital flight'. But our capital flight numbers provide a very conservative estimate of such movements: We will only identify these capital flows as capital flight if they are 'unrecorded'. Hence, apart from technical recording issues, we will only record that capital taken abroad in a hidden form, perhaps because it is illegal, or perhaps because it goes against social norms, or perhaps because it might be vulnerable to economic or political threat. Remember that our estimates provide minimum estimates of capital flight and might not pick up capital flight motivated by lower interest rates, except in the case where capital controls or other regulations would otherwise limit it.

Policy Impacts of Financial Liberalization

Interest in capital flight waxes and wanes. It was an important issue in the inter-war period (Kindleberger 1987) and, after a period of lying relatively dormant, then leaped to the fore with the traumatic 'Third World Debt Crisis' of the early 1980s. Dozens of articles and several books were published at that time, many of which demonstrated that in a number of countries, including Venezuela and Brazil, capital flight represented high proportions of increases in foreign borrowing (Lessard and Williamson 1987).

In the 1990s interest waned again, partly because it appeared that capital returned to several countries in which flight had previously been substantial. This return prompted a number of economists to conjecture that financial liberalization, and neo-liberal policies more generally, would lead to a repatriation of capital flight, and reduce further flight. Indeed, the notion that governments and policies more favorable toward large wealth holders would reduce capital flight is plausible. What this view missed, however, was the link between financial liberalization, financial crisis and capital flight. The Mexican, Russian and Asian Financial crises of the mid- and late 1990s, accompanied as they were by large amounts of capital flight, returned the phenomenon to the radar screens of economists and policy makers. Likewise, in this book, a matter of continuing interest will be precisely this nexus: what is the relationship between financial liberalization, financial crises and capital flight? In view of the dominant neo-liberal advocacy of financial liberalization, this set of questions becomes a further reason to study capital flight.

THE BOOK

The book is divided into three sections. Part 1 sets the stage for the case studies with a chapter on the impacts of capital account liberalization on income distribution and growth, by Kang-Kook Lee and Arjun Jayadev; the other chapter, by Edsel Beja, Jr., gives an in-depth overview of various measures and definitions of capital flight and a detailed description of the methodology used in the case studies of this book. Part 3 of the book, with chapters by James Boyce and Léonce Ndikumana, Eric Helleiner and Gerald Epstein, Ilene Grabel and Sundaram Kwame Jomo present possible remedies for the capital flight problem including debt forgiveness in the face of capital flight, capital controls and international cooperation to identify and repatriate capital flight.

If Part 1 sets the context, and Part 3 elaborates on solutions to the problems identified, Part 2 contains the book's core: seven case studies on capital flight from developing countries. Using a common definition and the 'residual method' of capital flight calculation, these chapters measure and discuss capital flight from Brazil, Chile, China, South Africa, Thailand, Turkey and the Middle East. Overall, these countries represent a broad range of cases geographically and in terms of experiences. While they are all semi-industrialized countries, these cases represent five continents and a range of economic types, from fairly free market economies like Chile, to strongly state-guided countries like China.

Setting the Stage

This book concerns capital flight in the 1980s and 1990s, the period of the rise of neo-liberalism. Among its key tenets is the liberalization of financial markets, including markets for international capital. This obviously sets a particular stage for the dynamics of capital flows and capital flight. In Chapter 2, Kang-kook Lee and Arjun Jayadev present a survey and new evidence on two key issues related to capital account liberalization: the impact of capital account liberalization on economic growth and the impact on income distribution, in particular, the share of income going to labor. Using various cross-country econometric models and indices of financial openness (including one newly developed by them), they find little evidence that capital account liberalization has positive effects on growth. Capital account openness provides no significant stimulus to growth even in the presence of typically proposed preconditions. By contrast, there is a persistent negative correlation between capital account liberalization and labor's share of national income, providing some support for the notion that labor's bargaining power is reduced when capital is more mobile.

Chapter 3 in this section, 'Capital Flight: Meanings and Measures' by Edsel L. Beja, Jr, is a comprehensive discussion and detailed presentation of the standard approaches to defining and measuring capital flight. This chapter not only presents important background information on the methods used by the authors of this book's case studies, but it will also be of great help to future researchers studying capital flight.

Case Studies: A Variety of Questions and Approaches

Although all the authors use the same methodology in deriving their quantitative estimates of capital flight, they ask a variety of questions about their estimates. Some of the chapters focus primarily on the determinants of capital flight while other chapters look at the impacts of financial liberalization. Others focus on political uncertainty and income distribution. Some chapters also investigate the costs of capital flight in terms of forgone output and investment. One author uses a comparative approach to understanding the deep structural determinants of capital flight. Yet another focuses primarily on the lessons that capital flight have to teach about class and political dynamics. Hence, one of the great strengths of this book is the common approach to measuring capital flight, combined with a richness of substantive discussions about the phenomenon.

The Cases

South Africa
Seeraj Mohammed and Kade Finnoff discover that capital flight in South Africa was relatively high, reaching, on average, almost 7 percent of South Africa's GDP. Paradoxically, there seemed to be more capital flight during the post-apartheid period, despite attempts by the government to adopt capital-friendly policies. The authors explain that distrust of government remains significant, and will likely stay so as long as inequality and poverty remain at high levels. Loosening of capital controls by the government has given wealth holders more opportunities for flight. The authors also suggest that the high levels of capital flight there may involve racial prejudice as well. Political and economic uncertainties are only part of the story. Mohammed and Finnoff argue that there are also structural factors involved: South Africa's mineral-based economy leads to highly concentrated wealth; this high concentration of wealth in a highly porous financial setting makes moving money offshore very easy.

Turkey
In their study of capital flight from Turkey, Anil Duman, Hakki C. Erkin and Fatma Gül Unal find that capital flight from 1971 to 2000 was comparatively low as a percentage of GDP (0.32 percent) but oscillated rather strongly (between 3 percent and 6 percent). The focus of their chapter is to identify the determinants of Turkish capital flight and explain the oscillations. The period between 1971 and 2000 was economically momentous for Turkey, with rather large changes in economic policy taking place during this period. Unlike a number of authors who have focused on net capital flight as being the most important measure of economic cost, Duman, Erkin and Gul Unal find that in the Turkish case it was the movements in and out that were most costly: they destabilized the Turkish economy and contributed to financial crises. They also find that, contrary to much mainstream writing, capital flight continued despite financial liberalization, a trend that was also observed in South Africa.

Thailand
Edsel L. Beja, Jr., Pokpong Junvith, and Jared Ragusett explore capital flight in Thailand from 1980 to 2000. They calculate that capital flight was very high in Thailand throughout most of the 20-year period, often over 10 to 15 percent of GDP in the 1990s. Indeed, they calculate that capital flight from Thailand has been so substantial that from 1985 on, Thailand has actually been a net creditor: there are more Thai-owned assets (capital flight) held abroad than Thai residents have borrowed from abroad. Of course, since this capital flight is hidden, this astonishing fact is not well known.

The authors study several other issues. They find that there is a link between capital inflows and capital flight: the more inflows there are, the greater the level of capital flight. They also find that financial liberalization and crises contribute to capital flight. In a new finding, they also discover that financial liberalization leads to greater volatility of capital flight. So, as in the Turkish study, it is not just the level of capital flight that is important, but also its volatility. Finally, the authors break new ground in this book by estimating the cost of capital flight in terms of forgone investment in the Thai economy: they find that the cost is large.

Chile
In 'A Class Analysis of Capital Flight from Chile, 1971–2001' Burak Bener and Mathieu Dufour focus on the political and power issues associated with capital flight, using capital flight as a lens through which to view the evolution of the political economy of Chile. As such they are not as interested in discovering the determinants of capital flight or in assessing the costs, as in the previously discussed chapters, but, instead, use capital flight as a window into the dynamics of class power in Chile during this

tumultuous period. They argue that since capital flight, at its core, is an attempt to evade social control over one's assets, they believe the conflict among different claimants on these assets, which is one aspect of the struggle for dominance among classes, to be an interesting focus for their analysis. In describing the history of Chile's political economy through the lens of capital flight, they identify four key factors that can help to explain capital flight from Chile: the extent of capital inflows, the state of domestic investment opportunities, capital controls and political risk. Using these factors, Bener and Dufour explain the ups and downs of capital flight from Chile. They find that economic crises and political instability contributed to a high level of capital flight, whereas the capitalist class preferred to stay in Chile as long as it felt secure and had good relations with the government.

Brazil
Deger Eryar's chapter on Brazil is important because Brazil was very highly in debt during the period under analysis, 1980 to 2001. Given its high foreign indebtedness, Brazil's capital flight clearly has costs in terms of lost foreign exchange needed to service debt. Eryar organized his analysis around different 'accumulation strategies' followed by the Brazilian authorities at various times. Many changes in strategy contributed to instability, which, Eryar argues, contributed to capital flight. Neo-liberal strategies of financial liberalization fared no better than other strategies. Eryar concludes by arguing that the only solution to capital fight is to generate more rapid economic development in Brazil. Like some of the other authors, he calls for the use of capital controls.

Middle East and North Africa
In this chapter, Abdullah Almounsor presents the first estimates of capital flight in Middle Eastern and North African countries. The analysis employs a development comparative approach to the countries of the region. In particular, it relates capital flight of each country to the model of development pursued. Resource-based industrialization states register the largest amount of capital flight, amounting to more than 273 billion of 1995 USD with accumulated interest earning capital flight of more than 935 billion of current USD. On the other hand, state-led development economies and balanced economies of the Middle East and North African (MENA) region show large negative capital flight of 102 and 112 billion 1995 USD, respectively. Capital flight under the first model is assisted by natural resource exporting rents, the capitalist orientation of most economies of the model and the monarchial character of most of their political systems. In contrast, capital flight under the last two models is driven by large negative trade misinvoicing and assisted by the inward-looking strategies of the two models, one-party or militarily controlled governments as well as the signifi-

cant capital controls characterizing the two models.

China

There have been numerous studies of China's capital flight, and Chunxiang Li, Andong Zhu, and Gerald Epstein present another one in this book. They find a similar pattern in capital flight found by other research, and, like others, find that it is extremely high, roughly 10 percent of GDP, and rather substantial relative to foreign direct investment (FDI). They discuss the interesting paradox that emerges from these findings: how can China have performed so brilliantly despite having such high levels of capital flight? Part of the answer is that a substantial amount of the capital fight is 'round-tripped', that is, it returns to China as foreign investment. The other part of the answer, emphasized by the authors, goes against the conventional wisdom, however. Whereas other authors blame the capital flight on government interference in the economy, including capital controls, the authors of this chapter suggest that it is government controls and management, including management of the capital account, that can help to explain massive Chinese economic growth, despite the high levels of capital flight. Fewer controls might have reduced capital flight in a statistical sense, but it is unlikely that they would have raised economic growth above its already blistering level.

Solutions

Given the persistent and in some cases rather larger levels of capital flight reported by these authors, what can be done to reduce the flight and the costs associated with it? Eric Helleiner gives the historical background to the development of arguments for capital controls. He shows how in the Bretton Woods Agreements, Keynes and White believed that controls of capital flight could only work if receiving countries helped the losing countries identify flight capital. The financial sector strongly opposed such rules and they were never passed. Helleiner suggests that now, with parts of the world still recovering from the Asian financial crisis and with heightened concern about the financing of terrorism and drugs, the powers that be might be more open now to rules and institutions to facilitate international cooperation to identify and recover flight capital than they have been in the last several decades.

Gerald Epstein, Ilene Grabel and Sundaram Kwame Jomo identify a broad set of policies, which they term 'capital management techniques', that can help regulate capital inflows and outflows. Many of these are simply prudential measures; others are strict controls over the capital account. They present several case studies that show that capital management techniques can be successfully applied and can help to stop capital flight.

In the final chapter of the book, James Boyce and Léonce Ndikumana discuss yet another strategy for dealing with accumulated foreign debt in the face of large outflows of capital. They show that when stocks of capital flight are taken into account, many sub-Saharan African countries are actually net creditors, not net debtors, as the standard analysis suggests! The problem of course is for these governments to get control over the capital flight assets, something which is very difficult. Instead, Boyce and Ndikumana suggest that governments implement the doctrine of odious debt. This doctrine states that governments should be allowed to cancel their debts if these had been acquired by dictators or others whose interests run counter to the bulk of the population. They argue that in many sub-Saharan African countries, this doctrine might well apply.

CONCLUSION

In the age of financial liberalization, capital flight, far from disappearing, has in fact remained high and even increased: this is the message of this book. Reducing capital flight and its costs in developing countries is a difficult challenge, but it is one worth trying to meet. Ultimately, promoting economic development and fighting capital flight must go hand in hand. The neo-liberal approach appears to be unsuccessful at doing either; it is time for something different, perhaps, even, for some of the ideas contained in this study.

NOTES

1. Boyce (1992).
2. We based our method on the work of Boyce and Ndikumana (2001).

REFERENCES

Boyce, James K. (1977), 'The Political Economy of External Indebtedness: A Case Study of the Philippines', Manila: Philippine Institute for Development Studies, Monograph Series, No. 12.

Boyce, James K. (1992), 'The Revolving Door? External Debt and Capital Flight: Philippine Case Study', *World Development*, **20** (3), 335–349.

Boyce, James and Leonce Ndikumana (2001), 'Is Africa a net creditor? New Estimates of Capital Flight from Severely Indebted Sub-Saharan African Countries, 1970–1996', *Journal of Development Studies*, **38** (2), 27–56.

Crotty, James and Gerald Epstein (1996), 'In Defence of Capital Controls', *Socialist Register*, reprinted in Leo Panitch, Colin Leys, Alan Zuege and Martijn Konings (eds) (2004), *The Globalization Decade; A Critical Reader*, London: The Merlin Press, pp. 80–110.

Crotty, James (1993), 'The Rise and Fall of the Keynesian Revolution in the Age of the Global Marketplace', in Gerald Epstein, Julie Graham and Jessica Nembhard (eds) for the Center for Popular Economics (CPE), *Creating a New World Economy: Forces of Change and Plans for Action*, Philadelphia: Temple University Press, pp. 163–80.

Kindleberger, Charles P. (1987), 'Capital Flight – A Historical Perspective', in Donald R. Lessard and John Williamson (eds), *Capital Flight and Third World Debt*, Washington, DC: Institute for International Economics, pp. 7–26.

Lessard, Donald R. and John Williamson (eds) (1987), *Capital Flight and Third World Debt*, Washington, DC: Institute for International Economics.

Schneider, Benu (2003), 'Measuring Capital Flight: Estimates and Interpretations', Overseas Development Institute, UK.

2. Capital Account Liberalization, Growth and the Labor Share of Income: Reviewing and Extending the Cross-country Evidence

Kang-kook Lee and Arjun Jayadev

INTRODUCTION

> *The next moment soldiers came running through the wood, at first in twos and threes, then ten or twenty together, and at last in such crowds that they seemed to fill the whole forest. Alice got behind a tree, for fear of being run over, and watched them go by.*
>
> Lewis Carroll (*Alice Through the Looking Glass*)

One of the most significant changes in the international economy over the last three decades has been the growing importance of international capital flows between countries. Flows to developing countries, less than $10 billion in 1973, experienced a 30-fold increase to over $300 billion in 1997.[1] This has been partly the consequence of improvements in financial technology and products, as evidenced by the vast increase in financial vehicles available to investors. A more important cause, however, has been the dismantling of barriers to cross-country capital flows in various parts of the world over this period, broadly subsumed under the label of capital account liberalization, a principle that has allowed capital to flow much more freely and in larger volumes across nations. This policy, in its various forms, has been spurred in part by the adoption of the Washington Consensus[2] by numerous policy makers in a variety of contexts, and in part by the conditionalities imposed by international lending institutions. While the forms and the pace of these deregulations have taken many constellations (see Epstein et al. 2003), it remains a fact that with few exceptions, countries have moved in the direction of opening up to international flows.

The predicted and perceived consequences of this explosion of financial activity have been contentious, both from a theoretical viewpoint and from the standpoint of its concrete empirical effects. Attention has largely focused on the growth impact of these developments drawing from various theoretical perspectives. A second concern has been its effects on macroeconomic stability, with the decade of the nineties seeing numerous calamitous financial crises. Only very recently have writers begun to examine its effects on income distribution and poverty.

This chapter draws from other work undertaken by the authors (see Lee 2003; Jayadev 2003) to address both the questions of growth and distribution. Using the method of cross-country regressions, we find that there is little evidence to suggest that capital account openness has a direct positive effect on growth, even under much talked-about preconditions. We present preliminary evidence that suggests a dissenting conclusion: where capital controls have been used as an active part of industrial policy, and under circumstances where such macroeconomic policy has been well managed, there is a significant positive effect on growth. We address the question of distribution by looking at the effect of capital account openness on factor shares. In keeping with the few studies that have been done drawing these linkages, we find that there is a systematic negative effect of capital account openness on the labor share of income, bolstering the argument, put forward by many, that a liberal financial regime may act to the detriment of workers.

Attempting to study the links between a policy variable such as capital account liberalization and national level outcomes involves a somewhat irreducible tension between the international scope of the former and the localized effects of the latter. That is to say, while full capital account liberalization presumably involves a similar (if not identical) set of deregulatory measures across countries, the specific channels and intensity with which these affect different countries diverge according to a large set of conditioning social, institutional and historical factors. As such, the research in this area is faced with the perhaps insurmountable problem of having to choose an empirical methodology that can address both of these issues. As a result, research tends to devolve into one of two methodologies: cross-country studies which attempt to study effects through structural equations so as to provide enough of a range of outcomes to be generalizable (if indeed this is possible) or country-specific (or more rarely region-specific) studies which attempt to establish the manner in which the policy changes have worked themselves out in a given country.

Given the flood of theoretical and empirical analyses that have been produced by researchers in the last decade and the vast array of the channels involved, the focus of this chapter is necessarily limited. We begin with a brief review of the key theoretical and empirical literature on the linkages between capital account liberalization on the one hand, and growth and distribution on the other. We concentrate on the numerous cross-country studies[3] that have been produced, before going on to present our analysis which uses a different (and more sophisticated) measure of capital account openness than has typically been employed.

REVIEWING THE LITERATURE

'Who are you?' said the Caterpillar.
This was not an encouraging opening for a conversation. Alice replied, rather
shyly, 'I – I hardly know, sir, just at present – at least I know who I was when I got
up this morning, but I think I must have been changed several times since then.

Lewis Carroll (*Alice in Wonderland*)

Growth

Theory
Following from Fischer (1930), capital mobility should benefit both borrowers and lenders as it enhances the efficiency of intertemporal decision making, raises returns to lenders and augments the savings of borrowers (Fischer 1998; Cooper 1999). In addition, open capital accounts should increase growth by enhancing the potential for risk diversification (Guitan 1997; Obstfeld 1994). As a result, one should expect both an increase in the growth rate across all countries and a reduction in macroeconomic volatility following capital account openness.

However, divergences from this outcome may result from imperfect capital markets (see, for example, Stiglitz 2000) or distortions in the real sector (Brecher and Diaz-Alejandro 1977). In the context of these alterations, capital account liberalization may in fact lead to more instability, with herd behavior and overborrowing (Kim and Wei 1999; McKinnon and Pill 1999; Eichengreen et al. 1997), and an inefficient allocation of capital resources. As such, when these prerequisites are not met, capital mobility may in fact be welfare-reducing.

Given this, much analytical attention has focused on the types of preconditions that must be in place[4] for capital account liberalization to increase growth and smooth macroeconomic unpredictability. More recent theory has attempted to shift the focus towards more indirect channels through which financial openness can enhance growth-increasing financial depth and development (Levine 1997) and promoting better governance and public policy (Dornbusch 1998; Kim 2000).

While the viewpoint endorsing capital account liberalization with caveats has become the dominant viewpoint, an alternative view is more critical of capital account liberalization. On the contrary, it is argued, capital controls should be seen as a necessary part of the development process, and as a central aspect of industrial policy (Crotty and Epstein 1996; Amsden 1989). As such, premature capital account openness reduces the ability of firms to undertake development policy and to move up the productivity ladder (Chang 2002), thereby reducing the rate of long-term growth. In addition, it is argued, rather than reducing macroeconomic volatility, capital account

Table 2.1 Important empirical studies of capital account liberalization

Study	Sample Size/ Period	Index	Effects	Preconditions and channels (o = statistically significant, x = statistically insignificant)
Grilli-Millesi Ferreti (1995)	61/1966–89	IMF dummy	Growth (x)	
Quinn (1997)	64/1960–89	Quinn's	Growth (o)	
Rodrik (1998)	More than 90/ 1960–89	IMF dummy	Growth (x) Investment (x)	Institutions (x)
Kraay (1998)	64/ 1985–97	Both and capital flows	Growth (x) Investment (x)	Institutions (x) Financial development (x)
Chanda (2001)	82/ 1975–95	IMF dummy	Growth (x)	Higher ethnic fragmentation (o)
Edwards (2001)	59/1980s	Both	Growth (o) TFP (o)	Higher level of growth (o)
Arteta et al. (2001)	59/ 1980s	Both	Growth (x)	Lower black market premium (o)
O'Donnell (2001b)	66/1971–94	IMF dummy, stock of foreign assets and liabilities	Growth (x)	Financial development (x)

Study	Sample	Measure	Effect on	Notes
Quinn et al. (2001)	76/1960–98	Quinn's	Growth (o)	Level of growth (x) Emerging market democracy (bad)
IMF (2001)	57/1980–99	IMF dummy, external assets	Growth (x) Investment (o) Financial development (o)	Institutions (x)
Klein and Olivei (2001)	69/1976–95	IMF dummy	Growth (o) Financial development (o)	Financial development (o)
Bekaert et al. (2002)	95/1980–97	Equity market opening date	Growth (o) Investment (o)	Financial development (x)
Edison et al. (2002a)	89/1976–95	Both	Growth (o)	
Edison et al (2002b)	57/1980–2000	Both, flows	Growth (x)	Level of growth (x) Institutions (x)
Klein (2003)	85/1976–95	Both		Inverse U-shaped relation of growth level
Prasad et al. (2003)	76/1982–97	Capital flows	Growth(x) Volatility on consumption (o)	

openness increases instability (at least in the short to medium-term) by exposing countries to speculative capital flows that exacerbate the business cycle (Palma 1998; Grabel 1997).

Empirical Research
Given the widely differing views held by researchers, a range of empirical projects have been undertaken to verify or reject the many hypotheses that have been put forward. For the most part, these projects have been cross-country studies, using a variety of different econometric methodologies. One particular sticking point has been the measurement of capital account openness, a topic to which we return later. Typically, researchers have used one of four indicators: actual flows of direct and portfolio investment, deviations from interest rate parity, a dummy variable for openness drawn from the International Monetary Fund's Annual Report on Exchange Arrangements and Restrictions and Quinn's (1997) index which codes various regulations from the IMF on a 0–4 scale.

Most empirical studies, using various policy variables, have examined the effect on growth with a standard cross-country regression framework.[5] These show only mixed results. The differences between studies seem to depend on the choice of sample, period and, most of all, capital controls indices (Grilli and Milesi-Ferretti 1995; Rodrik 1998; Quinn 1997; Edison *et al.* 2002a). More recent work attempts to shed light on the possible preconditions under which liberalization may spur growth (Edwards 2001; Arteta *et al.* 2001; IMF 2001; Kraay 1998; Chanda 2001, Klein and Olivei 2001; O'Donnell 2001b; Bekaert et al. 2001, Edison et al. 2002b; Prasad et al. 2003). Again the results of these studies are mixed.

Table 2.1 lists the key empirical studies on the effect of capital account liberalization (measured using these indicators) on growth. Perhaps the most striking feature of these studies is the lack of consensus on the issue. It appears that the impacts of financial openness on growth is highly sensitive to the time period in question, the sample of countries, the choice of indicator and the preconditions existing in countries which liberalize.

Just as noteworthy is the large number of studies searching for the linkages between financial openness and growth. In contrast, other crucial areas of interest, especially those to do with the relative welfare of groups and individuals affected by capital account openness, have not been addressed until very recently.

Distribution

Theory
With very few exceptions, current research largely ignores one of the more crucial concerns of the critics of open financial markets, namely that liberal

regimes may quite plausibly worsen the income distribution and the welfare of workers. Theoretically, from a neoclassical viewpoint, it is difficult to see how the direct effects of capital account openness might operate on the size distribution of income and even on a measure like poverty. For example, Cobham (2000) lists the potential linkages between openness and poverty. Allen (2002), in a comment on this issue, proposes that tracing the relationship between capital account liberalization and poverty is perhaps too onerous a task and suggests that first order relationships may be hard to find. Although gestures have been made towards understanding how different strata of society respond to and benefit from capital account openness (see, for example, Garrett 1995; Das and Mohapatra 2002), these are far from approaching the status of a theoretical viewpoint, at least in the mainstream literature on liberalization.[6]

By contrast, theoretical predictions may be drawn much more easily about another metric for the distribution of income: the factor shares of income.[7] In as much as the case for capital account liberalization is also the case for trade openness with the subscripts changed, one might expect homologous results to the effects of trade in the Hecksher–Ohlin model: capital account openness increasing the share of income going to labor (the abundant factor in developing countries) and increasing the share of income going to capital (the abundant factor in developed countries). To the extent that the labor share of income is a reflection of the income of the relatively less wealthy, we might expect to see a relative equalization of incomes in developing countries and between countries. Inequality in developed countries, by contrast, may rise.

While the Hecksher–Ohlin framework does provide an a priori theoretical prediction, it implicitly assumes that the division of production rents is a matter of the production technology. More recent works (Ortega and Rodriguez 2001; Harrison 2002) seek instead to explain the final division of factor shares as resulting from a bargaining game. As such, these models seek to formalize the arguments made by researchers such as Rodrik (1997) and Crotty and Epstein (1996) who suggest that capital account openness fundamentally changes the political economy of the country in question, to the detriment of the less mobile factor, labor. The imminent and plausible threat of capital strike causes workers and bargaining units to lose power and ex post, to lose their share of productive output. These ideas can be seen as one articulation of the familiar 'race to the bottom' hypothesis. Work by Bronfenbrenner (1997) and Choi (2001) appear to support this thesis in the case of US firms, in which increased capital mobility lowers the wage and bargaining power of labor unions.

Some authors (for example, Cobham 2000) see a differential impact of liberalization on the relatively high employment, small to medium enterprise sector (SMEs). To the extent that the labor share is higher in such firms, if capital account openness disrupts growth in this sector, there is a disproportionate effect on the labor share. To that extent, whether financial openness has an additional impact on labor share through the SMEs depends in large part on whether it provides more certainty or conversely increases volatility.

Table 2.2 (drawn from Jayadev 2003) lists the major theoretical positions on the effects of capital account openness on distribution.

Table 2.3 (also from Jayadev 2003) lists some of the cross-country studies that have been done to test these relationships. Perhaps most interestingly, given the lack of consensus in studies on growth, all the research listed concurs that rising inequality is a correlate of capital account openness. Whether the measure of inequality is the Gini coefficient, income shares or factor shares, there is a consistent finding that capital account openness contributes to increasing disparity. While it is difficult to lay out clear theoretical reasons to explain why financial liberalization affects interpersonal income distribution in this way, there are more solid linkages drawn for those results featuring factor incomes and the relative income shares of the top 20 percent of the population (see Das and Mohapatra 2002).

MEASURING CAPITAL ACCOUNT OPENNESS

'What's one and one and one and one and one and one and one and one and one and one?'
'I don't know,' said Alice. 'I lost count.'
'She can't do Addition,' the Red Queen interrupted.

Lewis Carroll (*Alice Through the Looking Glass*)

Capital account liberalization is usually taken to mean the removal of capital controls or restrictions that implicitly or explicitly restrain the international movement of capital. Typically, most measures of capital account liberalization can be divided into three types.

First, some authors (for example, Prasad et al. 2003) have sought to assess openness by measuring the actual flows of capital to and from the country in question. While this measure is likely on average to be correlated with financial openness, it confuses ex post and ex ante measurement. That is to say, capital account liberalization relates to how restrictive policies are towards capital flows (the only variable that policy makers have control over) and not how much capital actually traverses borders. Researchers who use this measure defend it by suggesting the *de facto* measures of openness capture the *de jure* measures as well as the effectiveness with which they are enforced.

A second line of empirical research, somewhat connected, revolves

Table 2.2 Predicted effects of capital account liberalization on income distribution

	Mainstream	Structuralist and Dependency	Marxian	Post-Keynesian
Income Distribution	Not main area of focus, but in developing countries, expected to eventually improve as more labor is incorporated into the market economy, and as the factor intensity of labor is higher. To the extent that capital account openness spurs growth, which in turn reduces poverty, there is likely to be a positive effect	Worsens in both labor and capital as well as in overall terms due to increasing incorporation of economy into global system. Also, differential negative effects on small/medium enterprise, thereby benefiting larger, lower employment business. More susceptibility to financial crises, which ultimately hurt labor	Labor–capital distribution worsens due to capital account deregulation and bargaining effects; ambiguous effect on overall distribution	More susceptibility to financial crises hurts labor disproportionately. Differential negative effects on small or medium–scale enterprise, thereby benefiting larger, lower employment business

Table 2.3   Cross-country studies on capital account openness and distribution

Study	Measure of Inequality	Result
Quinn (1997)	Gini coefficient	Inequality increases
Das and Mohapatra (2002)	Income quintiles	Inequality increases (middle income groups lose out)
Calderon and Chang (2001)	Gini coefficient	Inequality increases
Harrison (2002)	Labor share	Labor share declines
Diwan (2000)	Labor share	Labor share declines with crisis

around the integration of financial markets. The argument here is that countries with convergent returns are more open to capital flows and therefore the level of integration between rates of return is a measure of openness. Numerous authors (Bekaert 1995; Frankel and Macarthur 1988; Giavizzi and Pagano 1988; Cody 1990; Marston 1993, 1995) have followed this line of reasoning and utilize measures such as onshore–offshore differentials or deviations from covered interest parity to measure whether the economy is financially open. The problem, of course, is that while integration implies convergent rates, convergent rates do not imply integration. In addition, studies that equate market integration with openness assume implicitly that markets are complete, information is not distorted and the policy stance of the country is irrelevant for capital market integration – assumptions which are shaky at best.[8]

As a result of these complications, the most popular efforts to identify the presence of capital account restrictions have relied on the IMF's annual publication, 'Exchange Arrangements and Exchange Restrictions', which provides details on various regulations on capital account transactions across countries. It has represented the central source for various measures of financial openness (Rodrik 1998; Kraay 1998; Klein and Olivei 2001; Edwards 2001; Chanda 2001; Mody and Murshid 2002). Because of the qualitative nature of the data, these studies have constantly faced the problem of distinguishing among relative degrees of openness, and have come up with various responses, ranging from an outright ignoring of the problem (that is, treating it as a binary indicator) to providing various remedial measures.[9] Quinn's (1997) index remains the definitive study in this regard.

While Quinn's indicator is the most preferable index to use given its attempt to code for intensity, it is available in a reasonable time series for cross-country studies for only a handful of years. As a result, we use the same methodology that Quinn uses to develop a similar indicator of openness for the period 1973–1995. (For details on its construction, see Lee 2003 or Jayadev 2003.) This indicator is the basis of much of our analysis. Figure 2.1 details the movements in capital account openness over the last two and a half decades using this indicator. As can be seen, openness has increased in all groups of countries, with the early 1990s being the period of rapid opening up by the poorer groups, in keeping with other indicators.

ASSESSING THE ARGUMENTS

> *They hunted till darkness came on, but they found*
> *Not a button, or feather, or mark,*
> *By which they could tell that they stood on the ground*
> *Where the Baker had met with the Snark...*
>
> *In the midst of the word he was trying to say,*
> *In the midst of his laughter and glee,*
> *He had softly and suddenly vanished away –*
> *For the Snark *was* a Boojum, you see.*

Lewis Carroll (*The Hunting of the Snark*)

Assessing the Growth Impacts of Capital Account Liberalization

Testing direct growth channels
As mentioned in the review of the literature above, the central channel by which capital account liberalization is said to enhance growth is through access to greater financial opportunities for investment. We begin, therefore, by examining the effect of capital account liberalization on economic growth, investment, and efficiency of investment. Since growth regressions are varied (there have been at least 40 channels for growth identified by the World Bank), we use a very basic model that is used in other cross-country work. In this section, we report simple cross-country regressions, as much of the debate has focused on such models (see, for example, Rodrik 1998; Edwards 2001). In Lee (2003), this analysis is also repeated with panel regressions. The pooled OLS results are mostly consistent with these cross-country regressions, and while some fixed effects specifications provide opposing results to those given below, these are not very robust.[10]

The setup for the benchmark growth regression is:

$$Y_i = \alpha + \beta X_i + \gamma CAL_i + \varepsilon_I \qquad (2.1)$$

where CAL refers to the indicator for the capital account openness and X represents a vector of control variables.

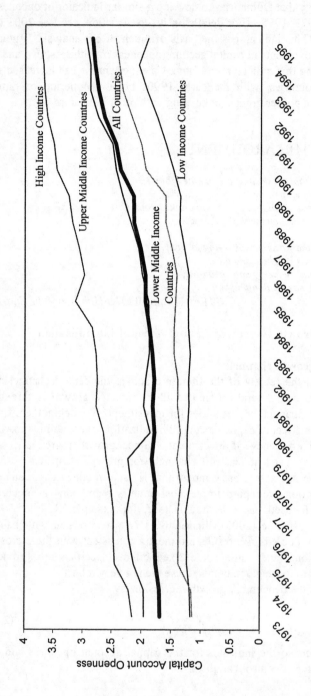

Note: *Capital Account openness ranges from a minimum of 0 (completely closed) to 4 (completely open). The heavy line is a simple average of openness in all countries in the sample.

Figure 2.1 Increasing capital account openness

The basic control variable set[11] used in our initial regressions includes the initial log of real GDP per capita, the average educational attainment for the period, institutional quality, and regional dummies. An extended control variable set includes inflation, the black market premium and other social variables such as ethnic fragmentation.

Table 2.4 reports the basic regression result using OLS estimation on the panel data. In order to cover the possible problems associated with using just one measure of openness, we report the results from using five different measures.[12]

The regression appears to suggest that by all the indicators, capital account liberalization appears to have no significant independent positive effect on growth. In additional work, not reported here, we repeat the exercise including a variable for the investment share of GDP as a determinant of growth. In previous work on growth equations, when this variable was included in the set of controls, the coefficient on capital account liberalization has been positive and significant (Quinn 1997; Edward 2001; Edison et al. 2002a). Omitting it has meant that the coefficient remains insignificant (Rodrik 1998; Kraay 1998; O'Donnell 2001a and Chanda 2001). This suggests that where the investment share of GDP is already large, capital account liberalization increases the growth rate. Our results mimic these conflicting results. Introducing investment share of GDP into the control vector leads to the capital account liberalization variable having a positive effect on growth, though only in the case of Quinn's index is this effect significant.

Considering this regression, does capital account liberalization increase the investment share of GDP? This is, after all, the key channel by which it is said to increase growth. Table 2.5 reports the results of such an investigation from an OLS estimation using the same dependent variables. As the results show, perhaps counter-intuitively, capital account liberalization has a negative effect on the investment share of GDP, and in two instances, a significantly negative effect. It is possible that this reflects capital flight, or perhaps the displacement of local investment by foreign competition, (Harrison 2002), but in either case, the logic runs counter to the general expectation of enhanced investment.

Nevertheless, our findings are not unusual. Most literature looking at the relationship between financial openness and investment does not find a consensus of a strong positive causal link.[13] It does not appear that actual flows can be said to enhance the investment share, and financial openness in turn may not even be a strong motivator of capital inflows (Mody and Murshid 2002).

Another essential direct channel by which capital account liberalization is said to affect growth is by enhancing economic efficiency. As mentioned in the literature review, it is argued that free international capital flows promote

Table 2.4 Capital account liberalization and economic growth with basic sets

Independent Variables	IMF capital account	IMF combined	Quinn's capital account	Quinn's overall account	Lee–Jayadev capital account openness index
Initial GDP per capita	-1.211* (-5.28)	-1.262* (-5.47)	-1.306* (-3.83)	-1.222* (-3.49)	-1.222* (-5.05)
Education ratio	0.021** (2.06)	0.022** (2.18)	0.011 (0.84)	0.011 (0.81)	0.021** (2.08)
Government anti-diversion Policy	8.380* (5.95)	8.403* (5.97)	7.645* (3.54)	7.964* (3.64)	8.421* (5.97)
Capital account Liberalization	-0.224 (-0.39)	0.017 (0.08)	0.373 (1.47)	0.045 (0.53)	-0.056 (-0.22)
East Asian dummy	2.813* (4.79)	2.722* (4.66)	2.566* (4.79)	2.6220* (4.64)	2.755* (4.92)

Latin American dummy	-0.020 (-0.05)	-0.014 (-0.03)	-0.166 (-0.30)	-0.133 (-0.24)	-0.024 (-0.05)
Sub–Saharan African Dummy	-1.819* (-3.84)	-1.810* (-3.82)	-2.650* (-3.20)	-2.629* (-3.10)	-1.814* (-3.83)
Adjusted R^2	0.583	0.582	0.576	0.560	0.583
No. of observations	108	108	60	60	108

Notes:

[a] Dependent variable: average real GDP per capita growth rate (from 1976 to 1995).

[b] t-value in parentheses, *: significant at 1% level, **: at 5% level, ***: at 10% level.

[c] GDP per capita growth rate rate: (log of real GDP per capita in 1995 – log of real GDP per capita in 1976)/19

[d] Initial GDP: log of GDP per capita in 1976.

[e] GADP: government anti–diversion index from ICRG, Hall and Jones (1999).

[f] Education ratio: secondary level education ratio of all population, from WDI.

[g] Quinn's indexes are for 1982 and 1988 for all countries, all years for OECD countries.

29

Table 2.5 *Capital account liberalization and investment with basic sets*

Independent Variables	IMF capital account	IMF combined	Quinn's capital account	Quinn's overall account	Capital account openness index
Initial GDP per capita	0.101	0.170	0.218	0.308	0.564
	(0.12)	(0.20)	(0.25)	(0.34)	(0.64)
Education Ratio	0.024	0.021	–0.042	–0.037	0.015
	(0.65)	(0.58)	(–1.19)	(–1.04)	(0.41)
Government Anti-Diversion Policy	0.915	1.324	7.594	7.122	1.822
	(0.18)	(0.26)	(1.35)	(1.27)	(0.35)
Capital Account Liberalization	–3.115	–1.318***	–1.032	–0.355***	–1.849**
	(–1.48)	(–1.62)	(–1.55)	(–1.66)	(–2.16)
East Asian Dummy	8.700*	8.737*	7.987*	8.335*	8.245*
	(4.02)	(4.07)	(5.72)	(5.78)	(4.05)

Latin American Dummy	-2.366	-2.745***	-2.645***	-2.502***	-2.487
	(-1.52)	(-1.75)	(-1.84)	(-1.74)	(-1.62)
Sub Saharan African Dummy	-3.163***	-2.851	-7.506*	-7.683*	-3.226***
	(-1.81)	(-1.64)	(-3.48)	(-3.57)	(-1.87)
Adjusted R-square	0.243	0.246	0.538	0.541	0.261
No. of observations	108	108	60	60	108

Notes:

[a] Dependent variable: average real GDP per capita growth rate (from 1976 to 1995).

[b] t-value in parentheses, *: significant at 1% level, **: at 5% level, ***: at 10% level.

[c] GDP per capita growth rate is percentage growth rate, calculated by (log of real GDP per capita in 1995 – log of real GDP per capita in 1976)/19

[d] Initial GDP: log of GDP per capita in 1976.

[e] GADP: government anti-diversion index from ICRG, Hall and Jones (1999).

[f] Education ratio: secondary level education ratio of all population, from WDI.

[g] Quinn's indexes are for 1982 and 1988 for all countries, all years for OECD countries.

efficiency by allowing for risk diversification and more competition (Obstfeld 1994; Guitan 1997). We test this notion in the manner of Edwards (2001) and Bekaert et al. (2002), by adding the investment variable and the interaction of investment and capital account liberalization. For lack of space, we do not report the full results here (see Lee 2003 for a more detailed analysis). The basic finding, however, is that the interaction term does not have a significant positive effect on growth.

The fact that neither of the two main channels linking financial openness to growth appears significant bolsters skepticism about the perceived growth effects of openness. These findings are not out of step with the growing acceptance among advocates and opponents of openness of the actual negligibility of its effects. Consider, as a preeminent example, the view of the IMF (Prasad et al. 2003): 'The main conclusions are that, so far, it has proven difficult to find robust evidence in support of the proposition that financial integration helps developing countries to improve growth and to reduce macroeconomic volatility.'

Does capital account openness work under certain preconditions?

Since our previous results do not provide any evidence to suggest that capital account openness spurs growth in and of itself, it is instrumental to assess the more moderate claim that under suitable preconditions, open policies enhance growth. As pointed out earlier, these preconditions typically involve notions of macroeconomic stability and 'sound' financial sector institutions and a general level of development. (Edwards 2001; Klein and Olivei 2001; Arteta et al. 2001).

In our test, we interact capital account liberalization and the variable representing the preexisting institutional structure. Accordingly, the test is of the form:

$$Y_i = \alpha + \beta X_i + \gamma CAL_i * Condition_i + \varepsilon_I \qquad (2.2)$$

$Condition_i$ represents the precondition variables.

For simplification, we focus on three of the capital account liberalization variables used in the previous exercise: the IMF dummy, Quinn's index and our capital account openness index.[14] The preconditioning variables are the initial level of GDP (proxying for the level of development), the education ratio (proxying for human capital) and the government anti-diversion policy index (proxying for institutional development). We leave the discussion of debt structure for the next subsection.

Table 2.6 reports the results. Interestingly, and once again contrary to the logic usually proposed, the interaction of all three variables with capital account openness leads to a decrease in the growth rate. That is to say, capital account liberalization appears to reduce growth in more developed

Table 2.6   Capital account liberalization, growth and some preconditions

Condition variables	IMF capital account	Quinn's capital account	Lee–Jayadev capital account openness index
Initial GDP			
Initial GDP	−1.013*	−0.767***	−0.853
	(−4.29)	(−1.72)	(−2.57)
Capital account liberalization	5.725**	3.300**	2.050***
	(2.11)	(2.12)	(1.79)
Initial GDP*capital account liberalization	−0.679**	−0.342***	−0.228***
	(−2.14)	(−1.85)	(−1.74)
Adjusted R^2	0.631	0.603	0.626
No. of observations	108	60	108
Initial GDP	−1.059*	−1.102***	−1.396**
	(−4.47)	(−2.15)	(−3.47)
Capital account liberalization	−11.297	−2.780	−6.060
	(−0.93)	(−0.57)	(−1.64)
Initial GDP*capital account liberalization	3.531**	1.044	1.612**
	(1.20)	(0.97)	(1.99)
Initial GDP^2*capital account liberalization	−0.252	−0.077	−0.100**
	(−1.44)	(−1.31)	(−2.30)
Adjusted R^2	0.635	0.675	0.641
No. of observations	108	60	108
Education ratio			
Education ratio	0.029**	0.044***	0.036***
	(2.52)	(1.91)	(2.16)
Capital account liberalization	1.923	1.456**	0.597
	(1.47)	(2.14)	(1.26)

Education ratio* capital account liberalization	−0.028** (−1.60)	−0.015** (−1.57)	−0.008 −1.20)
Adjusted R^2	0.623	0.596	0.620
No. of observations	108	60	108

Institutional development

Government anti– diversion policy	10.627* (6.72)	12.393* (3.86)	11.784* (5.19)
Capital account liberalization	3.990** (2.49)	1.888** (2.71)	1.142*** (1.93)
Government anti– diversion policy * capital account liberalization	−5.878** (−2.63)	−2.218** (−2.19)	−1.572*** (−1.91)
Adjusted R^2	0.639	0.613	0.628
No. of observations	108	60	108

Notes:
[a] Dependent variable: average real GDP per capita growth rate (from 1976 to 1995)
[b] T- statistics in parentheses; *: significant at 1% level, **: at 5% level, ***: at 10% level.
[c] Other variables reported in Lee (2003).

countries, in countries with higher levels of human capital and in countries with 'good' institutional structures. With regard to the first finding, our findings are similar to that of Klein (2003), who suggests that the relationship between growth and capital account openness is an inverted U curve, reflecting increasing and then decreasing marginal benefits from openness. We confirm his result in one instance (with our Modified Quinn Index).[15] Such a finding suggests that liberalization may be harmful in very poor countries which are macroeconomically and politically vulnerable. Middle-income countries may benefit from liberalization, but this finding is not robust to all indicators.

These four results are reported primarily because they stand so starkly against some of the standard expectations of neoclassical theory. This divergence is not atypical, however. Kraay (1998) is one study which finds similar results. Tests of other standard desirable preconditions do not provide any counter evidence for the whole sample.[16]

A typical precondition that is considered is the level of financial sophistication.[17] To look at this, we used standard measures of financial depth such as liquid liability to GDP and stock market development.[18] We find that interacting the level of financial depth with capital account openness does not lead to any significant results in this case. Another frequently cited precondition is the absence of corruption in the business environment.

Again, our analysis suggests no evidence that liberalization is helpful to growth in countries with less corruption overall,[19] in keeping with similar findings by Kraay (1998) and Edison et al. (2002b). Finally, we test for the interaction between capital account liberalization and macroeconomic distortions. More specifically, we test for its interacted effects with trade openness, black market premiums, the tariff rate and the non-tariff barrier index.[20] Once again, nearly without exception,[21] none of these variables appear significant in many specifications of the model. To the extent that this is the case, these results bring into question the typical preconditions that are considered in the 'orderly' or 'sequential' liberalization argument (McKinnon 1991; Arteta et al. 2001). Our results do not show any obvious preconditions for capital account openness to have significant and positive growth effects. The prescription of 'getting one's house in order' before inviting capital in appears reasonable a priori, except that it is unclear exactly what that involves.

To conclude the discussion on the growth effects of capital account liberalization, we assess the claims of the broad 'third school' that capital controls, under given preconditions, can be used to promote a high–growth development path. We test several possible contexts that might be related to success or failure of capital controls in the following section.

When may capital controls spur growth?

Researchers have suggested that capital controls may work best when there is a state with a high degree of autonomy and capability (Evans 1995). Extending beyond the insights of neoclassical political economy, it is argued that state intervention may lead to desirable results in cases where the state can prevent rent-seeking activity, be somewhat immune to pressures from strong interest groups, and enjoy a high degree of stability (Rodrik 1995; Chanda 2001). Such situations are most likely to occur in less fragmented societies.

In addition, researchers point out the effective government organization essential for the successful government intervention. They point to many constellations whereby a combination of strong capital controls, domestic financial control and industrial policy can spur investment and growth (Nembhard 1996).

Table 2.7 *Capital controls, growth and preconditions: ethnic homogeneity, institutional development and corporate debt ratio*

Independent variables	IMF capital account	IMF combined	Quinn's capital account	Quinn's overall account	Capital account openness index
Ethnic homogeneity					
Ethnic homogeneity index	−1.388	−0.363	−0.145	−0.599	−1.29
	(−0.97)	(−0.32)	(−0.08)	(−0.34)	(−0.84)
Capital controls	−2.976*	−1.15**	−0.996***	−0.24	−1.278**
	(−2.62)	(−2.61)	(−1.72)	(−1.43)	(−2.54)
Ethnic homogeneity index * capital controls	4.623**	1.577**	0.904	0.341	1.567**
	(2.54)	(2.31)	(1.02)	(1.29)	(2.26)
Adjusted R^2	0.648	0.647	0.587	0.568	0.646
No. of observations	103	103	59	59	103
Institutional development					
Government anti-diversion policy	4.749**	5.226*	3.520	3.415	5.496*
	(2.52)	(3.02)	(1.33)	(1.23)	(2.79)
Capital controls	−3.990**	−1.722*	−1.889**	−0.664**	−1.142***
	(−2.49)	(−2.76)	(−2.71)	(−2.43)	(−1.93)

36

Government anti-diversion policy * capital controls	5.878** (2.63)	2.628* (2.71)	2.218** (2.19)	0.882** (2.29)	1.572*** (1.91)
Adjusted R²	0.639	0.642	0.613	0.597	0.628
No. of observations	108	108	60	60	108
Corporate debt ratio					
Debt	-0.814** (-2.15)	-0.491*** (-1.95)	-0.193 (-0.55)	-0.354 (-1.27)	-0.288 (-0.87)
Capital controls	-1.321 (-1.34)	-0.565 (-1.20)	-1.285** (-2.64)	-0.360** (-2.31)	-1.238** (-2.50)
Debt* capital controls	1.215** (2.49)	0.673** (2.52)	0.347 (1.40)	0.144*** (2.10)	0.402 (1.68)
Adjusted R²	0.865	0.866	0.868	0.849	0.866
No. of observations	29	29	28	28	29

Notes:
a Dependent variable: average real GDP per capita growth rate (from 1976 to 1995).
b Ethnic homogeneity index: 1- ethnic fragmentation index from Krain (1997).
c Corporate debt ratio is debt/equity, from Demirgüç-Kunt and Maksimovic (1996), originally from International Finance Company.
d T- statistics in parentheses; *: significant at 1% level, **: at 5% level, ***: at 10% level.

Finally, another context within which capital controls may be useful is provided by Wade (1998), who claims that a high debt ratio which allows for ease of investment can only be managed in an environment of strict capital controls which are well managed and enforced by the government.

In order to assess these three channels, we perform the same tests to shed light on the specific institutional context within which capital controls are effective. We use the inverse of the capital account openness indices as measures of capital controls and interact them with preconditions required for capital controls to be successful in generating growth.

Table 2.7 provides partial evidence that capital controls may increase the growth rate in certain contexts. In regressions including a variable for ethnic homogeneity, it seems clear that capital controls can be used effectively to promote growth. Similarly the interaction term of 'government anti–diversion policy and capital controls' is significantly positive in almost all the regressions, although not significant in the non-OECD countries. It suggests that in countries with better institutions, proper capital controls might help minimize capital flight and that state-led development policies based on controls are more likely to be successful.[22]

Lastly, capital controls are more helpful in countries with a higher debt ratio. This probably reflects the fact that countries that followed a high debt model such as the East Asian and Scandinavian countries also adopted strict capital controls in order to do so successfully.

To summarize, our analysis suggests that there is little evidence to support the notion that liberalization of the capital account will have beneficial effects, even with the typical 'desirable preconditions'. There is slightly more evidence, by contrast, to suggest that capital controls may be used successfully as part of an alternative development path, such as that followed by many East Asian countries prior to liberalization in the early 1990s. It is useful here to mention the recent work of Gourinchas and Jeanne (2002). Assuming the benefits from capital account openness arising from the standard model, they calibrate it with the data available. They find that, for most countries, the average welfare gain from financial integration is only about 1 percent of current consumption. To conclude, our study provides little evidence that capital account openness aids growth. Even if this were the case, these benefits, the best evidence suggests, would be almost negligible.

Assessing the Distributional Impacts of Capital Account Liberalization[23]

> *Presently she began again. 'I wonder if I shall fall right through the earth! How funny it'll seem to come out among the people that walk with their heads downward! The Antipathies, I think –'*
>
> Lewis Carroll (*Alice in Wonderland*)

In order to test the various channels by which the labor share of income might be affected by the opening up of the capital account we specify a simple regression model on an unbalanced panel of countries. Our measure of the labor share is derived from the United Nations' system of national accounts, Table 103. Specifically, it is the item 'compensation to resident and non resident households' from the primary distribution of income accounts divided by gross domestic product. The data are pre-tax, and while they are supposed to capture the informal sector, in practice they do not, which is an important shortcoming. The regression model that we test is as follows:

$$LS_{it} = \alpha_i + \beta_1 X_{it} + \beta_2 Y_i + \beta_3 Z_{it} + \varepsilon_{it} \qquad (2.3)$$

where the vector X refers to a set of controlling macroeconomic and structural indicators, Y refers to the indicator of capital mobility and Z refers to the indicators of the channels by which we may expect capital account liberalization to affect labor's share of income. The impact of the means by which capital account openness affects the labor share of income is assessed by elaboration of the model, adding one variable at a time to its specification. The variable log (real GDP per capita) is used as a proxy for what may be termed a Kravis–Kuznets process. Both Kravis (1962, 1968) and Kuznets (1966) emphasize the process of development and structural change as the major reason behind the increase in wage ratios to GDP. First, with increasing capital–labor ratios and a production technology possessing an elasticity of substitution of less than unity,[24] the process of development leads mechanically to an increase in the labor share of income. However, both these authors point to other crucial structural shifts as well. These include a movement of labor away from agriculture into a position of wage labor (thereby reducing the proportion of the self-employed), demographic changes and urbanization (which increase the average age of retirement and women's participation) and the development of organized labor.

The other variables in the specification are self-evident. Current account restrictions, obtained from the IMF annual report on exchange restrictions, are a measure of the other major change in the international sector, namely trade liberalization. Crisis is defined, following convention, as a situation where the external value of the currency falls by more than 20 percent in a

Table 2.8 *All countries, OLS estimation, country fixed effects*

Dependent Variable: Compensation of Employees /GDP	1	2	3	4	5	6	7	8	9	10
Trend	(0.003)* (-3.3)	(0.002)* (-15.0)	(0.002)* (-9.3)	(0.002)* (-9.2)	(0.002)* (-8.4)	(0.002)* (-7.9)	(0.002)* (-8.1)	(0.002)* (-7.2)	(0.002)* (-6.5)	(0.003)* (-7.3)
Log (Real GDP per Capita)	—	0.078* (15.2)	0.064* (7.8)	0.058* (7.19)	0.053* (6.51)	0.056* (6.82)	0.064* (7.39)	0.085* (7.8)	0.082* (7.3)	0.069* (6.01)
Capital Account Openness	—	—	(0.011)* (-4.2)	(0.009)* (-3.12)	(0.009)* (-3.38)	(0.009)* (-3.31)	(0.009)* (-3.49)	(0.010)* (-3.09)	(0.009)* (-3.03)	(0.007)* (-3.31)
Current Account Restrictions	—	—	—	0.001 (-0.18)	0.0002 (0.06)	0.0004 (0.12)	(0.007)* (-2.2)	0.003 (1.60)	0.002 (0.6)	0.0004 (0.2)

	(1)	(2)	(3)	(4)	(5)	(6)	(7)	(8)	(9)	(10)
Crisis	(0.002) (-0.74)	(0.001) (0.76)	(0.002) (-0.5)	(0.011)* (-3.5)	(0.014)* (-4.0)	(0.012)* (-3.6)	—	—	—	—
Government Share of GDP	0.12* (3.05)	0.15* (4.75)	0.15* (4.8)	0.07** (2.46)	0.08* (3.05)	—	—	—	—	—
Budget Surplus	(0.003)* (-9.69)	(0.003)* (-10.1)	(0.003)* (-9.98)	(0.002)* (-7.5)	—	—	—	—	—	—
Real Interest Rate	0.0004* (3.32)	0.0005* (4.56)	0.0005* (4.59)	—	—	—	—	—	—	—
Exchange Rate	(0.0003)* (-2.64)	(0.0004)* (-3.33)	—	—	—	—	—	—	—	—
Financial Depth	0.063* (5.09)	—	—	—	—	—	—	—	—	—
R^2	0.64	0.63	0.59	0.56	0.55	0.53	0.52	0.52	0.47	0.001
Obs.	775	803	803	1102	1306	1316	1316	1347	2390	2885
No. of cross sections	70	73	73	81	86	86	86	87	117	140

year (Diwan 2000). The budget deficit and the government share of GDP are variables used to indicate the presence of government in order to measure the impact of government intervention and the spending of the public sector on the labor share. Finally, the exchange rate and the interest rate are introduced in order to analyze the effect of a change in relative prices on the labor share of income. Table 2.8 presents the result of this regression model for the period 1973–1995.

The fundamental result from this regression is that on average, capital account openness exerts a significant and negative effect on the labor share of income. More elaborate tests, reported in Jayadev (2003), show that controlling for trends and endowments and trying various robustness tests, capital account openness is strongly associated with declines in the labor share of income. The results also show, however, that the obvious ways whereby one may expect this result to hold[25] (by increasing the potential for crisis and by restricting government spending) are not significant transmission channels. Thus, crises enter the model with a negative sign in most instances, but they do not change the coefficient of capital account openness considerably, suggesting that, while there may be linkages between openness and crises, financial openness exerts an independent negative effect on the labor share. Similarly, while a larger government presence, as measured by the government share of GDP, affects the labor share of income positively as does government spending (measured by the budget deficit), neither of these variables reduces the coefficient on capital account openness, again suggesting that capital account openness has an independent negative effect on labor share. Finally, adding the relative price effects of openness, the real interest rate and the nominal exchange rate into the equation does not mitigate the effect either.

In most cases and specifications, therefore, increasing the potential for capital mobility has an independent and negative effect on the labor share of income, reflecting, perhaps, a decrease in the ability of labor to bargain over production rents. This is, prima facie, strong evidence for the claim that a liberal financial regime may work so as to reduce the relative power of labor versus capital. The exact manner in which this effect works, and the extent to which it matters will differ across countries, depends on the structure of the economy. Presumably the effect is stronger in countries with a large manufacturing sector and stronger labor unions.

To summarize, while crisis and reduced scope for expansionary policy both reduce labor share, as claimed by some, and while capital account openness may indeed contribute to both of these, in the period of study, it had an additional negative impact on the labor share of income. It is difficult to quantify the extent of the effect, given the ordinal definition of the labor share. Results using a standardized coefficient model reported in Jayadev (2003) show that the effect of capital account openness on the labor share is independently roughly the same as the effect of having a fir

At first cut therefore, the notion that capital account distribution-neutral or trivial may be questioned. This c qualitatively from the findings of Harrison (2002) in who controls only matter when interacted with general governme A potential reason for this difference may be precisely th indicator used here takes into account the intensity of controls.

This underscores the need to have a more nuanced indicator of the strength of controls; a binary indicator may obscure or miss out subtler relationships present in the data.

Given the predictions of standard trade models, we may expect that the effect of capital account openness on labor share is negative in high-income countries, but positive in developing countries. It is true that the loss of bargaining power is a problem that afflicts labor both in the North and the South. However, in developing countries there is a counteracting factor in the fact that factor intensity of capital is low, which will lead to an increase in the labor share with capital accumulation under conditions where the elasticity of substitution between labor and capital is less than one. In order to assess this, we repeat the estimation above with a sample restricted to developing countries. The results are given in Table 2.9.

Perhaps most strikingly, while the t-statistics on the capital accounts are not as large as with the whole sample, the coefficient on the capital account openness variable remains significant across most specifications, and more crucially, is negative. Capital account openness is associated with falling labor shares in developing countries as well, contrary to a prediction of regression to the mean that may be derived from standard Hecksher-Ohlin theory. That is to say, while one might expect a tendency for there to be a convergence in the labor share of income across countries arising from openness, there is little evidence to support this. Financial openness exerts a downward pressure on labor shares both in the North and in the South.

Finally, we repeat the analysis using five-year averages to control for cyclical effects. These are given in Table 2.10. The five-year averages show remarkably similar coefficients for the effect of capital account openness on labor share, suggesting that these effects are not only short-term. That is to say, the negative impact that capital account openness has on the share of income going to labor persists over time.

Table 2.9 All developing countries, OLS model with fixed effects

Dependent variable: Compensation of employees /GDP	Low income countries	Lower middle income countries	Upper middle income countries
Trend	−0.001	−0.002**	0.001
	(−1.6)	(−2.0)	(0.79)
Real GDP per capita	0.00075	0.0037*	0.0009
	(0.42)	(6.4)	(2.8)
Capital account openness	0.019	−0.018**	−0.023**
	(1.5)	(−2.5)	(−2.4)
Current account restrictions	0.0027**	−0.0069	−0.0089
	(1.9)	(0.1)	(−0.89)
Crisis	0.012	−0.023*	0.012
	(1.13)	(−3.2)	(1.3)
Government share of GDP	0.60*	0.13	−0.13
	(4.17)	(1.2)	(−1.03)
Budget surplus	0.0006	−0.007	−0.003
	(0.55)	(−10.3)	(−3.11)
Real interest rate	0.001**	0.0005*	0.001
	(2.22)	(2.97)	(3.5)
Nominal exchange rate	−0.00075	−0.00022	−0.00013
	(−0.83)	(−1.07)	(−1.8)
Liquid liabilities to GDP	−0.22**	0.044	−0.00049
	(−2.1)	(1.3)	(0.01)
R^2	0.07	0.57	0.04
Observations	121	162	120
No. of cross-sections	16	18	13

Table 2.10   Labor share model with five-year averages

Trend	−0.0028*
	(−6.15)
Log (real GDP per capita)	0.0822*
	(5.11)
Capital account openness	−0.0111*
	(−2.9)
Current account restrictions	−0.0004
	(−0.08)
Crisis	−0.0231**
	(−2.57)
Government share of GDP	0.0018*
	(4.23)
Budget surplus	−0.0013**
	(−2.44)
Real interest rate	0.0008*
	(3.79)
Nominal exchange rate	−0.0001*
	(−3.24)
Financial depth	0.0507*
	(3.58)
R^2	0.62
Observations	225
No. of cross–sections	53

CONCLUSION

The Bellman looked uffish, and wrinkled his brow.
If only you'd spoken before!
It's excessively awkward to mention it now,
With the Snark, so to speak, at the door!'

Lewis Carroll (*The Hunting of the Snark*)

The economic effects of capital account liberalization have been a matter of intense debate among economists for a decade. Standard theories have argued that liberalization and more open capital account should spur economic growth by encouraging more investment and economic efficiency, while reducing volatility. There is mounting evidence, including a slew of catastrophic financial crises over this period that gives reason to be skeptical about this claim.

In this chapter, we have made efforts to extend current empirical studies by constructing a sophisticated capital account openness index and attempting to shed new light on the potential preconditions that might accelerate growth. We find little evidence that capital account liberalization can spur growth in cross-country regressions. Even under some typical preconditions, we do not find evidence of the benefits of liberalization for economic growth. Finally, we present partial evidence that capital controls can spur growth in more homogeneous countries, and countries with better institutions, and higher corporate debt ratio. Cross-section studies appear to refute the mainstream argument for capital account liberalization, while panel regressions show mixed results. It is clear in any case that the empirical search for the growth effects of financial openness has been fruitless, despite the predictions of theory.

While capital account openness has an ambiguous impact on growth, there are clearer implications for its effect on factor shares. Specifically, liberalization is associated with a decreased share of productive income going to labor, even controlling for a wide range of factors and trends. This finding provides substantial support for the contention that liberalization may cause a decline in the political power of labor, thus allowing for a 'race to the bottom' scenario to emerge. If these results are somewhat distressing for labor, they also do come with a very large silver lining. One of the most painful facets of the changing political and economic climate in the last two decades for labor unions and working people is the fact that labor in the developed world seems to be hopelessly pitted against labor in the developing world with regard to many issues. Thus, for example, on such matters as international labor standards, sweatshops, and trade sanctions, there has often been bitter contestation between groups in the North and in the South with regard to appropriate policy. Our research suggests that on the issue of capital account liberalization at least, there is little conflict. To the extent that financial openness has negative effects on the labor share across many different economies in both the developed world and the developing world, there is a rare opportunity for cross-country labor solidarity to advocate for controls over capital or multilateral agreements to mitigate the depredations of an unregulated financial market.

APPENDIX

Table 2.A1 Variables and sources

Variable	Source
Growth effects	
Average real per capita GDP growth	World Development Indicators
Investment share of GDP	World Development Indicators
Average secondary school enrollment percent of total population	World Development Indicators
Liquid liabilities to GDP	Beck, Demirgüç-Kunt and Levine (1999).
Inflation: CPI growth rate	World Development Indicators
Black market premium	Easterly (2001)
Trade openness	World Development Indicators
GADP: Government anti-diversion index	Hall and Jones (1999)
Corruption	Knack and Keefer (1995)
Weberian state index	Evans and Rauch (1999)
Ethnic fragmentation	Krain (1997)
Land Gini	Deininger and Olinto (2000)
Corporate debt ratio	Demirgüc-Kunt and Maksimovic (1996)
DISTRIBUTION EFFECTS	
Labor share	United Nations National Account Statistics CD ROM
Real interest rates	IMF international financial statistics
Liquid liabilities to GDP	Beck, Demirgüç-Kunt and Levine (1999)
Nominal exchange rate	IMF international financial statistics
Budget surplus	World Development Indicators/ IMF international financial statistics
Crisis	Derived from Nominal Exchange Rate
Government share of GDP	Penn World Tables 6.0
Current account restrictions	Mody and Murshid (2000) from IMF annual report on exchange rate arrangements and restrictions

- Black market premium: Degree of distortion of the official exchange rate from the market exchange rate
- Trade openness: Own-import weighted average tariff and non-tariff on import and intermediate and capital goods
- Government anti–diversion index: Average of indices of law and order, bureaucratic quality, corruption, risk of expropriation and government repudiation of contracts from 84 to 94, based on the survey of International Country Risk Guide (ICRG).
- Corruption: Index developed by International Country Risk Guide (ICRG) as part of the political risk index
- Weberian state index: Index of bureaucratic and meritocratic nature of state organization using a coding methodology available at http://weber.ucsd.edu/~jrauch/webstate/codebook.html
- Ethnic fractionalization index: Operationalized by calculating the proportion of each ethnic group within the population, squaring it and summing these squared proportions. The index is obtained by subtracting this sum from 1
- Land Gini: Percentage of land held by percent of population
- Corporate debt ratio: Corporate debt/Corporate equity from International Financial Corporation

NOTES

We are very grateful to Mathieu Dufour for his extensive assistance in the construction of the capital account liberalization index, and to Gerald Epstein for his unstinting encouragement and insightful comments. We thank the Political Economy Research Insititute for financial support and Kade Finnoff for careful editorial assistance. All errors remain, as always, ours.

1. In real terms, using the US CPI deflator, the change is just as impressive, increasing roughly tenfold.
2. Williamson (2002) claims that Capital account liberalization was not part of the consensus. While this may be true, it rapidly became a *de facto* item on the agenda of the IMF in the 1980s.
3. In any case, it is also true that most of the relevant literature has used this methodology.
4. While varied, these preconditions typically reduce in shorthand to a notion of macroeconomic stability and 'sound' financial sector institutions (McKinnon 1991, Eichengreen and Mussa 1998).
5. For a comprehensive review of these, see Lee (2003).
6. By contrast, political scientists (Haggard and Maxfield 1996) have developed more elaborate narratives on the effects of financial openness on different groups in society.
7. Linkages between the factor share of income and the interpersonal share of income are often made in other contexts. Pikkety et al. (2003), for example, show that the reduction of inequality in France over the last two centuries has been largely due to a transfer of wealth from holders of rental income to the general population through the mechanism of an estate tax. Similarly, Rodriguez (2000) finds that much of the inequality in Venezuela in the last 3 decades is caused by the large share of income accruing to capital in that country.
8. See Eichengreen (2001) for more criticisms of this approach.

9.   Kraay (1998), for example, distinguishes only between major periods of change (five years of controls followed by five years of no controls).

10. Specifically, when we use a five-year average fixed effects model assuming country-specific unobserved effects, the coefficient of capital account liberalization is positive and significant; this is so with other control variables. However, the same model with annual data, four-year averages and ten-year averages show insignificant results. In the fixed effects model, we could not include institutional variables due to data availability. For a more extensive examination, see Lee (2003).

11. The sources for the data used are given in the Appendix.

12. These indicators and their sources are detailed in the Appendix.

13. Unlike studies that support it (Borensztein et al. 1998; Bosworth and Collins 1999) Carkovic and Levine (2001) report that the FDI does not spur domestic investment and Edison et al. (2002b) are also skeptical about the effect of capital inflows on growth. Rodrik (1998) and Kraay (1998) find the same negative result for investment.

14. We report the result of the regression in which the investment share is included, although excluding it does not change the results.

15. The setup for the model is: $y_i = \beta_1 + \beta_2 X_i + \beta_3 CAL_i Y_i + \beta_4 CAL_i Y_i^2 + \varepsilon_i$. If the hypothesis is correct, β_3 should be significantly positive and large while β_4 should be negative and small.

16. See Lee (2003) for details on non-OECD sub-samples.

17. For a more detailed exposition of the analyses cited in this section, see Lee (2003)

18. From Beck et al. (1999)

19. For corruption measures, we use the indicator created by Knack and Keefer (1995). Using Mauro's (1995) index, however, does not change the result.

20. See Appendix for details.

21. Regressing growth on the interaction between capital account openness proxied by the IMF dummy and the black market premium suggests that a large premium does reduce the effect of openness on growth.

22. These include East Asian countries such as Korea, a representative of the developmental state.

23. This section draws largely from the findings of Jayadev (2003).

24. Rowthorn (1999) shows that this is the case in most empirical research.

25. In certain cases, this effect does work through some obvious transmission mechanisms. For example, in Jayadev (2003), it is shown that the negative effect of capital account openness in developing countries is explained in part by its disciplining effect on government budgets.

REFERENCES

Alesina, A., V. Grilli and M. Milesi-Ferretti (1994), 'The Political Economy of Capital Controls', in L. Leiderman and A. Raizin (eds), *Capital Mobility: The Impact on Consumptions, Investment and Growth*, Cambridge, UK: Cambridge University Press, pp. 289–321.

Allen, Mark (2002), 'Comment on Cobham, "Capital Account Liberalization and Poverty" ', *Oxfam Discussion Papers*.

Amsden, A. (1989), *Asia's Next Giant: South Korea and Late Industrialization*, Oxford, UK: Oxford University Press.

Ariyoshi, Akira, Karl Habermeier, Bernard Laurens et al. (2000), 'Capital Controls: Country Experiences with their Use and Liberalization', IMF Occasional Paper No. 190.

Arteta, C., B. Eichengreen and C. Wyplosz (2001), 'When does Capital Account Liberalization Help more than it Hurts?', NBER Working Paper No. 8414.

Bekaert, Geert (1995), 'Market Integration and Investment Barriers in Emerging

Markets', *World Bank Economic Review*, **9**, 75–108.

Bekaert Geert, C. Harvey and C. Lundblad (2001), 'Does Financial Liberalization Spur Growth?', NBER Working Paper No. 8245.

Borensztein, E., J. De-Gregorio, and J. W. Lee (1998), 'How Does Foreign Direct Investment Affect Economic Growth?', *Journal of International Economics*, **45** (1), 115–135.

Bosworth, B., and Collins, S. (1999), 'Capital Flows to Developing Economies: Implications for Saving and Investment', *Brookings Institution Paper on Economic Activity* No. 1, 143–169.

Bronfenbrenner, K. (1997), 'The Effects of Plant Closing or Threat of Plant Closing on the Right of Workers to Organize', Mimeo, Cornell University.

Brecher, R. and C. Diaz-Alejandro (1977), 'Tariffs, Foreign Capital, and Immiserizing Growth', *Journal of International Economics*, **7** (4), 317–322.

Calderon, Cesar and Alberto Chong (2001), 'External Sector and Income Inequality in Interdependent Economies Using a Dynamic Panel Data Approach', *Economics Letters*, **71** (2), 225–231.

Carkovic, M. and R. Levine (2001), 'Does Foreign Direct Investment Accelerate Economic Growth?', Mimeo.

Carrol, L. (1865), *Alice in Wonderland*, London: Macmillan and Co.

Carrol, L. (1872), *Through the Looking Glass, And What Alice Found There*, London: Macmillan and Co.

Carrol, L. (1876*). The Hunting of the Snark*, London: Macmillan and Co.

Chanda, A. (2001), 'The Influence of Capital Controls on Long Run Growth: Where and How Much?', Mimeo, Brown University.

Chang, Ha Joon (2002), *Kicking Away the Ladder: Development Strategy in Historical Perspective*, London, UK: Anthem Press.

Choi, Minsik (2001), 'Threat Effect of Foreign Direct Investment on Labor Union Wage Premium', University of Massachusetts, Amherst: Political Economy Research Insititute Working Paper.

Cobham, Alexander (2000), 'Capital Account Liberalization and Poverty', Queen Elizabeth House, Oxford: Queen Elizabeth House Working Paper 70.

Cody, Brian J. (1990), 'Exchange Controls, Political Risk and the Eurocurrency Market: New Evidence from Tests of Covered Interest Rate Parity', International Economic Journal **42**, 75–86.

Cooper, R. N. (1999), 'Should Capital Controls be Banished?', *Brookings Papers on Economic Activity* No. 1, 89–125.

Crotty, James and Gerald Epstein (1996), 'In Defense of Capital Controls', *Socialist Register*, reprinted in Leo Panitch, Colin Leys, Alan Zuege and Martijn Konings (eds) (2004), *The Globalization Decade: A Critical Reader*, London: The Merlin Press, pp. 80–110.

Das, Mitali and Sanket Mohapatra (2002), 'Income Inequality: The Aftermath of Stock Market Liberalization in Emerging Markets', Columbia University Department of Economics Discussion Paper Series Discussion Paper No. 0102–42.

Deininger, K. and P. Olinto (2000), 'Asset Distribution, Inequality, and Growth', World Bank Discussion Paper No. 2375.

Demirgüç-Kunt, A. and Maksimovic, V. (1996), 'Stock Market Development and Firm Financing Choices', The World Bank Economic Review, **10** (2), 341–369.

Demirgüç-Kunt, A. and Maksimovic, V. (1998), 'Financial Liberalization and Financial Fragility', IMF Working Paper 98/93, Washington, US: International

Monetary Fund.
Demirgüç-Kunt, A. and Detragiache, E. (1998), 'Financial Liberalization and Financial Fragility', IMF Working Paper No. 98/83, Washington, US: International Monetary Fund.
Diwan, Ishac (2000), 'Labor Shares and Globalization', Mimeo, Prepared for the OECD Conference on Globalization and Inequality, Paris.
Diwan, Ishac (2001), 'Debt as Sweat: Labor, financial crises, and the globalization of capital', Mimeo, World Bank.
Dornbusch, R. (1998), 'Capital Controls: An Idea Whose Time is Past, in *Should the IMF Pursue Capital Account Convertibility*', Princeton Essays in International Finance, No. 207.
Easterly, W. (2001), 'The Lost Decades: Developing Countries' Stagnation in Spite of Policy Reform 1980–1998' *Journal of Economic Growth*, **6** (2), 135–157.
.Edison, H. J. et al. (2002a), 'Capital Account Liberalization and Economic Performance: Survey and Synthesis', NBER working paper.
Edison, H. J. et al. (2002b), 'International Financial Integration and Economic Growth', IMF Working Paper No. WP/02/145.
Edwards, S. (ed.) (2001), 'Capital Mobility and Economic Performance: Are Emerging Economies Different?', NBER Working Paper No. 8076.
Eichengreen, B. and M. Mussa (1998), 'Capital Account Liberalization and the IMF', *Finance and Development*, **35** (4), 16–19.
Eichengreen, B. and M. Mussa (2001), 'Capital Account Liberalization: What Do the Cross-Country Studies Tell Us?', *The World Bank Economic Review*, **15** (3), 341–365.
Eichengreen, B., M. Mussa, A. K. Rose and C. Wyplosz (1997), 'Contagious Currency Crises', NBER Working Paper No. 5681.
Epstein, Gerald, Ilene Grabel and K. S. Jomo, (2003) 'Capital Management Techniques In Developing Countries: An Assessment of Experiences from the 1990s and Lessons For the Future', University of Massachusetts, Amherst: Political Economy Research Insititute Working Paper No. 56.
Evans, P. B. (1995), *Embedded Autonomy: States and Industrial Transformation*, Princeton, US: Princeton University Press.
Evans, P. and Rauch, J. (1999), 'Bureaucracy and Growth: A Cross-national Analysis of the Effects of Weberian State Structures on Economic Growth', *American Sociological Review*, **64** (10), 748–765.
Fischer, S. (1998), 'Capital-account Liberalization and the Role of the IMF', in Kenen, P. (ed.), *Should the IMF Pursue Capital-account Convertibility?* Princeton Essays in International Finance, 207.
Fisher, Irving (1930), *The Theory of Interest*, New York, US: Macmillan.
Frankel, Jeffrey A. and Alan T. MacArthur (1988), 'Political vs. Currency Premia in International Real Interest Differentials: A Study of Forward Rates for 24 Countries', *European Economic Review*, **32**, 1083–1114.
Garrett, Geoffrey (1995), 'Capital Mobility, Trade, and the Domestic Politics of Economic Policy', *International Organization*, **49**, 657–687.
Giavazzi, Franceco and Marco Pagano (1988), 'Capital Controls and the European MonetarySystem', in Donald E. Fair and Christian de Boissieu (eds), *International Monetary and Financial Integration*, Dordrecht: Martinus Nijhoff, pp.261–289.
Gourinchas, P. and Olivier Jeanne, (2002), 'On the Benefits of Capital Market Integration for Emerging Market Economies', Mimeo, World Bank.
Grabel, Ilene (1997), 'Speculation-led Economic Development: A Post-Keynesian

Interpretation of Financial Liberalization in the Third World', *International Review of Applied Economics*, **9** (2), 127–149.

Grilli, V. and G. M. Milesi-Ferretti (1995), 'Economic Effects and Structural Determinants of Capital Controls', IMF Staff Paper, **42** (3), 517–551.

Guitan, M. (1997), 'Reality and the Logic of Capital Flow Liberalization', in C. P. Ries, and R. J. Sweeney (eds), *Capital Controls in Emerging Economies*, US: Westview Press, pp. 189–244, 189-244

Hall, R. and C. I. Jones (1999), 'Why Do Some Countries Produce So Much More Output per Worker than Others?', *Quarterly Journal of Economics*, **114** (1), 83–116.

Haggard, S. and S. Maxfield (1996), 'The political economy of financial internationalization in the developing world', *International Organization* **50**, 35–68

Harrison, Ann E. (2002), 'Has globalization eroded labor's share?', mimeo, University of California, Berkeley.

Harrison, Ann E. and Gordon Hanson (1999), 'Who Gains from Trade Reform: Some Remaining Puzzles', *Journal of Development Economics*, **59**, 125–154.

IMF (2001), IMF Economic Outlook 2001, Chapter 4.

IMF, Exchange Arrangements and Exchange Restrictions, Annual Reports (various editions)

Jayadev, Arjun (2003), 'The Impact Of Capital Account Liberalization on the Functional Distribution of Income', Mimeo, University of Massachusetts, Amherst and Political Economy Research Institute.

Kim, W. C. (2000), 'Does Capital Account Liberalization Discipline Budget Deficit?', mimeo, Harvard University.

Kim, W. C. and Wei, S. (1999), 'Foreign Portfolio Investors Before and During a Crisis', NBER Working Paper No. 6968.

Klein, M. and Olivei, G. (2001), 'Capital Account Liberalization, Financial Depth, and Economic Growth', Mimeo, Tufts University.

Klein, M. W. (2003), 'Capital Account Openness and the Variety of Growth Experience', NBER Working Paper No. 9500.

Knack, S. and Keefer, P. (1995), 'Institutions and Economic Performance: Cross-country tests using Alternative Institutional Measures', *Economics and Politics*, 7 (3), 207–227.

Kraay, A. (1998), 'In Search of the Macroeconomic Effects of Capital Account Liberalization', Mimeo, World Bank.

Krain, M. (1997), 'State-sponsored Mass Murder', *Journal of Conflict Resolutions*, **41** (3).

Kravis, Irving B. (1962), *The Structure of Income: Some Quantitative Essays*, Philadelphia, US: University of Philadelphia Press.

Kravis, Irving B. (1968), 'Income Distribution: I–Functional Share', in David L. Sill, (ed.), *International Encyclopaedia of Social Sciences*, **7**, 132–145, New York, US: Macmillan and the Free Press.

Krueger, Alan B. (1999), 'Measuring Labor's Share', NBER Working Paper No. 7006.

Kuznets, Simon (1966), *Modern Economic Growth: Rate, Structure, and Spread*, New Haven, US: Yale University Press.

Lee, Kang-Kook (2003), 'Does Capital Account Liberalization Spur Economic Growth, or Do Controls? Focusing on Conditions and Channels', Mimeo, University of Massachusetts, Amherst.

Levine, R. (1997), 'Financial Development and Economic Growth: Views and

Agenda', *Journal of Economic Literature*, **35** (2).

Marston, Richard C. (1993), 'Interest Differentials Under Bretton Woods and the Post-Bretton Woods Float: The Effects of Capital Controls and Exchange Risk', in Michael Bordo and Barry Eichengreen (eds), *A Retrospective on the Bretton Woods System,* Chicago, US: University of Chicago Press, pp. 515–546.

Marston, Richard C. (1995), *International Financial Integration: A Study of Interest Differentials Between the Major Industrial Countries,* New York, US: Cambridge University Press.

Mauro, P. (1995), 'Corruption and Growth', *Quarterly Journal of Economics*, **110** (3).

McKinnon, R. (1991), *The Order of Economic Liberalization*, Baltimore, US: Johns Hopkins University Press.

McKinnon, R. and Pill, H. (1999), 'Exchange Rate Regimes for Emerging Markets: Moral Hazard and International Overborrowing', *Oxford Review of Economic Policy*, **15** (3), 19–38.

Mody, A. and Murshid, A. P. (2002), 'Growing Up with Capital Flows', IMF Working Paper No. WP/02/75.

Nembhard, J. G. (1996), *Capital Control, Financial Regulation and Industrial Policy in South Korea and Brazil,* Westport, US: Praeger Publishers.

Obstfeld, M. (1994), 'Risk-Taking, Global Diversification and Growth', *American Economic Review*, **84** (5), 1310–1329.

O'Donnell, Barry (2001a), 'Financial Openness and Economic Performance', Trinity College, Unpublished PhD Thesis.

O'Donnell, Barry (2001b), 'Financial Openness and Economic Performance: Does Financial Depth Matter?', Trinity College, Unpublished PhD Thesis.

Ortega, Daniel and Francisco Rodriguez (2001), 'Openness and factor shares' Mimeo.

Quinn, Dennis (1997), 'The Correlates of Change in the International Financial Regulation', *American Political Science Review*, **91** (3), 531–551.

Palma G. (1998), 'Three and a Half Cycles of 'Mania, Panic, and [Asymmetric] Crash': East Asia and Latin America Compared', *Cambridge Journal of Economics* **22**, 789–80.

Pikkety, T., G. Postel-Vinay and J.L. Rosenthal, (2003), 'Wealth Concentration in a Developing Economy: Paris and France, 1807–1994', Mimeo.

Prasad Eswar , Kenneth Rogoff, Shang-Jin Wei and M. Ayhan Kose (2003), 'Effects of Financial Globalization on Developing Countries: Some Empirical Evidence', International Monetary Fund.

Rajan, R. S. (1999), 'Sand in the Wheels of International Finance: Revisiting the Debate in Light of the East Asian Mayhem', Mimeo.

Ries, C. P. and Sweeney, R. J. (eds) (1997), *Capital Controls in Emerging Economies*, Boulder, US: Westview Press.

Rodriguez, C.F. (2000), 'Factor Shares and Resource Booms: Accounting for the Evolution of Venezuelan Inequality', Mimeo.

Rodrik. D. (1995), 'Getting Interventions Right: How South Korea and Taiwan Grew Rich', *Economic Policy*, **20**, 55–107.

Rodrik. D. (1997), 'Has globalization gone too far?', Institute for International Economics.

Rodrik. D. (1998), 'Who Needs Capital Account Convertibility?' in Kenen, P. (ed), *Should the IMF Pursue Capital-Account Convertibility*? Princeton Essays in International Finance, No. 207.

Rodrik. D. (1998b), 'Making openness work', Policy Essays.

Rodrik. D. (2000), 'Factor Shares and Resource Booms: Accounting for the Evolution of Venezuelan Inequality', Mimeo.

Rowthorn, R. (2000), 'Unemployment, Wage Bargaining and Capital-Labour Substitution', Cambridge Journal of Economics, **23** (4), 413–425.

Reddy, S. and A. Dube (2000), 'Liberalization, Income Distribution and Political Economy: The Bargaining Channel and its Implications', Mimeo, Harvard University.

Stiglitz, J. E. (2000), 'Capital Market Liberalization, Economic Growth, and Instability', *World Development*, **28** (6), 1075–1086.

Wade, R. (1998), 'The Asian crisis: The High Debt Model Versus the Wall Street-Treasury-IMF complex', *New Left Review*, **228**, 3–24.

Williamson, J. (2002), 'Did the Washington Consensus fail?', Speech to the International Institute of Economics, November 6, 2002.

3. Capital Flight: Meanings and Measures

Edsel L. Beja, Jr.

INTRODUCTION

In this book, capital flight is defined as the net unrecorded capital outflows from a capital-scarce developing country. It is measured as the difference between the recorded sources and recorded uses of funds. This definition is by no means the only definition of capital flight, but it was chosen because of its close association with the research questions raised in this book. The task of illustrating what capital flight means to various developing countries is left to the country case studies (see Chapters 4 to 10); this chapter presents the various definitions and procedures used to estimate capital flight.

The chapter has four parts. After this introduction, Section 2 presents definitions of capital flight; in Section 3, the methods of estimating capital flight are discussed. Section 4 draws conclusions on our definition of capital flight.

MEANINGS OF CAPITAL FLIGHT

Capital flight is a complex phenomenon that is essentially unobservable. Often the reasons for engaging in capital flight are unclear. For these reasons, capital flight is a difficult object to pinpoint; it may be disguised as normal capital outflow or it may occur as pure flight, like trade misinvoicing, for example.

How do we make sense of this complexity? One strategy that scholars have used is to differentiate capital flight from capital outflows. A popular approach identifies capital flight as illegal and capital outflows as legal, while another approach defines capital flight as unreported (for example, the smuggling of currencies) and capital outflow as reported. The assumption is that capital flight is a distinct entity that can be identified so that domestic authorities can gain control over that capital. In this sense, capital flight represents lost income or revenue of the government. Capital outflows are to be expected and considered normal in the context of open and integrated economies, and it is capital flight per se that is interesting.

Another strategy is not to make any distinction at all, but rather to maintain that capital flight is a residual, or the net unrecorded capital outflow. The assumption is that capital flight takes place in the context of or is embedded in capital outflows. Thus, capital flight cannot be easily separated from capital outflows. What one gets as capital flight is merely a residual after attempting to account for capital and foreign exchange flows. In this sense, capital flight represents lost resources that could have been utilized in the domestic economy to promote economic activity. The notion that capital flight is a residual is interesting because of its implications for capital scarcity and the concomitant adverse consequences on the economy.

Capital Flight or Capital Outflow?

To distinguish capital flight from capital outflows, scholars have employed these broad criteria: volume, motive, and direction of the capital flows (see, for example, Cumby and Levich, 1987; Deppler and Williamson, 1987; Gordon and Levine, 1989).[1] The three variables are linked to one another, although we will treat them as separate categories in order to simplify the exposition that follows.

Capital flight in terms of volume
In terms of volume, capital outflows can be normal or abnormal. A normal capital outflow suggests investment portfolio diversification. In contrast, an abnormal capital outflow suggests a sudden or discrete outflow often set off by some adverse domestic or external economic condition. In addition, abnormal outflows typically occur in episodes of large outflows. Therefore, the nature of an abnormal outflow of capital defines it as capital flight. However, when there is capital outflow because better opportunities or higher returns are available elsewhere, it is considered normal. In this sense, there is no capital flight.

When the outflow is due to some discriminatory treatment of capital or due to fear, say, of a significant loss in the value of capital, there is capital flight (see, for example, Kindleberger 1937; Walter 1987). For instance, when capital holders suspect that there will be unfavorable and drastic changes in the economic policies of a country, they withdraw their investments and an upsurge in capital outflow takes place. In this case, the outflow is defined as capital flight. When massive amounts of capital pull out because of herd behavior brought about by panic or contagion, it is also capital flight. In short, the difference in the magnitude of the capital outflows is the key indicator for defining capital flight.

Deppler and Williamson (1987) stress that capital flight arises because of some concerns that if the capital is held in the country, it will experience a substantial or discrete loss in value. It is usual that an increase in expropriation risk, or the possibility that the government will seize assets through its fiscal powers, will scare away the capital holders. The important point is that the potential losses on the value of capital are perceived to be large relative to what was deployed in the economy. However, because of its subjective nature, this approach can be problematic if the concern is to have an 'objective' basis for decisions.[2]

The same can be said when there are expectations of large currency devaluations or concerns about unsustainable fiscal deficits. Capital holders anticipate future adverse conditions by pulling out their capital. Fear, suspicion or uncertainty makes capital flee to safer places, yet there is no presumption that capital flight is motivated by some irregular activity or hidden motive. The response of capital to risk and uncertainty defines capital flight.

Other scholars have extended the notion of risk to cover variables such as political instability, the possibility of war, uncertainties in developmental assistance or aid, and so on. (See, for example, Alesina and Tabellini 1989; Collier et al. 2001; Hermes and Lensink 2001; Lensink et al. 2000.) Political instability increases the perceived losses on capital and capital holders respond by pulling out their capital. Uncertainty in aid is manifested as private appropriation like conspicuous consumption or embezzlement of funds by the elite or by those who have access to such funds. In either case, political stability is undermined, raising risk and the perceived losses on capital, and capital holders respond by withdrawing their capital. In these cases, there are abnormal capital outflows that are therefore considered capital flight.

Hot money definition   An operational interpretation of abnormal capital outflows is Cuddington (1986), who considers hot money, or short-term capital outflows, as capital flight. Specifically, he defines capital flight as short-run speculative capital outflows. It involves hot money that is quick to respond to 'political and financial crises, heavier taxes ... tightening of capital controls, or [a] major devaluation ... or actual or incipient hyperinflation' (Cuddington 1986: 2).

The hot money definition refers only to funds that quickly respond to changes in the level of risk and returns. Short-term capital is most sensitive to unfavorable news or information that could have significant impacts on the value of capital. Money in equities and capital markets, for example, can be withdrawn quite easily and transferred to other investment areas. Thus, large and sudden outflows of short-term capital constitute capital flight. Nevertheless, short-term capital is also capital that returns quickly when conditions become acceptable for capital holders.

It is possible to broaden Cuddington's definition given global trends and advances in finance.[3] Hot money can be expanded to include long-term

capital. For example, long-term country bonds are not as sh[...]
investments, but they can be traded without much difficu[...]
bonds markets. In fact, when short-term and long-term se[...]
traded, not only is there little distinction in the volatility of [...]
also difficult to differentiate one from the other by simply ۱۰۰۰۰۰g
time series properties (see, for example, Claessens et al. 1993). Bond holders
can dispose of their holdings and transfer the capital elsewhere when a rise in
political risk makes a country bond unattractive. The same can happen when
there is an economic crisis. In any case, there is a sudden outflow of capital,
and that is defined as capital flight.

Capital flight as a motive

In terms of motive, capital outflows occur either because domestic residents
want to secure favorable returns to their capital, seek to evade taxes, or
intend to circumvent government authority like controls or regulations on
capital movements and foreign exchange. The desire to secure favorable
returns to capital abroad constitutes normal capital outflow as described
earlier, while seeking to evade taxes or circumvent government regulations is
an abnormal or irregular capital outflow, which is capital flight. The big
challenge, of course, is to uncover the motive for an action because in an
open economy, residents can engage in international transactions, including
making investments abroad. Provided the motive is identified, we can make
the following conjectures: if the motive is economic in nature (undertaken to
pursue favorable returns elsewhere), the capital outflow is not defined as
capital flight. If, on the other hand, the motive is to avoid government
control or evade payment of taxes and the like, or even to keep capital secret,
then it is defined as capital flight (see also Walter 1987, 1990).

Dooley definition   An application that highlights motive is that presented
by Dooley (1986: 15), who defines capital flight as that which is 'motivated
by the desire of residents to obtain financial assets and earnings on those
assets which remain outside the control of domestic authorities.' According
to this approach, abnormal risk (in the Kindleberger-Deppler-Williamson
sense) is not enough to define a capital outflow as capital flight; there must
exist an inconsistency between the actions of capital holders and what is
being reported to or recorded by the domestic authorities. Thus, the key
dimension to stress is the intention underlying capital outflows. The guiding
principle is whether the placement of capital abroad is done to evade the
control of domestic authorities on the capital; if so, the capital outflow is
capital flight.

In contrast to the volume-based definitions, the Dooley definition suggests
that some large and discrete capital outflows can be considered normal if
they are accounted for or reported to the domestic authorities. The converse

applies; that is, even if the volume of the capital outflow is small but goes unreported, the outflow is considered capital flight. After accounting for legitimate capital outflows, the Dooley definition measures what is considered pure capital flight.

Even if residents do not send or move any capital abroad, capital flight can still take place for as long as the earnings on current foreign assets (that is, previous capital flight) are not being reported to domestic authorities. The Dooley definition, however, is not useful when earnings on current foreign capital are reported but are not repatriated to the domestic economy because they are recorded as normal capital outflows.

Of course, changes in perceived risks or uncertainty concerning the performance of the domestic economy can factor into the motives for capital outflows, leading to the non-reporting or disguising of capital outflows to prevent the value of the capital from eroding.

An example is the differential tax treatment of domestic and foreign capital, with the latter enjoying little or no tax obligation. In this case, domestic capital holders withdraw their capital but return it in the guise of foreign investments. The differential treatment between domestic and external debt can also bring about a similar process (see, for example, Eaton 1987). If external debt is guaranteed by the government while domestic debt is not, capital holders can withdraw their capital and lend it to their government from abroad. The two examples illustrate what is called round-tripping of capital, which is a way to avoid risks and a form of capital flight (see, for example, Dooley 1986; Boyce 1992, 1993).

Legal or illegal flows   We can classify capital outflows as legal or illegal. A capital outflow sanctioned by the law and reported or recorded is not defined as capital flight. If it was neither sanctioned nor reported, or if it was reported but the information was inaccurately recorded or even manipulated, the outflow is defined as capital flight.

Of course, as Cumby and Levich (1987: 30) point out, 'illegal transactions need not be motivated by a desire to avoid domestic financial markets per se. The primary motivation for certain current account transactions may be the evasion of taxes, quotas, or laws regarding trade in illegal drugs or other activities, and these transactions necessarily generate a capital account dimension.'

If capital flight is motivated by the desire to evade taxes and if tax evasion is considered a crime, it follows that the Dooley definition refers to illegal capital outflows as well. The difficulty in dealing with illegal activities is precisely the fact that they are unrecorded or unreported. As mentioned earlier, illegal capital outflows can occur simultaneously with normal outflows, or may even occur within normal capital outflows.[4] However, extracting the illegal outflows from normal or legal capital outflows can be very difficult.

Systematic trade misinvoicing A category of illegal transactions is trade misinvoicing. It has been argued that the errors and omissions account of the balance of payments tables contains such information (see, for example, Cuddington 1986; IMF 1987). However, errors in recording trade data can occur even if there is no intent to manipulate the receipts.

What we are more concerned with is systematic trade misinvoicing which occurs because exporters or importers, or both, try to circumvent foreign exchange controls and obtain foreign currency that are eventually sent abroad. Bhagwati (1964), Bhagwati et al. (1974), and Gulati (1987) point out that exporters underinvoice while importers overinvoice trade transactions as a way of circumventing controls and regulations on foreign exchange. Thus, the motive for trade misinvoicing is related to the Dooley definition. Either type of trade misinvoicing is therefore defined as capital flight. The same applies to the underinvoicing of imports, which is done in order to avoid customs taxes and trade quotas and export overinvoicing, which in turn is done to obtain export subsidies or other concessions from the government, especially when such incentives are contingent upon meeting some performance-based criteria like exports revenue.

Whether transactions are done in collaboration with trade partners or counterparts is not an issue here. What such activities suggest is that capital flight can be undertaken through the systematic manipulation of trade information. Because government agencies do not have the capability to analyze every trade transaction and determine abnormal or irregular pricing of commodities, trade misinvoicing may be the least risky technique for capital flight.

Of course, there are other illegal activities that can bring about capital flight. For example, money laundering, trafficking in drugs and other contraband items and human trafficking involve foreign exchange transactions that result in capital flight. The nature of such activities implies that the information needed to estimate illegal activities would be very difficult and risky to obtain.

Direction of capital flows and capital flight

The third category distinguishes capital flows in terms of the general direction of flows. When capital flows are both ways, there is no presumption of capital flight. Like normal capital flows, a dual direction in the flows can be expected when capital is mobile and economies are open and integrated. In other words, capital flows into and out of the country are normal, especially when the economy is growing, and these should be encouraged (see, for example, FitzGerald and Cobham 2000).

On the other hand, when the capital flows are mainly or dominantly

outflows, there is a presumption of abnormality since large net capital outflows arise because of higher risks in the domestic economy, economic crisis, some uncertainties in government policies or some other adverse condition. In this context, the net outflow is abnormal and is defined as capital flight.

Another way to apply the directional categories is to consider the point of origin of capital, that is, with respect to the source country and the sender of capital (see, for example, Kindleberger 1937). In particular, capital inflows can be from developed or developing countries. A capital inflow from, say, a developed country can be either from residents or non-residents of the country. The same can be said for capital inflows into a country from a developing country. Similarly, capital outflows can be from developed or developing countries.

There are categories for senders of capital as well. A capital outflow from, say, a developed country can be either from residents or non-residents of the developed country. Similarly, capital outflow from a developing country can be from either residents or non-residents.

The convention is not to define capital outflows from developed countries as capital flight. However, the capital outflows from developing countries, in particular those that are undertaken by residents, are capital flight. In addition, in the current literature, it is usual not to differentiate capital outflows according to who is performing the activity (see, for example, Calvo and Mendoza 1996; Furman and Stiglitz 1998).

Mirror statistic or private assets in foreign banks Another version of the directional-type classification is the mirror statistic (see, for example, BIS 1984; Hermes and Lensink 1992). Hermes and Lensink (1992: 517) define capital flight as the change in the 'assets of non-bank residents of a country held at foreign banks' (for application see, for example, Gajdeczka 1989; Gajdeczka and Oks 1989); that is, when residents maintain foreign bank accounts, the capital held in foreign accounts is capital flight. Note that using information on bank accounts to measure capital flight assumes that private assets are held only in the form of bank deposits. In addition, the approach assumes that what is reported as the deposits of clients from other countries corresponds to the actual assets of non-bank residents held abroad. In other words, the assumption being made is that the nationalities of depositors are declared and reported, which may not be true in practice.

Capital Flight as Net Unrecorded Capital Outflow

The residual or broad definition
In contrast to the above categories of capital flight, other scholars have instead defined capital flight as the net unrecorded capital outflow (see, for

example, Erbe 1985; Morgan Guaranty 1986; World Bank 1985). This definition is often called the residual definition or broad definition of capital flight. Simply, items that cannot be accounted for in recorded capital inflows and recorded foreign exchange transactions are presumably reflected in the residual and therefore defined as capital flight.

The residual definition refers to an aggregate estimate of capital flight. It includes both short-term (hot money) and long-term (cool money) capital outflows.[5] Conceptually, the errors and omissions entry (EO) in the balance of payments (BOP) tables should capture the residual. However, given the nature of the unrecorded and illegal capital flows, the errors and omissions entry (EO_t) is ruled out as a measure of capital flight.

Moreover, the residual definition does not specify any property that suggests volume or motive, although it specifies the direction of the capital. In this sense, capital flight includes not only net unrecorded capital outflows but also resources that are lost from the domestic economy, which could have been employed to produce output and employment (see, for example, Chapter 6 of this book; Boyce and Ndikumana 2001).

MEASURES OF CAPITAL FLIGHT

Baseline Measures of Capital Flight

Different definitions of capital flight mean different measurement methods, and for that reason the estimates can vary. Even so, with good quality data, it is possible to get robust figures for all measurement procedures.

Table 3.1 presents a typology of the main procedures for estimating capital flight, corresponding to the six definitions that were discussed earlier. In this table, we find that capital flight can be estimated using the direct method or indirect method. The direct method takes data from the BOP tables or the Bank for International Settlements (BIS) tables. Two types of indirect measures are available: the derived method and the residual method. In the former, the capital flight estimate is the outcome after performing first-round measurements and adjusting the result using an imputed aggregate of domestic residents' foreign assets to obtain capital flight. The residual method arrives at capital flight after accounting for all capital inflows and recorded foreign exchange outflows.

Before elaborating on the different methods, we take note of the application of BOP principles. We stress this practice in order to avoid mistakes in the estimation procedures. First, we follow BOP reporting conventions. Current account balance (CA) refers to the balance of trade, services, other incomes, and current transfers. Net foreign investment (NFI) is the sum of net foreign direct investments (FDI), and net portfolio equities

(*PORT*).[6] SK_t is short-term capital of 'other' sectors.   The change in
international reserves (ΔRES) refers to the reserve assets, which include

Table 3.1   Capital flight measurement procedures

Direct method	Indirect method	
	Derived method	Residual method
Cuddington (1986)	Dooley (1986)	Erbe (1985)
		World Bank(1985)
Mirror statistic or BIS Method (BIS 1984)	Hermes and Lensink (1992)	Morgan Guaranty (1986)
	Trade misinvoicing (Bhagwati 1964; Gulati 1987)	

Note: See references for bibliography.

changes in holdings of gold, special drawing rights (*SDR*), foreign exchange
assets, reserve position in the IMF and other claims on non-residents (IMF
BOP lines 98–111).

However, total external debt (*DEBT*) follows the World Bank's reporting
convention. The variable $DEBT_t$ comprises the stock of long-term external
debt (*LTDEBT*), short-term external debt (*STDEBT*), and use of IMF credits.
The change in $DEBT_t$ ($\Delta DEBT$) represents increases in total external debt.
However, external debt flows (*ED*) can also be indirectly obtained from the
BOP.[7]

Second, we apply the BOP notation convention.[8] In particular, a positive
number is an inflow and a negative is an outflow.[9] Hence, CA_t is positive
when there is a surplus; it means an inflow of capital. A negative CA_t is a
deficit or an outflow of capital. Similarly, when NFI_t is positive, there is an
inflow of capital; when negative, there is an outflow of capital.   When
$\Delta DEBT_t$ is positive, there is an increase in external debt or an inflow of
capital. When it is negative, it means a decrease in external debt and implies
an outflow of capital.

Both ΔRES_t and errors and omissions (*EO*) follow the reverse sign
convention.   That is, a negative ΔRES_t means an accumulation of
international reserves or an inflow of capital; and positive ΔRES_t means a
reduction in international reserves, or an outflow of capital. Any unaccounted
capital or foreign exchange inflow is represented by a negative EO_t, and vice
versa.

Finally, we follow the convention in representing capital flight (an outflow) with a positive sign. If the estimated capital flight is negative, it means reverse capital flight; that is, there is net unrecorded capital or foreign exchange inflow to the country.

Direct Approach

Hot money or narrow measure

Cuddington (1986) measures capital flight as the sum of SK_t and EO_t (see also Ketkar and Ketkar 1989; Gibson and Tsakalotos 1993). Recall that hot money does not include long-term capital, but Cuddington includes EO_t because he argues that it accounts for the unrecorded SK_t outflows.[10] Thus,

$$KF_{H,\,t} = - SK_t - EO_t \qquad (3.1a)$$

Alternative versions of Equation 3.1a are available:

$$KF_{H,\,t} = - SK1_t - EO_t \qquad (3.1b)$$

$$KF_{H,\,t} = - SK_t - (PORT1_t + PORT_t) - EO_t, \qquad (3.1c)$$

where $SK1_t$ refers only to 'other assets' and $PORT1_t$ is net portfolio 'other bonds' and corporate equities (IMF BOP line 59–61). Among the narrow measures, Equation 3.1b is the narrowest for it considers only a subset of SK_t, while Equation 3.1c is the broadest of the narrow measure; that is, it is the middle estimate.[11]

Mirror statistic or BIS measure

The BIS method uses information on account deposits of BIS-reporting countries as a measure of private foreign assets, or capital flight. However, BIS reports data for 24 countries only, which is a problem in terms of the data coverage.

Alternatively, the BIS procedure can be performed using the IMF's International Financial Statistics. By utilizing the change in currency deposits of domestic residents in foreign banks, and including foreign exchange rate adjustments on the IFS data, we can obtain an estimate of the BIS measure of capital flight.

In similar fashion, Gajdeczka (1989), Gajdeczka and Oks (1989), and Sinn (1990) use annual outflows of capital into foreign deposit accounts, which is equivalent to the increase in recorded foreign bank currency deposits. Hermes and Lensink (1992) use private assets as a measure of capital flight, which is similar to the mirror statistic measure. Given the data limitations, the private assets approach can serve as a proxy for the BIS measure of capital flight.

Indirect Approach: Derived Measures

Dooley measure

Dooley (1986) measures capital flight in three steps. The first step is to obtain the total stock of capital outflows (*TKO*) and adjust it using the difference between external debt data reported in the World Bank's World Debt Tables (*WDT*) and that obtained from the BOP as an adjustment for debt data discrepancies,

$$TKO_t = RCNR \ (not \ FDI)_t + Diff\_WBIMF_t, \tag{3.2a}$$

where $Diff\_WBIMF_t = WDT \ figure_t - IMF \ figure_t$; $RCNR_t$ (*not FDI*) is the cumulative recorded non-FDI claims of non-residents.

Thus when $Diff\_WBIMF_t$ is positive, the BOP data underestimates total external debt with respect to the *WDT* and vice-versa. The difference in the external debt data is added to TKO_t to get a more accurate figure for capital flows. Note ΔTKO_t is net capital outflow. Note also that there are issues regarding the conversion of stocks to flows and comparing the results to actual flows (see Note 7). This issue will bring us to the debate on the appropriate data to use, but for now, we only point out that capital flight estimates could vary because of the different modes of data presentation.

The second step is to impute total recorded external assets (*EA*), using the interest earnings (*INTEARN*) on foreign assets reported in the BOP and utilizing an interest rate, *r*.

$$EA_t = INTEARN_t / r_t, \tag{3.3a}$$

where *r* can be the 90-day United States Treasury bill rate.[12] ΔEA_t gives the flow of external assets.[13]

The last step is to subtract Equation 3.3a from Equation 3.2a to obtain the Dooley estimate of (net stock) capital flight,

$$KF_{D, \ t} = TKO_t - EA_t \tag{3.4a}$$

and $\Delta KF_{D,t}$ gives the flow figures.

Following BOP convention, it can be shown that Equation 3.2a is equivalent to the residual method (see below). However, Dooley (1986), Hermes et al. (2003), and Murinde et al. (1996) include EO_t in their equations for ΔTKO_t;
that is,

$$\Delta TKO_t = ED_t + NFI_t - CA_t - \Delta RES_t - EO_t + Diff\_WBIMF_t, \tag{3.2b}$$

where $RCNR$ $(not\ FDI)_t \equiv ED_t + NFI_t - CA_t - \Delta RES_t - EO_t$.

However, in Dooley et al. (1986), EO_t is not included in the equation.[14] Also, in an earlier paper, Hermes and Lensink (1992) do not include EO_t in Equation 3.2b; and Chang et al. (1997), Claessens and Naude (1993), and Claessens (1997), working with BOP identities, show that ΔTKO_t should be

$$\Delta TKO_t = ED_t + NFI_t - CA_t - \Delta RES_t + Diff\_WBIMF_t \qquad (3.2c)$$

We think that Equation 3.2c is equivalent to Equation 3.2b and is therefore the correct specification for ΔTKO_t.

The second and third steps remain the same, but the flow figures are considered,

$$KF_{D,\ t} = \Delta TKO_t - \Delta EA_t. \qquad (3.4b)$$

An alternative to the Dooley measure is Khan and Ul Haque (1985), who use the flow version of the Dooley method but define ΔTKO_t as only SK_t like the Cuddington measure. The subsequent procedures are exactly the same as described earlier, thus

$$\Delta TKO_t = SK_t \qquad (3.2d)$$

$$KF_{KH,\ t} = SK_t - \Delta EA_t \qquad (3.4c)$$

Trade misinvoicing

The magnitude of systematic trade misinvoicing can be a measure of capital flight. As explained earlier, export underinvoicing and import overinvoicing are used as channels for capital flight. Import underinvoicing is technical smuggling, which can be a form of negative capital flight. In addition to pure capital flight, export overinvoicing can also occur when governments provide some incentives following performance-based indicators like export revenues.

Three steps are followed to compute trade misinvoicing. First, we obtain export and import discrepancies for a country in its trade with major trade partners using data from the IMF's Director of Trade Statistics (DOT):

$$DX_t = PX_t - CIF_t \cdot X_t \qquad (3.5a)$$

$$DM_t = M_t - CIF_t \cdot PM_t \qquad (3.5b)$$

where DX_t and DM_t are the total export and import discrepancies with trade partners, respectively; PX_t is the value of trading partner's imports from the country as reported by trade partners and PM_t are the value of the same trading partner's exports to the country as reported by trade partners; and X_t and M_t are the country's recorded exports to and imports from trade partners, respectively, as reported by the country. *CIF*, or the cif/fob factor, is the adjustment made to account for the cost of freight and insurance.

Second, we obtain global export discrepancies (*MISX*) and import discrepancies (*MISM*) by multiplying Equations 3.5a and 3.4b by the inverse of the shares of the major trading partners in the country's total exports and imports. We use industrial countries' trade data with the assumption that the information is more accurate than that obtained from non-industrial countries, thus

$$MISX_t = DX_t \, / \, X\_INDUS_t \qquad\qquad (3.6a)$$

$$MISM_t = DM_t \, / \, M\_INDUS_t \qquad\qquad (3.6b)$$

where X_INDUS_t is the share of industrial countries in the country's exports; M_INDUS_t is the share of industrial countries in the country's imports.

Finally, summing up export and import discrepancies from Step 2 gives us total trade misinvoicing (*MIS*) or capital flight:

$$KF_{MIS,t} = MIS_t = MISX_t + MISM_t \qquad\qquad (3.7)$$

Indirect Approach: Residual or Broad Measures

The residual or broad measure considers recorded capital inflows (that is, $\Delta DEBT_t$ and NFI_t) and recorded foreign exchange outflows (that is, CA_t and ΔRES_t). There are two types of residual measures of capital flight: the World Bank (1985) measure and the Morgan Guaranty (1986) measure.

World Bank measure
World Bank (1985) estimates capital flight as

$$KF_{WB,\,t} = \Delta DEBT_t + NFI_t - CA_t - \Delta RES_t \qquad\qquad (3.8a)$$

where $\Delta DEBT_t$ is the change in public and private external debts, covering $LTDEBT_t$ and $STDEBT_t$. $\Delta DEBT_t$ is equivalent to $ED_t + Diff\_WBIMF_t$ (again, see Note 7).

Several versions of Equation 3.8a are available, indicating differences in opinion on what BOP accounts are to be excluded from Equation 3.8a (see, for example, Eggerstedt 1995; Zedillo 1987; Walter 1987, 1990).

In Eggerstedt et al. (1995), for example, the change in assets held abroad by public institutions ($\Delta PUBLIC$) is subtracted from Equation 3.8a; that is,

$$KF_{E,\,t} = KF_{WB,\,t} - \Delta PUBLIC_t \tag{3.8b}$$

They argue that Equation 3.8a overstates capital flight when investments of, say, government-controlled corporations are considered official uses of funds. For Eggerstedt et al., $\Delta PUBLIC_t$ is similar to ΔRES_t. Or put another way, $\Delta PUBLIC_t$, unlike privately accumulated foreign assets, is within the control of the government (Dooley 1986) and is therefore not considered capital flight. Accordingly, $\Delta PUBLIC_t$ should be excluded from capital flight.

Similar to Eggerstedt et al., Conesa (1987) subtracts the change in assets of the official or public sector ($ASSETS_{PUBLIC}$) from Equation 3.8a; that is,

$$KF_{E,t} = KF_{WB,t} - \Delta ASSETS_{PUBLIC,t} \tag{3.8c}$$

Conesa broadens the contention made by Eggerstedt el al. by arguing that the public sector (not just government-owned corporations) cannot be involved in capital flight. In other words, the activities of the public sector that involve foreign exchange transactions are considered official transactions and therefore do not constitute capital flight.

Yet another version of Equation 3.8a is Zedillo (1987), who incorporates a BIS type or a mirror statistic type of adjustment. Zedillo subtracts the imputed interest earnings of identified residents with deposits abroad ($INTEARN_{DEPOSIT}$); that is,

$$KF_{Z,t} = KF_{WB,t} - \Delta EA_{DEPOSIT,t} \tag{3.8d}$$

$$EA_{DEPOSIT,t} = INTEARN_{DEPOSIT,t}/r_t \tag{3.3b}$$

where r is the 90-day United States Treasury bill rate (see Note 12). Equation 3.8d is similar to the Dooley method.

Clearly, the biggest challenge in estimating Equation 3.8d is obtaining the needed information for Equation 3.3b. As pointed out earlier, the mirror statistic and BIS method assume that domestic residents who have foreign deposits actually declare their nationality or alternatively that foreign banks indicate the nationality of their clients. In addition, both methods assume that domestic residents hold foreign assets as deposit accounts only, ignoring the possibility of other forms of assets. Equation 3.3b is particularly difficult because only identified individuals who hold accounts abroad or investments are considered.

An alternative to Equation 3.8d is to use Equation 3.3a; that is,

$$KF_{W,t} = KF_{WB,t} - \Delta EA_t \tag{3.8e}$$

Recall Equation 3.8e is the flow version of the Dooley method.

Morgan Guaranty measure

The Morgan Guaranty (1986) method subtracts changes in the banking sector's foreign assets ($\Delta BANKS$) from the World Bank measure,

$$KF_{MG,t} = \Delta DEBT_t + NFI_t - CA_t - \Delta RES_t - \Delta BANKS_t \qquad (3.9a)$$

By excluding $\Delta BANKS_t$ from Equation 3.9a, Morgan Guaranty is saying that the banking sector's accumulation of foreign assets or its involvement does not constitute capital flight. Morgan Guaranty, in fact, does not explain the rationale for the exclusion of $\Delta BANKS_t$.

There are two versions of the Morgan Guaranty method – Cline (1987) and Pastor (1990). Cline (1987) takes Equation 3.9a and makes adjustments on the current account. In particular, he excludes travel expenditures like tourism and border transactions ($TRAVEL$), FDI incomes ($FDIINC$), and other investment income ($OINC$),

$$KF_{C,t} = KF_{MG,t} - TRAVEL_t - FDIINC_t - OINC_t \qquad (3.9b)$$

where CA_t in Equation 3.9a is

$$(CA_t - TRAVEL_t - FDIINC_t - OINC_t).$$

Cline argues that $TRAVEL_t$ refers to transactions that domestic authorities cannot control and $FDIINC_t$ and $OINC_t$ are like official transactions, thus these three items do not constitute capital flight. The explanation for taking out $TRAVEL_t$, $FDIINC_t$, and $OINC_t$ from Equation 3.9b is not convincing and seems arbitrary. But excluding these three items obtains a capital flight estimate that may be understated because these are transactions under CA_t, although they are not part of the trade balance. CA_t is the relevant account in Equation 3.9a.

Pastor (1990) utilizes Equation 3.9a and adjusts it by adding implied earnings on SK_t (that is, Cuddington, above) net of reported investment income (that is, Dooley, above; see Note 12). In other words, Pastor does not consider reported earnings on capital held abroad as capital flight,

$$KF_{P,t} = KF_{MG,t} + \Delta[(1 + r_t)\cdot SK_t - EA_t] \qquad (3.9c)$$

Adjusting the Baseline Measures

All the baseline measures will give good estimates of capital flight when the data is unproblematic. However, there are errors in the data either because of data collection or reporting problems (see, for example, Boyce and Ndikumana 2001; Chang et al. 1997; IMF 1987, 1992; Morgan Guaranty 1986). In general, the errors in the data affect the current account or the capital account, or both.

Current account adjustment

Earlier, systematic trade misinvoicing was presented as a particular type of capital flight. Boyce (1993), Boyce and Ndikumana 2001, Chang et al. (1997), Claessens (1997), Gulati (1987) and Henry (1991) incorporate trade misinvoicing into baseline capital flight.

Recall that the first step is to compute DX_t and DM_t for a country in its trade with major trade partners, utilizing the CIF.

$$DX_t = PX_t - CIF_t \cdot X_t \qquad (3.5a)$$

$$DM_t = M_t - CIF_t \cdot PM_t \qquad (3.5b)$$

Then we compute the $MISX_t$ and $MISM_t$,

$$MISX_t = DX_t / X\_INDUS_t \qquad (3.6a)$$

$$MISM_t = DM_t / M\_INDUS_t \qquad (3.6b)$$

using trade data with industrialized country trading partners. MIS_t is the sum of equations 3.6a and 3.6b.

The adjustment for systematic trade misinvoicing is simply to add MIS_t to the baseline figure of capital flight. Thus if the World Bank measure is used (Equation 3.8a), adjusted baseline capital flight is

$$KF_{WB\_ADJ,t} = \Delta DEBT_t + NFI_t - CA_t - \Delta RES_t + MIS_t \qquad (3.10a)$$

Capital account adjustment

One adjustment in the capital account is for the impact of foreign exchange fluctuations on total external debt (see, for example, Chang et al. 1997; Claessens 1997, Morgan Guaranty 1986; Boyce and Ndikumana 2001). Long-term external debts ($LTDEBT$) are denominated in hard currency (for example, Euro, British pound, Japanese yen, United States dollar) and currency fluctuations affect their values across periods.

We adopt Boyce and Ndikumana's (2001) procedure in computing the foreign exchange-adjusted external debt (ATTD):

$$ATTD_{t-1} = \sum_{i = E, \text{Yen, UK}} [(\alpha_{i,t-1} \, LTDEBT_{t-1})(FX_{i,t}/FX_{i,t-1})] + \sum_{i = \text{USD, MULT, OTHER}} (\beta_{i,t-1} \, LTDEBT_{t-1})$$

$$+ \, IMF_{t-1}(SDR_t/SDR_{t-1}) + STDEBT_{t-1} \qquad (3.11)$$

where α_i is the proportion of $LTDEBT_t$ in, say, Euro (E) pound sterling (UK), and Japanese yen; β_i is the proportion of $LTDEBT$ in United States dollars (USD), multiple (MULT) and other currencies (OTHER); FX is the exchange rate between a hard currency to USD, so FX_t/FX_{t-1} is a ratio representing the exchange rate fluctuation between two periods; IMF_t is use of IMF credits; SDR_t/SDR_{t-1} is a ratio representing SDR fluctuation between two periods; and $STDEBT_t$ is short-term external debt. However, the currency composition for $OTHER_t$, $MULT_t$, and $STDEBT_t$ is not known.

All other things being equal, an appreciation in a hard currency relative to USD will reduce FX_t/FX_{t-1} and reduce $ATTD_{t-1}$ as well. In other words, the dollar value of external debt will be lower as a result of an appreciation of the other hard currencies relative to reported $DEBT_t$.

With Equation 3.12, the exchange rate adjustment on external debt ($ADEBT$) is

$$ADEBT_t = ATTD_{t-1} - DEBT_{t-1} \qquad (3.12)$$

Equation 3.12 gives an estimate on how much $DEBT_{t-1}$ was overstated or understated because of exchange rate fluctuations.

Subtracting Equation 3.12 from $\Delta DEBT_t$ gives the adjusted change in external debt ($\Delta DEBTADJ$),

$$\Delta DEBTADJ_t = \Delta DEBT_t - ADEBT_t \qquad (3.13a)$$

or using $\Delta DEBT_t = DEBT_t - DEBT_{t-1}$, it can be shown that Equation 3.13a is equal to

$$\Delta DEBTADJ_t = DEBT_t - ATTD_{t-1} \qquad (3.13b)$$

Either Equation 3.13a or 3.13b can be used to replace $\Delta DEBT_t$ in Equation 3.8a, thus

$$KF_{WB,t} = \Delta DEBTADJ_t + NFI_t - CA_t - \Delta RES_t \qquad (3.8f)$$

which gives the adjusted baseline capital flight.

Incorporating Equation 3.13a or 3.13b in Equation 3.10a, we have

$$KF_{WB\_ADJ,t} = \Delta DEBTADJ_t + NFI_t - CA_t - \Delta RES_t + MIS_t \qquad (3.10b)$$

Equation 3.10b gives an estimate of capital flight adjusted for exchange rate fluctuations and systematic trade misinvoicing.

Other Computations

Other computations can be performed for analyzing capital flight (see, for example, Boyce 1993; Boyce and Ndikumana 2001; Morgan Guaranty 1986). In particular, we calculate capital flight stock (*SKF*) and real capital flight (*RKF*) on, say, Equation 3.10b.

Real capital flight

RKF_t makes capital flight estimates comparable across periods. We use a deflator like the United States producer price index (*PPI*), thus[15]

$$RKF_t = KF_t / PPI_t \qquad (3.14)$$

Capital flight stock

If capital flight is put in an investment instrument, some earnings will be realized. Such earnings are additions to total capital flight. Thus, the following calculations are carried out on capital flight to account for such lost earnings,

$$SKF_t = [SKF_{t-1}(1 + r_t)] + KF_t \qquad (3.15)$$

where SKF_t includes accrued interest earnings at time t and r is the interest rate on 90-day United States Treasury bills.[16] Equation 3.15 is a measure of the opportunity cost of capital flight.

CONCLUSION

The discussion above showed that the concept of capital flight is complex. There are various definitions of capital flight, as well as different ways of estimating it. However, from among the definitions available, we picked a definition for this book: capital flight is the net unrecorded capital outflows from a capital-scarce developing country. It is measured as the difference between the recorded sources and recorded uses of funds.

Implicit in this definition is the notion that capital inflows that do not finance the current account, the recorded accumulation of foreign assets or the accumulation of international reserves (that is, official uses of capital) constitute capital flight. This definition is called the residual definition of capital flight, and the procedure we follow in estimating capital flight is the World Bank method. Adjustments in the procedure are made to correct for errors in the current and capital accounts.

Capital flight is capital sheltered abroad. It implies lost resources that could have been used to generate employment and produce goods and services. Consequently, capital flight represents lost potential government revenue that could have been used to provide public infrastructure and basic social services, which ultimately will support and enhance economic growth, or used to ease budgetary constraints in general.

Moreover, capital flight can worsen the capital scarcity problem in developing countries. It can also limit the capacity of developing countries to mobilize resources and access foreign capital, stunting economic growth. More importantly, capital flight can lead to a negative feedback process; that is, limited economic growth causes even more capital flight, which can further restrict economic growth and aggravate underdevelopment. Thus, from an economic point of view, there are important economic tradeoffs to capital flight.

It is interesting to note that developing countries that experience capital flight are often countries that are highly indebted. Indeed it is puzzling that substantial amounts of private capital are being accumulated abroad and not utilized in the domestic economy, while at the same time, the country is accumulating external debt. Since the elites are best able to transfer capital abroad (sheltering their wealth from the adverse consequences of capital flight), the rest of society often bears a disproportionate share of the burden of capital flight. Thus, from a social welfare point of view there are important redistributive dimensions to capital flight. What makes this situation more disheartening is that some analysts consider capital flight as an optimal portfolio decision that is normal and integral to globalization, deregulation and liberalization, and so they ignore or fail to see the adverse impacts of capital flight on society. Furthermore, because of weak, fragile or absent social institutions in developing countries, these negative consequences are likely to be large and to persist over time.

In short, in the context of developing countries, capital flight makes the twin goals of economic growth and development much more challenging to pursue. With developing countries already lagging on the development ladder, capital flight often pulls them several rungs down. In this context, capital flight is a threat to developing countries. Needless to say, policies must be implemented to halt, curb, or reverse capital flight.

Finally, a good definition and measure of capital flight must be able to capture the dimensions highlighted above. We think that the residual definition of capital flight and method used in this book goes far in satisfying this objective.

ACRONYMS

Δ	change
ADEBT	adjustment on external debt
ASSETS	total assets of official or public sector
ATTD	foreign exchange adjusted total external debt (stock)
BANKS	total foreign assets of banking sector
BOP	balance of payments
CA	current account
CIF	cif/fob factor
DEBT	total external debt (stock)
DEBTADJ	adjusted total external debt (stock)
Diff_WBIMF	difference between World Debt Tables and IMF total external debt
DM	total imports discrepancy
DX	total exports discrepancy
EA	total recorded external assets
ED	external debt (flow)
EO	errors and omissions
FDI	foreign direct investments
FDIIC	foreign direct investments income
FF	French franc
FX	foreign exchange
GM	German mark
IMF	International Monetary Fund
INTERN	interest earnings
KF	capital flight
LTDEBT	stock of long-term debt
M	total imports of country
MIS	total trade misinvoicing
MISM	total import discrepancy
MISX	total export discrepancy
MULT	multiple currencies
NFI	net foreign investments
OINC	other investments income
OTHER	other currencies
PM	value of trading partner's exports to country
PORT	net portfolio equities
PORT1	net portfolio 'other bonds'
PPI	producers' price index
PUBLIC	total foreign assets of public institutions
PX	value of trading-partner's imports to country
r	interest rate (90 day US Treasury bill)

RCNR	cumulative recorded non-FDI claims on non-residents
RES	international reserves
RKF	real capital flight
SDR	special drawing rights
SF	Swiss franc
SK	short-term capital, 'other' sectors
SK1	short-term capital, 'other assets'
SKF	stock of capital flight
STDEBT	stock of short-term debt
T-Bill	Treasury bill
TKO	total capital outflow
TRAVEL	travel expenditure (tourism and border transactions)
UK	British pound
USD	United States dollar
WB	World Bank
WDT	World Debt Tables
X	total exports of country
X_INDUS	share of industrial countries in country's total exports

NOTES

This chapter is based on Chapter 2 of my doctoral dissertation. I would like to thank James K. Boyce and Gerald Epstein for their advice. The usual disclaimers apply.

1. Some definitions apply a stock concept of capital flight, in particular Dooley (1986), Hermes and Lensink (1992), the mirror statistic and the Bank for International Settlements (BIS) definition (see, for example, BIS 1984). We are interested in the flow concept of capital flight, and so all the definitions used here will be expressed in terms of flows.
2. Mr Justice Potter Stewart in his concurring opinion in *Jacobellis* vs. *Ohio* (378 US 184, p. 197) said: 'I know [pornography] when I see it.' The same line of reasoning can be applied in deciding whether or not significant risk is the underlying concern for capital flight.
3. By making this adjustment, there is a risk of transforming the Cuddington definition of capital flight to a volume-type definition: large or abnormal capital outflows mean capital flight. Allowing for long-term capital flows still excludes direct investments (for example, multinational corporations). In other words, we broaden the definition to include financial assets. Furthermore, in an economic crisis, large outflows of capital could occur as asset prices decline; however, this decline in asset prices provides opportunities for a 'fire sale' (see Krugman 1992), thus capital inflows can occur. Both direct investments and capital inflows in a 'fire sale' are not covered in both the standard and expanded interpretation of Cuddington.
4. The same problem exists in illegal labor migration. There is an expanding literature on human trafficking. A review of concepts and empirical evidence can be found in Bautista and Beja (1998) and IOM (2000). Trafficking in human beings is difficult to isolate because it can occur through legal and illegal means and processes, and often without the knowledge of the victim.
5. Claessens et al. (1993) use 'hot money' for short-term capital and 'cool money' for long-term capital like foreign direct investment.

6. 'Net' refers to foreign residents' investments in the country and domestic residents' investments abroad. Thus an increase in foreign residents' FDI (into the country) has a positive sign, while an increase in domestic residents' FDI (abroad) has a negative sign. Net FDI, in this case, is the sum of the two figures. The same principle applies for portfolio equities.

7. See Chang et al. (1997), Cumby and Levich (1987) and BIS-IMF-OECD-WB (1994) with regard to using World Bank or IMF external debt data and related issues on debt stocks and debt flows.

8. The equations presented in this section follow the analytical presentation of the various estimation procedures. But on Excel, for example, capital flight is estimated as the row sum of the respective accounts.

9. The BOP 5th Edition groups the BOP entries in three parts: current account, financial account, and capital account. Credits are inflows, and thus carry a positive sign; debits, on the other hand, are outflows, and carry a negative sign. On the assets side, an increase is an outflow and is negative; a decrease is an inflow, and thus has a positive sign. On the liabilities side, however, an increase, or inflow, has a positive sign; a decrease, or outflow, has a negative sign.

10. But EO captures all unaccounted net inflows (net outflows), meaning it includes long-term capital flows, among others. In a way, the residual measure of capital flight is a complicated way of estimating EO.

11. The current BOP 5th Edition (published in 1993) emphasizes the type of financial instruments rather than their maturities, thus making it difficult to obtain accurate figures for short-term and long-term financial flows (although maturities are still reported for 'other' investments). The BOP 4th Edition (published in 1977), however, emphasized the maturity of instruments, so it was possible to obtain figures for short-term capital flows.

12. Equation 3.3a is sensitive to the r used. The 90-day US Treasury bill (T-Bill) can be a low rate of return on capital. While it is possible to realize a higher return on capital, the T-Bill rate is used to represent a definite rate of return.

13. See Chang et al. (1997) on issues regarding estimating EA.

14. Since EO is positive when there is unaccounted outflow, including it in Equation 3.2b may cause an upward bias on ΔTKO and on capital flight as well. The reverse happens when EO is negative. Most developing countries have positive EOs, and using Equation 3.2b may result in an overestimation of capital flight.

15. RKF is sensitive to the deflator used. It is important that the same deflator is used for all variables. An alternative deflator is the consumer price index (CPI).

16. We assume that capital flight has positive returns. Of course, some capital flight may end up financing private consumption. It is difficult to obtain such information. SKF is sensitive to the interest rate used.

REFERENCES

Alesina, Alberto and Guido Tabellini (1989), 'External Debt, Capital Flight, and Political Risk,' *Journal of International Economics*, **27** (3/4), 199–220.

Bank for International Settlements (1984), *BIS 54th Annual Report*, Geneva, Switzerland: Bank for International Settlements.

Bank for International Settlements, International Monetary Fund, Organization for Economic Cooperation and Development and World Bank (1994), *Debt Stocks, Debt Flows and the Balance of Payments*, Basle, Switzerland: BIS, IMF, OECD, WB.

Bautista, M. Cristina and Edsel L. Beja, Jr. (1998), 'The Trafficking of Women between Belgium and the Philippines: A Socio-economic Perspective' in *The Trafficking in Women between Belgium and the Philippines*, Final Report, Ateneo Human Rights Center, Ateneo de Manila University.

Beja Jr., Edsel, Pokpong Junvith and Jared Ragusett, 'Capital Flight from Thailand, 1980–2000, forthcoming in Gerald A. Epstein (ed.), *Capital Flight and Capital Controls in Developing Countries*, Chapter 6.

Bhagwati, Jagdish (1964), 'On Underinvoicing of Imports,' *Bulletin of Oxford University Institute of Economics and Statistics*, **26**, 389–397.

Bhagwati, Jagdish, Anne Krueger and Chaiyawat Webulswasdi (1974), 'Capital Flight from LDCs: A Statistical Analysis' in Jagdish Bhagwati (ed.), *Illegal Transactions in International Trade*, Amsterdam: North-Holland.

Boyce, James (1992), 'The Revolving Door? External Debt and Capital Flight: Philippine Case Study,' *World Development*, **20** (3), 335–349.

Boyce, James (1993), *The Political Economy of Growth and Impoverishment in the Marcos Era*, Manila, the Philippines: Ateneo de Manila University Press.

Boyce, James and Leonce Ndikumana (2001), 'Is Africa a Net Debtor? New Estimates of Capital Flight from Severely Indebted Sub-Saharan African Countries, 1970–98,' *Journal of Development Studies*, **38** (2), 27–56.

Calvo, Guillermo and Edwardo Mendoza (1996), 'Mexico's Balance of Payments Crisis: A Chronicle of Death Foretold,' *Journal of International Economics*, **41**, 235–264.

Chang, Kevin, Stijn Claessens and Robert Cumby (1997), 'Conceptual and Methodological Issues in the Measurement of Capital Flight,' *International Journal of Financial Economics*, **2**, 101–119.

Claessens, Stijn (1997), 'Estimates of Capital Flight and Its Behavior', *Revisita de Analisis Economico*, **12** (1), 3–34.

Claessens, Stijn and David Naude (1993), 'Recent Estimates of Capital Flight,' World Bank Working Paper No. 1186.

Claessens, Stijn, Michael Dooley and Andrew Warner (1993), 'Portfolio Capital Flows: Hot or Cold?' in Stijn Claessens and Sudarshan Gooptu (eds), *Portfolio Investment in Developing Countries*, World Bank Discussion Paper No. 223.

Cline, William (1987), 'Discussion', in Donald Lessard and John Williamson (eds), *Capital Flight and Third World Debt*, Washington DC: Institute for International Economics.

Collier, Paul, Anke Hoeffler and Catherine Patillo (2001), 'Flight Capital as a Portfolio Choice,' *World Bank Economic Review*, **15** (1), 55–80.

Conesa, Eduardo (1987), 'The Flight of Capital from Latin America: Causes and Cures,' Mimeo, Inter-American Development Bank.

Cuddington, John (1986), 'Capital Flight: Estimates, Issues and Explanation,' Princeton Studies in International Finance, No. 58, Princeton University.

Cumby, Robert and Richard Levich (1987), 'Definitions and Magnitudes: On the Definition and Magnitude of Recent Capital Flight', in Donald Lessard and John Williamson (eds), *Capital Flight and the Third World Debt*, Washington DC: Institute of International Economics.

Deppler, Michael and Martin Williamson (1987), 'Capital Flight: Concepts, Measurement, and Issues,' *Staff Studies for the World Economic Outlook*, International Monetary Fund, 39–58.

Dooley, Michael (1986), 'Country Specific Risk Premiums, Capital Flight and Net Investment Income Payments in Selected Developing Countries,' International Monetary Fund, unpublished manuscript.

Dooley, Michael (1988), 'Capital Flight: A Response to Differential Financial Risks,' *IMF Staff Papers*, **35** (3), 422–436.

Dooley, Michael, William Helkie, Ralph Tryon and John Underwood (1986), 'An Analysis of External Debt Positions of Eight Developing Countries through 1990',

Journal of Development Studies, 21, 283–318.

Eaton, Jonathan (1987), 'Public Debt Guarantees and Private Capital Flight,' *The World Bank Economic Review*, 1 (3), 377–395.

Eggerstedt, Susan, Rebecca Hall and Sweder van Wijnbergen (1995), 'Measuring Capital Flight: A Case Study of Mexico,' *World Development*, 23 (2), 211–232.

Erbe, Suzanne (1985), 'The Flight of Capital from Developing Countries,' *Intereconomics*, November/December, 268–275.

FitzGerald, Valpy and Alex Cobham (2000), 'Capital Flight: Causes, Effects, Magnitude and Implications for Development,' Department for International Development (UK).

Furman, Alejandro and Joseph Stiglitz (1998), 'Economic Crisis and Insights from East Asia,' *Brookings Papers on Economic Activity*, No. 2, 1–135.

Gajdeczka, Przemyslav (1989), 'Financial Flows to Developing Countries,' *Quarterly Review*, World Bank.

Gajdeczka, Przemyslav and Daniel Oks (1989), 'Domestic Deficits, Debt Overhand and Capital Outflows in Developing Countries', in Richard O'Brien and I. Iversen (eds), *Finance and the International Economy*, Oxford: Oxford University Press.

Gibson, Heather and Euclid Tskalotos (1993), 'Testing a Flow Model of Capital Flight in Five European Countries,' *Manchester School*, 61 (2), 14–166.

Gordon, David and Ross Levine (1989), 'The 'Problem' of Capital Flight – A Cautionary Note,' *World Economy*, 12, 237–252.

Gulati, Sanil (1987), 'A Note on Trade Misinvoicing', in Donald Lessard and John Williamson (eds), *Capital Flight and Third World Debt*, Washington DC: Institute for International Economics.

Henry, Lester (1991), *Capital Flight from the Third World: Case Study of Four Caribbean Countries*, Unpublished Ph.D. Dissertation, University of Massachusetts, Amherst.

Hermes, Niels and Robert Lensink (1992), 'The Magnitude and Determinants of Capital Flight: The Case of Six Sub-Saharan African Countries,' *De Economist*, 140 (4), 515–530.

Hermes, Niels and Robert Lensink (2001), 'Capital Flight and Uncertainty of Government Policies,' *Economics Letters*, 71 (3), 377–381.

Hermes, Niels, Robert Lensink and Victor Murinde (2003), 'Capital Flight: The Key Issues', in Andrew Mullineux and Victor Murinde (eds), *Handbook of International Banking*, Cheltenham, UK and Northampton, MA, USA: Edward Elgar.

International Monetary Fund (1987), *Report on the World Current Account Discrepancy*, Washington DC: International Monetary Fund.

International Monetary Fund (1992), *Report on the Measurement of International Capital Flows*, Washington DC: International Monetary Fund.

International Organization for Migration (IOM) (2000), 'Special Issue: Perspectives on Trafficking of Migrants, *International Migration*, 38 (3), Special Issue No. 1.

Ketkar, Suhas and Kusum Ketkar (1989), 'Determinants of Capital Flight from Argentina, Brazil and Mexico,' *Contemporary Policy Issues*, 7 (3), 11–29.

Khan, Mohsin and Nadeem Ul Haque (1985), 'Foreign Borrowing and Capital Flight: A Formal Analysis,' *IMF Staff Papers*, 32 (4), 606–628.

Kindleberger, Charles (1937), *International Short-term Capital Movements*, New York: Augustus Kelley.

Krugman, Paul (1992), *Currencies and Crises*, Cambridge, MA: MIT Press.

Lensink, Robert, Niels Hermes and Victor Murinde (2000), 'Capital Flight and Political Risk,' *Journal of International Money and Finance*, 19 (1), 73–92.

Morgan Guaranty Trust Company (1986), 'LDC Capital Flight,' *World Financial Markets*, March 13–15.

Murinde, Victor, Niels Hermes and Robert Lensink (1996), 'Comparative Aspects of the Magnitude & Determinants of Capital Flight in Six Sub-Saharan African Countries,' *Savings and Development Quarterly Review*, **20** (1), 61–78.

Pastor, Manuel Jr (1990), 'Capital Flight from Latin America,' *World Development*, **18** (1), 1–18.

Sinn, Stefan (1990), *Net External Asset Positions of 145 Countries*, Tubingen, Germany: Mohr (Paul Siebeck).

Walter, Ingo (1987), 'The Mechanisms of Capital Flight', in Donald Lessard and John Williamson (eds), *Capital Flight and the Third World Debt*, Washington, DC: Institute for International Economics.

Walter, Ingo (1990), *The Secret Money Market. Inside the Dark World of Tax Invasion, Financial Fraud, Insider Trading, Money Laundering, and Capital Flight*, New York: Harper Business.

World Bank (1985), *World Development Report*, Washington, DC: World Bank.

Zedillo, Ernesto (1987), 'Case Study: Mexico', in Donald Lessard and John Williamson (eds), *Capital Flight and Third World Debt*, Washington, DC: Institute for International Economics.

PART TWO

Capital Flight: Case Studies

4. Capital Flight from South Africa, 1980–2000

Seeraj Mohamed and Kade Finnoff

INTRODUCTION

This chapter presents an estimate of the wealth that left South Africa in the form of capital flight during the period 1980 to 2000. We adopt the residual method of calculating capital flight used in Boyce and Ndikumana (2001).[1] The residual or the broad measure is an indirect approach to measuring capital flight based on a comparison of the sources and uses of foreign exchange.[2] Previous studies of capital flight from South Africa (Smit and Mocke 1991; Fedderke and Liu 2002) have largely ignored the changing political context within which capital flight has occurred. By contrast our analysis suggests that the factors influencing capital flight have changed as a result of the successful political transition from white domination under the apartheid system to democratic rule during the period 1980 to 2000.

We suggest that the higher capital flight observed in the relatively more politically and economically stable period 1994 to 2000 (compared to the pre-democracy period 1980 to 1993) is reflective of the attitudes of wealthy white South Africans to the transition rather than of political and economic uncertainty.[3] We also show that changes in liquidity in global financial markets affected capital flight from South Africa. We argue that surges in net capital flows to South Africa are associated with higher levels of capital flight during the apartheid and post-apartheid periods. In addition, we draw on Fine and Rustomjee's (1996) discussion of the political economy of the industrialization process in South Africa to show how structural weaknesses in the economy may have contributed to capital flight. Therefore, a closer investigation of capital flight provides important insights into the political economy of South Africa during this period.

From 1980 to 2000, capital flight as a percentage of GDP was, on average, 6.6 percent a year. During the last 13 years of apartheid, from 1980 to 1993, average capital flight as a percentage of GDP was 5.4 percent a year. In the post-apartheid period, from 1994 to 2000, average capital flight rose to 9.2 percent of GDP per year.

Capital flight of such magnitude continues to impede South Africa's development. Capital flight negatively impacts the economy in the form of foregone private investment, tax revenue and potential public investment. The extent of accumulated capital flight from 1980 to 2000 was 36 percent of the value of cumulative gross fixed capital formation for the same period.[4] This level of capital flight represents an enormous sacrifice and missed opportunities for promoting South African growth and alleviating poverty.

A common explanation for capital flight from developing countries is that wealth holders move their wealth out of a country because of political and economic uncertainty. However, in South Africa, it seems that wealthy people moved more money out of the country during the relatively more stable post-apartheid period than during the turbulent 1980s when the struggle against apartheid, international pressure and economic sanctions intensified. The increase in capital flight of four percentage points from the earlier to later period suggests that wealthy South Africans wanted to move their assets outside South Africa's borders; either in anticipation of emerging macroeconomic distress, or more likely, in order to be safe from the changes brought about by a new democratically elected government. The wealthy seem to maintain a distrust of the South African government despite the government's efforts to create a business-friendly environment and despite their conservative approach to fiscal and monetary policy. This distrust will probably persist as long as the levels of inequality, unemployment and poverty in South Africa remain high (Terreblanche 2003). In addition, there are a host of complex psychological reasons, such as racial prejudice and feelings of lost power, which might be motivating wealthy South Africans to move their money offshore (ibid.).

Political and economic uncertainties may be part of the story, but they are not by themselves adequate explanations for capital flight from South Africa. In this chapter we wish to provide a more detailed exploration of the political economy of capital flight from South Africa from 1980 to 2000. The structure and institutions of the South African economy are central to this explanatory framework.

The rest of the chapter is structured as follows. The next section briefly outlines the capital flight literature specific to South Africa. Section three provides a short discussion of our method and data used for calculating capital flight. Section four contains an in-depth discussion and interpretation of our results aimed at explaining the reasons for capital flight from South Africa and the final section draws conclusions.

LITERATURE REVIEW

The theoretical debates on capital flight mainly focus on portfolio choice decisions. From this perspective, profit-maximizing investors will decide to

Table 4.1 Alternative measures and determinants of capital flight from South Africa

Author (s)	Method	Period	Macro instability	Risk and returns to investment	Political instability	Main finding
Khan (1991)	BOP, trade misinvoicing	1970 to 1985				Total capital flight 1970 to 1985 is $15.38 billion (1985 prices). Misinvoicing is a major channel for capital flight
Smit and Mocke (1991)	BOP, indirect, direct and derived	1970 to 1988	Average real growth rate over last three years, balance on CA and budget deficit, changes in gross foreign debt	Real exchange rate, real exchange rate minus PPP of real exchange rate, real domestic interest rates, difference between domestic and foreign short-term interest rates	Number of emigrants, number of European tourists	Total capital flight using derived measure from 1980 to 1988 is $6,099 billion

Study	Method	Period	Causes			Findings
Rustomjee (1991), Fine and Rustomjee (1996)	BOP plus errors and omissions and trade misinvoicing	1970 to 1988	Failed financial liberalization and debt default			Total capital flight from 1970 to 1988 is 7% of GDP. Causes include economic structure and global integration of SA's major corporations
Wood and Moll (1994)*	Trade misinvoicing	1970 to 1985				Capital flight from 1970 to 1985 is between $2 and $5 billion. Misinvoicing has been exaggerated by Khan (1991) and Rustomjee (1991)
Fedderke and Liu (2002)	BOP, indirect and derived	1960 to 1995	Growth	Exchange rate adjusted differential, overvaluation of exchange rate in terms of PPP	Political rights, index, political stability index (Fedderke et al., 1999)	Total capital flight from 1980 to 1989, using derived method, is $628 million, and from 1985 to 1995 as $462 million.

Note: * = no statistically significant effect. Wood and Moll do not provide reasons for capital flight but suggest that people are predisposed to evade exchange controls. They write, 'in countries where people are nervous about the long-run safety of their assets, capital drain will never be stopped…' (p. 41).

invest abroad when risk-adjusted returns abroad are higher. Therefore, capital flight is seen as a response to changes to an individual's portfolio arising from factors such as the fear of appropriation of assets, potentially higher taxes or perceived lower returns at home.

Most capital flight literature specific to South Africa utilizes the portfolio choice rubric. Khan (1991), Smit and Mocke (1991), Rustomjee (1991), Wood and Moll (1994), Fine and Rustomjee (1996), and Fedderke and Liu (2002) study various determinants of capital flight. These studies are of interest because they attempt to capture different features of capital flight – volume, motive and direction of capital flight – unique to the South African experience. These analyses focus on capital flows, macroeconomic instability, fiscal policy, risk and returns to investment, and political instability as the central motivating factors for capital flight. Table 4.1 outlines these studies and methods used.

Of particular interest to our analysis are the findings of Fine and Rustomjee on the one hand, and Federekke and Liu on the other. Fine and Rustomjee provide an informative discussion of the combination of factors that contribute to capital flight from South Africa. Their explanation of the causes of capital flight from South Africa include the structure of the economy, the degree of global integration of South Africa's major corporations and the country's failed attempt at financial liberalization in the early 1980s.

Fedderke and Liu, on the other hand, ignore the structural and institutional factors affecting capital flight from South Africa and focus on political uncertainty and risk. They consider capital inflows as an unconditional good and capital outflows as an unconditional bad. However, they do not make the link between surges of capital flows into South Africa and the instability in financial markets and volatility of the currency caused by these surges. Therefore, Fedderke and Liu fail to make the connection, which we show in this chapter, between changes in the liquidity in international financial markets and surges in net capital flows into and out of South Africa, on one hand, and capital flight on the other. We attempt to explain capital flight by considering the combination of political instability, structural weaknesses in the economy and changes in net capital flows into the economy.

The South African capital flight literature is helpful in building a better understanding of the volume and flow of capital flight. While Wood and Moll argue that capital flight has been relatively small, evidence from the rest of the literature indicates that by international standards capital flight from South Africa was high. Most authors agree that political instability is a major cause of capital flight. Yet, all of these perspectives, with the notable exceptions of Rustomjee (1991) and Fine and Rustomjee (1996), fail to specifically address the central political fact of the times: the white minority had control over capital and over the structural and institutional framework ɔices on the allocation of capital were made.

ᴇr, we examine capital flight over a period of time that
ᴛ the apartheid and post-apartheid eras. We argue that the
.....d capital flight are different before and after the fall of
ᴀᴘarᴛneid and show that during the post-apartheid period, when there was
greater political stability and the government had enacted economic policies
favored by the business sector, capital flight as a percentage of GDP rose to a
higher level. We also contribute to the existing literature on capital flight
from South Africa by extending the time period to 2000.[5]

METHOD AND DATA

This study employs the methodology outlined by Boyce and Ndikumana
(2001) to calculate capital flight from South Africa from 1980 to 2000. We
adopt the residual approach and adjust it by adding the value of trade
misinvoicing.[6] Capital flight is estimated using the following equation:

$$ADJKF_t = \Delta DEBT_t + NFI_t - (CA_t + \Delta RES_t) + MISINV_t \qquad (4.1)$$

where $\Delta DEBT$ is the change in South Africa's stock of external debt;[7] NFI is
net foreign investment; CA is the current account deficit; ΔRES is the change
in the net stock of foreign reserves; $MISINV$ is net trade misinvoicing.

Using the above approach we calculate the difference between total
capital inflows and recorded foreign exchange outflows. To obtain an
estimate for capital flight we add the change in debt from the previous year
to net direct and portfolio investment flows and subtract the current account
balance and the change in foreign reserves from the previous year. We then
add trade misinvoicing (calculated by comparing South Africa's reported
trade data to their trading partners' data) to capital flight to obtain an adjusted
capital flight ($ADJKF$) estimate.

The data used to calculate the change in stock of external debt is from the
IMF's International Financial Statistics (IFS). The IFS does not provide a
breakdown of long-term debt into the currencies it is held in, thus we are
unable to adjust debt for exchange rate changes in the currencies held against
the rand.[8] Net foreign direct investment was calculated using data from the
South African Reserve Bank (SARB).[9] Current account data and figures for
changes in reserves were obtained from the World Bank's World
Development Indicators (WDI).

The data used to calculate trade misinvoicing is from the IMF's Direction
of Trade Statistics (DOTS). Some authors have called into question the
quality of trade data from South Africa prior to democratic elections in 1994
(Wood and Moll 1994). Under the apartheid regime, a number of goods, inc-

Table 4.2 Capital flight calculations ($US millions)

Year	Change in debt	Net foreign investment	Current account	Change in reserves	Capital flight	Misinvoicing	Adjusted capital flight	Real adjusted capital flight
1980	-1656	-1307	3161	-1201	-4923	3334	-1589	-12130
1981	6241	-513	-4621	1101	9248	3757	13005	86702
1982	4766	1129	-3390	100	9186	3994	13180	77527
1983	2484	-534	-300	-1129	3379	2061	5440	28938
1984	2498	1060	-1802	428	4932	3937	8869	43475
1985	1383	-458	2317	606	-1997	4568	2571	10942
1986	-1921	-914	2828	146	-5808	4840	-968	-3470
1987	63	-1167	3347	-1407	-3045	2299	-746	-2323
1988	-886	-227	1504	715	-3332	4750	1418	3885
1989	-671	-293	1343	-528	-1780	6477	4697	11184
1990	-495	-101	2134	-355	-2375	4975	2600	5509
1991	-1265	284	2256	-1147	-2091	2289	199	376
1992	2284	-185	1967	-503	635	4094	4729	8196
1993	2284	434	1503	1341	204	3072	3276	5318
1994	2313	1968	112	-683	4852	7101	11953	17920

1995	3133	1233	−2205	−907	7468	7053	14520	19891
1996	292	1839	−1880	1272	2740	6451	9191	11768
1997	−487	7667	−2273	−4595	14049	7028	21076	25211
1998	−2520	2327	−2157	−920	2884	6671	9555	11033
1999	−4863	8434	−640	−4261	8472	6578	15050	16430
2000	−2942	−1262	−575	−544	−3085	8776	5691	5691

Source: Authors' computations using SARB data for net foreign investment, IFS data for change in debt, WDI for current account and change in reserves and IMF–DOTS data for misinvoicing. Real figures are calcutated using the South African producer price index (2000=100).

luding oil, were officially labeled as strategic and it was illegal to report statistics on these goods. It is likely that in an effort to circumvent sanctions a significant portion of international trade with South Africa may not have been reported.

Prior to 1998, trade data for South Africa were included in the trade of the South African Common Customs Area (SACCA). SACCA includes Botswana, Lesotho, Namibia, South Africa, and Swaziland. Beginning in 1998, SACCA trade data are reported separately as South Africa and SACCA excluding South Africa. In order to make the series consistent we add these two series together for the post-1998 period. South African trade accounts for the majority of SACCA trade.

DISCUSSION OF RESULTS

Our main results (Table 4.2) indicate that:

1. Capital flight was high during the period 1980–2000, averaging 6.6 percent of GDP.
2. Average annual capital flight as a percentage of GDP was higher following the transition to democracy in 1994 than it was in the period 1980 to 1993, indicating that the motivation for capital flight during the later period was different. Whereas capital flight during the earlier period may have been caused by political instability, during the later period it seems to have occurred because wealthy white South Africans were uncomfortable with the transition to democratic rule.
3. Capital flight as a percentage of GDP peaked during the 1980–85 period when there was a surge in the volume of short-term bank lending, as South Africa became a preferred destination for international lenders after the Latin American debt crisis. It peaked again during the 1994–2000 period when South Africa received large portfolio capital flows as a result of the increased liquidity in international financial markets in the 1990s.
4. The structural weaknesses in the economy may be an important factor in explaining why wealthy South Africans choose to take their wealth out of South Africa rather than investing within the country.

Figure 4.1 shows the trends in capital flight (ADJKF).[10] Capital flight exhibits substantial volatility over the 20-year span, peaking in 1981–1982, in 1984 and again in 1997. The troughs in capital flight occur in 1980, 1986 and 1991. Capital flight remained high during two periods, from 1980 to 1985, at 10.3 percent of GDP, and from 1994 to 2000 at 9.2 percent of GDP. The amount of capital that left South Africa for the period 1980 to 2000 adds up to $370 billion (in year 2000 US dollars).

1980–1985

From 1980 to 1985 capital flight from South Africa averaged 10.3 percent of GDP. During this period the vast majority of capital flight occurred with increasing levels of debt. Debt rose during the early 1980s as the government took on a large share of short-term loans for large projects (Fine and Rustomjee 1996). Foreign short-term loans to private borrowers also increased significantly as South Africa was perceived favorably by international lenders for a few years after 1982, when some other developing countries were defaulting on their debt.

Figure 4.2 graphs changes in debt and capital flight. The trend in debt levels closely followed the trend in capital flight, suggesting, at the very least, that they were codetermined from 1980 to 1985. The real effective exchange rate (REER) seems to have been affected by the increased levels of debt as well. In Figure 4.7 we see that, due to the surge in net capital flows, especially in short-term debt, both capital flight as a percentage of GDP and the REER followed a similar trend from 1980 to 1985, with capital flight lagging by a year. From 1984 to 1985 we see how the collapse of net capital flows led to a sharp decline in the REER and capital flight.

During this early period, misinvoicing also followed capital flight closely. Figure 4.3 shows misinvoicing rising in 1981–1982, falling in 1983 and rebounding to reach a peak in 1985. During this time, misinvoicing was driven by underinvoicing of exports to industrialized countries.

The macroeconomic environment of South Africa was particularly volatile during the 1980s. South Africa had high current account deficits and a growing debt burden from the 1970s (Lowenberg 1997). The apartheid government, which faced increased international isolation, borrowed heavily to finance a number of large investments. One of these investment projects was Sasol, a project to produce oil from coal.[11] The government also spent large amounts on its military and the state-owned arms industry to support its aggression in the Southern African region and within South Africa. These expenses were in addition to the waste and inefficiency associated with maintaining the apartheid system. The apartheid government attempted a liberalization of financial markets in 1980 but was forced to abandon this policy in 1985 when the debt crisis occurred.[12]

At the same time that South Africa was experiencing economic instability, the anti-apartheid struggle was undergoing a resurgence. There was ongoing mobilization of students from 1980 while the renascence of political trade unionism led to a series of strikes in 1981. In 1983, the United Democratic Front, a national alliance of community organizations (women's, youth, civic and cultural organizations) and trade unions, was launched. The intensification of the struggle led to the apartheid state declaring a state of emergency in 1985.

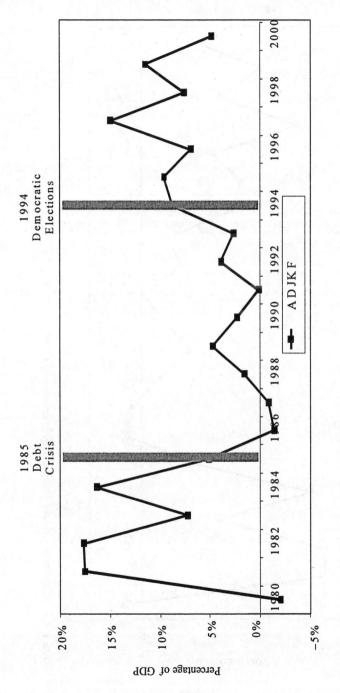

Figure 4.1 Capital flight as percentage of GDP

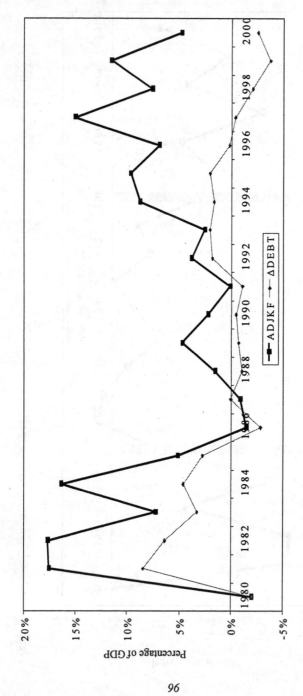

Figure 4.2   Capital flight and change in debt as ratio of GDP

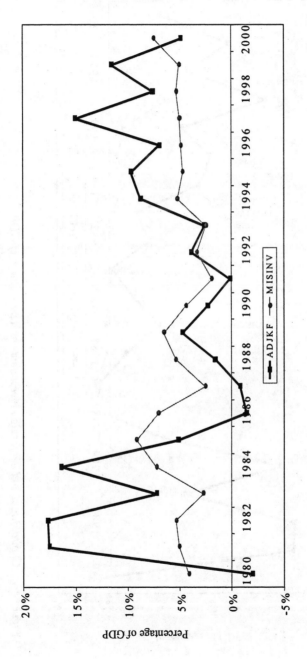

Figure 4.3   Capital flight and misinvoicing as ratio of GDP

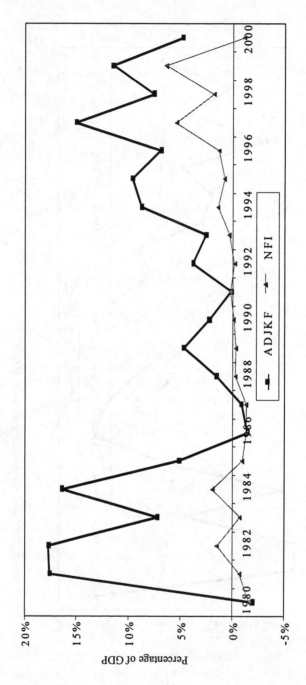

Figure 4.4   Capital flight and net foreign investments as a percentage of GDP

The combination of political and economic instability contributed to the development of the debt crisis in 1985 as lenders and other investors became less willing to invest in South Africa. Pressure by anti-apartheid organizations in other countries put pressure on banks to stop lending to South Africa and to disinvest (see Figure 4.4). The success of the disinvestment campaign in developed countries increased during the early 1980s with 47 US companies leaving between 1984 and 1985[13] (see Jenkins 1990).

It seems that economic problems and the anti-apartheid struggle reinforced one another (see Figure 4.5). On the one hand, the weakening economy and the debt crisis fueled the struggle internally. On the other hand, the intensification of the struggle, which was met by severe repression by the apartheid state, fueled economic problems and provided ammunition for anti-apartheid activists to push for the imposition of further economic sanctions and disinvestment by the international community.

1986–1993

The period after 1985 until 1993 was marked by less volatility in capital flight. The most dramatic changes in capital flight occurred at the start and end of this period. From 1985 to 1986, capital flight declined by 6 percent of GDP. Conversely, from 1993 to 1994 capital flight increased by 6 percent of GDP.

Capital flight as a percentage of GDP was negative in 1986 and 1987 despite high levels of resistance to apartheid and the continuation of the apartheid government's state of emergency (see Figures 4.1 and 4.5). From 1986, South Africa was forced to run a trade surplus because of the foreign exchange difficulties that had resulted from the dearth of capital flowing into the country after the 1985 debt crisis. Repayment of debt, attempts to build up foreign reserves and net outflows of investment also contributed to lower levels of capital flight (see Figures 4.2, 4.4 and 4.6). As in the 1980–1985 period, capital flight and the REER were affected by similar factors. Between 1986 and 1993, capital flight and the REER seemed to respond to the reduction in capital flows leaving the country and the maintenance of a positive trade balance during this period.

The negative levels of capital flight did not last long. There was a resurgence in capital flight as a percentage of GDP in 1988 and 1989 when misinvoicing as a percentage of GDP increased (see Figure 4.3). The introduction of the General Export Incentive Scheme (GEIS) in 1990 had an interesting influence on capital flight because it affected the behavior of firms involved in misinvoicing.[14] The GEIS led to significant overinvoicing of exports from 1990 to 1994 as exporters tried to take advantage of the export subsidies provided by the government.[15] Unfortunately, the level of

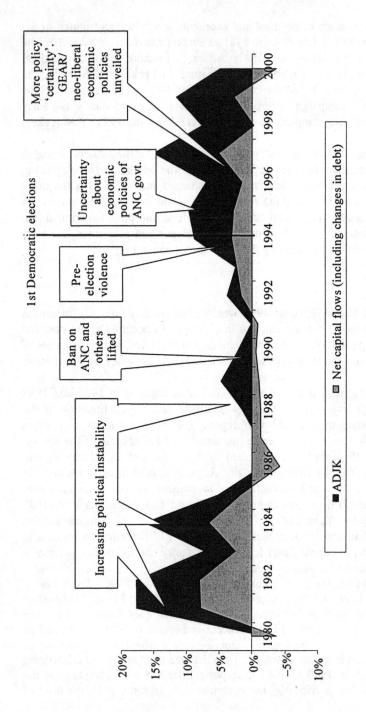

Figure 4.5   Political events, net capital flows and capital flight as a percentage of GDP

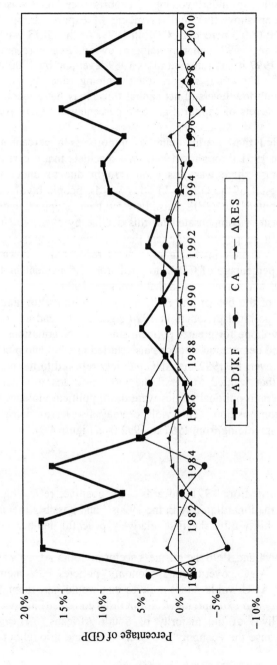

Figure 4.6 Capital flight, current account and changes in reserves as a percentage of GDP

overinvoicing of exports as a result of the GEIS is not known currently. However, the change in misinvoicing behavior can be inferred from the significant decline in underinvoicing of exports once GEIS was introduced. Our calculations show that underinvoicing of exports dropped from 3.3 percent of GDP to 0.3 percent of GDP in 1993. As the GEIS was phased out between 1994 and 1997, underinvoicing of exports as a percentage of GDP increased; by 1997 it had returned to its 1989 level and by 2000 it was up to 5.2 percent.[16] Therefore, export overinvoicing due to the GEIS in combination with low levels of net capital flows may have accounted for the relatively low levels of capital flight as a percentage of GDP from 1990 to 1993.

We also find that overinvoicing of imports as a percentage of GDP increased from 1991 through to 1994. We speculate that this rise may have occurred because there was less capital flight due to underinvoicing of exports as a result of the GEIS. In other words, people involved in capital flight who wanted the GEIS subsidy may have stopped underinvoicing exports and instead compensated for this decline by overinvoicing imports. Our argument is supported by the fact that the level of import overinvoicing dropped off once underinvoicing of exports recovered. Overinvoicing of imports, as a percentage of GDP, dropped from 3.5 percent in 1994 to 2.3 percent in 1995 and stayed around that level until 2000.

The lifting of the ban on the ANC and other political organizations and the release of political prisoners in 1990 signaled the end of apartheid and ushered in new hope for greater political stability. Negotiations over a new constitution and democratic elections also started in 1990 and picked up pace in 1991. However, by 1992 the ANC publicly referred to the existence of a 'third force' that wanted to derail the movement towards democracy. It seemed that certain political parties were using political violence to improve their negotiation position. This violence may also have contributed to the increase in misinvoicing from 1991 to 1992 (see Figure 4.3).

1994–2000

Net capital flows from 1991 onwards were positive, reflecting the strong growth in international liquidity in the 1990s[17] and possibly the expectations of political stability after the first relatively peaceful democratic elections, were held.[18]

Between 1994 and 1996 the business sector in South Africa was relatively unsure of the ANC government's economic policies. Its members were afraid that the ANC would adopt policies that would hurt them, nationalize private property and expropriate wealth in order to redistribute wealth and to improve the lives of the majority of South Africans. They were also concerned because the economy had been in decline throughout the 1980s.

The Nationalist Party had increased public debt significantly during the pre-election period as it attempted to buy votes on a large scale. There were fears that the new ANC government would increase debt further in an attempt to improve the lives of the majority of South Africans.

After the democratic elections in 1994, the African National Congress (ANC) government chose to adopt neoliberal economic policies to appease local business interests and to attract foreign investors. They did increase social spending and delivery of basic services but within the constraints of tight fiscal policy. They also supported development of a black business elite by promoting black ownership of businesses and implementing affirmative action policies. These policies have recently been integrated into a more comprehensive program for black economic empowerment. However, the overall structure of the South African economy, which had failed to significantly diversify out of the mining and mineral industrial sectors, had not changed much during the 1994 to 2000 period.

From 1994 to 1995, capital flight and the REER did not follow a similar trend (see Figure 4.7). The REER did not respond to the surge in net capital flows from 1993 and continued to decline. This may have been due to political instability before the elections and uncertainty about the new government's policies.

The adoption of neoliberal economic policies in the Growth, Employment and Redistribution (GEAR) program in 1996 reassured the business community about the ANC government's economic policies. Around the same time, political violence was brought under control and a degree of political stability was achieved. The recovery in the REER from 1996 to 1997 in response to the very large increase in net portfolio flows may well have been due to improved investor sentiment. However, contagion from the Asian financial crisis and the subsequent financial instability in several developing countries seem to have caused a decline in the REER of the rand after 1997.

Despite the achievement of political stability and the adoption of the types of economic policies that the business community wanted, misinvoicing continued at the same level as in 1994 and 1995. It is interesting to note that misinvoicing is fairly constant from 1994 to 1999 because it indicates that wealthy elites behaved differently in the post-election period. During the pre-election period misinvoicing was volatile and responded to significant events affecting the economy. However, during the post-election period misinvoicing remained relatively high and constant. The behavior of the wealthy elites after the elections seemed to indicate a sustained effort to build up wealth reserves outside of South Africa rather than a knee-jerk response to larger problems as in previous years. A possible reason for this is that a large proportion of the business community in South Africa continued to have fears and insecurities about the new democratically elected government.

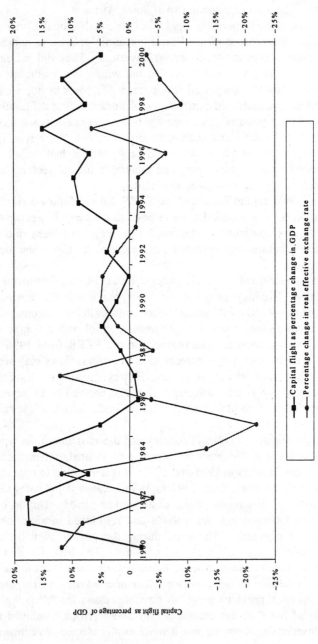

Figure 4.7 Movements in capital flight and the real effective exchange rate

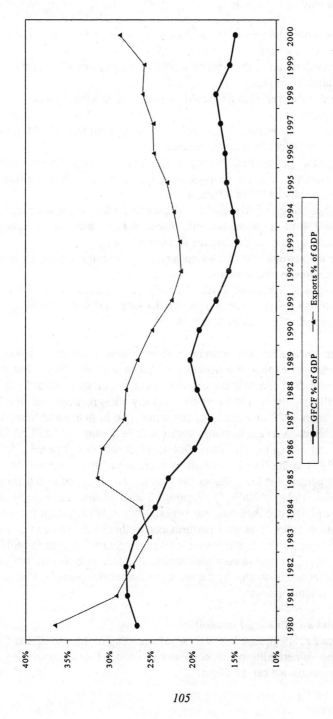

Figure 4.8   Exports and gross fixed capital formation as a percentage of GDP

They feared that:[19]

- they would be punished for their support or at least their failure to oppose apartheid;
- nationalization of their assets would be seen as just because they had benefited from apartheid;
- the need to redistribute wealth would lead to sequestration of their assets;
- measures to ensure black economic empowerment would have a negative affect on their businesses;
- the new government would force them to invest in low-return investments aimed at redistributing wealth or improving the lives of the majority of South Africans;
- the need to invest in social and economic infrastructure and programs would lead to unmanageable fiscal deficits and macroeconomic instability that would damage their businesses;
- tax rates would sky-rocket to pay for improving access to health, education and basic needs;
- the new government would be unable to control people who had been oppressed and exploited for so long and that there would be persistent instability in South Africa.

However, uncertainty and insecurity about a new government's policies are not enough to explain the behavior of South African elites. The poor performance of the South African economy is an important motivating factor for capital flight. Figure 4.8 shows that wealthy elites reduced their level of investment from 1982 onwards. At the same time business and household savings declined. Average business saving as a percentage of GDP declined from 6 percent during the turbulent 1980 to 1993 period to 5 percent during the period 1994 to 2000 while household average savings as a percentage of GDP was 3 percent for the 1980 to 1993 period and dropped to 0.8 percent for the period 1994 to 2000. [20] Figure 4.8 also shows that exports as a percentage of GDP declined over the period 1980 to 1982, except for a one-year rebound in 1985. The poor performance of the South African economy may have reinforced the determination of wealthy South Africans to build up offshore assets. At the same time, capital flight contributed to the poor performance of the economy by depleting resources the country needed for investment in future growth.

Capital flows and financial instability
South Africa's reintegration into the global economy at the end of apartheid increased the vulnerability of the economy to financial crises, providing the incentive for increased capital flight.

There were two occasions during the last two decades when there were crises in the South African financial system: the debt crisis in 1985 and the currency crisis in 2001. Both crises were caused by inadequate capital controls and were preceded by surges in net, short-term capital flows and sudden sharp declines in these flows.

The surges in net capital flows to South Africa during the early 1980s and after 1994 (see Figure 4.5) contributed to the growth in capital flight in both periods. The peaks in capital flight in 1982 and 1997 were clearly the result of the peaks in net capital flows into South Africa in those years (see Figure 4.5). The flows absorbed into the economy after 1994, which were largely in the form of short-term portfolio investment, led to lower real interest rates and a boom in credit to the private sector. However, as can be seen in Figures 4.8 and 4.9, these flows were not utilized for productive purposes.[21] Mohamed (2003) shows that the surge in net capital flows was associated with increased consumption, imports of goods and services and capital flight and not with productive investment in the economy.[22] The surge in net capital flows could not last; it collapsed in 2000. This collapse in capital flows probably contributed to the increase in misinvoicing from 5 percent of GDP in 1999 to 7.5 percent of GDP in 2000.

Wealthy South Africans may have engaged in capital flight in order to hold their assets in economies that are less vulnerable than South Africa to financial crises and contagion. This reason has been used by companies to explain their decision to move their primary listing from the Johannesburg Stock Exchange to the London Stock Exchange.[23] They claim that they want to reduce currency and other risks associated with being listed in South Africa, which is classified as an emerging market

The ANC government believed that foreign investment was important for further industrialization of the South African economy and seemed to pay very little attention to whether foreign investment was short-term or long-term. The government adopted neoliberal economic policies, which included little control over capital movements by non-residents, to attract foreign investment. The result of these policies was wasteful use of the surge in portfolio flows by private borrowers, a currency crisis in 2001 and more capital flight.

The policy conclusion that can be drawn from this discussion is that capital controls are necessary in South Africa as they may reduce capital flight by addressing the country's vulnerability to financial crises and contagion. Unfortunately, the same companies that are listed offshore continue to push for open capital markets.

Attitudes of the elite and capital flight

Another important reason for capital flight by wealthy South Africans has been mentioned above: the lack of faith of South African elites in the South

African economy, whose doubts about the future of the economy contribute towards weakening the economy even further. Their views are reinforced by social problems associated with poverty, like high levels of crime and corruption, and may also be exacerbated by racist views about the 'black' government's ability to govern the country and manage economic policy. Many racists may have further doubts about the future because of the greater role played by black South Africans in senior management positions in all spheres of the economy. These issues are continually raised in the South African media with white South Africans, tourists, business people and emigrants often being accused of 'badmouthing' South Africa abroad and providing a negative picture of the country to foreign investors. In most cases, tensions that arise between government and the white business community are not usually overtly about race; however, more often than not, issues of race lurk just below the surface.[24]

Structural weaknesses contributing to capital flight
There are serious structural weaknesses in the economy that affect accumulation and contribute to capital flight. It is worthwhile to explore these structural weaknesses in the South African economy further to understand some of the reasons why there may be capital flight rather than productive investment. The roots of these weaknesses lie in the type of industrialization that occurred within the context of South Africa's racist economic policies.

Fine and Rustomjee (1996) provide a very good framework for understanding the structural weaknesses of the South African economy. They organize their ideas around the existence of a minerals and energy complex (MEC) at the core of the South African economy. Fine and Rustomjee argue that the MEC includes the mining and energy sectors and a number of associated subsectors of manufacturing.[25] They make the point that most economic analyses of South Africa point to a decline in the mining sector and a greater role for manufacturing and services after World War II. However, the type of manufacturing and services that have developed are closely associated with, and often dependent on, the mining and energy sectors. Viewed from this perspective, the role of mining and energy in the economy has actually increased.

The strength of Fine and Rustomjee's analyses is their description of the MEC as a system of accumulation in which they show a close relationship between ownership and control of the few conglomerates. These conglomerates include the industrial and financial interests that control most of the South African economy. They discuss the history of industrialization in South Africa and the role played by key corporations and the state in developing the MEC and how the influence of the key corporations in the MEC extends into the financial sector.[26] They argue that through the control of the core sectors and of finance, these conglomerates were able to extend their control to other sectors.[27]

The high level of concentration in the South African economy along with the domination of the MEC imposed serious limitations on the success of industrial policies aiming to diversify industry.[28] Industrial concentration limits the ability of firms not within the dominant conglomerates to expand. The conglomerates also limit competition in the economy by suppressing competitors and buying up new entrants. Physical and other forms of infrastructure in the economy are geared towards the requirements of the MEC and may increase the costs associated with non-MEC activities.

Fine and Rustomjee note that a major weakness of the MEC as a system of accumulation was its failure to diversify out of the MEC into downstream manufacturing. They write:

> The evolution of the MEC has left the economy with both strengths and weaknesses. The strengths arise out of the productive and infrastructural capacities that have been built up around its core sectors. The weaknesses arise from the failure of this to be vertically integrated forward into the rest of the economy...the result has been an internationally uncompetitive consumer goods industry and limited capacity across a range of intermediate and capital goods. In addition, the scope of infrastructural provision, broadly interpreted to include the full range of what are normally public utilities as well as housing, health, education and welfare, is extremely limited as a consequence of apartheid. (Fine and Rustomjee 1996, p. 252)

The implication of the failure of the conglomerates that control most of South Africa's economy to diversify out of the MEC is that there has been relative stagnation in the economy with declining investment in new activities and limited replacement of old capital stock. Not only do these problems lead to capital flight, they are also reinforced by capital flight. Figure 4.9 shows capital flight as percentages of gross fixed capital formation (GFCF). The average capital flight is 34 percent of GFCF per year for the entire period. During the early period from 1980 to 1985, capital flight as a percentage of GFCF averages 39 percent, dropping to 9 percent from 1986 to 1993. During the latter period, from 1994 to 2000, capital flight as a percentage of GFCF averages a high of 58 percent. On the whole, it is clear that a very large amount of investment has been foregone in South Africa as a result of the magnitude of capital flight.

Fine and Rustomjee estimate that the average capital flight from South Africa between 1970 and 1988 was 7 percent of GDP per year. They write that the high level of capital flight 'indicates the global nature of South Africa's major corporations and their longstanding failure to promote diversification out of indigenous strengths in and around the MEC core' (p. 247). They add, 'The lack of industrial investment and diversification has its counterpart in the over-bloated financial system and corporate capacity to

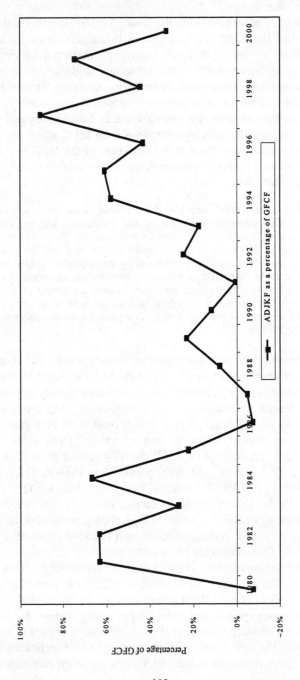

Figure 4.9   Capital flight as ratio of gross fixed capital formation

transfer funds abroad whether through transfer pricing, false invoicing of trade or other methods' (ibid.). They succinctly summarize how the limitations of the structure of the South African economy contribute towards capital flight.

In addition to these structural reasons, an important explanation for large capital flows from South Africa is the deep integration of South African capital with capital in industrialized countries.[29] This level of integration means that moving wealth and assets offshore is relatively easy for many wealthy South Africans. Our calculations indicate that the lowest level of misinvoicing was 1.9 percent of GDP for the period investigated. Therefore, it seems to us that capital flight may be the standard operating procedure for many of the large South African importing and exporting firms.

Diaz-Alejandro's (1984) discussion of capital flight from Latin America is relevant to South Africa as well. Those engaged in capital flight escape the burden of contributing (through taxation) to investments that develop the country. The burden is shifted to people who keep their wealth in the country. In addition, capital flight from South Africa entrenches MEC and the structural weaknesses in the economy. The holders of capital choose not to invest in diversifying the South African economy or further developing the economy. They stunt economic development by shifting the cost of development to the rest of society. At the same time, they pressure the government to adopt neoliberal policies that limit state spending and stifle demand.

CONCLUSION

Our interpretation of the data and South African economic history leads us to believe that capital flight from the South African economy has been rampant. We show that it was affected by the ebb and flow of capital flows into and out of the economy. Capital flight peaked in periods when there were peaks in net capital flows in South Africa. We also show that misinvoicing, even when using a conservative estimate, was an important source of capital flight that remained consistently high. We believe that tracking misinvoicing provides important insights into how wealthy South Africans engaging in capital flight behaved before and after the 1994 democratic elections.

Wealthy South Africans have made a concerted effort to build up wealth outside South Africa, despite the relative political stability and the adoption of neoliberal policies that they favor. We believe that racism, fear and a sense of loss of power are important explanations of capital flight. In addition, the structural weaknesses of the South African economy that limited diversification and stifled investment are central to our explanation of capital flight. The control by a few white-owned and controlled conglomerates that have power over the major financial institutions in the country and also have deep ties with capital in advanced industrial countries provides an important reason for capital flight.

NOTES

We gratefully acknowledge the support and guidance of Gerald Epstein and the Political Economy Research Institute. Thanks to Arjun Jayadev for help providing valuable feedback and editorial assistance.

1.   See Beja, Chapter 3, of this book.
2.   Operationally, we compute capital flight as the sum of change in external debt, foreign investment inflows, current account surplus and change in international reserves.
3.   See Terreblanche (2003) for a discussion of white attitudes during the post-apartheid period.
4.   Cumulative totals for capital flight (including misinvoicing) and gross fixed capital formation are obtained by simply adding the nominal values for each year from 1980 to 2000 respectively. We do not consider potential rates of return on domestic capital or capital held overseas.
5.   The latest period investigated in the South African capital flight literature ends at 1995 (see Fedderke and Liu 2002).
6.   We modify Boyce and Ndikumana's (2001) calculation to obtain a more conservative estimate for trade misinvoicing. Boyce and Ndikumana's calculation assumes that the levels of trade misinvoicing for the African countries they examine are the same in developed and developing countries. In order to provide a conservative estimate of capital flight from South Africa, we assume that there is no misinvoicing of trade to and from developing countries.
7.   Boyce and Ndikumana (2001) use an adjusted change in external debt variable to revalue foreign debt taking into account cross–currency exchange rate fluctuations. South African debt data decomposed by different currencies was not available for the time period we were investigating.
8.   Global development finance (GDF) has available decomposed debt data from 1994.
9.   IFS only has data for South Africa from 1985.
10.   Capital flight in our discussion of results refers to adjusted capital flight (ADJKF), which includes misinvoicing.
11.   The apartheid government built Sasol 1, Sasol 2 and Sasol 3 at great expense to ensure that they had enough oil in a situation when sanctions were escalating.
12.   The apartheid government was forced to call a four-month moratorium on $14 billion short-term loan repayments in August 1985. This moratorium was later extended to March 1986. The debt crisis was a direct result of the surge in liquidity when South African borrowers were plied with short-term loans after the Latin American debt crisis.
13.   According to Jenkins (1990, p. 279), seven US companies left South Africa in 1984, 40 left in 1985, 49 left in 1986, 58 left during 1987 and almost 80 left in 1988. By 1987, 20 percent of British firms in South Africa had left.
14.   GEIS was a subsidy to promote manufactured exports. The levels of subsidy were higher for goods with higher levels of value-added. The introduction of GEIS as a 'general' incentive was indicative of the apartheid state choosing a more market-oriented approach to industrial policy and their rejection of alternate views that called for a more targeted approach to industrial policy (for more on this debate, see Black 1993).
15.   This information was obtained in private communication with people who had administered GEIS in the South African Government's Department of Trade and Industry. They mentioned a number of drawn–out court cases as a result of charging exporters with fraud for claiming GEIS subsidies when they had overinvoiced exports. Wood and Moll (1994) also refer to overinvoicing due to GEIS.

16. Authors' calculations.
17. See Palma (2000) for a discussion of the massive rise in liquidity in global financial markets in the 1990s.
18. International investor sentiment towards South Africa improved once the government had adopted the market-driven Growth, Employment and Redistribution (GEAR) program and may have contributed to further growth in short-term capital flows after 1996. It is ironic that these capital flows spurred by improved investor sentiment contributed to capital flight.
19. See Terreblanche (2003) for a discussion of white South African business attitudes and fears.
20. Author's calculation using SARB annual data on corporate and household savings.
21. Gross fixed capital formation (GFCF) as a percentage of GDP does increase by 2 percent from 1993 to 1998, possibly in response to the increased access to debt as a result of the increase in net capital flows. However, after 1997 when net portfolio flows peak, GFCF declines back to 15 percent of GDP – the lowest level for the period from 1980 to 2000.
22. Mohamed (2003) notes that from 1999 to 2000 net portfolio flows into South Africa reduced significantly and were actually negative in 2001. He argues that this sudden drop in portfolio flows may have been an important reason for the currency crisis in South Africa in 2001 when the rand depreciated by 35 percent relative to the US dollar.
23. ABSA (1999) says that international investors demand risk premiums on funds invested in emerging markets. When local companies list offshore they are seen to attract '…keener interest by foreigners' (p.6).
24. Thabo Mbeki's column, 'Letter from the President', has an article called 'Empowerment good for the economy and the nation' in the 5–11 December 2003 issue of the ANC's newsletter '*ANC Today*'. This article provides an interesting insight into the tension between business and the ANC government about policies like empowerment and continued white domination of the economy.
25. The writers use input–output tables to establish the linkages between the core MEC sectors and associated sectors and allocate a number of industries within the MEC that have traditionally been allocated to manufacturing although they are directly attached to mining and energy. They provide the example of metal fabrication that is allocated to manufacturing in traditional classification systems but which in reality is directly attached to mining because it follows on from the ore–making process.
26. During the post-World War II period, the development of Afrikaner nationalism, the apartheid state's support for Afrikaner business, and the conflict–cooperation relationship between the apartheid state and English capital, which dominated the economy, is important for understanding the specific form of industrialization that occurred in South Africa. During the interwar period, the Afrikaner nationalist movement chose to build Afrikaner political and economic influence by supporting the development of large corporations. After the Nationalist Party took power in 1948, English capital was forced to accommodate Afrikaner capital because of their political power. The apartheid state invested directly in the mining and energy sectors and developed financial institutions in order to foster the development of a powerful Afrikaner corporate sector. This process carried on through most of the post-War period and locked South Africa into a form of industrialization that was centered on the mining and energy sectors. It led to increased interpenetration of English and Afrikaner capital from the 1960s, which intensified with the disinvestments by foreign capital. This industrialization was based on large–scale, capital and energy–intensive investments. This type of large-scale capital and energy intensive investment still dominates the South African economy today despite a change in government and unemployment of close to 40 percent.
27. Innes (1984) also provides a detailed account of the concentration of South African industry through his vivid history of the Anglo–American Corporation.
28. Inadequate diversification out of core MEC sectors and low GFCF was accompanied by increased financial market activity. During the 1980s, financial institutions played an exaggerated role in the economy that supported further concentration in the economy. South African capitalists were influenced by trends of hostile takeovers and merger and

acquisitions in many industrialized economies and the earlier trends towards diversified conglomeration in the 1960s and early 1970s. The increasing number of disinvestments by US and British companies from the South African economy during the 1980s fueled this trend towards further concentration. This further entrenched the inability of the economy to diversify out of the MEC.

29. There have always been strong links between the families that own the holding companies controlling the largest, most powerful companies in South Africa and powerful businesses in developed countries. Colonialism and imperialism explain this enduring relationship. Wealthy South Africans have maintained or built strong ties with European and US businesses over a long period of time. Large finance houses like Citibank and Barclays Bank have historical and long-term interests in South African businesses. They have financed South African mining houses since the discovery of diamonds in the 1830s and have had and continue to have representatives on the boards of the major South African conglomerates or their subsidiaries.

REFERENCES

Abayi, Ibi S. (1997), 'An analysis of external debt and capital flight in the severely indebted low income countries in Sub-Saharan Africa', IMF Working Paper No.WP/97/68. www.imf.org/external/pubs/ft/wp/wp9768.pdf.

ABSA (1999), 'Implications of the migration to London of South African companies', *Economic Spotlight*, **27**, Johannesburg, South Africa: ABSA Bank.

Alesina, A. and G. Tabellini (1989), 'External debt, capital flight and political risk', *Journal of International Economics*, **27** (3–4), 199–220.

Black, Anthony (1993), 'The role of the state in promoting industrialisation: selective intervention, trade orientation and concessionary industrial finance', in Lipton, M. and Simkins, C. (eds), *State and Market in Post Apartheid South Africa*, Johannesburg, South Africa: Witwatersrand University Press.

Boyce, James and Leonce Ndikumana (2001), 'Is Africa a net creditor? New estimates of capital flight from severely indebted Sub-Saharan African countries, 1970–96', *Journal of Development Studies*, **38** (2), 27–56.

Collier, Paul, Anke Hoeffler and Cathy Pattillo (2001), 'Flight capital as a portfolio choice', *The World Bank Economic Review*, **15** (1), 55–80.

Diaz-Alejandro, Carlos (1984), 'Latin American debt: I don't think we're in Kansas anymore', *Brooking Papers on Economic Activity*, No. 2, pp 335–403.

Dornbusch, Rudiger (1987), 'Comment', in Lessard, D.R. and Williamson, J (eds), *Capital Flight and Third World Debt*, Washington, US: Washington Institute for International Economics.

Fedderke, J., R. de Kadt and J. Luiz (1999), 'Indicators of Political Liberty, Property Rights and Political Instability in South Africa: 1953–1997', ERSA Working Paper No. 4, University of the Witwatersrand.

Fedderke, J. and W. Liu (2002), 'Modelling the determinants of capital flows and capital flight: with an application to South African data from 1960 to 1995', *Economic Modeling*, **19**, 419–444.

Fine, Ben and Zavareh Rustomjee (1996), *The Political Economy of South Africa: From Minerals and Energy Complex to Industrialisation*, Boulder, US: Westview Press.

Innes, Duncan (1984), *Anglo-American and the Rise of Modern South Africa*, New York, US: Monthly Review Press.

Jenkins, C. (1990), 'Sanctions, economic growth and change', in Nattrass, N. and Ardington, E. (eds), *The Political Economy of South Africa*, Cape Town, South Africa: Oxford University Press.

Khan, Brian (1991), 'Capital flight and exchange controls in South Africa', Research Paper 4, Center for the Study of the South African Economy and International Finance, London School of Economics.

Lowenberg, Anton (1997), 'Why South Africa's apartheid economy failed', *Contemporary Economic Policy*, **15** (3), 62–72.

Mbeki, Thabo (2003), 'Empowerment good for the economy and nation', in ANC Today (The online newsletter of the African NationalCongress), **3** (48) available at www.anc.org.za/ancdocs/anctoday/2003/at48.html.

Mohamed, Seeraj (2003), 'Capital inflows since the end of apartheid and the 2001 currency crisis', mimeo, presented at the Trade and Industry Policy Strategies and the Development Policy Research Unit's 2003 Annual Forum in Johannesburg, South Africa.

Palma, Gabriel (2000), 'Three routes to financial crises: The need for capital controls', Center for Economic Policy Analysis, New School University, Working Paper No. 17, (RePEc:cepawp:2000–17).

Rustomjee, Zavareh (1991), 'Capital flight under apartheid', *Transformation*, **15**, 89–103.

Smit, B.W. and B.A. Mocke (1991), 'Capital flight from South Africa: magnitude and causes', *South African Journal of Economics*, **59** (2), 101–117.

Terreblanche, Sampie (2003), A History of Inequality in South Africa: 1652–2002, Pietermaritzburg, South Africa: The University of Natal Press.

Wood, E and T. Moll (1994), 'Capital flight from South Africa: is underinvoicing exaggerated?', *South African Journal of Economics*, **62** (1), 28–45.

Databases

Direction of Trade Statistics (DOTS) CD-ROM 2003
Global Development Financial (GDF) CD-ROM 2002
International Financial Statistics (IFS) (Online), http://ifs.apdi.net/imf/logon.aspx
South African Reserve Bank, Balance of Payments data (Online), www.resbank.co.za
World Development Indicators (WDI) CD-ROM 2003

5. The Determinants of Capital Flight in Turkey, 1971–2000

Anil Duman, Hakki C. Erkin and Fatma Gül Unal

INTRODUCTION

Financial markets are considered an important force for generating economic growth and development. Conventional theory suggests that given free and open capital markets, capital will flow from capital-abundant advanced economies to capital-scarce developing countries. However, when there is capital flight, these flows move in the opposite direction, thereby becoming an undesirable resource-transfer mechanism. Even though there have been several discussions of the potential effects of capital flight on investment and economic development, capital flight from individual countries remains a largely unexplored area.

This chapter examines the determinants of capital flight from Turkey. Various authors have explored the impact of capital flows on financial crisis and economic volatility. Akyuz and Boratav (2002)[1] argue that capital flows were the main reason for the recent financial crisis in Turkey. Also, Boratav and Yeldan (2002) claim that capital movements contributed to rising external and domestic instability. Yet, all these investigations focus on capital flows or a narrow definition of outflows, namely hot money,[2] rather than on capital flight. We consider capital flight to be any net capital outflow that is conducted unofficially and therefore never appears on the books. This definition encompasses a broad range of outflows, from the proceeds of illegal activities to capital earned in an otherwise legal way, but whose owners want to place it out of the reach of government officials or creditors. This redefinition of capital flight is our first departure from the existing literature on Turkey. In addition, while the majority of the literature on capital flight from Turkey explores the effects of capital flows on the functioning of the economy, our attention will be focused primarily on the determinants of capital flight.

The remainder of the chapter is structured in five parts. Section two discusses several different definitions of capital flight and reviews the method we employed to estimate it. Section three presents a description of the methodology. Section four presents an overview of the magnitude of the capital flight in Turkey from 1971 to 2000 and significant factors determining it, and section five draws conclusions.

THE MEASUREMENT OF CAPITAL FLIGHT

There is no consensus on the definition of capital flight or its measurement. Some studies suggest a distinction between capital flight and 'normal' capital outflows, which are based on considerations of portfolio diversification of residents[3] (Lessard and Williamson 1987). A similar view emphasizes the abnormal or illegal nature of outflows (Kindleberger 1987). However, it is difficult to empirically distinguish between normal and abnormal or illegal capital outflows. Therefore, many studies assert that normal and abnormal capital outflows should be assessed together (World Bank 1985; Morgan Guaranty 1986). Besides, for countries that are struggling with large current account deficits and external debt payments, any capital outflow creates a bottleneck. As a result of the lack of consensus in defining and measuring capital flight, there are five widely accepted methods of estimating capital flight. The first method was developed by Dooley (1986)[4] and estimates abnormal or illegal capital flight by looking at the difference between World Bank data on the change in external debt stock and the amount of external borrowing reported in the balance of payments statistics. The second method is the hot money method, which was used by Cuddington (1986) to measure capital flight. The hot money method adds up net errors and omissions and non-bank private short-term capital outflows and is based on the premise that capital flight, being illegal, will be reflected in errors and omissions in the balance of payments accounts. Next, there is the trade misinvoicing method, which includes trade misinvoicing in the estimate of capital flight. The fourth measure, the asset method, reports the total stock of assets held by residents in foreign banks as capital flight. Finally, the residual method estimates the amount of capital flight from a country by analyzing the difference between recorded sources and uses of capital flows.

The major shortcoming of the Dooley and hot money methods arises from the conceptual premise that there is a distinction between abnormal and normal flows. We do not believe that this differentiation is useful since what really matters for most developing countries is the lack of financial resources. Both the asset and trade methods are too narrow and overlook significant elements of capital flight. The residual method has the advantage of reflecting the macroeconomic structure by examining the debt stock, which is an important indicator of economic fragility for countries like Turkey.

This chapter does not distinguish between normal and abnormal capital outflows and employs the residual method to estimate capital flight.[5] The definition and method of estimation of capital flight used here are taken from the World Bank (1985) and Ndikumana and Boyce (1999), who define capital flight as '... mechanisms by which residents of a country seek to evade domestic social control over their assets by transferring them abroad'. The standard measure of capital flight is improved by taking into account trade misinvoicing[6] and inflation. The residual method is particularly relevant for Turkey given that it considers external borrowing in the calculation of capital flight. Turkey is a highly indebted country and the debt dynamics play an important role in the country's economic and political cycles, which we will turn to in the next section.

METHODOLOGY

We compute total capital flight by adding the change in external debt outstanding ($\Delta DEBT$) to net foreign investments (NFI), and subtracting total recorded foreign exchange outflows, which comprise the current account deficit (CA) and the change in international reserves (ΔRES). Therefore;

$$KF_t = \Delta DEBT_t + NFI_t - (CA_t + \Delta RES_t) \tag{5.1}$$

A positive estimate from equation (5.1) would mean capital flight out of the country, while a negative estimate would mean reverse capital flight. We make further adjustments for errors in the data. Long-term external debt is acquired from different countries and expressed in their respective currencies; exchange rate fluctuations therefore affect the value of total external debt across periods.[7] The impact of foreign exchange rate fluctuations on external debt ($ADEBT$) is estimated in line with Ndikumana and Boyce (1999).

$$\Delta DEBTADJ_t = DEBT_t - ADEBT_{t-1} \tag{5.2}$$

Then equation (5.1) is re-estimated taking the adjustment in debt into consideration:

$$KF_t = \Delta DEBTADJ_t + FDI_t - (CA_t + \Delta RES_t) \tag{5.3}$$

Next, we adjust the capital account figures since export and import data could be erroneous because of systematic trade misinvoicing. Ndikumana and Boyce (2001) present the steps to calculate the export and import discrepancies and we follow the same procedure for Turkey. Therefore,

$$DX_t = PX_t - CIF^*X_t$$
$$DM_t = M_t - CIF^*PM_t$$
$$MIS_t = DX_t + DM_t \qquad (5.4)$$

DX and DM are the total export and import discrepancies, respectively. PX is the value of the trading partner's imports from Turkey and PM is the value of the trading partner's exports to Turkey. X and M are Turkish exports to and imports from major trading partners, correspondingly. CIF is the c.i.f./f.o.b. factor used to adjust export data for cost of freight and insurance. Lastly, adding the discrepancies of exports and imports gives us equation (5.4), which is total trade misinvoicing.

Equation (5.4) is added to Equation (5.3) to obtain adjusted capital flight.

$$AdjKF_t = KF_t + MIS_t \qquad (5.5)$$

Lastly, we calculate real capital flight to make estimates comparable across periods. We use the producer price index (PPI) with a base of 1995 as deflator.

$$Real\ KFlight_t = Adj\ KFlight_t / PPI_t \qquad (5.6)$$

THE DETERMINANTS OF CAPITAL FLIGHT IN TURKEY

Trends in Capital Flight

Capital flight as a percentage of GDP has on average been moderate for Turkey. However, it fluctuated sharply over the period under study; these movements can be explained within the context of different economic and political developments. Recent Turkish economic history can be divided into three phases reflecting the diverse macroeconomic policies implemented in each stage. The first stage starts in the late 1960s with import substitution industrialization and ends in 1980 with the military coup. The second stage is marked by trade liberalization and export-led growth strategies, and ends in 1989, when Turkey fully liberalized its capital account, leading to the third stage, which is characterized by financial openness and crises. However, before moving to a detailed examination of each phase, it would be useful to look at the general developments in capital flight and its determinants.

As can be seen in Figure 5.1, Turkey experienced a steady inflow of capital until the second half of 1976, when the trend was reversed, and the economy experienced a steady increase in capital outflows which reached a record high of 5.19 percent of GDP in 1977. Total real capital flight, with

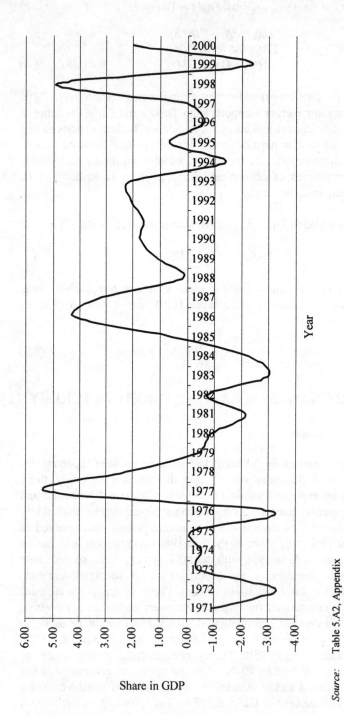

Source: Table 5.A2, Appendix

Figure 5.1 Capital Flight with misinvoincing (percentage of GDP)

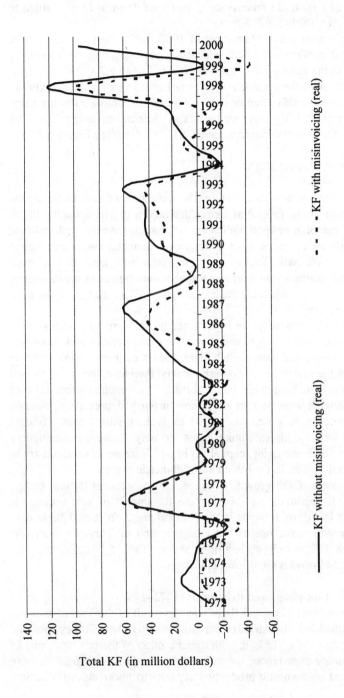

Source: Table 5.A2, Appendix

Figure 5.2 Capital flight with and without misinvoicing

- - - KF with misinvoicing (real)
—— KF without misinvoicing (real)

the inclusion of total trade misinvoicing, increased from $–33.98 million to $60.8 million (see Table 5.A2, Appendix).

Capital flight after the military coup of 1980 was modest, but there were massive capital outflows in 1986 and 1987, corresponding to increasing levels of debt in the same years, as can be seen in Figure 5.2.

In the 1990s, with the notable exceptions of crises years, capital flight out of the country was positive and unstable. Figure 5.1 demonstrates the sharp fluctuations in capital flight during the era of financial openness. In 1998 capital flight values reached approximately $121 million (see Figure 5.2).

Determinants of Capital Flight

Even though there is no agreement on the definition of capital flight, the existing literature points to a set of factors that appear to trigger capital flight. Most studies examine several indicators of macroeconomic and political instability, differences in the rates of return on financial assets and lagged capital flight. We will follow a similar path and look at the main macroeconomic indicators in Turkey to analyze the trends in capital flight. In addition, we will include trade misinvoicing as well as changes in the level of external borrowing.

Macroeconomic instability can be detected by growing imbalances in the economy such as rising budget and current account deficits and inflation.[8] Each of these may accelerate capital flight from a country. High inflation directly erodes the real value of domestic assets; therefore, the residents will have an incentive to hold their assets abroad. Increasing current account deficits may trigger expectations of future currency depreciation, causing residents to remove their financial assets to avoid wealth losses. Budget deficits may lead to higher future taxes or may influence inflationary expectations; in both scenarios, capital flight will increase as residents try to avoid a potential decline in the real value of domestic assets.

We will consider GDP growth, inflation, current account deficit, budget deficit and trade misinvoicing. To capture the impact of macroeconomic policy changes and developments in the political arena on capital flight over the period we will make use of our categorization of Turkey's economic history into the different phases identified above. Table 5.1 summarizes this categorization and reveals significant indicators.

Import substitution phase and debt crisis (1972–1980)
The low average level of capital flight was the result of the inward-looking, domestic demand-led industrialization policy (ISI) that Turkey pursued between 1972 and 1980. Indeed, with the exception of the last two years of the decade, Turkey experienced net capital inflows. Economic policies were aimed at expanding domestic production capacity to foster industrialization.

During this period, the major economic groups of the country, industrial workers, bureaucratic elites, industrial capitalists and peasants, had established alliances on the basis of a state-managed system (Senses 1991; Ozcan, Voyvoda and Yeldan 1999). Heavy public investment in manufacturing was accompanied by the active discouragement of foreign direct investment. The state implemented these policies via state-owned economic enterprises (SEEs) and controlled the prices of goods produced by the SEEs. The controlled price mechanism aimed at motivating industrialization by lowering production costs. As pointed out by Metin-Ozcan et al. (2001), domestic production was heavily protected through the use of import quotas and fixed exchange rates. The government also tried to maintain the value of the lira through extensive foreign exchange controls.

These policies came to a halt in 1977, when net capital inflows were dramatically transformed into net capital outflows, and capital flight hit a record high of 5.19 percent of GDP. The price controls for the commodities produced by SEEs[9] were causing operational losses and hence increasing the budget deficit, which was under further stress from the emerging oil crisis. Growing public deficits and investment had been financed by borrowing heavily from the Central Bank and by short-term external borrowing. From 1972 to 1978 the budget deficit as a percentage of GDP grew from 1.67 percent to 3.34 percent while the current account balance deteriorated from 0.11 percent to −4.57 percent. This resulted in a payments crisis and required a suspension of foreign exchange transfers for imports. By 1976, the current account deficit was no longer sustainable and the country was running short of foreign exchange. The current account deficit doubled in 1977, quickly plunging the country into debt. External debt reached 22.1 per cent of GDP in 1978 with the second oil crisis, while inflation increased almost fivefold. These developments led to increased capital flight by the end of the ISI period.

Export overinvoicing and import underinvoicing decrease the current account deficit and thus diminish capital flight. These forms of trade misinvoicing were prevalent in Turkey for the entire ISI period with the exception of 1977 when exports were underinvoiced and imports were overinvoiced, which seems reasonable considering that this was a year of serious foreign exchange shortage.[10] Total capital flight increased from $54.8 million to $60.8 million in real terms with the inclusion of total trade misinvoicing.

The foreign exchange crisis of 1977–1980, coupled with civil unrest and political instability, came to an end with the adoption of an orthodox stabilization package by a new military regime. Two stand-by agreements were signed with the IMF in April 1978 and July 1979 to solve the liquidity problem while efforts were made to stabilize the economy. Steps were taken in the direction of a more flexible interest and exchange rate policy.

Table 5.1 *Macroeconomic indicators and capital flight*

	Year	GDP growth	Inflation	BOP/ GDP	Budget deficit/ GDP	Debt/ GDP	Total trade mis./GDP	KF/ GDP
Averages	Import Substitution	2.41%	26.32%	-1.41%	-2.51%	15.60%	-0.93%	-0.06%
	Export-Led Growth	2.08%	49.94%	-2.27%	-3.69%	36.72%	-1.76%	-0.13%
	Financial Liberalization	1.87%	75.97%	-0.57%	-6.26%	42.44%	-0.72%	1.52%
	2000	5.79%	54.92%	-0.68%	-11.45%	58.32%	-3.11%	2.00%
	1972	4.68%	11.67%	0.11%	-1.67%	16.50%	-2.08%	-3.31%
	1973	0.64%	15.44%	0.46%	-1.43%	15.51%	-2.45%	-0.43%
	1974	3.03%	15.82%	1.65%	-1.42%	12.41%	-1.16%	-0.54%
	1975	4.72%	19.20%	-1.36%	-1.04%	10.84%	-0.17%	-0.19%
Import Substitution	1976	8.07%	17.36%	-2.99%	-1.55%	11.24%	-1.25%	-3.12%
	1977	1.30%	27.08%	-3.27%	-4.82%	18.80%	0.51%	5.19%
	1978	-0.51%	45.28%	-4.57%	-3.34%	22.10%	-0.76%	2.27%
	1979	-2.67%	58.69%	-1.32%	-4.79%	17.37%	-0.08%	-0.36%
Crisis	1980	-4.60%	110.2%	-1.97%	-3.07%	26.98%	-1.09%	-0.84%

	Year							
Export-led	1981	2.41%	36.58%	−4.80%	−1.48%	28.94%	−0.41%	−2.15%
Growth	1982	1.02%	30.84%	−2.97%	−2.48%	30.62%	−0.61%	−0.70%
	1983	2.39%	31.40%	−1.52%	−3.48%	33.04%	−1.48%	−2.97%
	1984	4.09%	48.38%	−3.16%	−8.25%	36.08%	−4.28%	−2.29%
	1985	1.74%	44.96%	−2.10%	−5.84%	38.69%	−3.23%	0.56%
	1986	4.61%	34.62%	−1.33%	−2.47%	43.56%	−0.95%	4.17%
	1987	7.13%	38.85%	−1.68%	−3.14%	47.10%	−2.52%	3.15%
Crisis	1988	−0.07%	73.67%	−0.89%	−2.99%	45.50%	−1.31%	0.17%
	1989	−1.90%	63.27%	1.49%	−3.30%	38.85%	0.96%	1.10%
Financial	1990	6.86%	60.31%	0.64%	−3.00%	32.81%	−0.42%	1.73%
liberalization	1991	−0.66%	65.97%	−1.74%	−5.29%	33.74%	−0.99%	1.64%
Phase I	1992	4.35%	70.07%	0.17%	−4.33%	35.59%	−0.43%	2.08%
	1993	6.40%	66.10%	−0.54%	−6.72%	38.24%	−0.94%	2.15%
Crisis	1994	−6.88%	106.3%	−4.96%	−3.90%	51.07%	−0.29%	−1.39%
	1995	5.59%	88.11%	1.55%	−4.08%	43.58%	0.45%	0.66%
Financial	1996	5.41%	80.35%	−1.29%	−8.38%	43.99%	−1.57%	−0.59%
liberalization	1997	5.93%	85.73%	−1.28%	−8.48%	44.81%	−1.43%	0.04%
Phase II	1998	1.57%	84.64%	−1.33%	−8.40%	48.68%	−1.20%	4.87%
Crisis	1999	−6.11%	64.87%	1.07%	−13.02%	55.52%	−2.02%	−2.35%
	2000	5.79%	54.92%	−0.68%	−11.45%	58.32%	−3.11%	2.00 %

Although the rise in nominal interest and exchange rates did not prevent negative real interest rates or appreciation of the real exchange rate, these steps were still significant in terms of the direction of change and can be seen as early signs of what was to come in the 1980s.

Export-led growth

In 1980, Turkey started to implement a liberalization agenda that was to have a substantial impact on capital flight. Even though the level of capital flight was not on average significantly different from that of the previous macroeconomic phase, there was a net outflow of capital from Turkey after 1985. The policy shifts of the period were instrumental in causing this change. In 1980, restrictions on the trade sector were eliminated and the industrialization strategy shifted to an outward-looking, export-led growth strategy. According to Kirkpatrick and Onis (1991), the main objectives of the government were a reduction in state involvement in productive activities, an increased emphasis on market forces and the attraction of foreign investment. Key among the series of measures introduced was the devaluation of the currency by nearly 50 percent. Price controls on most SEE products were removed.[11] A third set of measures involved institutional changes, most important of which was the creation of a Money and Credit Committee, which was given responsibility for making decisions on economic policy, previously the domain of the Council of Ministers.

One of the major steps towards deregulating the financial system was taken on July 1, 1980, when the government removed all controls on commercial bank interest rates and allowed them to be determined by market forces. These initial attempts were not successful and resulted in an imme-diate crisis in 1982, when numerous money brokers who engaged in financial intermediation collapsed, together with a number of smaller banks. The crisis caused a marked decrease in net capital inflows compared to the previous year, from 2.15 percent to 0.7 percent of GDP. The benchmark of Turkish liberalization in this period was the opening of the current account. Current account liberalization undeniably affected not only the volume, but also the composition of Turkey's trade. The share of trade in GDP rose from 11 percent of GDP in 1972 to 29.14 percent in 1988. While both the shares of exports and imports steadily increased, export numbers almost tripled from 1972 onwards. Thanks to the increased export volume, the current account deficit declined to 0.89 percent of GDP in 1988. In addition, with the exception of 1984, there was an improvement in the budget deficit; nevertheless, it remained high on average compared to the ISI period. The rapid resurgence of growth and the improvement in the balance of payments were insufficient to overcome unemployment and inflation, which remained serious problems. The official unemployment rate fell from 15 per cent in 1979 to 11 percent in 1980, but, partly because of the rapid growth of the labor force, unemployment rose again, to 13 percent in 1985 (Senses 1996). Inflation fell to about 25 percent from 1981 to 1982 period, but climbed again to more than 30 percent in 1983 and more than 40 percent in 1984. Although inflation eased somewhat in 1985 and 1986, it remained one of the primary problems facing economic policy makers. The debt share in GDP hit 43.56 percent in 1986 and increased further to 47.1 percent the following year. As a result, capital fleeing the country reached an average of 2.63 percent between 1985 and 1987, peaking at 4.17 percent in 1986.

Another factor contributing to the change in the trend of capital flows was the problem of trade misinvoicing. Overinvoicing exports and underinvoicing imports had remained a problem in Turkey throughout the 1970s and 1980s. In 1972, 7.8 percent of all exports were overinvoiced. By 1984, this figure jumped to 25 percent due to generous export subsidies. At the beginning of 1985, capital flight with misinvoicing increased to $4.55 million in real terms from a net capital inflow of $16.5 million in the previous year.

The export-led growth path, which was dependent on wage suppression, depreciation of the domestic currency and extremely generous export subsidies, had reached its economic and political limits by 1988.[12] Anti-labor legislations of the early 1980s were instrumental in lowering production costs and squeezing domestic absorption[13] (Boratav and Yeldan 2002). International competitiveness in this era was based on low labor costs, which destroyed the earlier coalition that had existed between labor and capital.[14] A continued erosion of wage incomes – a process started by the 1980 military regime – characterized the 1983–87 period. The way out of the impasse turned out to be the liberalization of the capital account in 1989, and the full convertibility of the Turkish lira was ultimately realized at the beginning of 1990.

Financial liberalization and the crisis of 1994
However, full-fledged capital account liberalization created problems for the Turkish economy. The unregulated opening of domestic financial markets increased their fragility. There were a number of reasons for this. The public sector's share in financial markets was high; the commercial banking sector was the largest holder of public securities, and was operational in marketing the T-Bills in reverse repo operations. In addition, the arbitrage opportunities and high interest rates that were a by-product of the fiscal system generated short-term capital flows and worsened economic instability (Onis 1996). At the same time, the high interest rates offered by government bonds and treasury bills created a rentier economy and diverted economic activity from the real sector to the financial sector. There were adverse changes in the composition of fixed investments vis-à-vis non-tradables; most of the increase in private investment was in housing, not manufacturing.

According to Yeldan (2002a), financial cycles dominated the growth process.

The rate of growth of GDP was meager in 1988 and 1989; it increased to 6.86 percent in 1990, but then fell to –0.66 percent in 1991 and continued to fluctuate thereafter. Parallel with this trend was the cyclical behavior of consumption and investment. Private capital accumulation peaked in 1993, reaching 35 percent of GDP; however, this was immediately followed by a contraction in 1994 to 9.1 percent of GDP (Cizre-Sakallioglu and Yeldan 2000). Public investment expenditure declined by 20 percent in 1988 and did not recover until 1997. Private investment, on the other hand, was not sustain- able. The overall expansion of private capital accumulation followed a modest trend and could not provide sustained invigoration to the overall economy.

The average rate of inflation during the first phase of financial liberalization was 65.14 percent. The current account deficit was not a major problem and was low compared to what it had been in the earlier years of export-led growth. The decrease in the volume of exports was accompanied by an even larger decline in imports, so that the balance of payments did not deteriorate. The major deterioration was in the budget deficit, which jumped to an average of 4.53 percent of GDP. Debt levels fell slightly.

The period is exceptional in terms of capital flight figures. Before 1994, which is recorded as a crisis year, capital had continued to leave the country. In 1993, capital flight had reached 2.15 percent of GDP. The same year saw a deterioration in the capital account deficit when the import share in GDP doubled relative to the export share. Coupled with a huge rise in the budget deficit to 6.72 percent of GDP, it became impossible to roll over the debt and the crisis unfolded.

It is believed that the 1994 crisis was caused by capital outflows due to deteriorated confidence in the Turkish economy. A stand-by agreement signed with the IMF in March was not successful in lowering inflation or reducing the volatility of financial markets. The First Deputy Managing Director of the IMF, Stanley Fischer stated, while on a visit to Turkey, that the country was 'not an option for stand-by'. The reason behind this rejection, as noted in the Turkish media, was the IMF's finding that Turkey had been inconsistent in applying the economic policies suggested by IMF (Yeldan 2002b).

Recovery and 1999 crisis

According to Akyuz and Boratav (2002), the recovery came fast. From 1995 to 1997, the economy enjoyed three years of good economic performance and around 7 percent of GDP growth. The Asian Crisis put an end to the recovery; net capital inflows slowed down and the growth rate fell to 1.57 percent in 1998. Government debt had grown rapidly, approaching 50 percent of GDP; two-thirds of this was domestic debt. The banking system was extremely fragile and was working with a high-risk margin. To roll over its debt, the government had to offer high interest rates, thus fueling high inflation, even though there was little economic activity in the real sector. The public deficit continued to worsen, averaging 7.3 percent of GDP. This was again followed by massive capital flight in 1998 amounting to 4.87 percent of GDP.

The fallout from the Russian crisis and a devastating earthquake pushed the economy into a deep recession. Finally, Turkey launched an exchange rate-based disinflation and stabilization program designed, engineered and monitored by the IMF. The program's target was to lower the rate of inflation to 25 percent inflation by 2000 from 68.8 percent at the end of 1999.

Accordingly, the Central Bank committed itself to a no-sterilization policy so that liquidity available in the economy would be managed by interest rate signals in smoothly operating financial markets. It was expected that rising interest rates would invite foreign investors thereby allowing for monetary expansion.

As Boratav and Yeldan (2002) point out, in its first ten months, the program was successful in attaining its monetary, fiscal and exchange rate targets. The domestic currency appreciated, helped by an 'explosion' of net capital inflows from non-residents that reached $15.5 billion during the first ten months of 2000. This was reflected in the Central Bank's balance sheet as a net increase in external assets of 53 percent, and in the monetary base by 46 per cent between February and mid-November. Although inflation fell only to 32.7 percent, interest rates fell significantly faster, bringing relief to the government's budget. The economy enjoyed a positive net capital inflow of $12.5 million in the first ten months.

However, disinflation, currency appreciation, and exceptionally low interest rates created a strong surge in domestic demand, causing imports to increase by 32 percent from 1999 to 2000, while export growth was nil. In 2000, the total volume of trade was $80 billion and the average share of total trade in GDP had risen from an average of 31.12 percent in the 1990s to 41.15 percent in 2000. That year, exports financed only half of the country's imports. By mid-November, the IMF had started to express some concern, causing foreign bankers to call in short-term loans. This was the beginning of the new crisis (Yeldan 2002). The trends in the data for this period show a clear relationship between liberalization and the emerging crisis of the 1990s. Interestingly, the overinvoicing of exports ceased to be a problem, although the underinvoicing of imports continued to rise. Average export overinvoicing was 4.1 percent in the 1980s; by 2000, this had changed to export underinvoicing of 4.9 percent. For the 1970s import underinvoicing averaged about 11 percent, and even though this figure fell slightly in the 1980s, it increased afterwards to 13.9 percent in 2000. Throughout the

1990s, with the exception of the crisis years of 1994 and 1999, capital flight with misinvoicing averaged $28.5 million in real terms.

The debt structure and capital flight followed similar trends. Like the volume and share of capital flight in GDP, Turkey's debt continued to increase throughout the 1980s and 1990s until 2000. The average share of dollar-denominated debt in GDP increased from around 39.18 percent in the 1980s to 45.18 percent in the 1990s. In 1999, dollar-denominated debt was 55.5 percent of GDP; in 2000, it was 58.3 percent, signaling an even more rapid increase at the end of the period. In the 1990s Turkey's debt structure also changed. Until 1992, public and publicly guaranteed debt had constituted more than 95 percent of all long-term debt in Turkey. Only after this year did private non-guaranteed debt rise, reaching 35 percent of all long-term debt in 1999.[15]

Although both net foreign direct investment (FDI) and net portfolio investment (PI)[16] remained low, their share in GDP increased in the 1990s relative to the 1980s. For the entire period, FDI averaged only about 0.25 percent of GDP. However, there was a slight but steady increase from 0.2 percent to 0.37 percent of GDP in the 1980s and 1990s. PI followed a similar trend with more fluctuations, plummeting in 1998, a year of financial crisis, to −3.3 percent. In 1999, net PI recovered and reached almost 2 percent.

Lastly, even though there was no substantial change in the magnitude of capital flight, it became increasingly volatile in the 1990s. Turkey experienced persistent reverse capital flight in the 1970s; the 1980s saw persistent capital flight out of the country. However, the 1990s showed an oscillation between sudden inflows and outflows of capital, which, we believe, is important in explaining the financial crisis that occurred during this period.

CONCLUSION

We investigated the determinants of capital flight from Turkey, using the method employed in Ndikumana and Boyce (2002) for the period 1971–2000. The analysis demonstrates that capital flight surged during the country's financial crises. When we look at different macroeconomic phases in Turkey's history, we see that capital flight as a share of GDP grew steadily as the country changed its macroeconomic policies from an import substitution strategy to a more open one, rising from −0.06 percent to 1.52 percent, and finally reaching 2 percent in 2000.

Even though the highest capital flight to GDP ratio was recorded in 1977 at 5.19 percent, the general trend in the import substitution industrialization period was negative capital flight (that is, a net capital inflow). As the economy became more open, particularly after capital account liberalization, not only did the volatility of capital flight increase, but Turkey also experienced net capital outflows.

In addition, we find that macroeconomic and political instability were important determinants of capital flight in Turkey. Macroeconomic instability can be detected by rising imbalances in the economy such as growing budget deficits, increased debt and rapid inflation, and all three indicators showed a rising trend throughout the 1980s and 1990s as macroeconomic policies became more liberal and financial markets more open. Inflation increased from 26 percent in the ISI period to 75 percent during the era of financial liberalization; budget deficits grew from 2.5 percent to 11.45 percent in the same period, and Turkey's indebtedness increased from 15.6 percent in 1970s to almost 60 percent by 2000.

This conclusion suggests that Turkey's macroeconomic policies had a profound impact on capital flight. Neoliberal policies have been the dominant paradigm in offering solutions to macroeconomic problems for the last two decades in Turkey. Even though financial liberalization was seen as a panacea for capital bottlenecks, the Turkish experience illustrates that the level of capital flight rose and became more volatile with the increased openness of capital markets.

APPENDIX

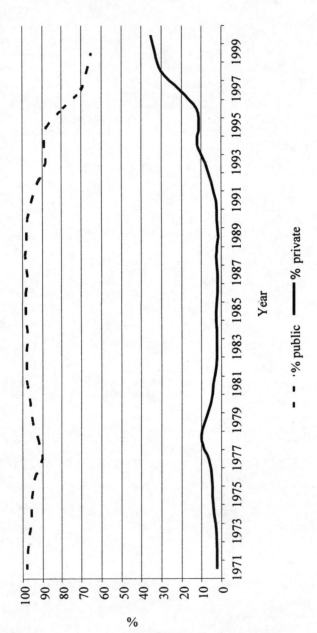

Figure 5.A1   Composition of long-term debt (1971–1999)

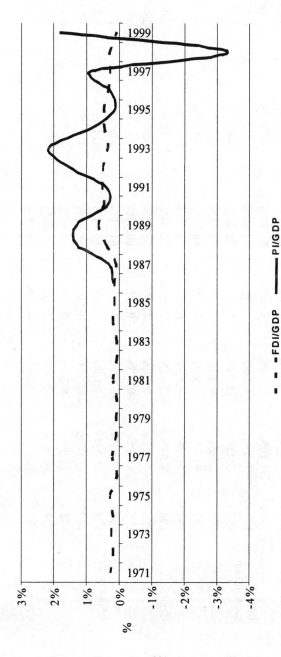

Figure 5.A2   Share of foreign direct investment and portfolio investment in GDP (1971–1999)

135

Table 5.A1 Stylized facts and descriptive statistics for trade 1972–2000

	Year	Xmis/X	Mmis/M	X/Trade	M/Trade	Total Mis./Trade	Total Mis./GDP
	1972	−7.80%	−25.07%	37.10%	62.90%	−18.66%	−2.08%
	1973	−3.92%	−29.20%	38.59%	61.41%	−19.45%	−2.45%
	1974	−1.10%	−11.03%	28.86%	71.14%	−8.17%	−1.16%
Import	1975	5.58%	−3.28%	22.82%	77.18%	−1.26%	−0.17%
substitution	1976	−3.41%	−11.74%	27.64%	72.36%	−9.44%	−1.25%
	1977	2.00%	4.78%	23.22%	76.78%	4.13%	0.51%
	1978	−5.37%	−8.39%	33.23%	66.77%	−7.38%	−0.76%
	1979	17.67%	−9.29%	30.84%	69.16%	−0.97%	−0.08%
Crisis	1980	6.70%	−12.25%	27.46%	72.54%	−7.04%	−1.09%
	1981	−5.61%	−0.27%	34.46%	65.54%	−2.11%	−0.41%
	1982	−6.79%	−0.07%	39.51%	60.49%	−2.73%	−0.61%
	1983	−10.61%	−3.33%	38.42%	61.58%	−6.13%	−1.48%
Export-led	1984	−25.31%	−7.13%	40.06%	59.94%	−14.41%	−4.28%
growth	1985	−11.66%	−11.02%	41.38%	58.62%	−11.28%	−3.23%
	1986	2.60%	−8.23%	40.20%	59.80%	−3.88%	−0.95%
	1987	−6.35%	−12.06%	44.20%	55.80%	−9.53%	−2.52%
Crisis	1988	3.21%	−10.66%	44.44%	55.56%	−4.49%	−1.31%

Financial liberalization	1989	12.84%	-2.86%	40.95%	59.05%	3.57%	0.96%
	1990	2.93%	-4.23%	35.92%	64.08%	-1.66%	-0.42%
	1991	5.82%	-10.88%	39.37%	60.63%	-4.31%	-0.99%
	1992	7.58%	-7.36%	37.46%	62.54%	-1.76%	-0.43%
	1993	3.41%	-7.58%	34.33%	65.67%	-3.80%	-0.94%
Crisis	1994	3.53%	-4.35%	43.82%	56.18%	-0.89%	-0.29%
	1995	5.08%	-0.95%	37.71%	62.29%	1.32%	0.45%
Financial liberalization	1996	0.17%	-6.81%	35.26%	64.74%	-4.35%	-1.57%
	1997	-0.17%	-5.52%	35.04%	64.96%	-3.65%	-1.43%
	1998	6.01%	-8.92%	37.03%	62.97%	-3.39%	-1.20%
Crisis	1999	6.71%	-13.55%	40.13%	59.87%	-5.42%	-2.02%
	2000	4.90%	-13.90%	33.75%	66.25%	-7.55%	-3.11%
	Mean	0.30%	-8.45%	35.97%	64.03%	-5.33%	-1.18%
	Median	2.60%	-8.23%	37.10%	62.90%	-4.31%	-1.09%
	St. Dev.	8.35%	6.89%	5.75%	5.75%	5.59%	1.17%
	Min.	-25.3%	-29.20%	22.82%	55.56%	-19.45%	-4.28%
	Max.	17.67%	4.78%	44.44%	77.18%	4.13%	0.96%
Mean	1970s	0.46%	-11.65%	30.29%	69.71%	-7.65%	-0.93%
	1980s	-4.10%	-6.79%	39.11%	60.89%	-5.80%	-1.49%
	1990s	4.11%	-7.02%	37.61%	62.39%	-2.79%	-0.88%
	2000	4.90%	-13.90%	33.75%	66.25%	-7.55%	-3.11%

Table 5.A2 Data used for Capital flight Estimation

Year	KF /GDP	DEBT /GDP	FDI ($ millions)	Current account ($ millions)	Reserves ($ millions)	KF without misinvoicing (real)	KF with misinvoicing (real)
1972	-3.31	16.50	43.43	123.77	-699.20	-8.32	-22.38
1973	-0.43	15.51	78.68	615.14	-696.20	15.18	-3.21
1974	-0.54	12.41	87.78	-633.71	407.64	5.39	-4.71
1975	-0.19	10.84	114.13	-1595.39	993.17	-0.25	-1.91
1976	-3.12	11.24	10.39	-1989.24	81.97	-20.33	-33.98
1977	5.19	18.80	142.44	-3074.08	438.99	54.80	60.80
1978	2.27	22.10	81.38	-1213.19	-57.59	36.33	27.25
1979	-0.36	17.37	117.57	-1356.60	7.75	-4.12	-5.25
1980	-0.84	26.98	18.22	-3408.71	-92.41	2.05	-8.32
1981	-2.15	28.94	95.51	-1916.14	8.25	-14.55	-18.21
1982	-0.70	30.62	55.20	-935.10	-147.94	-0.69	-5.64
1983	-2.97	33.04	45.97	-1897.48	-134.69	-11.28	-22.55
1984	-2.29	36.08	112.75	-1409.38	717.50	14.39	-16.48
1985	0.56	38.69	98.48	-1004.13	78.18	30.79	4.55

138

1986	4.17	43.56	125.00	−1465.00	−540.00	48.20	39.23
1987	3.15	47.10	106.00	−806.00	−580.00	59.93	33.26
1988	0.17	45.50	354.00	1596.00	−1153.00	15.63	1.77
1989	1.10	38.85	663.00	961.00	−2710.00	1.66	13.11
1990	1.73	32.81	700.00	−2625.00	−943.00	34.72	27.91
1991	1.64	33.74	783.00	272.00	1199.00	42.53	26.46
1992	2.08	35.59	779.00	−974.00	−1484.00	42.52	35.21
1993	2.15	38.24	622.00	−6433.00	−308.00	58.35	40.51
1994	−1.39	51.07	559.00	2631.00	−203.00	−14.88	−18.72
1995	0.66	43.58	772.00	−2338.00	−4660.00	3.54	11.13
1996	−0.59	43.99	612.00	−2437.00	−4544.00	17.42	−10.47
1997	0.04	44.81	554.00	−2679.00	−3343.00	27.39	0.69
1998	4.87	48.68	573.00	1984.00	−441.00	121.55	97.42
1999	−2.35	55.52	138.00	−1360.00	−5204.00	−5.54	−42.86
2000	2.00	58.32	112.00	−9819.00	2934.00	95.84	37.42

NOTES

We thank James K. Boyce, Gerald Epstein, Léonce Ndikumana, and members of the Capital Flight Working Group for their valuable comments and suggestions. The authors are responsible for any mistakes in the chapter.

1.   Akyuz and Boratav (2002) assert that sudden changes in the direction of capital flows trigger financial crises in a highly indebted country such as Turkey.
2.   This essentially focuses on short-term assets and does not take into account the acquisition of foreign long-term financial and real assets. This could lead to an understatement of capital flight.
3.   These include any portfolio or direct investment by residents or domestic commercial banks. Williamson maintains that capital flight is motivated by the desire to avoid losses that may occur as a result of government expropriation, unexpected changes in exchange rate or interest rate policies, and so on.
4.   According to Dooley, capital flight can be defined as the amount of externally held assets appropriated with the purpose of transferring wealth out of the country.
5.   See Beja, Chapter 3, this book.
6.   Export underinvoicing and import overinvoicing lead to an overstatement of the current account deficit; export overinvoicing and import underinvoicing lead to its understatement. If the current account deficit is overstated, capital flight will be too low whereas if it is understated, capital flight will be too high.
7.   For example, an appreciation of the US dollar would, everything else constant, lead to an increase in capital flight figures.
8.   Of course, the list is not exhaustive and there are certainly other indicators for macroeconomic imbalances (that is, exchange rate overvaluation); however, in the case of Turkey, these variables remain more relevant for capital flight.
9.   The cheap intermediate goods produced by SEEs were one of the main channels of subsidizing the private sector.
10. Exporters preferred to keep their foreign exchange earnings underreported and importers preferred to get more foreign exchange reserves by over-reporting.
11. A second set of measures concerned domestic prices, with reductions in the subsidies on fertilizers and petroleum products. The regulation of the prices of the manufactured goods was abolished.
12. The next year, 1989, witnessed general strikes all over the country and the government had to raise the salaries of public employees. The private sector, at least partially, was also forced to follow a similar pay structure. All political parties in the 1989 national elections declared populist programs.
13. The share of wage-labor in manufacturing value-added declined from an average rate of 35.6 percent in 1977–80 to 20.6 percent in 1988, and average mark-up rates (gross profit margins as a ratio of current costs) in manufacturing increased from 31 percent to 38 percent.
14. For a broader explanation on the earlier coalition, see Boratav (1983) and Boratav, Keyder and Pamuk (1984).
15. See Figure 5.A1 in Appendix.
16. See Figure 5.A2 in Appendix.

REFERENCES

Akyuz, Yilmaz and Korkut Boratav (2002), 'The Making of the Turkish Financial Crisis', UNCTAD Discussion Paper No. 158.
Alam, Imam and Rahim M. Quazi (2003), 'Determinants of Capital Flight: An Econometric Case Study of Bangladesh', *International Review of Applied Economics*, 17 (1), 85–103.

Bicer, Gul, Erol Balkan and Erinc Yeldan (2002), 'Patterns of Financial Capital Flows and Accumulation in the Post-1990 Turkish Economy', Hamilton College Working Paper No. 02/02.

Boratav, Korkut, C. Keyder and S. Pamuk (1984), *Krizin gelişimi ve Türkiye'nin alternatif sorunu/* Istanbul: Kaynak Yayınları.

Boratav, Korkut and Oktar Turel (1993), 'Turkey', in Lance Taylor (ed.), *The Rocky Road to Reform: Adjustment, Income Distribution and Growth in the Developing World*, Cambridge, MA: MIT Press, pp.143–165.

Boratav, Korkut and Erinc Yeldan (2002), 'Turkey, 1980–2000: Financial Liberalization, Macroeconomic (In)Stability and Patterns of Distribution', unpublished mimeo.

Cizre-Sakallioglu, Umit and Erinc Yeldan (2000), 'Politics, Society and Financial Liberalization: Turkey in the 1990s', *Development and Change*, 31 (2), 481–508.

Cizre-Sakallioglu, Umit and Erinc Yeldan (1999), 'Dynamics of Macroeconomic Disequilibrium and Inflation in Turkey: The State, Politics and the Markets under a Globalized Developing Economy', www.econturk.org.

Cuddington, John T. (1986), 'Capital Flight, Issues and Explanations', *Princeton Studies in International Finance*, No. 58, Princeton, NJ: Princeton University Press.

Dooley, Michael P. (1986), 'Country Specific Risk Premiums, Capital Flight, and Net Investment Income Payments in Selected Developing Countries', Washington DC: IMF, unpublished manuscript.

Edwards, Sebastian (2001), 'Exchange Rate Regimes, Capital Flows and Crisis Prevention', NBER Working Paper, No. 85 (29).

Elekdag, Selim (2002), 'Capital Flight, Monetary Policy and Currency Crisis', John Hopkins University Working Paper, No. 2002/198.

FitzGerald, Valpy and Alexander Cobham (2000), 'Capital Flight: Causes, Effects, Magnitude and Implications for Development', Queen Elizabeth House Working Paper No. 25.

Guaranty, Morgan (1986), 'LDC Capital Flight', *World Financial Markets*, 2, 13–16.

Hatiboglu, Zeyyat (1990a), 'A Theory of Growth and its Validation by the Turkish Experience', Institute of Business Economics, Istanbul University, Istanbul.

Hatiboglu, Zeyyat (1990b), 'Comments on Conventional Economics in the Light of the Turkish Experience', Institute of Business Economics, Istanbul University, Istanbul.

Hermes, Niels, Robert Lensik and Victor Murinde (2002), 'Flight Capital and its Reversal for Development Financing', WIDER Discussion Paper No. 2002/99.

Kindleberger, Charles P. (1987), 'A Historical Perspective', in D.R. Lessard, and J. Williamson (eds), *Capital Flight and Third World Debt*, Washington, DC: Institute for International Economics, pp. 7–26.

Lessard, Donald R. and John Williamson (1987), *Capital Flight and Third World Debt*, Washington DC: Institute for International Economics.

Metin-Ozcan, K., E. Voyvoda, and E. Yeldan (2000), 'On the Patterns of Trade Liberalization, Oligopolistic Concentration and Profitability: Post-1980 Turkish Manufacturing', Mimeo, Bilkent University.

Metin-Ozcan, K., E. Voyvoda, and E. Yeldan (2001), 'Dynamics of Macroeconomic Adjustment in a Globalized Developing Economy: Growth, Accumulation and Distribution, Turkey 1969–1998', *Canadian Journal of Development Studies*, 22 (3), 217–253.

Ndikumana, Leonce and James Boyce (1999), 'Is Africa a Net Creditor? New Estimates of Capital Flight from Severely Indebted Sub-Saharan African

Countries: 1970–1996', *Journal of Development Studies,* **38** (2), 27–56.

Ndikumana, Leonce and James Boyce (2002), 'Public Debts and Private Assets: Explaining Capital Flight from Sub-Saharan African Countries', University of Massachusetts, Department of Economics and Political Economy Research Institute, Working Paper No. 32 (www.umass.edu/peri/pdfs/WP32.pdf) *World Development*, January 2003.

Onis, Ziya and Colin Kirkpatrick, (1991), 'Turkey' in Paul Mosley, Jane Herrigan and John Toye (eds), *Aid and Power, The World Bank and Policy- based Lending,* London, New York: Routledge Publishers, pp. 9–37.

Onis, Ziya (1996), 'Globalization and Financial Blow-ups in the Semi-periphery: Turkey's Financial Crisis of 1994 in Retrospect', *New Perspectives on Turkey,* 15 (Fall), 1–23.

Ozlale, Umit and Erinc Yeldan (2004), 'Measuring Exchange Rate Misalignment in Turkey', *Applied Economics,* **36,** 1839–1849.

Schneider, Benu (2003), 'Resident Capital Outflows: Capital Flight or Normal Flows? A Statistical Interpretation', Overseas Development Institute Working Paper No. 195.

Senses, Fikret (1991), 'Turkey's Stabilization and Structural Adjustment Program in Retrospect and Prospect', *The Developing Economies*, 29 (3), 211–234.

Senses, Fikret (1996), 'Structural Adjustment Policies and Employment in Turkey', Middle East Technical University ERC Working Paper No. 96 (01).

Tanner, Evan and Shigeru Iwata, (2003), 'Pick Your Poison: The Exchange Rate Regime and Capital Account Volatility in Emerging Markets', IMF Working Paper No. 03/92

Yeldan, Erinc (2001), 'On the IMF-directed Disinflation Program in Turkey: A Program For Stabilization and Austerity or a Recipe for Impoverishment and Financial Chaos?', unpublished mimeo, Bilkent University.

Yeldan, Erinc (2002a), 'Patterns of Financial Capital Flows and Accumulation in the Post 1990 Turkish Economy', unpublished mimeo, Bilkent University.

Yeldan, Erinc (2002b), 'Behind the 2000–2001 Turkish Crisis: Stability, Credibility, and Governance for Whom?', Paper presented at the IDEAs Conference, Chennai.

Yenturk, Nurhan (1995), 'Short-term Capital Flows and their Impact on Macroeconomic Order: A Comparison between Turkey and Mexico', *Bogazici Journal, Review of Social, Economic and Administrative Studies,* 9 (2), 67–84.

World Bank (1985), *World Development Report 1985,* Washington DC: World Bank.

Databases

Direction of Trade Statistics (DOTS) CD-ROM 2003
Global Development Financial (GDF) CD-ROM 2002
International Financial Statistics (IFS) (Online), www.ifs.apdi.net/imf/logon.aspx
Central Bank of Turkey (Online), www.tcmbf40.tcmb.gov.tr/cbt-uk.html
World Development Indicators (WDI) CD-ROM 2003

6. Capital Flight from Thailand, 1980–2000

Edsel L. Beja, Jr., Pokpong Junvith and Jared Ragusett

INTRODUCTION

We measure capital flight from Thailand from 1980 to 2000 and analyze the relationships between capital flight and capital inflows, economic growth, crisis, and financial liberalization. We define capital flight as net private unrecorded capital outflows from a capital-scarce developing country, measured as the difference between the recorded sources and uses of funds. This definition is commonly referred to as the 'residual' definition of capital flight (see, for example, Erbe 1985; Morgan Guaranty 1986; World Bank 1985).

As discussed in Chapter 3, there are several definitions of capital flight: capital flight as the undeclared stock of external assets of domestic residents (Dooley 1986); capital flight as only 'hot' money (Cuddington 1986); capital flight as illegal activities like trade faking (see, for example, Bhagwati 1964; Gulati 1987); and capital flight as a 'mirror' statistic of domestic residents' deposits abroad (BIS 1984). In this particular case study, we choose to use the residual definition and measure of capital flight because net unrecorded capital outflows suggest the extent of lost funds that could have been invested in the domestic economy to generate additional output and employment.

Many studies investigate capital flight because of its link with external debt (see, for example, Lessard and Williamson 1987; Boyce 1992). Highly indebted countries like Mexico, Brazil, Argentina, or the Philippines have experienced significant capital flight. Thailand, however, is not a highly indebted country, so presumably capital flight would not be an important concern for the country. Yet our research shows that Thailand experienced a sizeable amount of capital flight in real terms for most of the period covered in the study.

To the best of our knowledge, there are no studies specifically on capital flight from Thailand. Studies like Morgan Guaranty (1986) and Schneider (2003), for example, contain estimates of capital flight, including from

Thailand, but they do not discuss capital flight specifically from this country. We illustrate in this chapter why capital flight is an important concern for Thailand; to this end, we explore five issues linked to capital flight.

The first issue we explore is the link between capital inflows and capital flight. While capital inflows can directly influence capital flight, it is possible that these inflows will be accumulated, especially when the economy is expanding, but will exit in the future when economic conditions are no longer favorable to capital (such as an economic crisis). In this latter scenario, we would expect capital flight to be substantial. In the case of Thailand, our study confirms this contention: when there was an economic expansion, capital inflows were larger than capital flight; when there was an economic crisis, capital flight exceeded capital inflows.

The second issue is the relationship between economic growth and capital flight. Conventional analysis suggests that economic growth implies high returns to capital, both domestic and foreign, and an attractive investment environment in general. As such, we expect capital not to flee in a high growth environment. In the case of Thailand, our research confirms this argument: economic growth and capital flight are inversely related.

Furthermore, we explore the relationship between economic crises or shocks, in particular the 1983–87 banking crisis and 1997–98 Asian financial crisis,[1] and capital flight. In both cases, our research supports the notion that economic crisis induces capital flight. In the case of Thailand, capital flight was especially high during these economic crises.

We then go on to explore the relationship between financial liberalization and capital flight. Conventional analysis suggests that favorable policy changes (like opening the capital account and financial market integration) will discourage capital from fleeing. The alternative view is that financial liberalization produces an environment that is relatively volatile for capital flows, creating uncertainty, and making the economy vulnerable to economic crises and thus capital flight. Our research supports the latter argument: in the case of Thailand, financial liberalization resulted in high and volatile levels of capital flight.

Finally, we explore the potential contribution of capital flight if it were instead invested in the domestic economy. Put another way, how much additional output and employment could have been generated in Thailand if the capital that fled had been repatriated, or if capital had not fled but had been invested in the country? Our research demonstrates that there would have been substantial potential gains for the Thai economy if capital flight had been repatriated or invested in the country.

This chapter has five sections. Following this introduction, Section 2 presents a description of the methodology, and Section 3 presents the data and results. Section 4 presents our analysis, particularly presenting relationships between capital flight and capital inflows, economic growth, economic shocks or crises, and financial liberalization policies. Section 5 draws conclusions.

DESCRIPTION OF THE METHODOLOGY

We measure capital flight as the residual of total capital inflows and recorded foreign exchange outflows. The sum of net additions to external debt ($\Delta DEBT$) and net foreign investments (NFI) constitute total capital inflows, and the current account balance (CA) and international reserves accumulation (ΔRES) constitute recorded foreign exchange outflows.[2] Thus,

$$KF_t = \Delta DEBT_t + NFI_t - (CA_t + \Delta RES_t). \tag{6.1a}$$

Estimates from equation 6.1a are called baseline capital flight. Positive estimates imply capital flight; negative estimates imply 'reverse' capital flight (i.e. net unrecorded capital inflows).

Data used to estimate Equation 1a might contain errors, in particular errors in the capital account and in the current account. Some adjustments are therefore needed to correct them.

In the capital account, one adjustment concerns total external debt. Long-term debts are acquired from different countries and expressed in their respective denominations; as such, currency fluctuations will affect their respective values across periods. Accordingly, we compute the foreign exchange adjusted external debt in time $t–1$ (FX_DEBT) to obtain adjusted external debt ($\Delta DEBTADJ$) in time t.[3]

$$\Delta DEBTADJ_t = DEBT_t - FX\_DEBT_{t-1} \tag{6.2}$$

All other things constant, the appreciation of a hard currency relative to the US dollar increases estimates for equation 2. Since $DEBT_t$ is what is normally reported, $\Delta DEBTADJ_t$ captures unreported debt inflows. Accordingly, Equation 6.1a is re-estimated as

$$KF_t = \Delta DEBTADJ_t + FDI_t - (CA_t + \Delta RES_t). \tag{6.1b}$$

Estimates from Equation 6.1b are called baseline capital flight with adjusted external debt.

The other adjustment concerns the current account. Specifically, export and import data could be inaccurate because of systematic trade misinvoicing either through import overinvoicing or export underinvoicing. As such, capital flight also takes place through these means. Import underinvoicing represents technical smuggling undertaken to evade custom duties and restrictions, which can be interpreted as a form of reverse capital flight. Export overinvoicing may be a response to government incentives that reward industries based on performance indicators like export revenues.

Three steps are required to compute trade misinvoicing. The first is to compute export and import discrepancies for Thailand in its trade with major trading partners.

$$DX_t = PX_t - CIF \cdot X_t \qquad (6.3a)$$

$$DM_t = M_t - CIF \cdot PM_t \qquad (6.3b)$$

where DX_t and DM_t are the total export and import discrepancies, respectively; PX_t is the value of the trading partners' imports from Thailand as reported by trade partners, and PM_t is the value of the trading partners' exports to Thailand as reported by trade partners; X_t and M_t are Thailand's exports to and imports from major trading partners, respectively, as reported by the country.[4] CIF is the c.i.f./f.o.b. factor to adjusting export data for cost of freight and insurance.

The second step is to calculate the global export and import discrepancies for trade misinvoicing by multiplying these discrepancies with the inverse of the shares of the major trading partners in Thailand's exports and imports.

The last step is to find the sum of export and import discrepancies from the second step to get total trade misinvoicing; that is,

$$MIS_t = DX_t + DM_t \qquad (6.4)$$

We then add this calculation to Equation 6.1b to obtain total adjusted baseline capital flight (*Adj KFlight*),

$$Adj\ KFlight_t = KF_t + MIS_t \qquad (6.1c)$$

We also compute real capital flight (*RKF*) in order to make estimates comparable across periods by deflating Equation 6.1c using the United States producer price index (PPI) with a base year of 1995,[5]

$$RKF_t = Adj\ KFlight_t / PPI_t \qquad (6.5)$$

We note that capital flight is like capital invested abroad, thus such capital will earn some return. We compute the stock of capital flight (*SKF*), which is accumulated capital flight and the interest earnings on capital flight.

$$SKF_t = [SKF_{t-1} \cdot (1 + r_t)] + Adj\ KFlight_t \qquad (6.6)$$

where r is the interest rate on the 90-day United States Treasury bill.[6] Equation 6.6 is an estimate of the total opportunity cost of capital flight at time t.

CAPITAL FLIGHT FROM THAILAND: DATA AND RESULTS

Description of the Data

In this section, we describe the data on Thailand's external debt, net foreign investment, current account and international reserves accumulation. The data we use were compiled from the IMF's Direction of Trade Statistics CD-ROM (2003), International Financial Statistics (online) and the World Bank's Global Development Finance CD-ROM (2002) and World Development Indicators CD-ROM (2003).

External debts outstanding
Thailand's total external debt grew from $8.3 billion to $23.3 billion during the 1980s (Table 6.1). In 1990 total external debt stood at $28.1 billion and grew swiftly to $100 billion by 1995. For the period 1995 to 1999, Thailand's total debt averaged $103.8 billion. By 2000, total external debt had declined to $79.7 billion.

Table 6.1 presents a breakdown of total external debt according to long-term and short-term loans as well as the use of IMF credits. Thailand's long-term external debt grew significantly over the years and remained a significant share of total external debt in the period 1980 to 2000. In 1980, long-term debt stood at $5.6 billion. It increased to $13.1 billion in 1985 and expanded further, reaching $17.1 billion in 1989. Following a jump in 1991 to $25.2 billion, long-term debt expanded throughout most of the 1990s, peaking at $72 billion in 1998, with significant increases throughout the period 1994 to 1998. Only in 1999 did external debt show some decline. In 2000, long-term external debt was $61.7 billion. For both decades, long-term debt was a significant portion of total external debt.

Short-term debt saw significant increases from 1980 to 2000, especially in the early 1990s, falling gradually after 1995. Short-term debt, however, never reached 50 percent of total external debt. From 1980 to 1987, it remained fairly steady, averaging about $3 billion. This value began to accumulate gradually beginning in 1988, growing to $14.7 billion by 1992, with its peak at $44.1 billion in 1995. In 2000, Thailand's short-term debt decreased to $14.9 billion.

Table 6.1 External debt and other capital flows

Year	Long-term debt	Short-term debt	Use of IMF credits	Total debt	Net foreign investment	Current account	Change in reserves
1980	5,645.8	2,303.0	348.3	8,297.1	244.0	(2,076.3)	(73.5)
1981	7,115.6	2,878.0	858.0	10,851.6	304.0	(2,571.1)	(305.9)
1982	8,347.9	3,041.0	846.3	12,235.2	220.0	(1,003.1)	(46.5)
1983	9,544.0	3,305.0	1,040.4	13,889.4	366.0	(2,873.5)	(118.0)
1984	10,535.5	3,551.0	903.4	14,989.9	436.0	(2,108.6)	131.5
1985	13,187.0	3,200.0	1,121.6	17,508.6	205.0	(1,537.3)	316.0
1986	14,583.0	2,840.0	1,069.3	18,492.3	360.0	247.0	773.2
1987	16,693.7	2,664.0	972.4	20,330.1	1,021.0	(366.5)	1,429.2
1988	16,247.5	4,800.0	331.0	21,378.5	1,573.0	(1,654.4)	1,906.6
1989	17,104.3	6,112.0	45.3	23,261.6	3,249.0	(2,497.9)	3,395.9
1990	19,771.4	8,322.4	0.7	28,094.5	3,024.0	(7,281.1)	3,750.1
1991	25,210.8	12,492.2	0.0	37,703.0	2,218.0	(7,571.5)	4,134.4
1992	27,057.1	14,726.9	0.0	41,784.0	2,715.0	(6,303.4)	2,790.4
1993	30,003.8	22,634.2	0.0	52,638.0	4,716.0	(6,363.6)	4,256.2

1994	36,354.4	29,178.8	0.0	65,533.2	1,475.0	(8,085.4)	4,841.0
1995	55,943.5	44,095.0	0.0	100,038.5	5,079.0	(13,553.9)	6,658.5
1996	65,122.5	42,613.1	0.0	107,735.6	4,472.0	(14,691.5)	1,705.9
1997	69,434.2	37,836.0	2,428.7	109,698.9	8,383.0	(3,021.1)	(11,747.3)
1998	72,017.6	29,659.9	3,238.5	104,916.0	7,713.0	14,242.5	2,639.7
1999	69,919.3	23,418.0	3,421.3	96,758.6	7,395.0	12,427.9	5,243.8
2000	61,733.4	14,880.0	3,061.8	79,675.2	4,397.0	9,369.3	(2,115.4)

Notes:

a Sources of raw data: Global Development Finance CD-ROM (2002) and International Financial Statistics (online).

b Positive number suggests an inflow; a negative suggests an outflow. A positive change in reserves means an accumulation of (or increase in) reserves. External debt data are stock volumes. The other columns are flows.

Net foreign investment
Net foreign investment (NFI) was $244 million in 1980 and grew to $436 million in 1984, with a decrease in 1982 of $84 Million (Table 6.1). Following another decline in 1985, NFI picked up again and rose to $1 billion in 1987. From 1988 to 1997, NFI averaged $3.7 billion, reaching its peak of $8.4 billion in 1997. Thereafter, NFI began a downturn, dropping as low as $4.4 billion in 2000.

Current Account
The current account (CA) was in deficit over the course of the period considered, with the exceptions of 1986 and from 1998 to 2000 (Table 6.1). The average deficit between 1980 and 1985 was $2 billion; between 1987 and 1997, it was $6.5 billion. In 1986, there was a surplus of $247 million; however, the following year, the deficit on the current account returned and steadily worsened, reaching $7.3 billion in 1990. The deficit reached its highest levels in 1995 and 1996, when it stood at $13.6 billion and $14.7 billion, respectively, due to substantial reductions in exports. In 1997, the deficit contracted to $3 billion and in 1998, Thailand witnessed a surplus of $14.2 billion. Although the current account remained in surplus to 2000, in that year, the surplus decreased to $9.4 billion.

Accumulation of foreign reserves
From 1980 to 1983, there were outflows in foreign reserves of about $543.9 million (Table 6.1). From 1984 to 1996, there was a steady accumulation of foreign reserves starting with an increase of about $131.5 million in 1984 and peaking at $6.6 billion in 1995. Table 6.1 shows that there was a large decline in foreign reserves in 1997 ($11.7 billion) and again in 2000 ($2.1 billion).

Description of the results

Using Equation 6.1b, we compute estimates of baseline capital flight with adjusted external debt (Table 6.2). Figure 6.1 shows the trend of adjusted baseline capital flight as a share of gross domestic product (GDP), which relates capital flight to the size of the economy. Notice that the pattern shows a cyclical movement in capital flight; on the whole, however, the trend suggests overall flight. Notice also that between the 1980s and 1990s, there is an apparent difference in the character of the trend, with the latter decade exhibiting some systematic volatility.

Table 6.2 presents other capital flight calculations, namely real capital flight (RKF) and stock of capital flight (SKF). In 1980, RKF was $399.2 million. Real capital flight rose to $2.2 billion by 1982, dipping back down to $802.7 million in 1983, with a jump in 1985 and again in 1986 to $5.1

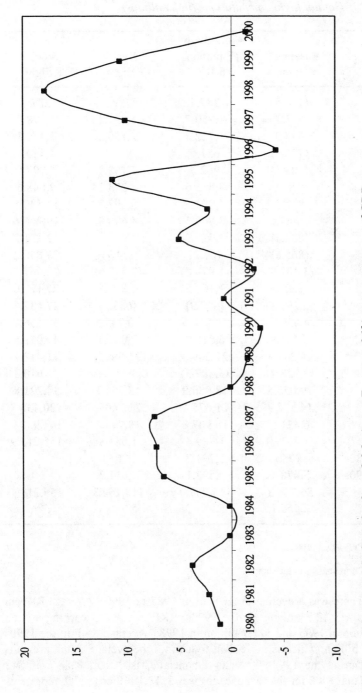

Figure 6.1 Capital flight with adjusted debt (using Equation 6.1b) as a percentage of GDP

Table 6.2   Capital flight computations (in $ millions)

Year	Baseline Kflight	Adj. Kflight (Equation 6.1c)	Real Kflight	Stock Kflight
1980	(106.5)	287.4	399.2	287.4
1981	593.2	1,250.7	1,591.2	1,578.6
1982	647.0	1,722.3	2,150.2	3,470.3
1983	(735.3)	651.0	802.7	4,420.4
1984	(703.5)	962.3	1,158.0	5,797.8
1985	870.4	3,616.6	4,373.2	9,848.6
1986	817.5	4,093.5	5,097.8	14,530.1
1987	1,063.1	3,869.3	4,695.8	19,246.6
1988	(608.4)	1,590.9	1,856.3	22,121.2
1989	(865.6)	(67.2)	(74.7)	23,850.2
1990	(3,401.6)	(1,973.6)	(2,117.6)	23,667.7
1991	120.7	1,700.5	1,820.6	27,122.0
1992	(2,297.8)	(622.9)	(663.3)	27,437.5
1993	4,950.2	10,240.5	10,745.6	38,556.1
1994	1,443.8	6,810.0	7,057.0	47,012.5
1995	19,371.8	21,809.8	21,809.8	71,412.7
1996	(4,228.2)	(3,387.3)	(3,311.2)	71,610.3
1997	19,072.5	18,980.9	18,554.1	94,221.8
1998	14,532.9	21,675.4	21,740.6	120,438.7
1999	6,431.6	18,907.8	18,795.0	144,958.9
2000	(1,211.7)	1,789.4	1,681.8	155,213.9
Ave. 1980s	97.2	1,797.7	2,205.0	
Ave. 1990s	5,478.4	9,593.1	9,611.2	
Total	55,756.3	113,907.4	118,162.3	155,213.9
Average	2,655.1	5,424.2	5,626.8	

Note: US PPP 1995 = 100.

Source: Computations of the authors.

billion. There was a decline in RKF from 1987 to 1990. Average RKF in
the 1980s was $2.2 billion. In the 1990s, RKF increased, reaching around
$21.8 billion in 1995 and $21.7 billion in 1998. Average RKF in the 1990s
was $9.8 billion, which is more than four times the average in the previous
decade. During the 1997–98 Asian Financial Crisis, total RKF was $42
billion. Total RKF for the two decades was $118.1 billion, which represents

Table 6.3   Trade misinvoicing (in $ millions)

Year	Export misinvoicing	Import misinvoicing	Total trade misinvoicing
1980	(35.0)	(35.0)	(70.0)
1981	19.9	479.0	498.8
1982	96.1	273.2	369.4
1983	(39.1)	628.7	589.7
1984	(110.3)	1,016.5	906.3
1985	365.0	743.9	1,108.9
1986	395.5	603.7	999.2
1987	28.0	162.3	190.3
1988	(315.5)	1,847.5	1,532.0
1989	(667.7)	1,780.5	1,112.8
1990	(899.8)	1,370.5	470.7
1991	(1,358.1)	2,411.9	1,053.8
1992	(774.0)	2,573.9	1,799.9
1993	69.4	4,021.8	4,091.2
1994	1,056.4	2,467.1	3,523.4
1995	1,040.8	1,753.4	2,794.2
1996	2,490.9	1,988.8	4,479.7
1997	2,497.1	1,211.5	3,708.6
1998	2,243.6	(638.4)	1,605.3
1999	2,802.6	3,058.5	5,861.2
2000	2,088.9	1,474.8	3,563.7
1980s ave	(26.3)	750.0	723.7
1990s ave	916.9	2,021.9	2,938.8
Total	10,994.8	29,194.2	40,189.0
Average	523.6	1,390.2	1,913.8

Note: For exports, positive numbers mean underinvoicing and negative numbers mean overinvoicing. For imports, positive numbers mean overinvoicing and negative numbers mean underinvoicing.

Source: Authors' computations

a substantial loss of capital to Thailand. SKF in 2000 was $155.2 billion.[7] This estimate represents the opportunity cost of capital flight.[8]

In addition, we take note of trade misinvoicing. Average misinvoicing in Thailand for the two decades was $1.9 billion.[9] Estimates in Table 6.3 show that overall trade misinvoicing increased over the two decades. In the 1980s, average total trade misinvoicing was $723.7 million and in the 1990s, it was $2.9 billion.

Table 6.3 suggests that export underinvoicing and import overinvoicing are regular sources of capital flight through trade. But it is interesting that there was some export overinvoicing in some years in the 1980s and early 1990s. This finding may illustrate the notion that trade misinvoicing was undertaken to cover price uncertainties and risks in the export market. But more interestingly, export underinvoicing is large particularly in the latter part of the 1990s, while import overinvoicing is large particularly in the early 1990s.

CAPITAL FLIGHT FROM THAILAND: ANALYSIS

Capital Inflows and Capital Flight

We further examine the link between capital inflows and capital flight. In Figure 6.2, we find that Thailand experienced a swift expansion of capital inflows beginning in the late 1980s, as the country became increasingly outward-oriented and integrated into global trade and finance. Following a brief slump in inflows in the early 1990s, capital inflows grew very rapidly. The turning point for capital inflows seems to have occurred in 1995, when capital inflows declined and continued to do so in 2000. Although some capital, particularly net foreign investments (NFI), continued to flow into Thailand, the total inflows were nowhere near pre-crisis levels. Total capital inflow was negative after 1999.

External debts have clearly comprised a greater share in capital inflows from 1980 to 2000. NFI only began to increase its share in capital inflows in the late 1980s, coinciding with the end of the rule of Prime Minister General Prem Tinsulanonda (1979–1988). Democracy and sound macroeconomic policies marked the economic boom that started in 1988. It is also noteworthy that after the Plaza Accord in 1985, Japanese firms started to relocate their foreign investments to Thailand, and subsequently, Taiwanese and South Korean foreign investments followed suit. While an increase in NFI is clear, change in total external debts ($\Delta DEBT$) play a much more significant role in driving capital inflows.

The structure of Thailand's total external debts is shown in Figure 6.3 (see Table 6.1). From 1980 to 2000, long-term external debt unambiguously comprised a greater share of Thailand's external debt position. The share of short-term external debt increased from 1986, reaching a maximum of approximately 44 percent in total external debt in 1995 and 1996.

There is clearly a rise in short-term indebtedness as the country experienced sustained economic growth from 1986 to 1995. This finding is

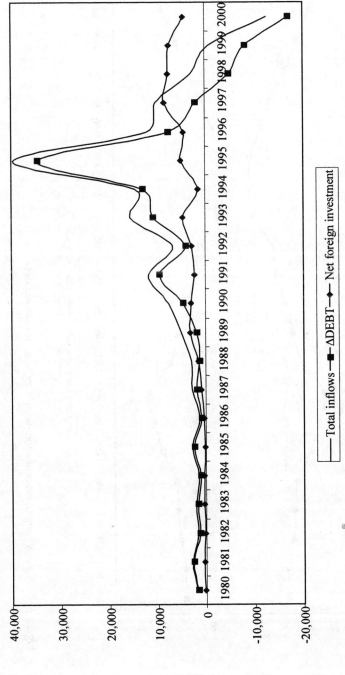

Figure 6.2   Composition of capital inflows (in $ millions)

155

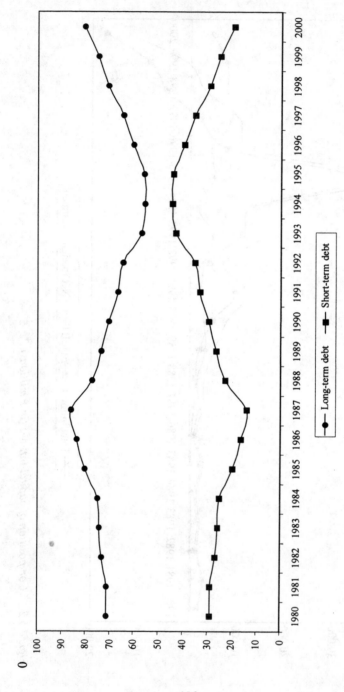

Figure 6.3: Share of long- term and short-term debt to total external debt

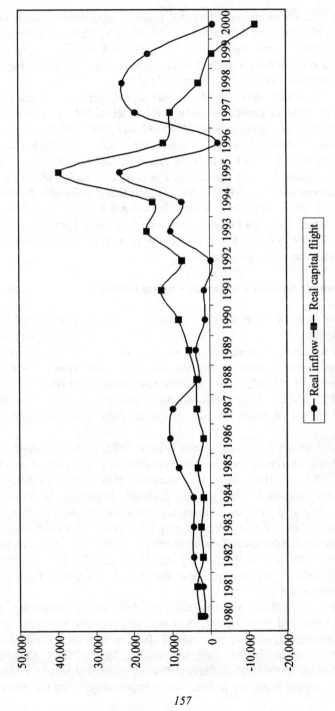

Figure 6.4 Real capital inflows and real capital flight (in $ millions)

- ● - Real inflow - ■ - Real capital flight

consistent with the common notion that financial liberalization leads to the acquisition of more short-term debt (see, for example, Wade 1998; Wade and Veneroso 1998). Large short-term debt creates vulnerability: an economic shock could drive debtors to reclaim or refuse to reissue debt. If that happens, we have a precondition for an economic crisis.

Figure 6.4, which shows trends in real capital inflows and real capital fight (RKF), tells an interesting story. We observe that in some periods, RKF exceeded real capital inflows (1985–87 and 1997–2000) and in other periods, real capital inflow was greater than RKF. We think that this situation illustrates that RKF is not only fueled by real capital inflows. Such a situation is possible when capital flight is driven by capital already in the domestic economy that is fleeing. This suggests that it is possible for foreign capital to be accumulated in a country for an undetermined period only to flee in the future when, for instance, economic conditions deteriorate.

Indeed Figure 6.4 illustrates that there is a close year-to-year trend between RKF and real capital inflows.

Does Economic Growth Discourage Capital Flight?

We explore the question of whether economic growth dampens capital flight. The relationship is expected to be negative since economic growth raises incentives for capital to remain in the domestic economy, and consequently, discourages flight. To examine this link, we obtain growth rates of real gross domestic product (RGDP) and the share of real capital flight (RKF) to RGDP (RKRGDP). RGDP allows a comparison of growth rates over time, while RKRGDP shows the relative burden of capital flight to the economy over time.

Figure 6.5 shows the trends. From 1980 to 1985, growth declined while RKRGDP was increasing, a trend that became most pronounced in 1985. Between 1986 and 1995, there was sustained high growth as RKRGDP declined and remained low; growth declined, beginning in 1996 and becoming negative as the financial crisis deepened, reaching an unprecedented low point in 1998. During this period, RKRGDP rose, also reaching an unprecedented and alarming level in 1998. There was a recovery in 1999, but with little capital coming into Thailand, RKRGDP and growth declined in 2000. Therefore, we argue that there is a negative relationship between growth and capital flight.[10]

Three periods, 1985, 1986–1990 and 1997–1998 are of interest in Figure 6.5. In the first and third periods, there was an economic slowdown and a severe recession, respectively, in Thailand. Both periods are associated with the banking crises in Thailand (see, for example, Jansen 2000). Of course, these periods are qualitatively different. But it appears that when a recession takes place, capital is pushed to flee. More importantly, when the recession

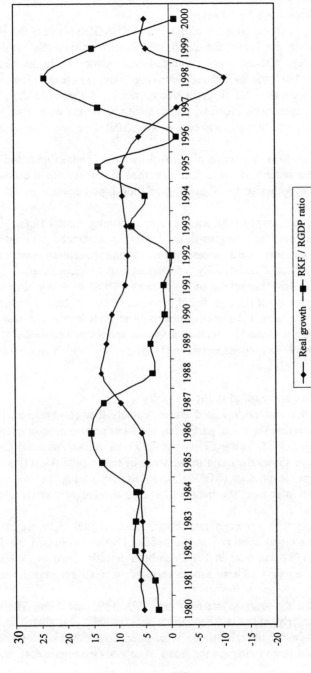

Figure 6.5 Real growth (in percentages) and real capital flight as a share of real GDP

is severe and intensifies or is prolonged, even more capital is pushed to flee. From 1986 to 1990, there was sustained high growth and it appears that capital was discouraged from fleeing.

Figure 6.5 also shows an interesting trend in RKRGDP between the 1980s and the 1990s. In the 1980s, there appeared to be no systematic pattern in RKRGDP, except that the highs coincided with economic shocks like the devaluations in 1981 and the 1983–87 Banking Crisis. However, after 1992–93, the trend appears to be different. In particular, the trend in the 1990s appears to be a systematic cycle, with each swing becoming wider over time. We argue below that the wider swings in RKRGDP were linked to financial liberalization.

Again, we confirm that economic growth reduces capital flight, and vice versa. But the pattern is more complex than it seems. In the case of Thailand, we hypothesize the following relationships between growth and capital flight.

First, declining growth rates can lead to declining capital flight. This condition arises because low growth rates would not attract capital into the country and therefore there is less capital flight. Second, significantly declining growth rates that steadily worsen can lead to intense capital flight. A recession can drive capital out of the country. Third, recovery can reduce capital flight because of the significant potential returns to capital within the country. Fourth, sustained growth, especially at high levels, can result in lower capital flight. Finally, negative economic shocks induce capital flight. A negative shock can increase risk and uncertainty, which make capital flee.[11]

Economic crises and capital flight

We highlight the contention raised above, namely that economic crises or shocks induce capital flight. In particular, we focus on two economic crises, namely the 1982–87 Banking Crisis and 1997–98 Asian Financial Crisis. Figure 6.5 above shows the trend in the share of real capital flight (RKF) to real gross domestic product (RGDP), or RKRGDP, during the two crises periods; we can infer from the trend that during an economic crisis, capital flight increases.[12]

In order to argue that an economic shock induces capital flight, we have to consider the historical context. In the 1980s, Thailand devalued the Baht twice, first in 1981 and later in 1985. In both periods, there was a rise in RKRGDP (Figure 6.5). These shocks resulted in relatively high levels of capital flight.

In the 1990s, the years to consider are 1993, 1995 and 1996. The year 1993 is particularly important because it was in this year that Thailand pursued full financial liberalization. With liberalized financial flows there were sudden and large swings in the flows of capital (see Figure 6.4), and in the case of Thailand, large and volatile capital flight (see below). 1995 and 1996 are also interesting years. In 1995, China devalued the renminbi and in 1996, Japan devalued the yen. We think that successivedevaluations in China and Japan led to the export shock of 1996, when Thailand experienced negative growth in exports for the first time. Also, during this period, there was a surplus of semi-conductors (Thailand's main export) on the world market, causing prices of these exports to decline and reducing Thai export earnings (see, for example, Ito 2000). These years are important because they represent a turnaround in the Thai economy. Indeed, Ito (1999, 2000) argues that 1996 marked the turning point that eventually led to the speculative attack on the Baht in 1997. He points out that the current account deficit in 1996 (about 8 percent of GDP) was the same size as the deficit that led to the Tequila Crisis in Mexico in 1994. Suffice it to say that the speculative attack on the baht in 1997 led to the financial crisis.

Economic Liberalization and Capital Flight

Financial regulation, governance and capital flight
Figures 6.1 and 6.6 illustrate that movements in capital flight (and real capital flight) are different before and after 1992. Except in the mid-1980s, when there was a rise in capital flight due to an economic crisis, capital flight in the pre-1992 period was relatively low. In fact, the levels were below the two-decade period average.

In Figure 6.6, we see that after 1992, capital flight was more significant in size and had large fluctuations, with figures way above the average of the 1990s and the two-decade period average. We argue that the structural change in the movement of capital flight might be due to institutional changes in the country's financial system. Financial liberalization in the early 1990s allowed for large flows of capital. Accordingly, this had significant implications for the movement and size of capital flight.

In terms of financial integration, the World Bank (1997) classified Thailand in the 'high-medium' income category during the mid-1980s. Alba et al. (1999) suggest that the country already had reasonably open current and capital accounts and liberal treatment of foreign direct and portfolio investment. They point out that the foundations for significant changes in the financial sector were laid as early as 1986.

Important policy changes in the financial sector started in 1990. In that year, for example, Thailand accepted the IMF Article VIII obligations, leading to comprehensive financial reforms. Thus, for instance, there were reductions in tax treatment of dividends, royalty payments, capital gains and interest payments on foreign debentures. In 1991, the repatriation of investment funds, interest and loan repayments by foreign investors was fully liberalized. In addition, the Investment Promotion Act was amended to

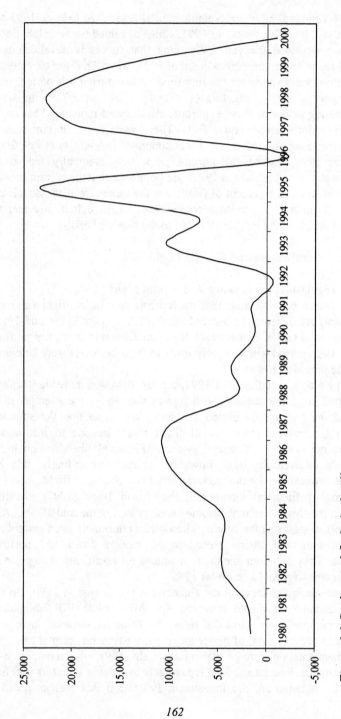

Figure 6.6 Real capital flight (in $ millions)

encourage more foreign investment. Likewise, around the same period, the Bank of Thailand (BOT) relaxed interest rate controls, having already abandoned the ceiling on the commercial bank deposit rate in 1989–91. In 1992, BOT finally abandoned the ceiling on financial and credit companies' deposit and lending rates and on commercial banks' lending rate; it also relaxed portfolio restrictions on the scope of activities and the portfolio composition of commercial banks. In addition, policies to create a competitive environment for a domestic financial market were launched. These policy changes included granting financial companies the autonomy to conduct leasing business, and permitting commercial banks to expand their operations (for example, they could undertake underwriting, issuance and distribution of debt securities, and they could act as selling agents of mutual funds, among others).[13]

Another important financial liberalization policy was the Bangkok International Banking Facility (BIBF) program in 1993. The BIBF program enabled commercial banks and firms to access foreign funds with relative ease. It also favored short-term capital (Alba et al. 1999). With high interest rates, tax breaks, and the exchange rate of the Baht fixed, foreign exchange rate risk was eliminated, encouraging large amounts of short-term and long-term capital to enter Thailand. Alba et al. (1999) point out that such policy changes resulted in a moral hazard problem because the policies favored short-term foreign borrowing and made borrowers ignore exchange rate risks because the Baht was artificially fixed. They argue that the BIBF program was indeed one important policy change that resulted in volatile and unstable financial flows. With our results, we argue that the adoption of liberalization policy can explain the higher magnitude of capital flight in the 1990s. Needless to say, financial liberalization has been identified as a major cause of the 1997 economic crisis.

As we noted earlier, Thailand faced two economic crises between 1980 and 2000. Comparing the two crises, we noted that in the 1983–87 Banking Crisis, Thailand experienced relatively lower capital flight than in the 1997–98 Asian Financial Crisis. In the latter period, there were larger swings in capital flight. We further argue that the structural difference in the levels of capital flight was the result of financial liberalization, which created high volatility and unpredictability and dependence on foreign capital.

Volatility of capital flight
In this section, we investigate the volatility of capital flight. We use data from Tables 6.1 and 6.2. Data in Table 6.2 indicate that average real capital flight in the 1980s was $2.2 billion and in the 1990s, $9.6 billion, over four times the level of the previous decade. The average for the two decades was about $5.6 billion. Over time, there was indeed a change in the level of real capital flight (see Figures 6.1 and 6.6). We argued earlier that there is a link

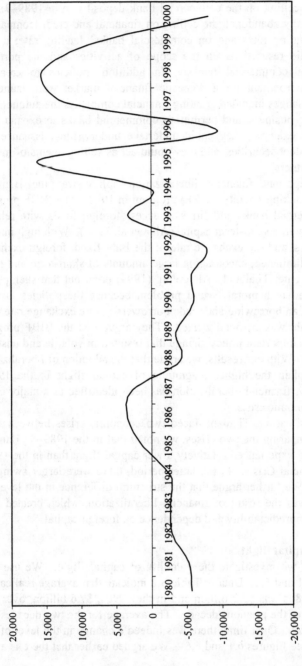

Figure 6.7 Capital flight deviations from the mean (in $ millions)

between financial liberalization and capital flight. We further argue that financial liberalization increases the volatility of capital flight.

To highlight abnormal fluctuations in real capital flight in the 1990s, we show that the expected returns on real capital flight are 'abnormal,' meaning expected returns far exceed the average return. In doing this, we follow Fatehi and Gupta (1992), who utilize the mean value of capital as proxy for the expected returns. Accordingly, we obtain the mean of real capital flight, which is $5.6 billion, and compute deviations of real capital flight from the mean. We obtain ± 1 standard deviation of real capital flight, which is $7.8 billion. Obviously, ± 1 standard deviation is somewhat arbitrary; however, our purpose is to set a marker against which we can compare the mean deviation of real capital flight and, at the same time, stress significant deviations during the period considered. When the marker is breached, we consider the level to be significant. When the marker is breached repeatedly, we consider the situation to be volatile.

Figure 6.7 shows that in the post-liberalization period (that is, post 1992–1993), the deviation of real capital flight from its mean exceeded ± 1 standard deviation. In the other periods, the mean deviation of real capital flight was within range. The figure shows that real capital flight in this period was relatively more volatile, especially in the latter part of the 1990s. Thus we argue that financial liberalization increases the volatility of capital flight.

Foregone Output and Employment

In this section, we estimate foregone output and employment due to capital flight.[14,15] If flight capital had been repatriated and invested in Thailand, or if there had been no capital flight, additional output and employment could have been generated. In other words, suppose we assume that capital flight was invested in the domestic economy, what would have been its impact in terms of output and employment? To obtain the potential additional output due to the repatriation (or investment) of flight capital, we need the incremental capital output ratio (ICOR).[16] To obtain the potential additional employment of capital flight, we need the incremental labor-capital ratio (ILCR).[17]

Table 6.4 shows that if the estimated flight capital in 1980 had been repatriated or had not fled, Thailand would have obtained an additional output of $355.1 million. If flight capital in 1981 had been invested in the country, $634 million worth of output would have been generated. These findings mean that Thailand's GDP could have been higher than what was reported for 1980 or 1981. The same logic applies to the other years.[18] Moreover, an initial investment in one year can continue to generate output until it is fully depreciated. For instance, an initial investment of $399.2

Table 6.4 Potential additional output and employment (in millions)

Year	Real capital flight	Additional output in year t	Ratio to GDP	Stream of output in year t	Stock of output by year t	Additional employment
1980	399.2	355.1	1.1	355.1	355.1	43.8
1981	1,591.2	634.0	1.8	728.6	1,083.6	211.3
1982	2,150.2	693.2	1.9	1,025.3	2,108.9	327.2
1983	802.7	258.8	0.6	895.3	3,004.2	90.4
1984	1,158	270.9	0.6	635.8	3,640	130.6
1985	4,373.2	1,661.2	4.3	2,272.2	5,912.3	590.7
1986	5,097.8	1,936.5	4.5	3,493.8	9,406	723.4
1987	4,695.8	4,296.7	8.5	10,152.1	19,558.1	547.6
1988	1,856.3	1,601.6	2.6	8,065.9	27,624	262.6
1989	(74.7)	–	–	3,917.1	31,541.1	–
1990	(2117.6)	–	–	2,109.6	33,650.7	–
1991	1,820.6	782.4	0.8	1,870.5	35,521.2	17.9
1992	(663.3)	–	–	1449.6	36970.8	–
1993	10,745.6	4,322.9	3.5	5,473.9	42,444.7	643
1994	7,057	3,510.9	2.4	10,183.9	52,628.6	307.1
1995	21,809.8	10,972.5	6.5	21,241.5	73,870.2	193.9

1996	(3,311.2)	–	–	11,958.6	85,828.8	–
1997	1,554.1	7,518.3	5.0	24,621.1	110,449.9	608.6
1998	21,740.6	8,709.4	7.8	33,051	143,500.9	797.1
1999	18,795	13,296.8	10.9	71,664.2	215,165.1	602
2000	1,681.8	706.9	0.6	43,286.5	258,451.6	–
Total	118,162.3	61,528	–	258,251.6	258,251.6	6.097

Note: Authors' computations using raw data from the World Development Index CD-ROM and Thailand's National Economic and Social Development Board

million in 1980 (capital flight) would continue to generate a stream of output in succeeding years, about $94.5 million in 1981. With an additional output of $634 million from 1981 repatriated flight capital, Thailand would have gained a total stream of additional output of $728.6 million in 1981, or a total stock of output of $1 billion by 1981. In 1982, repatriated flight capital from 1980 would have continued to generate some output, about $46.2 million and the same for 1981 repatriated capital, about $285.7 million. Counting additional output from 1982 repatriated capital flight at $693.2 billion, Thailand would have obtained a total stream of output of $1 billion in 1982, or a total stock of additional output of $2.1 billion by 1982. The same logic applies for the succeeding years.[19] By 2000, past capital flight would have generated $61.4 billion in output, or a total stock of additional output of $258.2 billion by 2000. As a share of real gross domestic product (RGDP), the potential output in 1980 would be 0.6 percent of RGDP; that in 1981 would be 1 percent of RGDP. Counting the streams of output by 1981, we get 1.2 per cent of GDP in 1981. The potential output in 2000 would be 0.7 percent of RGDP. As expected, during years of high levels of capital flight, the potential output would indicate significant shares of GDP. These numbers suggest large increases in potential output with repatriated capital flight.

Also if the estimated flight capital in 1980 had been repatriated or had not fled, but was invested in the country, Thailand would have created an additional 43,800 jobs in 1980. We estimate that there were 200,000 people unemployed in 1980 (extrapolated using figures from the World Development Index), thus unemployment could have been cut by about 22 percent. In 1981, with an estimated 335,000 unemployed, 211,300 jobs could have been created; in other words, about 63 percent of the unemployed could have got jobs in 1981. For these two years, a total of 255,100 jobs could have been created with repatriation of capital flight. In 1999, about 602,000 jobs could have been created. About 986,000 people were unemployed in 1999 (International Financial Statistics Online), and again, a significant proportion of the unemployed could have found jobs if capital had been repatriated or invested in the country. Table 6.4 shows that we obtain a total of about 6 million potential jobs between 1980 and 2000.

With these results, we therefore argue that capital flight implies significant losses in jobs and output. We furthermore argue that for Thailand, the repatriation of flight capital (or the investment of this capital within the country) can be a valuable aid in realizing increased employment and development.

CONCLUSION

Using the residual method, we estimated capital flight from Thailand from 1980 to 2000. We found that during the two decades period, total real capital flight from the country was $118.1 billion. Accounting for interest earnings (assuming the amount was fully invested abroad), we arrived at a total stock of capital flight of $155.2 billion in 2000, or about 1.5 times real gross domestic product (RGDP) in 2000. By any measure, this amount suggests large opportunity costs of capital flight.

We investigated five issues in the chapter. First, we examined the relationship between capital inflows and capital flight and found a close year-to-year trend between capital inflows and capital flight. This situation illustrates that RKF is not only fueled by real capital inflows. Such a situation is possible when the capital flight is driven by capital already in the domestic economy and is fleeing. Next, we asked whether economic growth discourages capital flight and whether economic crisis induces capital flight. Our answers to the two questions were in the affirmative. In the case of Thailand, we suggested how these were linked: (1) a declining growth rate can lead to declining capital flight; (2) when the declining growth rates worsens and becomes severe, capital flees and flight intensifies; (3) economic recovery can reduce capital flight; (4) sustained growth rates, especially at high levels, can result in declining capital flight; and (5) economic shocks induce capital flight. We also explored the question of whether financial liberalization increases the volatility of capital flight. Our results indicated that in the case of Thailand, the volatility of capital flight increased under financial liberalization. Finally, we calculated the potential losses of output and employment due to capital flight. Our estimates show that capital flight from Thailand was indeed substantial. The repatriation of capital flight (or investing it in the country) could mean more output and employment. Our total estimate of foregone output is $61.5 billion by 2000, or an average of 2.3 percent of GDP for the whole period. We also estimated that total foregone employment was 6 million between 1980 and 2000, or approximately 15 per cent of total unemployment for the same period. By any measure, capital flight implies large foregone opportunities in Thailand. If capital had not fled or if capital flight had been repatriated and invested in Thailand, it could have generated more economic growth and more jobs in Thailand.

However, there remain more questions for future research. In particular, it would be worth exploring the extent to which capital flight was fueled or driven by external debt, and vice versa; that is, whether or not there is a 'revolving door' relationship between capital flight and capital inflows in Thailand (see, for example, Boyce 1992). It would also be worth exploring how changes in Thailand's trade policies and the world market have influenced systematic trade misinvoicing.

NOTES

We thank James K. Boyce, James Crotty, Gerald Epstein, Gerald Friedman, Carol Heim, James Heintz, Léonce Ndikumana, Peter Skott, and members of the Capital Flight Working Group at the University of Massachusetts Amherst for comments. The usual disclaimers apply.

1. See, for example, Alba et al. (1999) for the 1983–1987 Thai Banking Crisis, Montes (1998) for the 1997–1998 Asian Financial Crisis and Jansen (2000) for a comparison of the 1983–1984 and 1997 financial crises in Thailand.
2. Total external debt refers to long-term and short-term debt, and use of IMF credits. Long term and short-term debt covers public debt, private publicly guaranteed debt, and private non-guaranteed debt. NFI is the sum of net direct foreign investments (FDI) and net portfolio equities investments (PORT). Net FDI is FDI by non-residents into the country (inflow) and FDI of residents' abroad (outflow). PORT covers portfolio equities investments of non-residents into the country (inflow) and portfolio equities investments of residents' abroad (outflow).
3. See Chapter 3 for details of the estimation procedure.
4. We consider trade data with industrialized countries on the assumption that the information is reasonably accurate compared to trade data with developing countries (see, for example, Boyce 1993; Boyce and Ndikumana 2001).
5. Other indices can be utilized as deflator. It is important that the same index for deflating figures is used throughout the estimation procedure.
6. Of course, it is possible to get higher returns on the capital. The 90-day US Treasury Bill rate can be the minimum rate of return or guaranteed return on investment.
7. Note that the starting stock of capital flight affects the subsequent stock of capital flight. Cline (1995) follows a different approach in which the stock is not allowed to become negative.
8. Clearly, there is a private gain for those who engage in capital flight. An estimate of the private gain can be subtracted to get a more accurate estimate of the opportunity cost.
9. In the literature, trade misinvoicing is also called secondary capital flight. Primary capital flight refers to baseline capital flight (see Equation 6.1a).
10. Correlation analyses between RKRGDP and growth rates, and between real capital fight and growth rates, show a negative relationship. We ran Granger tests and results showed that movements in RKRGDP were Granger-caused by growth rates, but not the reverse. Also movements in real capital flight were Granger-caused by growth rates, but not the reverse. These findings were consistent using one to three lags. Note that we have a limited number of observations (only 21 years).
11. Positive external shocks can reduce capital flight. D'Arista (1996) discusses the pro-cyclical nature of business cycles and volatility of capital flows.
12. Note that capital flight was increasing before the crisis.
13. For a detailed discussion of this issue, see Alba et al. (1999) and Jensen (2000).
14. We acknowledge James K. Boyce for the suggestion.
15. Clearly, there can be other possible tradeoffs. If capital did not flee, there could be more resources for public services (public education, health services). To illustrate the tradeoff relationship at the aggregate level, we consider total output and employment. It is possible to disaggregate potential increases in output and employment according to sectors.
16. ICOR indicates how much output is generated per unit of capital. It is computed as the ratio of net fixed capital formation and change in GDP. The reciprocal of ICOR is the marginal product of capital. Capital flight divided by ICOR gives the potential additional output due to full capital flight repatriation. Clearly, this procedure is an approximation of the potential additional output. We assume that the repatriated capital will be invested in some productive activity and generate some positive output in the current year and a

stream of output in the future. We use the fixed capital depreciation rate as an adjustment to net fixed capital in computing the stream of output. When GDP declines or when net fixed capital formation is negative in a particular year, ICOR is also negative. To avoid this problem, we use the previous five-year average of ICOR as proxy for that year.

17. ILCR indicates how much employment is generated per unit of capital. It is computed as the ratio of change in employment and net fixed capital formation. Capital flight multiplied by ILCR gives the potential additional employment due to capital flight (full) repatriation. Clearly, this procedure is only an approximation of potential additional employment. Again, we assume that capital fight (full) repatriation will generate employment as it generates output. When GDP declines or when net fixed capital formation is negative in a particular year, ILCR is also negative. To avoid this problem, we use the previous five-year average of ILCR as proxy for that year.

18. Some years have negative capital flight and we assume no capital repatriation for those years. Table 6.4 assumes that the repatriated capital flight is used in productive investments. It is possible that some amount of repatriated capital goes into consumption. This aspect is a limitation of the calculations.

19. Excel files for ICOR and ILCR are available from the authors.

REFERENCES

Alba, Pedro, Leonardo Hernandez and Daniela Klingebiel (1999), 'Financial Liberalization and the Capital Account: Thailand 1988–1997', Policy Research Working Paper No. 2188, World Bank.

Bank for International Settlements (1984), *BIS 54th Annual Report*, Geneva, Switzerland: Bank for International Settlements.

Bhagwati, Jagdish (1964), 'On the Underinvoicing of Imports', *Bulletin of the Oxford University Institute of Economics and Statistics*, **26**, 389–397.

Boyce, James (1992), 'The Revolving Door: External Debts and Capital Flight: Philippine Case Study', *World Development*, **20** (3), 335–345.

Boyce, James (1993), *The Political Economy of Growth and Impoverishment in the Marcos Era*, Manila, the Philippines: Ateneo de Manila University Press.

Boyce, James and Leonce Ndikumana (2001), 'Is Africa a Net Creditor? New Estimates of Capital Flight from Severely Indebted Sub-Saharan African Countries, 1970– 96', *Journal of Development Studies*, **38** (2), 27–56.

Chang, Kevin, Stijn Claessens and Robert Cumby (1997), 'Conceptual and Methodological Issues in the Measurement of Capital Flight', *International Journal of Financial Economics*, **2**, 101–119.

Cline, William (1995), *International Debt Reexamined*, Washington, DC: Institute for International Economics.

Cuddington, John (1986), 'Capital Flight: Estimates, Issues and Explanation', Princeton Studies in International Finance No. 58, Princeton University.

Cumby, Robert and Richard Levich (1987), 'Definitions and Magnitudes: On the Definition and Magnitude of Recent Capital Flight' in Donald Lessard and John Williamson (eds), *Capital Flight and the Third World Debt*, Washington, DC: Institute of International Economics.

Deppler, Michael and John Williamson (1987), 'Capital Flight: Concepts, Measurement, and Issues', *Staff Studies for the World Economic Outlook*, Washington, DC: International Monetary Fund, 39–58.

D'Arista, Jane (1996), 'International Capital Flows and National Macroeconomic Policies', Otaru University of Commerce (Japan): Institute of Economic Research

Discussion Paper No. 32.

Dooley, Michael (1986), 'Country Specific Risk Premiums, Capital Flight and Net Investment Income Payments in Selected Developing Countries', International Monetary Fund (unpublished manuscript).

Erbe, Suzanne (1985), 'The Flight of Capital from Developing Countries', *Inter-economics*, November/December, 268–275.

Fatehi, Kamal and Manoj Gupta (1992), 'Political Instability and Capital Flight: An Application of Event Study Methodology', *The International Executive*, **34** (5), 441–461.

Gordon, David and Ross Levine (1989), 'The 'Problem' of Capital Flight – A Cautionary Note', *World Economy*, **12**, 237–252.

Gulati, Sanil (1987), 'A Note on Trade Misinvoicing' in Donald Lessard and John Williamson (eds), *Capital Flight and Third World Debt*, Washington, DC: Institute for International Economics.

Ito, Takatoshi (1999), 'Capital Flows in Asia', NBER Working Paper No. 7134, National Bureau of Economic Research.

Ito, Takatoshi (2000), 'Principal Causes of Asian Export Deceleration', in Dilip Das (ed.), *Asian Exports*, Manila: Asian Development Bank.

Jansen, Jos (2003), 'What do Capital Inflows do? Dissecting the Transmission Mechanism for Thailand, 1980–96', *Journal of Macroeconomics*, **25** (4), 457–480.

Jansen, Karel (2000), 'Thailand Crisis: Two Crises Compared', *Chulalongkorn Journal of Economics*, **12** (3), 1–25.

Lessard, Donald and John Williamson (eds) (1987), *Capital Flight and the Third World Debt*, Washington, DC: Institute for International Economics.

Montes, Manuel (1998), *The Currency Crisis in Southeast Asia*, Singapore: Institute of Southeast Asian Studies.

Morgan Guaranty Trust Company (1986), 'LDC Capital Flight', *World Financial Markets*, March, 13–15.

Schneider, Benu (2003), 'Measuring Capital Flight: Estimates and Interpretations', Working Paper No. 154, Overseas Development Institute (UK).

Wade, Robert (1998), 'The Asian Debt and Development Crisis of 1997: Causes and Consequences', *World Development*, 26 (8), 1535–1553.

Wade, Robert and Frank Veneroso (1998), 'The Asian Crisis: The High Debt Model Versus the Wall Street-Treasury-IMF Complex', *New Left Review*, March/April (228), 3–23.

World Bank (1985), *World Development Report*, Washington, DC: World Bank.

World Bank (1997), *Private Capital Flows to Developing Countries: The Road to Financial Integration*, Washington, DC: World Bank.

Databases:

Bank of Thailand, www.bot.or.th
Direction of Trade Statistics CD-ROM (2003)
Global Development Financial CD-ROM (2002)
International Financial Statistics (Online), www.ifs.apdi.net/imf/logon.aspx
National Economic and Social Development Board, www.nesdb.go.th
World Development Indicators CD-ROM (2003)

7. A Class Analysis of Capital Flight from Chile, 1971–2001

Burak Bener and Mathieu Dufour

INTRODUCTION

Capital flight is a captivating phenomenon to study. The desire for concealment that is displayed in the act of capital flight lends it a dimension that is absent from other capital flows in that it gives onlookers an insight into the motivations of the capital holder beyond the mere desire to maximize a return. The fear of expropriation, in one form or another, that drives capital flight allows for a complex analysis of the environment within which it is generated. It is to such an analysis, with a particular focus on the Chilean experience in the last three decades, that this chapter is dedicated.

Chile, during the last three decades of the twentieth century, stands out as an interesting case study. For the greater part of that period (from 1973–90), the country was under a dictatorship. It received sizeable capital inflows and had fairly strict capital controls for many of those years. These are all factors that have traditionally been employed as explanations and justifications for the occurrence of capital flight. On the other hand, Chile has for a long time been the darling of the proponents of neoliberalism, who hail it as an example of what neoliberal macroeconomic policies can achieve when they are employed 'in the proper fashion'. It is cited for its sound fundamentals and the sympathy it seems to elicit from international investors, both of which suggest a fairly clean and open investment environment scarcely conducive to capital flight. At the outset, Chile therefore seemed to be a good experimental subject from which information could be garnered on the relative strength of these different influences.

A more careful analysis reveals a much richer reality. Each of the specific factors we mention above, be it the political structure or the existence of capital controls, is certainly important, but the impact of each is deeply influenced by the idiosyncratic nature of the context in which it operates. Their classification into the conventional categories of contributing or inhibiting factors is therefore mistaken. Furthermore, other factors, notably institutions and power struggles among different classes, which have not been highlighted as much in previous analyses, play essential roles. We believe that, at least in the Chilean case, it is misleading to focus on capital flows alone while ignoring both the set of circumstances in which they take place and the way in which the institutional arrangements are devised. A much better understanding of the determinants of capital flight can be achieved by investigating the specific ways in which economic agents interact with each other and with the government. Consequently, we concentrate our analysis around a historical account of the evolution of the Chilean economy and its institutions, using a class analytical framework.

This chapter seeks to demonstrate why and how class, as a theoretical category, is the appropriate entry point to the analysis of the economic processes surrounding and determining the phenomenon of capital flight in Chile. In particular, conflicts among classes and the ways in which these conflicts are reflected onto their relations with the state and the institution-building process in Chile constitute the main framework of the study. Since capital flight, as we interpret it, is at its core an attempt to evade social control over one's assets, we believe the conflict among different claimants on these assets, which is one aspect of the struggle for dominance among classes, to be an appropriate locus for our analysis.

Several determining factors stand out from this exercise, four of which we deem central to the explanation of capital flight in Chile. These are the extent of capital inflows, the state of domestic investment opportunities, capital controls, and political risk. We then embed these determinants into a larger narrative where we show how they affected the occurrence of capital flight in Chile in the last three decades. This approach stands in contrast with the existing analyses of capital flight from Chile. Whereas the latter tend to try to distil the influence of different factors from their capital flight estimates using various statistical methods (e.g. Schneider 2001), our analysis is more historically oriented. Consequently, in addition to the production of a new set of capital flight estimates, using a method not heretofore employed, our study furthers the analysis of the financial sector of the Chilean economy by linking the phenomenon of capital flight more closely to the concurrent political economic reality.

The chapter proceeds as follows. Different definitions of capital flight are surveyed in the first section. Our estimates, along with some methodological considerations, are laid out and contrasted with some existing capital flight estimates in the next section, and analyzed in the following section. The last section draws conclusions.

ON THE NOTION OF CAPITAL FLIGHT

Despite the widespread use of the term 'capital flight' in development literature, there is scarcely any agreement on the exact nature of the phenomenon.[1] This state of affairs can be partly attributed to irreducible divergences in theoretical standpoints, which lead their respective proponents to label different subsets of capital outflows as capital flight, and also to different political and analytical objectives. Its origin notwithstanding, the absence of consensus has forced economists wishing to make use of the concept of capital flight to first lay out their personal view on its analytical nature, and then to justify their chosen approach, often on the basis of the same factors causing the lack of definitional convergence. As we find ourselves in the same position as our predecessors, we devote this first section to a statement of the definition we use in the present study, as well as an elaboration of some of the reasons which have led us to make this choice.

The definition of capital flight we adopt in this study can be seen as a hybrid of different conceptual stances existing in the literature. Starkly put, we consider as capital flight any net capital outflow that is conducted unofficially and therefore never appears on the books.[2] This definition encompasses a broad range of outflows, from the proceeds of illegal activities to capital earned in an otherwise legal way, but hidden by its owners so as to put it out of reach from government officials (or certain creditors). At a certain level then, such net outflows could perhaps be better viewed as capital evasion, notwithstanding the exact motivation for it. Nevertheless, as is explained further below, these unrecorded flows have more in common than just a desire of their owner to hide them. There is an inherent fear of confiscation associated with a lot of these flows, so that the term 'flight' seems an appropriate descriptor for the phenomenon under study.

At the root of our interest in such a definition for the analysis of the pattern of capital flows in and out of Chile is the fact that it incorporates the flows which occur out of the reach of the authorities, and therefore represent net drains on Chile's capital stock over which they have no control. Of course, any capital outflow can be viewed as such a drain in some respect, notwithstanding the reason why it is conducted or whether or not it 'increases global efficiency' (see Schneider 2001), and the actual degree of control a government can exercise on them is always relative. Nevertheless, we believe that unrecorded outflows are qualitatively different from official ones in that not only do they escape the purview of government officials, but they occur outside any social controls. In effect, they disappear from view, never to be seen in Chile again unless those responsible for the flight of capital decide to return it. The fact that unrecorded outflows lay beyond the reach of most other members of Chilean society lends them a greater permanency than recorded ones, so that they can be said to constitute a more important leakage out of the Chilean economy. If those unrecorded outflows are sizeable, they could seriously impede the functioning of the Chilean economy. In our opinion, this potentially deleterious effect warrants a detailed study of the level and fluctuation of unrecorded outflows, as well as its determinants. Thus exposited, our definition excludes recorded flows that could be due to what is sometimes euphemistically referred to as 'increases in the risk structure', which is in fact how some economists actually define capital flight. In other words, giving 'flight' a literal meaning, these authors argue for a definition that would comprise any flow resulting from the owner's desire to remove capital from a country in response to an adverse change in the conditions under which investment is conducted in that country,[3] including those that are recorded. This approach certainly seems sensible for the study of financial crises, for example, and the different phenomena preceding and surrounding them. Our interest, however, lies more in the study of the evolution of the processes surrounding the flight of capital in Chile over a long period. Consequently, although a portion of our analysis concerns itself with short-run outflows responding to a sudden situational change, its purpose goes beyond what this alternative definition would allow.

Another group of economists restrict their definition of capital flight to illegal transactions, such as smuggling (e.g. Bhagwati 1964; Bhagwati, Krueger and Wibulswadia 1974; both cited in Schneider 2001). Although we wholeheartedly agree that the proceeds of illegal activities should be conceptualized as forming an integral part of capital flight, they by no means constitute its entirety. Other unrecorded flows, such as the transfer of government funds abroad by corrupt officials, also fall into the category of irrecoverable losses for an economy, the importance of which has been argued for above. Consequently, the proceeds of illegal activities form a subset of our estimates of capital flight.

As this last comment highlights, our capital flight estimates comprise different components that are analytically distinct. According to our definition, for example, both smuggling and fiscal fraud involving foreign currencies should appear in the estimate, but one would be hard-pressed to argue that they have the same determinants. To circumvent that problem, we distinguish between the 'trade-related' (misinvoicing of imports and exports) and 'financial' components of capital flight, and analyze them separately.[4]

Trade misinvoicing implies additional conceptual difficulties as a category of capital flight. First, the only way to calculate misinvoicing is to assume that international trade statistics reported by some countries (namely 'industrialized countries' as categorized in the IMF's *International Financial Statistics*) are more reliable than those stated by Chile. Second, one needs to further presume that the discrepancy observed between Chile's and its 'reliable' trading partners' accounts will hold precisely in all trade relations of Chile. We are uncomfortable with both of these presumptions. In fact, even if we assume that industrialized countries' commercial accounts are more credible, it seems quite bizarre to suppose that a similar proportion of trade is misinvoiced with the other trade partners: if their controls are much worse than those of the industrialized countries, would not there be more opportunities for misreporting? In any case, given that the method we employ seems like the best option, short of an in-depth analysis of the Chilean trade sector, and that misinvoicing seems to be an important phenomenon in Chile, we still report and analyze the misinvoicing estimates, but separately from the other components of capital flight. To note, the 'financial' components of capital flight are by contrast derived using data reported for Chile alone, so there is no value judgment that has to be made regarding comparative statistical reliability.[5]

BASIC EMPIRICAL TRENDS

The foregoing discussion in which we described our conceptualisation of capital flight was conducted at a fairly theoretical level. Before we go on to a description of the empirical results we obtain when we look at unofficial flows from Chile, a few words on the way in which our theoretical stance is operationalized are probably warranted. We therefore open this section by stating the estimation method we employ. We then present our estimates of capital flight, along with some relevant empirical trends, and compare them with other estimates present in the literature.[6]

In this study, we make use of the method developed by Boyce and Ndikumana (1997, 2000, 2002). They use a residual method, whereby capital flight is calculated as the difference between gross inflows and outflows in the following manner:

$$KF = FDI + \Delta DEBT - (CADEF + \Delta RES) \tag{7.1}$$

where net foreign direct investment (*FDI*) and increases in foreign debt (*DEBT*) represent net inflows, while the current account deficit (*CADEF*) and the change in reserves (*RES*) are seen as outflows; finally, *KF* stands for 'financial' capital flight. To be able to make inter-temporal comparisons, the debt totals are adjusted for changes in the exchange rates of the currencies comprising them, and the formula is computed in real terms. Finally, account has to be taken of the fact that trade may be misinvoiced. Technically, our capital flight estimates should be modified in such a way as to have a true measure of the current account deficit.[7] However, following the reservations we expressed above concerning the practice of jointly estimating the 'trade-related' and 'financial' components of capital flight, we keep them separate for the most part and analyze them accordingly.

This residual method accounts for all recorded net inflows, as well as the amount of those net inflows that are held as official reserves. In a sense, it tracks all the foreign exchange that enters and leaves the country through official channels. Consequently, a positive number implies that some of the foreign exchange that was recorded as entering the country eventually disappeared from view. It is this lost foreign exchange that we label as unrecorded outflows of capital.

The general picture which emerges from our estimation is, as demonstrated in Figures 7.1 and 7.2 and Table 7.A1, one of a relatively low average (especially compared with some of the other countries covered in this book), punctuated by a few short-lived spikes. 'Financial capital flight' is low throughout the period, except around the debt crisis of 1982 and the Asian crisis, as well as for a short period of time during the mid-1980s (see Figure 7.2). With the exception of a short time at the end of the 1970s, misinvoicing also remains low throughout the entire period under study. Common low averages notwithstanding, it can also be seen that both components of capital flight are not correlated, which validates our strategy to analyze them separately.

Although methodological differences preclude direct comparisons, these results are consistent with existing estimates of capital flight from Chile.[8] Cuddington (1986), employing a measure of capital flight encompassing short-run flows and errors and omissions,[9] and taking his data from the IMF balance of payments statistics, estimates capital flight to be negative from 1975 to 1981, turning positive only in 1982. Similar conclusions are reached by Pastor (1989),[10] who uses a measure that resembles ours, but in his analysis all outflows generated by residents are seen as capital flight,[11] and no consideration is given to potential misinvoicing problems. The only period during which our estimates diverge is the mid-1980s, where he finds negative amounts of capital flight while we estimate positive ones. Our estimates are also in line with Benu Schneider's (2001) estimates, except for the second half of the 1980s. Though she never precisely describes the measure she uses, we suspect it to be relatively similar to that of Pastor. Finally, using a method closely resembling ours, and accounting for misinvoicing, Mahon (1996) generates estimates that are consistent with ours, except for a few scattered years.

Most authors, and certainly the four just mentioned, analyze the capital flight trends for the whole period and treat it as a single entity. We believe that this way of approaching the problem is inadequate, as it obscures the changes Chile underwent during this period. More precisely, we believe that in order for the phenomenon of capital flight to be analyzed properly, the Chilean experience during the last three decades should be divided into seven sub-periods, which are further developed in the next section.

We start by analyzing the years during which Allende's socialist government was in power. Given the important policy changes following the advent of the authoritarian regime, we treat the years under military rule

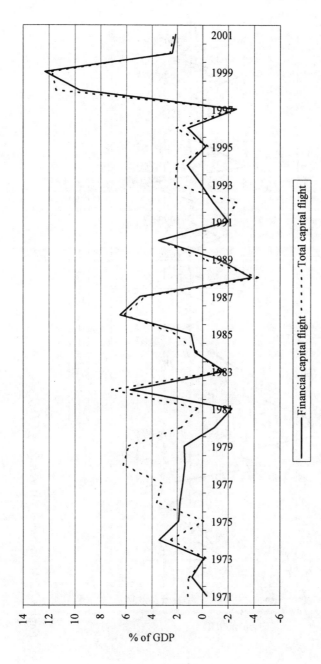

Figure 7.1 Financial and total capital flight (as shares of GDP)

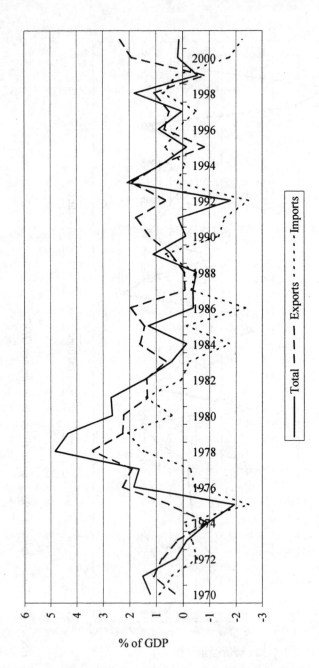

Figure 7.2 Misinvoicing (as a share of GDP)

differently from the Allende period. However, the policy regimes followed during the dictatorship were far from uniform. In fact, we identify three different policy regimes following Silva (1993 and 1996): 'gradual' liberalization (1973–75), 'radical' neoliberalism (1976–81) and 'pragmatic' neoliberalism (1983–88/90). Because of the special constraints imposed by the debt crisis, we also treat 1982 as a separate sub-period. Finally, we analyze the era after the military regime and once again treat the years surrounding the Asian Crisis of 1997–98 independently.

Trade Misinvoicing

(See Figure 7.2 and Tables 7.A1 and 7.A3, in the Appendix.) One of the basic tenets of the neoliberal development strategy followed during and after the dictatorship in Chile has been to open up the national economy, which since the Great Depression had been highly protected under an import substitution industrialization (ISI) strategy, to global markets at a drastic pace. As a result, total trade volume as a ratio of GDP more than tripled (from 14 to 44 percent) in the first three years of the Pinochet government, when import tariffs were virtually abolished. Three decades of structural integration into the world market resulted in an economy where imports and exports added up to more than half of the national income. However, as we report below, contrary to conventional expectations, liberalization has not been a very efficient cure against illegal activity in international commercial relations of Chile.

It can be said that there existed, to some extent, fairly chronic export underinvoicing (EU) between 1970 and 2001 in Chile, which, on average, amounted to 1 percent of GDP or $0.5 billion (measured in 1995 US dollars) for each year. Only in five years out of thirty-two did the country not suffer from capital flight due to export misinvoicing. Import overinvoicing (MO), on the other hand, was not significant in the same period. According to our estimations, MO was negative for two-thirds of the period, and accounted, on average, for $100 million (in 1995 US dollars) of negative capital flight (i.e. unrecorded inflows into Chile). In short, trade misinvoicing was mainly driven by exports in Chile, and caused on average a trade-related capital flight of 0.75 percent of GDP every year.

To sum up, the 'Chicago Boys' period[12] clearly stands out in terms of the amount of misinvoicing. Hence, it can be argued that, except for the 1976–1982 period, net misinvoicing was not a significant source of the drain on capital in Chile. We think that this structural property of trade misinvoicing provides us with another justification for separating it from the financial form of capital flight.

'Financial' Capital Flight

Figure 7.1 illustrates our first crucial finding about 'financial' capital flight in Chile: in the immediate aftermath of the Asian crisis (and its offshoots in Russia and Brazil), specifically 1998 and 1999, the country experienced exceptionally high volumes of capital flight – on average, 11 percent of its GDP. It is exceptional since pre-1998 capital flight averaged only 0.78 percent of GDP. Hence, we prefer to analyze the impact of the Asian crisis separately from the previous period.

Figure 7.3 provides a graphical outline of 'financial' capital flight from Chile during the 26-year period stretching from Allende's socialist government until the outbreak of the Asian crisis (see also Table 7.A1 in the appendix). It is quite remarkable that we observe very low capital flight when there was a socialist government in power. This may be partially explained by very low levels of foreign capital entering the country in that period. In the first two years of military junta (particularly in 1974), there was significant flight of capital from Chile: indeed, our calculations detected a spike from 0 to 4 percent. After 1974, as liberalization reforms accelerated, capital flight consistently declined and eventually arrived at negative numbers in 1980 and 1981. This period is particularly interesting in the sense that low and negative capital flight was experienced in the face of huge inflows of capital.

During the debt crisis and the prolonged transition to democracy, when the country witnessed popular unrest and a long process of negotiations among the elite (military, business, landlords and a few key politicians) to determine the future of the country, there were once again relatively high levels of capital flight from Chile, in particular, in 1986, 1987 and 1990. Wide fluctuations reflect the nation's unstable political and economic situation during this transition. With the advent of electoral politics, which at the same time ensured the continuation of neoliberalism, capital flight ceased again to be an issue in Chile – until the Asian crisis. In two years (1998–99), $15 billion (over 10 percent of GDP) left the country through unofficial channels. Over the next two years, this number dropped to $3 billion, partly because external funds dried up.

To sum up, a first glance at the data seems to suggest that financial capital flight seems to be quite reflective of Chile's macroeconomic environment. Economic crises and political instability tend to cause a high level of capital flight, whereas the capitalist class prefers to stay in Chile as long as it feels secure and it has good relations with the government. We now proceed to analyze some of the underlying determinants of capital flight in more detail.

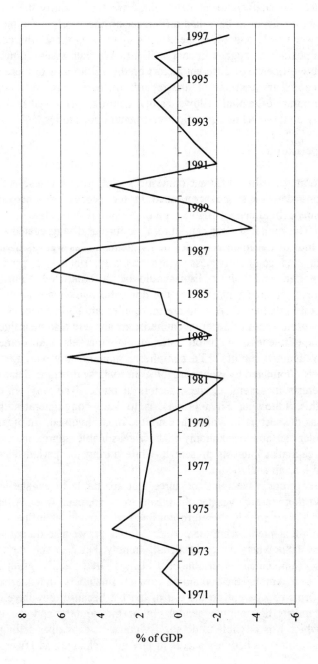

Figure 7.3 Pre-Asian crisis financial capital flight (as a share of GDP)

CORE ANALYSIS

To conduct our analysis of capital flight,[13] we first identify the individuals and groups we deem to have had an impact on the level of capital flight in Chile between 1971 and 2001, specifically identifying those who could have been in a position to engage in capital flight. We then assess in more detail the possible influence of different factors on the willingness of these actors to conduct capital transactions off the record. In particular, we focus on the level and nature of capital inflows, capital controls, perceived political risk, and finally on the level of domestic investment opportunities.[14]

The Perpetrators

There are at least four different domestic social groups whose actions and motivations deserve to be scrutinized in the process of uncovering the mechanisms behind capital flight: capitalists, landowners, state officials, and workers. The capitalist class can, in turn, be further disaggregated according to the nature of the main activities of its members, as well as their market orientation and competitiveness. More precisely, financiers, primary products exporters and industrialists should be differentiated. Furthermore, industrialists producing mainly for the domestic market are likely to have different interests than those who are more internationally oriented. Finally, the policy preferences of different capitalist groups will also be influenced by their competitiveness, both on international markets and domestically, especially against imports. To complicate matters, however, the Chilean economy is dominated by giant conglomerates whose diversified nature gives them interests in several of these sectors at once. The way we chose to resolve this, following Silva (1996), is to lend conglomerates the same interests as the sectors in which they are the most involved. In other words, we consider the above taxonomy to be a reasonable approximation of the different capitalist interests present in Chile during the period under study and adopt it as an analytical tool.

Of these groups, we focus on three that are liable to engage in capital flight. Workers rarely ever had the means to do so, even when Allende was in power. Their role is therefore confined to a potential influence on the policies implemented during the period. Moreover, we also do not study the actions of landowners in great detail, mainly because the development strategies promulgated under Pinochet always put capitalist groups on the center stage. Among the remaining groups, financiers and internationally oriented firms can be put on the top of the list because they have both the financial means to smuggle capital out of the country and the channels through which it is possible to do so. By contrast, capitalists selling mainly in domestic markets had less access to foreign exchange and fewer contacts in financial markets than financiers and internationally oriented firms.

A widespread belief, popularized by Dependency theorists (e.g. Cardoso and Faletto 1978), is that the Latin American bourgeoisie has remained relatively weak, unorganized and dependent on the state – a primary reason why capitalism is underdeveloped, or developed in its own perverse way, on the continent. What this vision could imply, for our purposes, is that private businesspeople are not powerful enough to engage in large amounts of capital flight.[15] The potential validity of this view for other Latin American countries notwithstanding, it certainly does not apply to Chile, where business organization is much more developed than in any other Latin American country, especially with respect to its institutionalization and political influence (Silva 1999).

Dominant sections of the Chilean elite started to get organized as early as the early nineteenth century in four peak business associations: landowners in the *Sociedad Nacional de Agricultura* (SNA) in 1830s, merchants in the *Cámara Nacional de Comercio* (CNC) in 1850s, miners in the *Sociedad Nacional de Minería* (SONAMI) and finally industrial capitalists in the *Sociedad de Fomento Fabril* (SFF) in 1880s. Moreover, these associations tended to unite with each other under the umbrella organization *Confederación de la Producción y Comercio* (CPC) whenever working masses started to become powerful enough to influence state policy – which happened for the first time in 1935 when the Great Depression propelled labour unions to instigate a radical shift in economic policy towards the left (Silva 1996).

In the second half of the twentieth century, the CPC expanded its membership and command by embracing the Construction Chamber in the 1960s and, more importantly, the financial capitalists' peak organization, *Asociación de Bancos e Instituciones Financieras* (ABIF) in the 1980s. This was part of an effort to control the direction of economic policy against, first, the reformists (Eduardo Frei government, 1964–70), who nationalized the copper industry and increased the extent of redistributive policies, and then the socialists (Salvador Allende government, 1970–73), who initiated a much more profound and large-scale program of nationalization and land reform which put the fortunes of all business associations into great danger.

Later in this section, we analyze the relationships between CPC and the dictatorship, its economic technocrats as well as with the succeeding liberal-democratic governments. As we will elaborate there, the most important feature of the CPC, for our purposes, is the fact that it managed to accommodate the different visions of its members so as to retain unity among them, especially since the 1960s. This prevented sectoral conflicts from triggering the breakdown of the CPC as an effective policy-pursuing entity.

It is widely believed that autocracy is more conducive to capital flight, as state officials have a greater ability to enrich themselves at the expense of society.[16] While there have certainly been several instances of dictatorial regimes looting their country, we do not agree with the necessity implied by the conventional prejudice. It is worthwhile stressing that there have been many so-called democratic governments that were highly corrupt as well as many autocratic regimes where high state officials did not particularly enrich themselves.[17] This is highlighted in our analysis of the state sector in Chile during the last three decades which went through both dictatorial and democratic (liberal and socialist) governments. In any case, notwithstanding the nature of the regime, state officials also could have engaged in capital flight, perhaps through the fraudulent use of international loans, for example, so their actions will have to be examined as well.

In addition to domestic actors, foreign investors can also engage in capital flight; this may play an important role in an economy relying heavily on foreign investment such as that of Chile. Arguably, the desire of foreign investors to hide a portion of the funds they take out of the country depends on many factors, some of which are unrelated to the economic conditions prevailing in Chile. Nevertheless, given the existence of serious legal impediments to rapid investment liquidation in Chile throughout most of the years we study, it is possible that in times of crisis (either in Chile or in other locations that matter for these investors) some foreign investors choose to smuggle some of their financial assets out of the country.

In short, the potential perpetrators we will focus on are the financiers, the internationally oriented capitalists, foreign investors and state officials. As is shown below, the ability of any of these groups of individuals to illegally smuggle capital out of the country depends on the amount of power they wield. Consequently, this ability will vary through time, following the fortunes of different groups and the outcomes of the class struggles taking place.

Factors Underlying Capital Flight

As implied by its specific definition used in this study, capital flight refers to unrecorded flows of capital. In other words, it is driven by the wish of capital owners to escape social control over their assets. We identify four factors which we deem to be important structural influences on the desire, as well as the ability, of capital owners to engage in capital flight.

Our measure of capital flight tracks foreign exchange as it enters and leaves Chile and labels as capital flight any inflow that is not matched by an outflow or an increase in reserves in a given period. Consequently, only the flows which occur in a given year enter into the calculation of capital flight for that year, although the capital itself may be transferred abroad at a different moment, so the level of inflows has an important influence on the amount of capital flight. That said, foreign exchange can change hands a few times during a year, so particular inflows may not be directly linked to unrecorded capital outflows. For example, a domestic firm might choose to default on its debt by hiding money abroad, buying foreign exchange that was earned by the exports of another firm (possibly during a previous year) in the process.

A second determinant of capital flight is the state of domestic investment opportunities. We expect capital owners to be more eager to flee if their own country is less able to provide alternative forms of assets to be invested in, such as that made available by the banking sector and the stock market. In our view, there is no single index that can capture the general attractiveness of an economy to domestic investors. We therefore make an assessment based on different indicators of the quality of investment opportunities. Interest rate differentials between the country under study and a referent country (often the USA) or group of countries, and variations in the exchange rates, are two indicators that are often used as proxies for the attractiveness of investment in domestic currencies. We find both to be inadequate, which is why we make recourse to several indicators, which vary in importance across the different time periods we analyze. Interest rate differentials are of dubious significance because they are driven by multiple considerations in addition to those pertaining to returns on capital, represent only the return to a certain type of investment, and lack a clear correlation with the actual investment climate (e.g. the return on physical investment). Similarly, the usefulness of real exchange rate fluctuations is undermined by the inherent difficulty of establishing a correct valuation of the exchange rate. Moreover, we believe that these fluctuations do not constitute an independent mechanism underlying capital flight; they are an integral element and a reflection of the general process we are trying to outline.[18]

The third factor that we would like to stress is one that has particular significance for Chile, namely capital controls. Although capital controls vary widely, they can be broadly classified as controls on inflows and controls on outflows. Strict controls on capital outflows invite higher capital flight, simply because the lack of controls makes the flight – unrecorded outflows – redundant in many cases. In other words, the decision of capital owners to conduct capital flight may be partly predicated on their desire to circumvent capital controls, so that the greater the controls on outflows, the greater the incentive to engage in capital flight. Controls on inflows, on the other hand, work in the opposite way because they imply unrecorded capital inflows.

Finally, the fourth element to consider, the 'political security of capital', is perhaps the most critical for our analysis. What we mean by 'political security' in the context of capital flight is the extent to which domestic owners of foreign capital feel safe about the fate of their ownership rights. Of course, this feeling of security is directly related to the nature of the government in place. Dictatorships, for example, by closing all sorts of democratic regulatory channels, can provide an exclusive environment in which a small minority exploits the opportunities of a nation. Such an extreme case, where the repressive regime has no or very little legitimacy in the eyes of the people, can ironically render capitalists insecure, creating a strong motivation to move their capital outside the country, where it is safer.

Class Analysis

Chile's economic performance is often described as a perfect example of the transformation that cleverly devised policy can bring to developing countries. Such a description obscures the fact that far from implementing one set of 'sound policies', Pinochet's government modified its approach at least three times during the dictatorship that lasted from 1973 to 1990. Moreover, Pinochet's control was preceded by the short-lived socialist experience (1970–73), and it was followed by a set of economically liberal but politically democratic policies. In other words, Chile's development strategy in the last three decades has been far from linear, going through many ups and downs, as several accounts of its economic history for that period bring out. This chapter aims to complement the existing accounts through an analysis focusing on capital flows before, during and after Pinochet's reign. More precisely, the analysis is broken up into the seven sub-divisions mentioned in the previous section.

Unitad Popular (1970–73)

Between the Great Depression and the accession to power of the Allende government in 1970, Chile more or less pursued a classic import substitution strategy. The domestic economy, which was dominated by oligopolistic conglomerates,[19] was highly regulated and protected from international competition by high tariff barriers. Industrialists and other capitalists producing for domestic markets were the dominant factions of capital, and the model was also supported by landowners whom the trade barriers protected from cheap food imports, and by workers, for whom the barriers provided relatively high paying jobs. This arrangement became strained during the 1960s under the reformist governments that preceded Allende. As Chilean politics became increasingly polarized between different interest groups, including diversely oriented segments of the industrial bourgeoisie, landowners and labour, the coalition of radical left-wing parties, *Unitad Popular*, led by Allende, won the 1970 elections with the support of working classes. During its three years in power, Allende's government launched a series of far-reaching policies, including radical land reform and the widespread nationalization of key industries of the Chilean economy.

These policies are commonly expected to scare capital off. However, our findings, somewhat surprisingly, do not hint at significant levels of capital flight in those years. In fact, on the contrary, we found negative numbers for 1971 and 1973, and a relatively low level of capital flight in 1972. This has been for us a fairly unanticipated discovery, especially for the very end of the period, when social strife and exclusion of capital, and hence heightened uncertainty, reached their peak.

First of all, it is well worth mentioning that we believe there exist reasons for not counting on the national statistics for this period (1973, in particular, when social turmoil further ascended). We think that, under extraordinarily chaotic political and economic circumstances, state officials may have basically stopped recording balance of payments (BOP) flows, and hence our capital flight calculations (which are, except for debt statistics, based on official BOP reports) might not reflect the actual amount of capital flight from Chile. Remarkably high capital flight in 1974 points to the validity of this hypothesis. In other words, as many groups within the capital-owning classes were calmed by the intervention of the military junta, they were possibly convinced to keep their capital in Chile (or even to bring some of the capital that has been already smuggled back to home, causing negative capital flight). One would therefore expect to observe lower amounts of capital flight than those we report. However, since 1973 transactions might actually have been recorded in 1974, our estimations for 1974 (3.4 percent of GDP) might be artificially boosted.

Another explanation for unexpectedly low levels of capital flight under the socialist regime is the presence of comprehensive capital controls on both inflows and outflows (IMF 1971–74). Whereas it is quite hard to tell which side of the controls were enforced more strictly and efficiently in practice, these controls, as mentioned in the previous section, potentially cancel each other out in terms of their effect on capital flight. Moreover, despite the fact that controls on outflows generate incentives for capital owners to carry their money abroad illegally, we also think that the socialist government was quite determined as well as successful in their attack on the bourgeoisie, which significantly hindered illicit capital movements.

The panic caused by the socialist regime was obviously not the sole reason why the Chilean elite were induced to flee. The comprehensive nationalization of major industries and a land reform dramatically limited investment opportunities for private capital in Chile, which surely encouraged the flight of capital.

'Gradualist' neoliberalism in the early Pinochet era (1974–75)
The aggressive leftist policies of the Allende government, in particular the wide nationalization program, further polarized the left and right. Consequently, erstwhile divided capitalists, along with landowners, formed a coalition to oppose Allende's reforms. The fear of losing their assets, as the regime of private property came under attack, pushed them to overcome their

differences and form a united front against the government. They first attempted to do so through traditional channels, partly using the Christian Democrats (a centrist party in power from 1964 to 1970) as the mediator between them and the government. When this failed, they turned to more radical options and a subset of the capitalist class initiated discussions with the military conspirators, whom they supported when they took over the government in September 1973.

The leaders of the anti-Allende business coalition, internationally competitive firms which favored a gradual opening of the economy to international markets, successfully managed to get their policies implemented by the Pinochet government following the coup. Moreover, given the broad nature of the conservative coalition, gradual liberalization policies can be seen as a compromise by different factions of capital (by those who benefited from protection and the internationally competitive firms) as well as by the rentiers and landowners. Consequently, for a few years after the coup, the government attempted to gradually move away from import-substitution strategies (ISI) towards a policy of liberalized markets mixed with protection policies. The officially stated aim was to dismantle trade barriers, but only gradually and in a way that did not destabilize the economy, so that only the inefficient would be adversely affected.

The unity of the broad front started to erode immediately after the military takeover and right after the new rules were established, a fierce rivalry among the leading groups headed off, with each group trying to get their favored policies implemented. Despite the fact that internationally oriented groups were in the lead most of the time, this competition generated a high degree of uncertainty regarding future economic policies, an uncertainty which was further exacerbated by the high degree of political repression. This general atmosphere may partly explain the spike in capital flight in 1974, which was largely financed by the major debt inflow ($1.4 billion or nine percent of GDP) originating mainly in the USA, as aid to the Pinochet government.

In addition, despite the significant position it possessed within the capitalist coalition and the preferential treatment received by the economic elite in power, the domestic financial sector remained fairly underdeveloped throughout the period – particularly because it had been extensively damaged by the socialist government. Thus, the limited opportunities at home may have pushed some capital owners to leave Chile to invest abroad.

Our general framework gives two possible explanations for the virtual decline in financial capital flight in the following year. First, capital controls on outflows were mildly relaxed, placing a downward pressure on capital flight. Second, and for us more significantly, the group that was most likely to contribute to capital flight, that is internationally oriented capitalists (since they had the means), basically stopped leaving Chile when they started to become increasingly dominant within the coalition backing the military government. The next section explores how these tendencies further developed as the direction of economic policy was increasingly influenced by a group of neoliberal technocrats, the Chicago Boys, who had extremely close ties with internationally oriented financiers.

Birth of the Chilean model: 'Radical' neoliberalism (1976–81)

Economic policy changed fundamentally after mid-1975, as the internationally minded elements of the coalition captured Chile's leadership through different means, not the least of which was a closer association with Pinochet, who in turn used them to bolster his political power. The creation in 1974 of the so-called *financieras*, financial intermediaries whose interest rates were, unlike the rest of the banking sector, deregulated, along with the increase in the availability of foreign funds, allowed the few conglomerates (especially, the BHC and Cruzat-Larraín groups) who took advantage of the changing economic climate to expand their business activities (Silva 1993, 1996; IMF 1975–78). At a time when oil shocks hit industrialists the hardest, those conglomerates were able to increase their economic power to a degree that allowed them to take the leadership of the capitalist coalition. In his efforts to gain absolute power, Pinochet bid on them, hoping that they could deliver sufficient economic growth and prosperity to offer him legitimacy. He therefore appointed radical neoliberal technocrats, known as the 'Chicago Boys' – at once linked to both financial conglomerates and monetarists by ideology – to key ministries and agencies, and allowed them to implement policies desired by the financiers at a drastic degree and pace: financial deregulation, privatisation, deflation, and trade liberalization.

The ensuing policy switch was nothing short of astounding. For example, differential tariffs were abolished and replaced by a very low (eventually 10 percent) across-the-board rate. Inflation, as measured by the GDP deflator, steadily decreased from more than 330 percent in 1975 to 57 percent three years later, and even 13 percent in 1981.[20] When domestically oriented oligopolies were severely hurt by rising interest rates, declining prices as well as growing foreign competition, internationalist conglomerates, given their financial resources, were able to buy relatively cheaply some of the firms that went under during the 1974–75 depression. Similarly, when the government proceeded to privatize what remained of the state sector after the firms requisitioned by the Allende government had been returned to their owners, they were in a privileged position to capture a large number of sound firms at a bargain.[21]

Most of the capitalists and landowners, hurt by high interest rates and reductions in protection, protested against this policy change, but the exclusionary nature of the political regime appears to have insulated the technocrats from pressure by business.[22] Although they were shut out of decision-making like the rest of the non-financial conglomerates, those groups whose assets were concentrated in export activities also benefited from the liberalization policies, and they tacitly supported them. The immediate results of the radical neoliberal policies were disastrous, as shown by the major economic downturn in 1975, but thereafter the neoliberal model delivered growth, so the narrow base of support for the regime was sufficient for Pinochet to withstand the opposition. The solidity of the support was such that other conglomerates eventually decided to join the ball and reorient themselves to global markets.

To summarize, the primary characteristic of this era was, for our purposes, the high level of political stability which increased the confidence of the Chilean elite in the economic policies that followed and in the general progress of the economy. With the consolidation of Pinochet's rule and the advent of financiers (and their technocrat offshoots) to power, financial capital flight steadily decreased and ultimately became negative in the last two years before the debt crisis. What is especially striking about this period is that this remarkably decreasing trend in financial capital flight was attained in the face of unprecedented inflows of foreign capital in the Chilean economy (averaging 11 percent of GDP from 1978 to 1981). Indeed, substantial inflows of international capital (mainly in the form of long-term private bank debts) in the late 1970s and early 1980s fueled Chile's development under the monetarist model.

Financial conglomerates were able to further extend their activities, and the deregulation of the banking sector in 1977–78, which removed caps on foreign borrowing, allowed them to channel huge amounts of funds into the country, which were then lent to businesses undergoing restructuring and to consumers for import purposes. This led to a swelling of private debt to unparalleled levels, at the same time that austerity measures were being taken to reduce public debt. Interestingly, the presence of capital controls that forbade capital inflows with a maturity of less than two years, along with high reserve requirements for short- and medium-run loans,[23] did not seem to do much to stymie those capital inflows.[24] Moreover, controls on outflows were being slashed (while most of the controls on inflows were kept), which might have generated a negative bias on capital flight.

Two other major developments that allowed financial capitalists to widen their economic supremacy were the privatization boom in the second half of 1970s as well as the purchase of domestically oriented firms which went bankrupt during the severe economic crisis in the first year of the military government. The privatization of companies that were either established as public enterprises or nationalized by the *Unitad Popular* in the early 1970s was one of the corner-stones of the neoliberal program. Besides its ideological significance (in terms of dismantling socialism completely in Chile), it greatly contributed to the redistribution of national resources to the rentier class. In addition, the same government which helped the financial capitalists during the severe 1974 crisis has been quite reluctant to help the domestically oriented firms (also associated with the ISI policies as well as the socialist government) which ended up being purchased by the financial conglomerates.

Both of these channels, closely monitored by the technocratic elite, created an economy which was run essentially by internationally oriented financial capitalists who, by taking loans from abroad (financed by the petrodollar boom in the international economy), to which they had preferential access, were able to continue investing at home. In short, 'radical' neoliberalism relied, more than anything else, on the exclusion of a vast majority of the society from political as well as key economic channels; and incentives to leave Chile and engage in capital flight were, in these circumstances, considerably weakened for privileged groups which possessed significant levels of capital and also had access to international markets. However, the debt crisis of 1982 was to lead to the sudden and painful collapse of this structure.

In addition, this period of intense deregulation saw a swelling in misinvoicing, particularly export underinvoicing. This is somewhat counter-intuitive since the abolition of trade barriers could be thought of as decreasing the incentives to engage in illicit trade. However, when we consider that the decrease in controls also implies a decrease in surveillance, then our results do not appear so strange. In fact, it may simply have been the case that the increase in scope for misinvoicing dominated the negative influence that the decrease in trade barriers had.

1982 Debt Crisis
The euphoria came to an end when the hasty change in the US monetary policy in 1981 led to the drying up of international capital inflows. Chilean interest rates sky-rocketed as a result of its monetary policy, which had pegged the money supply to international reserves. The financial institutions, which were having a hard time servicing their debts, supported this policy. This in turn rendered other firms incapable of rolling over their debt and made them go under in a sort of domino process culminating in the debt crisis. The government had to buy a large number of bankrupt corporations and their outstanding debts to Western bankers to preserve Chile's credibility on international markets.

The abrupt collapse of the economy led most capitalists, who just a few years before had jumped on the neoliberal bandwagon, to reverse their stance and demand major policy changes. Pinochet finally yielded in 1983, when the popular protests backing the demands for reform became too strong to ignore.   Under the massive political uncertainty caused by declining popularity and legitimacy of Pinochet's leadership in the eyes of Chilean people, the amount of capital which left the economy amounted to 5.7 percent of GDP, the second largest on record (after 1986) in the pre-Asian Crisis history of Chile. We hypothesize that the main factor behind this sizeable figure was the financial capitalist class, which, having accumulated large amounts of debt in the previous radical neoliberal period, smuggled most of its wealth outside Chile just before it was swept away, both economically and politically, by the crisis.

'Pragmatic' neoliberalism (1983–90)

Beginning in 1982, organized business started, once again, to come to the forefront, replacing financiers as the leading capitalist branch. Indeed, in sheer contrast to the earlier technocratic 'Chicago Boys' period, economic administration came under direct control of the CPC to the extent that many actual leaders of its branches started to head the ministries of Economy and Finance.

In the immediate aftermath of the crisis, this coalition led by internationally minded capitalists (mainly exporters with a heavier concentration in fixed assets such as logging, fishing and mining), and to a certain degree, by some producers for domestic markets, managed to induce a policy switch from the government. In July 1983, the CPC publicly introduced a formal economic recovery program called *Recuperación económica*, which proposed more 'pragmatic' policies to deal with the crisis, such as a devaluation of the exchange rate[25] to enable exporters to expand their activities and bring more foreign exchange in the country. This had deleterious effects on all the firms whose debt was denominated in dollars, so they also proposed that heavily indebted firms be bailed out, notably through generous debt rescheduling programs. Interest rates were brought down, even to the point of allowing some inflation,[26] hitherto anathema for Chilean policymakers.

At the same time, a large chunk of private debt was made public, partly through the transfer of bad loans from financial institutions to the central bank and the nationalization of many bankrupt financial firms, which led the government back into deficit spending. Finally, fairly stringent capital controls, especially regarding debt contracting and repayment, were instituted and only relaxed in 1985 (IMF 1984–86).[27] Overall, the whole package, especially the devaluation of the Chilean Peso, benefited exporters and domestic market producers, and dealt a hard blow to the financial sector, which lost its grip on the policymaking process for good.

In the first couple of years after the debt crisis, capital flight from Chile, after its peak in 1982, remained negative (1983) or quite low (1984, 1985); and this was attained (except for 1983) in the face of continuing foreign debt flows into the country. In our view, the principal cause was the reshuffle in the hierarchy among capitalist factions: the rentiers, who were in the best position to engage in capital flight in 1982, descended from their leading position to be replaced by export-oriented industrial firms, which favored more pragmatic liberal policies that allowed for some inflation and import tariffs as well as more stringent capital controls. Moreover, during this early phase of 'pragmatic' neoliberalism, no major capital-owning group, including the internationally oriented industrialists, appeared strong enough to pursue significant amounts of capital flight.[28]

Between 1985 and 1988, the leading subject matter of the negotiations between the military government and business elite was the privatisation of state-owned enterprises. As the date of the plebiscite on the continuation of Pinochet's rule approached (1988), business leaders were obviously becoming increasingly less patient about realizing their agenda. They made it increasingly clear that they supported the current form of government. After all, Pinochet had given in to their demands and Chile was back on the path of economic growth.

Yet, in spite of the uninterrupted efforts of the government to satisfy the demands of the internationally oriented industrialists, as well as the rather quick recovery from the severe recession of the debt crisis, political unrest did not die out in Chile. Hence, economic recession and political strife after the debt crisis created a high level of uncertainty about the future of the dictatorial regime, an uncertainty which lasted until Pinochet agreed to hold a plebiscite in 1988.

Another line of negotiations – critical in setting the political context of the 1980s – was carried out between the elite and the opposing coalition of center-left political parties. Leaders of this democratic coalition, although their popular support rested mainly with the masses, who had been severely hit by the crisis, 'promised' the bourgeoisie to give up comprehensive economic reform in exchange for the transition to democracy. However, during this heightened bargaining process, capitalists, who did not feel safe, chose to leave, which resulted in consistently rising capital flight after 1984. In 1986 and 1987, capital flight reached 6.5 percent and 4.9 percent of GDP respectively.

Political turbulence and the resulting policy ambiguities were somewhat alleviated after Pinochet was compelled to consent to the plebiscite in 1988. Our estimations indicate, for the following two years (i.e. 1988 and 1989), negative amounts of capital flight, to which, without doubt, this improved state of political security contributed to a large extent. Another factor behind the sharp reversal in capital flight was the second wave of privatisation of the firms nationalised during the crisis. The privatization process began in 1985, but went slowly for the first few years due to the inability of the domestic bourgeoisie and the reluctance of the foreign bourgeoisie to make long-term investment in Chile. When export-oriented conglomerates started to purchase these enterprises, funds that may have ended up outside Chile instead stayed at home.

In the very last year of military rule, when the first democratic elections in 17 years were held in Chile, there was another spike in the level of capital flight (3.5 percent of GDP). This could be attributed to a last bid on the part of the friends of the military junta to get their money out of the country in response to the uncertainty they faced regarding the way this wealth would be treated by the incoming government. Certainly, the CPC, despite its virtual accord with the opposition about the future of economic policy, supported Hernán Bűchi (formerly a business leader himself) for the elections. As the next section shows, it became immediately clear that their concerns were redundant, and they chose to invest within Chile in the 1990s.

'Democratic' neoliberalism (1991–97)

In an effort to garner the support of the military as well as the bourgeoisie, the center-left coalition, the *Alianza Democratica*, had to make many concessions in the design of their post-dictatorship economic strategy, which, though they ultimately failed to keep capitalists from campaigning for Pinochet, did ensure a continuity in the economic model followed by the government elected in 1990. Consequently, throughout the 1990s, the focus on exports and the commitment to generally pragmatic free-market policies remained the central tenet of the development strategy in Chile. This can be exemplified by the installation of an unremunerated reserve requirement (URR)[29] between 1991 and 1998, an asymmetric capital control designed as a tax on short-run capital inflows, which basically served to maintain a low exchange rate, with interest rates high enough to keep inflation at desired levels (Ariyoshi et al. 2000; Soederberg 2002). In fact, the only important divergence from the policies followed in the 1980s was the gradual liberalization of financial transactions.[30] It can be argued, however, that even this policy was not really at odds with the rest of the development model, as the rationale behind the controls of the 1980s no longer applied (Soederberg 2002).

The first half of 1990s, or to be precise, the period stretching from the 1990 elections to the Asian crisis in 1997, was a period of very rapid export-led economic expansion, accompanied by a domestic investment boom under fundamentally diminished uncertainty and a surge of FDI. This led to an exceptionally confident atmosphere, further encouraged by the political transition to a democratic process, which added to the presence of good investment opportunities as money poured in, decreased the incentive for capital flight. Consequently, throughout the entire period, capital flight was either negative (1991, 1992 and 1995) or quite low (1993, 1994 and 1996) in the face of substantial net inflows of foreign capital into Chile. Unlike the late 1970s when a similar trend was observed, however, the major form of capital inflows took the form of foreign direct investment (gradually increasing from 2 percent to 6.5 percent of GDP) rather than bank loans. The domestic bourgeoisie, just like foreign investors, seem to have preferred to invest in this safe environment.

Another very widely discussed feature of the Chilean development strategy in the 1990s has been the URR, which has been praised as the example of perfect controls on capital inflows. The URR, which was kept in place until the Asian crisis, affects our calculations in two important ways. First, controls on inflows, in general, have a negative effect on capital flight. Second, since foreign investors are required to deposit a certain amount of the money they bring in with the central bank of Chile, a requirement which is particular to the URR, this has an additional negative bias on our estimations, for the accumulation of foreign reserves is one of the two ways in which foreign currency is officially utilized. Hence, the implementation of a URR contributed significantly to the low level of capital flight in this period.

Asian Crisis and its aftermath (1998–2001)
The Asian crisis of 1997 was a devastating external shock for many countries, and Chile was no exception. The economy, which had already started to stagnate in the year before the crisis (the country's GDP had declined by 4 percent), was hit hard: in real terms, national income contracted by 12 percent in 5 years. The neoliberal 'miracle' was suddenly in tatters. Although there was little political uncertainty, confidence in economic prosperity and progress was very low. Under these tough circumstances, Chile experienced a colossal flight of capital in 1998 and 1999: 9.6 percent and 12.3 percent of its GDP, respectively. Major debt build-up in those two years probably contributed to this process. Despite the fact that inflows into Chile (especially foreign direct investment which fell to under 1 percent of GDP) dried up during the crisis, capital flight remained over 2 percent of GDP in 2000 and 2001.

The confidence in the economy was undermined further due to the backlash of bad memories from the 1982 debt crisis, in which numerous corporations had been swept away. However, the question remains as to why so many panicked investors preferred, in the absence of tight controls on capital outflows, to utilize unofficial channels to remove their money from Chile. We believe that many of these firms (domestic and foreign) favored unofficial means because these enabled them to hide capital from their creditors as loans were pulled back.[31] Finally, the abandonment of capital controls on inflows (that is, the URR) by the government, in a bid to retain and attract foreign capital, which was already exceedingly nervous due to the crisis, removed the negative influence the controls exerted on capital flight, further contributing to the record levels of capital flight.

CONCLUSION

Quite evidently, capital flight is, by its very nature, a difficult phenomenon to grasp. Flows motivated by a desire to evade social and political control on the part of their perpetrators are unlikely to be recorded anywhere and can therefore only be inferred by looking at the discrepancies between different sets of data. Measurement problems notwithstanding, we believe that one's understanding of a country's politico-economic dynamics can be much enriched by an analysis of unrecorded outflows precisely because of the holder's fear of expropriation and the factors that are at the root of this apprehension.

In this chapter, we have endeavored to demonstrate how the shifting power relations among capitalists in Chile had a determining influence on the amount of unofficial outflows. We have also underlined the importance of other factors, such as the existence of capital controls on inflows and the quality and abundance of domestic investment opportunities. Financial capital flight was found to be relatively low when the dominant capitalist class, who also had preferential access to foreign exchange, was secure in its position. By contrast, capital flight levels rose significantly around the period of the debt crisis, when these capitalists were uprooted, as well as for a few years in the second half of the 1980s, when there was a high degree of political uncertainty. Interestingly, misinvoicing remained fairly low throughout the period, except in the latter half of the 1970s, when the current account was the most liberalized. Another interesting result is that we found no evidence of a general negative impact from the presence of capital controls, aside from the biases we mention. On the contrary, it was when controls were most stringent that we witnessed the lowest amount of capital flight.

We consider our analysis to be a first pass at gaining a more complete understanding of the functioning of some of the hidden aspects of the financial sector of the Chilean economy. There certainly is much scope for further research, possibly along the lines of an even finer division of the time periods to analyze the shifts in dominance with greater precision. A more detailed account of some of the practices of the financial institutions during that period would certainly also shed more light on the actual way in which capital flight may have been conducted.

APPENDIX

Table 7.A1 'History' of capital flight

Year	Subperiod	Financial capital flight (% of GDP)	Misinvoicing (% of GDP)	Total capital flight (% of GDP)
1971	Democratic socialism	-0.3	1.5	1.2
1972		0.8	0.3	1.1
1973		-0.1	-0.1	-0.2
1974	Gradual neoliberalism	3.4	-1.0	2.5
1975		1.9	-1.9	-0.1
1976		1.8	1.8	3.6
1977		1.6	1.6	3.2
1978	Radical neoliberalism	1.4	4.8	6.2
1979		1.5	4.3	5.8
1980		-0.9	2.7	1.8
1981		-2.3	2.7	0.4
1982	Debt crisis	5.7	1.4	7.1
1983	Pragmatic neoliberalism	-1.7	0.4	-1.3
1984		0.6	-0.1	0.5

Year				
1985		0.9	1.3	2.2
1986		6.5	-0.4	6.1
1987	Pragmatic neoliberalism	4.9	-0.4	4.5
1988		-3.8	-0.5	-4.3
1989		-1.2	1.1	-0.1
1990		3.5	-0.1	3.4
1991		-2.0	0.2	-1.8
1992		-0.8	-1.8	-2.6
1993		0.1	2.1	2.2
1994	Democratic neoliberalism	1.2	0.8	2.0
1995		-0.2	-0.1	-0.4
1996		1.2	0.9	2.1
1997		-2.6	0.0	-2.6
1998		9.6	1.8	11.4
1999		12.3	-0.6	11.8
2000	Asian crisis	2.4	0.2	2.6
2001		2.1	0.1	2.3

Sources: International Financial Statistics, World Development Finance and authors' own calculations.

Table 7.A2 Components of capital flight (in constant 1995 US dollars)

Years	Change in debt	Net FDI	Change in reserve assets	Current account balance	'Financial' capital flight	Total misinvoicing	Total capital flight
1971	217	−213	523	−636	−119	518	399
1972	1,687	−3	136	−1,452	298	94	392
1973	1,114	−14	−267	−815	−40	−65	−105
1974	4,125	−1,492	−89	−782	1,422	−397	1,026
1975	1,333	123	195	−1,201	336	−345	−9
1976	1,082	−2	−958	343	408	420	828
1977	1,850	35	−112	−1,201	460	479	939
1978	3,977	360	−1,423	−2,213	437	1,515	1,952
1979	4,364	437	−1,665	−2,233	568	1,689	2,256
1980	5,294	292	−2,183	−3,390	−431	1,262	831
1981	6,352	569	−114	−7,445	−1,181	1,391	211
1982	3,022	569	2,042	−3,412	2,044	515	2,560
1983	1,096	188	−133	−1,591	−482	119	−363
1984	3,521	92	−429	−2,899	159	−35	124
1985	2,093	190	−136	−1,881	201	285	486
1986	2,516	408	179	−1,552	1,496	−89	1,407
1987	1,216	1,119	−83	−929	1,287	−98	1,190

Year							
1988	-1,120	1,165	-924	-283	-1,126	-149	-1,275
1989	-563	1,610	-646	-814	-391	361	-30
1990	3,109	1,158	-2,406	-550	1,195	-38	1,157
1991	-300	788	-1,148	-107	-756	65	-691
1992	2,272	935	-2,503	-1,022	-372	-809	-1,181
1993	1,561	1,383	-177	-2,665	65	962	1,027
1994	2,665	2,637	-2,982	-1,621	644	416	1,060
1995	-0.4	1,942	-740	-1,350	-148	-92	-240
1996	690	4,235	-1,098	-3,024	789	609	1,399
1997	39	4,764	-3,193	-3,522	-1,913	23	-1,890
1998	7,316	1,090	2,083	-3,725	6,676	1,253	7,928
1999	4,041	3,042	700	93	7,819	-351	7,468
2000	2,556	44	-291	-703	1,554	123	1,677
2001	1,251	581	537	-1,069	1,271	80	1,351

Note: *Entries are in million US dollars.

Sources: International Financial Statistics, World Development Finance and authors' own calculations.

Table 7.A3 Components of misinvoicing

Year	Export underinvoicing			Import overinvoicing		
	In current US $	In constant (1995) US $	% of GDP	In current US $	In constant (1995) US $	% of GDP
1971	117	375	1.1	44	143	0.4
1972	91	282	0.8	-61	-188	-0.5
1973	33	97	0.2	-56	-162	-0.3
1974	-137	-367	-0.9	-11	-30	-0.1
1975	39	94	0.5	-179	-440	-2.5
1976	224	521	2.3	-43	-101	-0.4
1977	256	558	1.9	-36	-79	-0.3
1978	522	1061	3.4	223	455	1.5
1979	471	884	2.3	429	805	2.1
1980	613	1054	2.2	121	207	0.4
1981	435	685	1.3	449	706	1.4
1982	330	489	1.4	18	26	0.1
1983	131	186	0.7	-47	-67	-0.2
1984	309	424	1.6	-335	-459	-1.7
1985	236	314	1.4	-22	-29	-0.1

Year						
1986	351	457	2.0	-419	-546	-2.4
1987	-15	-20	-0.1	-62	-78	-0.3
1988	-14	-18	-0.1	-108	-132	-0.4
1989	127	150	0.5	179	211	0.7
1990	373	423	1.2	-407	-461	-1.3
1991	608	665	1.8	-548	-600	-1.6
1992	277	296	0.7	-1,034	-1,104	-2.5
1993	833	869	1.9	89	93	0.2
1994	437	447	0.9	-30	-31	-0.1
1995	-526	-526	-0.8	434	434	0.7
1996	475	466	0.7	146	143	0.2
1997	383	369	0.5	-360	-346	-0.5
1998	779	740	1.1	539	512	0.7
1999	-538	-504	-0.8	163	153	0.2
2000	1344	1233	1.9	-1,210	-1,111	-1.7
2001	1574	1411	2.4	-1,485	-1,332	-2.2

Note: *Monetary entries are in million US dollars.

Source: Direction of Trade Statistics (IMF).

NOTES

We wish to thank the members of the Capital Flight Working Group for many insightful suggestions and comments. Quite evidently, any mistake remains our own. This is a shortened version of a longer study. The complete study can be accessed on the website of the Political Economy Research Institute (PERI) at the University of Massachusetts, Amherst.

1. For a thorough treatment of different alternatives, see Chapter 3 by Beja in this book.
2. This definition parallels the one used by Boyce and Ndikumana (1997, 2000).
3. An example of this conception may be found in Cuddington (1986).
4. Both components will be outlined with greater precision in the next section. As an aside, let us stress that we are well aware that some of the capital flight not linked to trade is not directly taking place in the financial sector. Bribes readily come to mind as an example of a source of capital flight that neither originates from trade nor from financial transactions. Nonetheless, as is made clear below, we believe that in Chile, the greater proportion of the capital flight unrelated to trade takes place in the financial sector.
5. The only exception is our assumption that the World Bank provides better 'foreign debt' data than the IMF (following Boyce and Ndikumana 2001).
6. For a detailed description of the residual method, as well as the procedure employed to calculate misinvoicing, see chapter 3 by Beja in this book.
7. As aforesaid, we estimated trade misinvoicing by comparing the import and export statistics reported by Chile to those reported by its trading partners, restricting our analysis to 'industrialized countries'. Taking the latter to be the 'true' numbers, we then weighted the differentials by the share of Chilean trade with the industrialized countries. The resulting number is what we take as our estimate of misinvoicing.
8. Our results and data are available on demand.
9. It should be noted that except for the adjustments we make, our method is essentially equivalent to the errors and omissions residual reported in the IMF balance of payments statistics.
10. Pastor employs data from the IMF's International Financial Statistics, as well as the World Bank's Debt Tables.
11. By contrast, we consider net flows in our calculation of capital flight, without distinguishing between resident and non-resident capital holders.
12. Thus has been called by many commentators (e.g. Silva 1993, 1996) the 'radical' neoliberal period spanning between 1976 and 1982, after the technocrats whom Pinochet put in charge of formulating economic policies and running governmental institutions and the university where most of them studied.
13. As the following analysis centers on financial capital flight, 'capital flight' will be used as a synonym for 'financial capital flight'. The trade-related component will be denominated as 'misinvoicing'.
14. Let us stress that our analysis of the general structure and path of Chile's economy relies to a great extent on excellent studies by Eduardo Silva (1993, 1996, 1999). His proficient approach (especially, the classification of dominant classes in Chile and the periodization of the Pinochet era) provided us with a fertile framework with which to analyze capital flight from Chile.
15. We do not argue that fragmented business is unable to flee their capital; however, we think that it is much more difficult for them (than for organized capitalists) to escape from the authority of the government.
16. For an example of a variant of this view, see Lensik et al. (1998), who analyze the impact of political variables on capital flight. They consider the positive link between autocracy and capital flight to be so self-evident they do not provide any theoretical support for it, merely stating that the correlation between the two variables should be positive and then proceeding with their estimates.
17. For example, while Turkey can be seen as a democratic country with a long history of deep-rooted corruption, state officials in many communist countries did not accumulate serious personal wealth from their position.

18. For a more detailed commentary on these alternative measures, see the longer version of the article.

19. The largest were Edwards, Matte, Banco Hipoteracio de Chile (BHC) and Lúksic groups, among which Edwards' group was the most powerful.

20. World Bank: World Development Indicators.

21. Extensive privatization did not take off until mid-1975 and it was almost completed in less than a year. Perhaps the most critical element of this process, for the mounting fortunes of internationalist conglomerates, was the privatization of banks, which enabled them to dominate the entire economy.

22. We do not imply that radical neoliberal policies were devised by autonomous economic technocrats liberated from the pressures of the self-interested/short-sighted bourgeoisie. On the contrary, the 'Chicago Boys' formulated and implemented those policies that were particularly beneficial for a privileged group of capitalists, namely the internationalist conglomerates. The authoritarian regime enabled the economic technocracy to serve as the direct representative of one subsection of the bourgeoisie.

23. IMF (1981).

24. In fact, Edwards and Cox-Edwards (1987) go as far as to say that capital controls were irrelevant for the most part and that banking regulation, or the lack thereof, is to blame for the debt crisis. This, however, remains a contentious issue in the economics literature.

25. Given its ingenuity, one of the ways in which this devaluation was achieved and maintained probably deserves mention: a scheme of debt repatriation whereby Chileans could buy the right to buy foreign debt in New York, which was badly undervalued at the time, and sell it to their local bank for Pesos (see Harberger 1993 for details).

26. Measured by the GDP deflator, inflation was above 20 percent for most of the 1980s and only fell below the 10 percent threshold in 1995. (World Bank; World Development Indicators).

27. See Gallego et al. (1999) for more details.

28. In other words, no single group achieved the hegemonic position previously held by financial capitalists with respect to their hold on foreign exchange and control of foreign transactions. In view of the stringency of capital controls imposed by the government, such a position of force might have been necessary to circumvent them.

29. The URR required investors to hold a fixed proportion of the investment in the form of reserves, earning no interest, at the central bank, for a fixed period (usually a year).

30. Even though a URR was put in place in 1991, other restrictions were removed simultaneously and in subsequent years.

31. Admittedly, there is an alternative explanation for the large numbers observed during the crisis years, which pertains to the way we measure capital flight. Changes in exchange rates allow for possible capital gains arising from currency exchanges or from the exchange of assets denominated in different currencies. For example, suppose that one exchanges euros for US dollars; subsequently, the dollar appreciates, so that when the reverse transaction is made, the individual ends up with more euros. The IMF data we use makes provisions for capital gains only when they are realized, such as when the last transaction in the example occurs. However, non-realized capital gains are not captured at all. Consequently, if such capital gains are realized later (but not recorded), not only will they not appear in official statistics, but they will also not be computed in capital flight estimates based on the residual method. In the case of capital gains, this would imply a downward bias in capital flight estimates, while unrecorded capital losses would imply an overestimation of capital flight. Such biases are likely to be most important during periods of crisis as well as when rapid and unexpected changes in exchange rates occur. If there were many unrecorded capital losses during the Asian crisis, then this would present an alternative explanation for our large estimates of capital flight. We would like to thank Florian Kaufmann for pointing this out to us.

REFERENCES

Argosin, Manuel (1998), 'Capital Inflows and Investment Performance: Chile in the 1990s', in R. Ffrench-Davis and H. Reisen (eds), *Capital Flows and Investment Performance: Lessons from Latin America*, OECD Development Studies Centre, pp. 111–146.

Ariyoshi, Akira, Karl Habermeir, Bernard Laurens et al. (2000), 'Capital Controls: Country Experiences with their Use and Liberalization', IMF Occasional Paper No. 190.

Boyce, James and Léonce Ndikumana (1997), 'Congo's Odious Debt: External Borrowing and Capital Flight in Zaïre', *Development and Change*, **29** (2), 195–217.

Boyce, James and Léonce Ndikumana (2001), 'Is Africa a Net Creditor? Estimates of Capital Flight from Severely Indebted Sub-Saharan African Countries, 1970–96' *Journal of Development Studies*, **38** (2), 27–56.

Boyce, James and Léonce Ndikumana (2002), 'Public Debts and Private Assets: Explaining Capital Flight from Sub- Saharan African Countries', University of Massachusetts, Department of Economics and Political Economy Research Institute, Working Paper No. 32, (www.umass.edu/peri/pdfs/WP32.pdf), *World Development*, January 2003.

Cardoso, Fernando H. and Enzo Faletto (1978), *Dependency and Development in Latin America*, Berkeley, California: University of California Press.

CIA World Factbook (2002), available at www.cia.gov/cia/publications/factbook.

Cuddington, John (1986), 'Capital Flight: Estimates, Issues and Explanations', *Princeton Studies in International Finance*, No. 58, Princeton University: Department of Economics.

Daniels, Anthony (2000), 'Of All the Dictators...: Why the Left Singles Out Pinochet', *National Review*, February 7.

Edwards, Sebastian (1998), 'Capital Flows, Real Exchange Rates and Capital Controls: Some Latin American Experiences', NBER Working Paper, No. 6800.

Edwards, Sebastian and Alejandra Cox-Edwards (1987), *Monetarism and Liberalisation: The Chilean Experiment*, Cambridge: Ballinger.

Gallego, Fransisco, Leonardo Hernandez and Klaus Schmidt-Hebbel (1999), 'Capital Controls in Chile: Effective? Efficient?' Central Bank of Chile Working Paper, No. 59.

Harberger, Arnold (1993), 'Secrets of Success: A Handful of Heroes', *American Economic Review*, **83** (2), 343–350.

IMF (1971–78), *Annual Report on Exchange Restrictions*.

IMF (1979–88), *Annual Report on Exchange Arrangements and Exchange Restrictions*.

IMF (1989–98), *Exchange Arrangements and Exchange Restrictions*.

Kant, Chander (2002), 'What is Capital Flight?' *The World Economy*, **25** (3), 341–358.

Lensik, Robert, Niels Hermes and Victor Murinde (1998), 'Capital Flight and Political Risk', SOM Research Reports, No. 98c34, University of Groningen.

Mahon, James E. (1996), *Mobile Capital and Latin American Development*, Pennsylvania: Penn State University Press.

Pastor, Manuel (1989), 'Capital Flight and the Latin American Debt Crisis', mimeo, Washington, D.C.: Economic Policy Institute.

Schneider, Benu (2001), 'Measuring Capital Flight: Estimates and Interpretations', mimeo, London: Overseas Development Institute.

Silva, Eduardo (1993), 'Capitalist Coalitions, the State and Neoliberal Economic Restructuring: Chile, 1973–1988', *World Politics*, **45** (4), 526–559.

Silva, Eduardo (1996), *The State and Capital in Chile: Business Elites, Technocrats and Market Economics*, Boulder: Westview Press.

Silva, Eduardo (1999), 'Organised Business, Neo-Liberal Restructuring and Redemocratisation in Chile', in Fransesco Durand and Eduardo Silva (eds) *Organized Business, Economic Change and Democracy in Latin America*, University of Miami: North-South Center Press, pp. 217–252.

Soederberg, Susanne (2002), 'A Historical Materialist Account of the Chilean Capital Control: Prototype Policy for Whom?', *Review of International Political Economy*, **9** (3), 490–512.

8. Capital Flight from Brazil, 1981–2000

Deger Eryar

INTRODUCTION

Only a few months before the 2002 presidential elections in Brazil, the former US Secretary of Treasury, Paul O'Neill, made a statement reflecting his suspicions about the uses of foreign capital inflows in developing countries. His skepticism as to the efficacy of providing further aid to countries like Brazil was based on the assumption that additional money pumped into the Brazilian economy would end up in Swiss Bank accounts.[1] In short, Mr O'Neill was concerned about potential capital flight from Brazil. Yet, he did not give any explanation, apart from the so-called 'Lula Effect', for the readiness with which external funds coming into Brazil would leave the country.

This chapter will attempt to provide a framework within which the determinants of capital flight from Brazil from 1981 to 2000 can be analyzed. The aim is not to justify the above statement by showing how Lula's economic policy proposals would have been conducive to capital flight, but to show that the existing structure of the economy, especially after the implementation of the Real program in 1994, had already been effective in triggering capital flight by increasing macroeconomic instability in Brazil Although there has been a significant amount of research as to the impact of the transformation of Brazil's economy during the 1990s on macroeconomic variables, this contribution to the literature is different for a number of reasons. First, the amount of capital flight from Brazil from 1983–2000 is measured using the residual method corrected for trade misinvoicing (see Beja, Chapter 3). Furthermore, an institutional-historical analysis is developed to explore the macroeconomic dynamics of the period and to show how the changes in the domestic economic structure accompanied by the volatility in foreign capital flows to Latin America induced domestic residents to engage in capital flight from Brazil.

Generally speaking, capital flight seems to be affected by a loss of confidence in the overall economy. In other words, if the residents of a country perceive macroeconomic instability as a threat to their holdings of domestic assets, they try to switch to holding foreign assets to protect the value of their assets from any sudden changes in government policy, changes that may take the form of a freeze on assets in the banking system or a postponement of interest payments on public debt. Under the conditions of huge external liabilities, such as those of Brazil, then even flight capital of US$1 can be considered a loss to the economy. Given the importance of capital flight for Brazil, this chapter seeks to explain Brazil's failure to attain a stable accumulation path after the debt crisis within a broad macroeconomic framework. Specifically, its emphasis will be on how changes in accumulation strategies from 1981 to 2000 induced residents to engage in capital flight by creating macroeconomic instability in Brazil.

CAPITAL FLIGHT

What is Capital Flight and how is it Measured?

The lack of consensus regarding its definition means that there are a variety of measures of capital flight. Dooley's method (1986) intends to distinguish between normal and abnormal capital flows. According to this method, the assumptions made about the motives of individuals who take their assets beyond the control of domestic authorities constitutes the basic rationale behind capital flight. Therefore, capital flight is measured as the total amount of externally held assets of the private sector that generate income not recorded in the balance of payments statistics of a country. An alternative measure of capital flight is the 'hot money' method (Cuddington 1986), which measures capital flight by adding up net errors and omissions and non-bank short-term capital flows. This method also distinguishes between normal and abnormal outflows, with the latter believed to show up in net errors and omissions. On the other hand, by emphasizing short-term flows only, this method makes an additional assumption about the normal character of medium and long-term flows.

This chapter uses the residual method, which measures capital flight by comparing the sources of capital inflows (that is, net increases in external debt and net inflows of foreign investment) with their uses (that is, the current account deficit and additions to foreign reserves). The amount by which the sources of capital inflows exceed the uses constitutes estimated capital flight. That is,

Capital flight (KF) = (Change in Debt + Net Inflow of Foreign Investment) – (Current Account Deficit + Change in Reserves)

Additionally, since misreported trade figures enable domestic actors to engage in capital flight by providing both a source and mechanism, capital flight figures are adjusted for trade misinvoicing. Trade misinvoicing is determined by comparing trade data from both the importing and exporting countries. Importers are assumed to be involved in capital flight by reporting a higher value for imported goods, while exporters engage in capital flight by reporting lower values for exported goods. Accordingly, comparing trade data of Brazil with the reported data by the industrial countries makes it possible to account for the amount of capital flight based on both underinvoicing of exports and overinvoicing of imports (Ndikumana and Boyce 2002). Therefore,

$$\text{Adjusted Capital Flight} = KF + \text{Misinvoicing}$$

In other words, capital flight in this chapter refers to all resident capital outflows from Brazil, excluding recorded investment abroad (Ndikumana and Boyce 2002). By using this method, it becomes possible to overcome the distinction between normal and abnormal capital flows since the focus will be on the amount of unrecorded capital outflows resulting from structural macroeconomic problems in Brazil rather than on the specific motives of groups or individuals who engage in capital flight. This method also makes it possible to avoid limiting the analysis to short-term capital outflows as in the 'hot money' method, since the long-term outflows contribute even more to the depletion of resources needed for growth in the domestic economy (Hermes et al. 2002).

Why is Capital Flight Important?

In the final quarter of the twentieth century, macroeconomic conditions in Latin America were closely linked to fluctuations in the region's capital inflows. During the second half of the 1970s and in the early 1980s, the region received massive inflows of external credit. This came to an abrupt halt in 1982, giving way to a severe, widespread shortage of external financing.[2] According to Frenkel (2002), the lack of external finance from 1982–90 set the agenda for changes in domestic development strategies culminating in stabilization programs. Supply limitations as a result of foreign exchange scarcity led to slow growth and high inflation in most of the region (Taylor 1999). The stabilization programs of the 1980s attempted to reconcile the external financing constraints with the achievement of three conflicting targets: debt service, inflation reduction, and recovery of a positive rate of growth. Capital flight was particularly crucial in these times, as the countries severely constrained by the lack of international funds after the debt crisis most needed resources to finance economic growth.

External finance started to become abundant again in early 1990s due to the increase in liquidity in international capital markets. Palma (2002) points to the increase in the value of assets of institutional investors between 1988 and 1996 and the relatively low rates of return on capital in developed countries as reasons for this. An additional factor was the development of new financial instruments. At the same time, capital flight started to lose its importance in the literature since most of the developing countries had regained their access to international capital flows and were renegotiating their debts to international commercial banks. Developing countries were able to use the abundant external resources both to sustain their growth rates and debt payments; capital flight no longer presented a problem.

Despite the positive changes in international capital markets, the capital flows would not have been directed to Latin America if the countries in the region had not made the necessary changes to their macroeconomic policies. The combined effects of liberalization of both capital and current accounts, the gradual withdrawal of the state from the markets along with massive privatization and deregulation in most markets attracted external capital to Latin America in the 1990s. However, these changes in the international environment and gradual financial integration of Latin America with the global economy also generated increased domestic economic fragility and vulnerability to international shocks.

From 1991 to 1994, a new wave of capital entered the region, only to be followed by another sharp contraction in late 1994 and early 1995. In the wake of the crisis in 1996 and 1997, capital again became abundant. Then, with the onset of the Asian crisis in the second half of the 1997, the Russian crisis in August 1998, and the Brazilian one in 1999, capital inflows to the region continued to exhibit considerable volatility (ECLAC 2002). These changes in the structures of both international capital flows and the domestic economies were important influences on capital flight. Particularly, the crisis period saw significant jumps in the amount of capital flight from many developing countries (Hermes et al. 2002).

CAPITAL FLIGHT FROM THE BRAZILIAN ECONOMY, 1983–2000

Analytical Framework

In identifying the determinants of capital flight from Brazil, it is necessary to give an account of how the specific configuration of the Brazilian economy between 1983 and 2000, along with the volatility of international capital flows, induced domestic residents to engage in capital flight. The structural impact of macroeconomic instability on capital flight is emphasized, without necessarily singling out the motives of individual actors. In the literature, different indicators have been used to capture the level of instability of the macroeconomic structure. These indicators include, among others, the inflation rate, budget deficit, interest rate, and the exchange rate. Instead of exploring them as independent indicators and evaluating their separate impacts on macroeconomic stability over a given period, this chapter explores how the combined effects of these indicators under a particular accumulation strategy can induce capital flight.[3]

The government and its interventions in the economy play a crucial role in ensuring the continuous accumulation of capital. To have a better understanding of macroeconomic instability in Brazil, it is also necessary to examine the dynamic relationship between accumulation strategies and various forms of government intervention. However, the different paths taken by the government as an institution are both enabled and constrained not only by the domestic actors in the economy but also by the international actors and their strategies. Therefore, the combined effects of the above indicators on macroeconomic instability, and hence on capital flight, can be better understood by investigating the interplay between the state and domestic capital and their access to international capital flows. Such a framework can be more helpful in exploring the determinants of capital flight than a formal analysis of individual indicators, which does not necessarily capture the impact of the changing institutional and historical context.

Periodization

To capture the impact of the different accumulation strategies pursued in Brazil, the period of time under investigation is divided into two parts. The first period, 1981–89, is best described as a transitional period during which Brazil tried to find a solution to the problems of the state-led development strategy that had been the dominant accumulation strategy for the last 50 years. To cope with stagnant growth and a high chronic inflation rate (and sometimes hyperinflation), especially after the international debt crisis triggered by the Mexican default in August 1982, Brazil pursued a mixture of orthodox and heterodox stabilization policies; these policies, however, did not have a significant impact on growth and inflation rates (see Table 8.1).

The second period is characterized by the adoption of neoliberal policies, including current and capital account liberalization, deregulation and privatization, which took place throughout the 1990s. The same period is called the 'growth-cum-foreign saving' period since the above domestic policy changes were accompanied by renewed access to international capital flows in the early 1990s (Pereira et al. 2002). This section is further divided into two sub-periods. 1990–94 was not very different from the preceding period in terms of inflation and growth rates in spite of substantial policy changes (Table 8.1). The last period, 1995–2000, is best characterized by the new accumulation strategy that ushered in the full-fledged implementation of

Table 8.1   Inflation, growth and labor productivity

Years	Inflation (GDP deflator)	Growth in real GDP per capita	Productivity growth
1948–1980	45.3	4.40	4.1
1981–1989	341.2	1.28	0.6
1990–1994	1643.6	–0.77	1.0
1995–2000[a]	8.96	1.2	2.8[b]
1990–2000[a]	653.3	0.63	1.8[b]

Notes:
[a]Own calculations for the 1995 to 2000 period.
[b]Figure goes up to 1999

Source: Vernengo 2003

neo-liberal policies to promote both stable growth and low inflation accompanied by continuous flows of international capital.   Only in this period was Brazil able to create a political consensus on neo-liberal policies among the different groups in society, mostly through the implementation of a successful stabilization policy that was reflected in low and stable inflation rates.

However, the internal mechanism of this strategy, the high interest rates used to attract foreign capital, along with a deteriorating trade balance in the face of an overvalued currency, set the parameters for a fragile domestic economy. Additionally, the substantial integration of the Brazilian economy into the international financial architecture, together with growing external liabilities, made the country more vulnerable to the contagion effects of the major financial crises of this period. In the end, Brazil was forced to switch to a floating exchange rate system to curb the speculative attacks on the real. The only success of this period was in terms of lower inflation rates; indeed, all the efforts to liberalize the economy culminated in lower growth rates, even in comparison to the 'lost decade' of the 1980s (Vernengo 2003).

The rest of the chapter investigates the determinants of both the magnitude and volatility of the capital flight from Brazil during these periods. The aim is to discover the links between capital flight and the combined effects of macroeconomic indicators and to analyze how macroeconomic instability arising out of different economic and institutional settings can be conducive to capital flight.

Real Capital Flight

Table 8.2 gives estimates of real capital flight from Brazil during the period under study.

Table 8.2   Estimates of capital flight

Years	Capital Flight (in 1995 US$ billions)	Capital Flight as a share of GDP (%)
1981–2000	5.7	1.08
1981–1989	2.85	0.83
1990–2000	8	1.29
1990–1994	5.75	1.2
1995–2000	9.95	1.36
1996–2000	16	2.22

Source: Based on author's calculations.

The residual method, corrected for misinvoicing, is used to calculate the annual amount of capital flight from Brazil from 1981 to 2000. Real capital flight, measured in 1995 US dollars, shows an annual average of $5.7 billion. However, the figures differ significantly at different periods (see Table 8.2 and Figure 8.1). In the first period (1981–89), the annual average is only about $2.8 billion; the figure rises to $10 billion in the last period ($16 billion if 1995, when the country experienced reverse capital flight, is excluded). Real capital flight peaks in 1998, reaching almost $43 billion.

Capital Flight as a share of GDP

Capital flight as a share of GDP provides an indicator of the opportunity cost of capital flight relative to the overall level of economic activity (see Table 8.2 and Figure 8.2). For the entire period the annual average of capital flight is slightly above 1 percent of GDP. However, a comparison of the sub-periods shows that most of the capital flight occurred when Brazil was undergoing the fully-fledged implementation of neoliberal policies. In this period, excluding 1995, the average annual capital flight as a share of GDP is twice as much as that for the whole period.

Trade Misinvoicing

All of the estimates of capital flight above include misinvoicing. The main assumption regarding the importance of this issue lies in the fact that trade

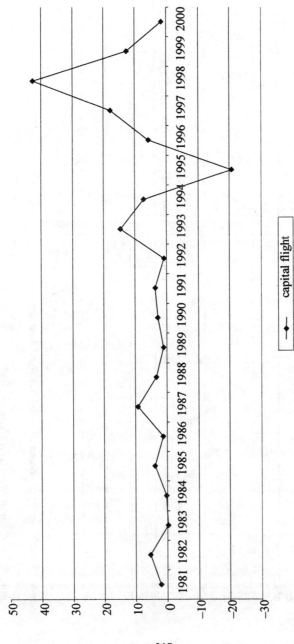

Source: Author's own calculations based on IMF and World Bank data.

Figure 8.1 Capital flight (in 1995 US$ billions)

217

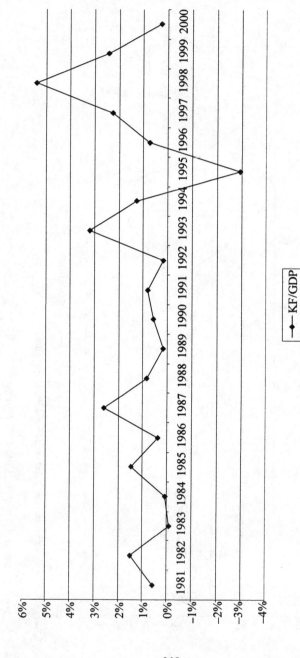

Source: Author's own calculations based on IMF and World Bank data.

Figure 8.2   Capital flight as a share of GDP

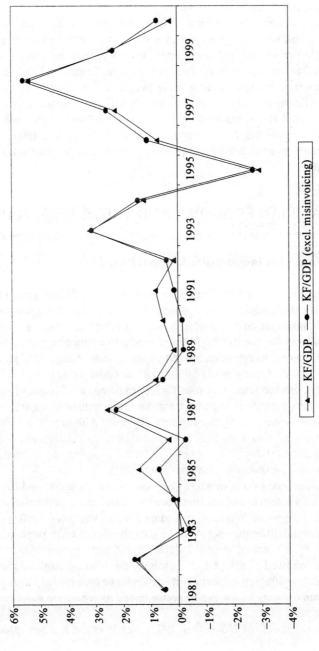

Source: Author's own calculations based on the IMF and World Bank data.

Figure 8.3 Capital Flight as a share of GDP with and without misinvoicing

misinvoicing, in the face of macroeconomic instability, can be considered a source for capital flight. Either through export underinvoicing or import overinvoicing, residents of a country can hide foreign currency from domestic authorities (see Figure 8.3).

When comparing the capital flight estimates with and without misinvoicing (both in real terms and as a share of GDP), the overall impact for the whole period does not seem important. Whereas the yearly average estimation of capital flight is US$5.7 billion as indicated in Table 8.2, the same average for misinvoicing is no more than US$56 million (0.056 percent of GDP). However, trade misinvoicing is still an important factor in explaining capital flight, particularly for the years between 1983 and 1992, when Brazil was severely constrained by the lack of access to international funds. A more detailed analysis of this observation will be undertaken later in the chapter.

THE BRAZILIAN ECONOMY AND THE DETERMINANTS OF CAPITAL FLIGHT

Import Substitution Industrialization (ISI) Period

In the ISI period, which lasted until the early 1980s, different governments pursued fairly successful state-led industrial development strategies through unorthodox interventionist policies. A striking feature of state-led development was the massive build-up of productive capacity, particularly in the areas of energy, heavy industry and capital goods (Palma 2002). These investments, either directly made by the state or under its supervision by the private sector, created important uses for external capital. This development strategy rested on political support from domestic industrial capital, which was under the protection of the military regime. Although the industrial working class was also a partner in this coalition, its relative share of the benefits was minimal due to the oppressive military regime and its immediate impact on working-class organizations (Baer 2001).

As a consequence of this massive state-led industrialization, and the large size of Brazil's internal market, the country experienced particularly rapid growth after the Second World War (Palma 2002). Vernango (2003) points out the substantial difference between the growth rates of GDP per capita and productivity in this era of state-led development strategy and those of the periods that followed (Table 8.1). However, the internal contradictions of this accumulation strategy, especially its dependence on external funds given the inadequate capacity of the export sector, made its long-term sustainability rather difficult.

With the oil shock of November 1973, Brazil entered a new phase of development. New president Geisel tried to sustain the development process of Brazil as the new administration tried to keep up with its higher oil bills by maintaining high growth rates. In 1975, he introduced the Second National Development Plan, which focused on making new investments to expand productive capacity in the near future. Instead of engaging in an austerity adjustment program to cope with the dramatic decline in the country's terms of trade, the government opted for a growth policy that resulted in a rapid expansion of the country's international debt (Baer 2001). Brazil's external indebtedness initially worsened after the sudden interest rate increases in 1979, and then became a major problem after the international debt crisis triggered by the Mexican default in 1982 (Figure 8.4).

The 'Lost Decade': Struggling with the Debt Crisis (1981–89)

This period, which was characterized by high levels of inflation and stagnant growth rates, is frequently referred to as the 'lost decade'. Brazil was unable to pursue high growth rates after 1980 because productive investments could not be undertaken, given the lack of foreign capital flows after the debt crisis and the related changes in the institutional capacity of the state in this new context. Under the previous accumulation strategy, the state had been very effective in promoting investment in the economy both directly through state-owned corporations (in key industries such as energy, steel, mining and railroads) and also indirectly through different forms of subsidies to the private sector. Until 1982, the state was still able to finance its interventions in the domestic economy through external borrowing.

After the debt crisis, however, the state faced a growing problem of public deficits (operational budget deficits). This became more explicit when the government assumed the debts of the private sector right after the debt crisis.[4]This transfer of external liabilities from the private sector to the government deserves particular attention to understand the dynamics between the government and capitalist sector during the crisis of accumulation. The government's particular form of intervention at this stage paved the way for future problems of accumulation. To cover its interest payments, the state had to reduce its financing of investment and its social expenditure. In other words, the economy needed to shrink. The investment rate declined from 24 percent in 1980 to 16.7 percent in 1989 as a percentage of GDP (Pereira and Bresser 1996). Similar adjustment policies were implemented mostly through military interventions in other developing countries that suffered from balance of payments problems. Ironically, how ever, the implementation of adjustment policies was one of the main factors contributing to the end of Brazil's military regime in 1985. Although the public deficit was reduced by severe cuts in public investment and social spending, the transition to democracy in 1985 and the adoption of populist

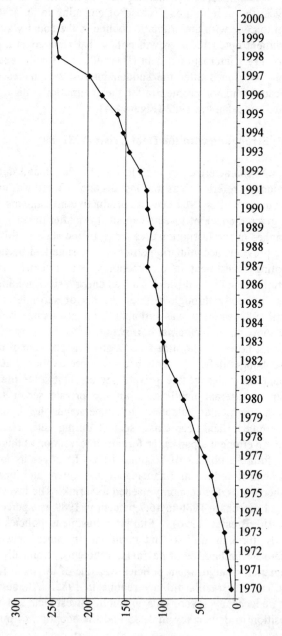

Source: World Bank debt tables from various years.

Figure 8.4 Total external debt (in 1995 US$ billions)

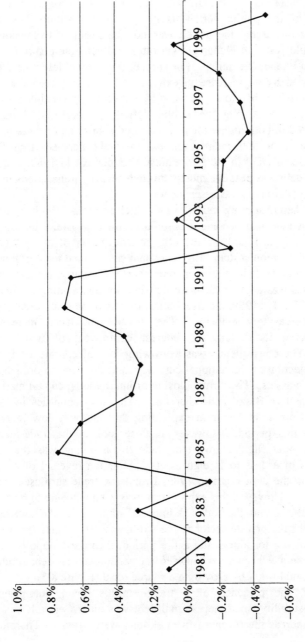

Source: Author's own calculations based on the IMF and World Bank data.

Figure 8.5   Total misinvoicing as a share of GDP

policies in the Sarney administration (1985–89) resulted in higher public deficits after 1984.[5]

The size of the public deficit emerges as an important indicator of macroeconomic instability in Brazil. However, the main problem was not the magnitude of the public deficit itself, but its opportunity cost and financing. For one thing, the deficit was not the result of expansionary policies that could result in higher growth rates and generate a surplus that could be used to finance the deficit. For another, the public deficit could no longer be financed by an increase in external debt, as had been the case before the debt crisis; it had to be financed by increasing internal debt or by printing money. Financing the public deficit by increased domestic borrowing resulted in both higher interest rates and shorter maturity terms of bonds. The interest on both internal and external debt increased from 0.85 percent as a share of GDP in 1979 to almost 12.3 percent in 1989, and the financing of the debt was possible mostly through security transactions in the overnight market (Pereira and Bresser 1996).

On the other hand, printing money would fuel an already high inflation rate. Inflation, which had become a chronic problem in Brazil during the mid-1970s, was related mainly to the oligopolistic power of many sectors and also to the indexation system. Both mechanisms enabled most groups in the economy to protect their relative income shares.[6]Similarly, indexation of government bonds was another factor responsible for aggravating the public deficit (Baer 2001). By 1989, the fiscal crisis in which the state found itself had become increasingly evident. The government faced increasing difficulty financing its deficit, the interest component of which was unsustainable. The consequence was a growing loss of confidence in the economy, the rejection of the national currency, and the need to protect the value of domestic assets. The virtual closing of international capital markets to finance the debt in Brazil and other Latin American countries in 1982 seems to be an important factor in explaining the relatively low level of capital flight in this period. However, a close look at the trade-related component of capital flight shows that trade misinvoicing was the only important means of access to foreign assets. After the reversal of capital inflows following the debt crisis in 1982, Brazil ran trade surpluses every year from 1983 on. However, this export surplus was an outcome of both the massive devaluations and the reduced imports, rather than the increased competitiveness of the private sector in the world markets. Since there was export underinvoicing for almost the entire period, then these trade policies that aimed to generate foreign exchange to repay the external debt actually contributed to capital flight by providing a source for it (Figure 8.5).

Furthermore, the presence of a trade surplus could not provide macroeconomic stability since the external debt was almost entirely a state responsibility, whereas the revenues from exports were private. Therefore, the persistence of the fiscal deficit contributed to macroeconomic instability throughout the period. Particularly, the spike in capital flight in 1985 corresponds to the increase in total internal debt as a share of GDP. This rise in the volume of internal debt was mostly influenced by the expansion of social spending during the transition to democracy. Another period of significant capital flight in 1987 can also be related to the moratorium on external debt payments. Since the debt-service ratio in 1986 had reached over 90 percent of exports in Brazil and there was little access to 'new money' in international capital markets, the government, which owned a significant portion of the external debt, had to suspend its payments on medium and long-term debt. In both cases, macroeconomic instability, which manifested itself mostly in the government's difficulties in financing the public deficit, provided an environment favorable to capital flight.

Despite the steep inflation rates for this period, there is no clear line of causation between high inflation and macroeconomic instability. There are two reasons for this. First, through the system of indexation, those actors who financed the public deficit were protected from any erosion in the value of their assets. Second, the oligopolistic structure of the manufacturing sector made it possible for producers to pass their cost increases on to the consumers. Hence, the persistence and acceleration of inflation is regarded, not as an individual factor contributing to macroeconomic instability, but as an indicator of the fiscal problems of the government.

Liberalization in the Face of High Inflation (1990–94)

The election of Collor in 1990 marked the beginning of a new era in Brazil: the gradual introduction of neoliberal economic policies in Brazil. The new president announced a comprehensive program to deal with chronic high inflation, high public deficits and stagnant growth rates. The Collor government also began a process of trade liberalization, which was based on the removal of subsidies for exports and staggered reductions in tariffs.

His program included a temporary freeze on wages and prices, aimed at reducing the rate of inflation. To reduce the budget deficit, Collor gradually reduced all fiscal incentives (for imports, exports, agriculture and industry) and eliminated the indexation of taxes to reduce tax evasion. One novel feature of this program was an 18-month monetary moratorium that affected about 80 percent of domestic financial assets[7] and which can be thought of as a moratorium on domestic debt since most of the public debt was financed in the overnight markets. However, due to the absence of popular support for this policy, it lasted only two months (Pereira and Bresser 1996). The pressure from various socio-economic groups led the govern- ment to release many frozen financial assets ahead of schedule. Despite this, a budget surplus was recorded for the first time in 1990. However, this surplus was mostly due to artificial or temporary measures, such as the once-and-for-all tax on financial assets, the suspension of debt servicing accomplished by the assets freeze, and the lateness of government payments to suppliers (Baer 2001). The immediate impact of these policies can be seen in the rise in capital flight between 1990 and 1991. The ad hoc surplus in the budget was not enough to convince various actors that macroeconomic stability had been achieved. The successive shocks and price/wage freezes were not accompanied by the necessary structural fiscal adjustments; the policies aimed at fiscal and monetary austerity were insufficient to attain a reversal of expectations, which was crucial for an effective stabilization program. Thus, these heterodox stabilization programs rapidly lost their credibility (Baer 2001).

The same period also saw renewed access to international capital after the rescheduling of Brazil's debt and the gradual opening up of the capital account. Yet, since the government could not generate the much needed confidence in the economy, the increased inflow of external funds induced residents to initiate a new wave of capital flight. Additionally, in 1992, escalating corruption charges and private scandals led to the resignation of President Collor, contributing to the overall decline in confidence. In 1993, the amount of capital flight as a share of GDP rose to above 3 percent.

Plano Real (1995–2000)

The Plano Real, the new plan initiated in the summer of 1994 by Cardoso, the winner of the presidential elections held that year, has been the most successful in stabilizing the economy. From the outset, its central premise was that only by slashing inflation could an attractive investment climate be created for foreign investment by multinationals in Brazil, and only massive inflows of such productive capital from abroad could provide a sound basis for long-term domestic growth (Rocha 2002). Figure 8.6 shows both the growing amount and the composition of inflows. Although a substantial amount of capital inflows came in the form of portfolio flows immediately after the country's renewed access to international capital markets, FDI became the dominant component of capital inflows following the massive privatization of the Cardoso era.

The program attempted to curb inflation by different means. First, the new currency was pegged to the US$ to lower inflationary expectations. The indexation system was dismantled to reduce inflation inertia. These policies were initially successful: inflation rates declined rapidly, aggregate demand expanded, and the country seemed poised for an extended period of growth stimulated by capital inflows. Stabilization was supplemented by trade liberalization and the overvaluation of the real due to massive capital inflows (Saad-Filho and Morais 2000).

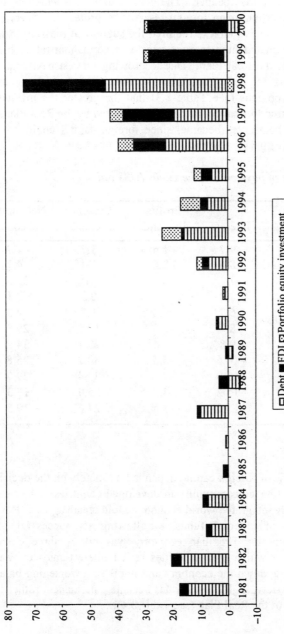

Source: IMF Financial Statistics and World Bank debt tables.

Figure 8.6   Net capital flows (in 1995 USD billions)

However, there was a huge jump in imports due to overvaluation of the currency. Between 1994 and 2000, Brazil ran steady trade deficits. Although an exchange rate peg can fight inflation in the short run, it worsens the trade balance by making imports cheaper. The combination of a widening trade deficit and the need to build up foreign reserves to protect the overvalued currency against speculative attacks required the support of massive inflows of capital that necessitated high interest rates as a permanent rather than a temporary feature of the Real Plan. Due to growing interest payments and repatriation of profits, the deficit on current account also soared in the same period. It became obvious (see Table 8.3) that the greater the inflows of foreign capital required to finance the deficits generated by the Real Plan, the larger the deficits themselves became, since foreign capital could not but aggravate the negative balances it financed (Rocha 2002).

Table 8.3   Balance of payments in the 1990s (US$ billions)

Year	Trade balance	Interest	Profits dividends	Current account	Net capital account
1990	10.7	−9.7	−1.6	−3.7	−4.7
1991	10.5	−8.6	−0.6	−1.4	−4.1
1992	15.2	−7.2	−0.7	6.1	25.2
1993	13.3	−8.4	−1.9	−0.5	10.1
1994	10.4	−6.3	−2.4	−1.7	14.3
1995	−3.4	−8.1	−2.5	−17.9	29.3
1996	−5.5	−9.8	−2.4	−23.1	34.2
1997	−8.3	−10.6	−5.5	−30.7	25.8
1998	−6.5	−11.9	−7.0	−33.4	29.7
1999	−1.2	−15.2	−4.0	−25.4	17.3
2000	−0.6	−15.0	−3.5	−24.6	19.3

Source: Rocha (2002).

The continued inflow of foreign capital depended ultimately on the decisions of the international finance community in developed countries. A crisis in any part of the highly integrated world economy could create a panic, leading to the withdrawal of external funds. Following its successful price stabilization program, the Brazilian economy was hit by three external shocks, after each of which the authorities raised interest rates to reduce capital outflows, slow down the economy and improve a worsening balance of payments. Ultimately, high interest rates became a permanent rather than a temporary feature of the Real Plan (see Table 8.4).

Table 8.4   Real interest rates (1990–2000 for all countries, except 1995–2000 in Brazil)

Country	Average	High
Indonesia	4.9	49.1
Korea	6.2	18.1
Malaysia	2.6	8.6
Thailand	3.9	15
Philippines	5.5	17
Mexico	5.5	29.6
Brazil	18	40.6

Source: IMF (2003).

Since the success of a stabilization program depends on continuous foreign capital inflows, the interest rate was the main instrument for attracting these flows. However, each surge in the interest rate in the face of crisis worsened the fiscal fragility of the state, which depended mostly on domestic debt to finance its deficit. These high interest rates also aggravated the situation of industrial capital, particularly those sectors that had to compete with cheap imports as the result of an overvalued domestic currency.

It is also clear from Table 8.5 that the public deficit was not fiscal, but monetary Most of the deficit was comprised of interest payments as a result of high real interest rates; the problem of a high level of public domestic debt was compounded by the sterilization policies used by the central bank in the face of growing capital inflows.

Table 8.5   Deficit and public debt (% of GDP)

Year	Primary deficit	Operational deficit	Net public debt
1994	5.3	1.4	29.2
1995	0.4	–4.9	30.5
1996	–0.1	–3.8	33.3
1997	–1.0	–4.3	34.5
1998	0.01	–7.5	42.4
1999	3.2	–9.4	49.5
2000	3.5	–1.2	52

Source: Vernengo (2003).

An important element of the new growth strategy was the privatization of state-owned enterprises, a policy that attracted more foreign capital especially after 1996. The government also relied to a large extent on the privatization process to deal with the growing budget deficit. This process had already begun in the early 1990s, but accelerated as it was expanded to include public utilities such as telecommunications or power distribution. Along with privatization, mergers and acquisitions were the other sources of growing FDI. Overall, FDI was geared towards buying existing plants, rather than building new ones and thus expanding production and boosting employment (Rocha 2002). One can argue that the receipts from the mere change in ownership of capital, if not reinvested in domestic productive activity, would simply add to the holdings of external funds ready to flee the country in the form of capital flight.

In attempting to identify the determinants of capital flight after the implementation of the Real Plan, the reversal of capital flight in 1995 deserves special attention. In December 1994, the world witnessed the first major crisis in a developing country – Mexico; the immediate response was a speculative attack on the Real. However, the Cardoso administration was successful in countering this with a dramatic increase in real interest rates (up to 40.6 percent when average inflation was around 22 percent in 1995), and also by depleting its foreign exchange reserves (Rocha 2002). This earned Cardoso the approval of the international community, an approval that seems to have been shared by the residents of Brazil who started to sell their foreign assets and acquire domestic assets to benefit from the new opportunities in their home country. Nevertheless, the increase in interest rates also paved the way for future macroeconomic instability by generating huge public deficits from 1995 onwards.

After the Mexican crisis, Brazil had to cope with two more crises in the years that followed. Similar defense mechanisms – hikes in interest rates – made the government's task more difficult by increasing its domestic debt burden. An overvalued currency further worsened the trade deficit and denied Brazil the option of generating foreign exchange from trade. At the same time, the share of external debt held by the private sector was growing. Alternative ways for the government to curb budget deficits were to slash public expenditure and speed up the privatization process.

The impact of high interest rates on the structure of internal public debt in the face of growing budget deficits, the growing balance of payments deficits that resulted from an overvalued currency, and a ratio of foreign debt to GDP that was approaching debt-crisis level were the factors that contributed to economic instability and loss of confidence in the sustainability of the new growth strategy.[8] Under these conditions, first the Asian crisis, and then the Russian crisis the following year triggered capital flight from Brazil in 1997 and 1998. After a renewed speculative attack on the real following a moratorium declared by one of the states towards the end of 1998, the government abandoned its defense of the currency and allowed it to float early in 1999. Nonetheless, capital flight in 1999 was not as intensive as it had been the previous year.

This relative decline in the capital flight even in the face of continuous capital inflows and a consistently worsening macroeconomic instability can be better understood if we look at the private sector's attempts to reduce their risk. To secure its rollover after the Asian and Russian crises, about a third of the domestic debt was now indexed to the US$. Although it was widely accepted that the currency had been overvalued throughout the Real Plan, banks that had been large holders of dollar-linked government debt in their portfolios reported record profits as a result of future positions taken in anticipation of the depreciation of the currency (Kregel 2001). On the other hand, the IMF bailout of $41.5 billion in 1998 also created the impression that Brazil did not need to be afraid of another debt crisis.

CONCLUSION

This chapter has attempted to explore the determinants of capital flight from Brazil between 1981 and 2000 and to show that capital flight is stimulated by growing macroeconomic instability, which induces residents to engage in capital flight by creating a loss of confidence in the overall economy. Instead of a formal statistical analysis, a historical and institutional analysis of the given period was used to investigate the relationship between individual macroeconomic indicators and the changes in capital flight. The choice of historical-institutional analysis is justified by recognizing that macroeconomic instability has always been an outcome of structural changes in the accumulation process, whose dynamics are both enabled and constrained by the interplay between the state on the one hand, and domestic and international actors on the other. By looking at specific historical-institutional settings it is possible to gain a better understanding of why a country cannot generate enough surpluses to cover its external liabilities, or why, in the first place, these countries need external funds to finance their growth strategies. Only after making this broader analysis can we conceptualize capital flight as an effect rather than a cause of the structural problems of developing economies, such as that of Brazil.

One of the major discoveries of this analysis has been the persistence of capital flight over the entire period. Although the volume of capital flight on average seems to have been relatively low in comparison to other developing countries, its peak was reached during a period when the Brazilian economy had been successfully integrated into the world economy as a result of major institutional changes, particularly capital account liberalization. Although the state had implemented all the required policy changes to attract foreign capital to bridge its 'resource gap', the same period also witnessed a continued loss of confidence by the residents of Brazil regarding the overall functioning of this new growth strategy. If capital flight is considered a major problem for developing countries, especially in times when these countries need the foreign exchange to cover their external liabilities, then any policy proposal to reverse capital flight should go hand in hand with other policy changes to shift the direction of accumulation towards a more productive, employment-generating and equity-enhancing growth process.

NOTES

I would like to thank all members of the Capital Flight Group and Nuria Malet for their valuable suggestions and comments on earlier drafts of this chapter. The usual disclaimers apply.

1. Latin American Weekly Report, 6 August 2002.
2. The region remained practically isolated from international capital markets between the debt crisis in Mexico (1982) and the signing of the first Brady Plan to restructure external debt in 1990 (Frenkel 2002, p.256).
3. An accumulation strategy defines a specific economic growth model complete with its various extra-economic preconditions and also outlines a general strategy appropriate to its realization (Jessop1990).
4. In the early 1980s, private firms paid their debts in local currency to the government, usually at an overvalued exchange rate. This practice, in addition to shifting the foreign debt to the state, subsidized the private sector and increased the budget deficit (Pereira and Bresser 1996).
5. 8.3 percent in 1979, 2.7 percent in 1984, and 12.4 percent in 1989 (all figures show the public deficit as a ratio of GDP).
6. Even the organized sections of the working class had some limited benefits from the indexation system (Baer 2001).
7. Eighty percent of all deposits in the overnight market, transaction and savings accounts were frozen for 18 months, receiving during this period a return of the prevailing rate of inflation plus 6 percent a year (Baer 2001).
8. Vernengo (2003) points to the explosive growth of foreign debt in two quite different accumulation strategies. The first one occurred at a time when state-led development was complete for the most part, and the second one took place after the implementation of an outward-oriented neoliberal strategy based on entirely different priorities.

REFERENCES

Baer, Werner (2001), *The Brazilian Economy: Growth and Development*, Westport, CT: Praeger.

Cuddington, J. T. (1986), 'Capital Flight, Issues and Explanations', *Princeton Studies in International Finance*, **58**, Princeton, NJ: Princeton University.

Dooley, M. P. (1986), 'Country-specific Risk Premiums, Capital Flight, and Net Investment Income Payments in selected Developing Countries', Washington, DC: IMF, Unpublished manuscript.

ECLAC (2002), *Globalization and Development*, Santiago, Chile: United Nations, Economic Commission for Latin America and the Caribbean.

Frenkel, Roberto (2002), 'Capital Market Liberalization and Economic Performance in Latin America', in J. Eatwell and L. Taylor (eds), *International Capital Markets*, New York: Oxford University Press.

Hermes, Niels, Robert Lensink and Victor Murinde (2002), 'Flight Capital and its Reversal for Development Financing', UN-WIDER, Discussion Paper 99.

IMF (2003), 'The IMF and Recent Capital Account Crises', Evaluation Report, Washington, DC: International Monetary Fund.

Jessop, Bob (1990), *State Theory: Putting the Capitalist State in its Place*, University Park, PA: Pennsylvania State University Press.

Kregel, Jan (2001), 'The Brazilian Crisis: From Inertial Inflation to Fiscal Fragility', Working Paper, Jerome Levy Economics Institute.

Mahon, J., Jr. (1996), *Mobile Capital and Latin American Development*, Pennsylvania: The Pennsylvania State University Press.

Ndikumana, Léonce and James K. Boyce (2002), 'Public Debts and Private Assets: Explaining Capital flight from Sub-Saharan African Countries', University of Massachusetts, Department of Economics and Political Economy Research Institute, Working Paper 32, www.umass.edu/peri/pdfs/WP32.pdf, *World Development*, January 2003.

Palma, Gabriel (2000), 'The Magical Realism of Brazilian Economics: How to Create a Financial Crisis by Trying to Avoid One', CEPA Working Paper Series 17.

Palma, Gabriel (2002), 'The Three Routes to Financial Crises: The Need for Capital Controls', in J. Eatwell and L. Taylor (eds), *International Capital Markets,* New York: Oxford University Press.

Pereira, L., C. Bresser and Yoshiaki Nakano (2002), 'Economic Growth with Foreign Saving', www.bresserpereira.org.br.

Pereira, L. and C. Bresser (1996), *Economic Crisis and State Reform in Brazil*, Boulder: Lynne Riener.

Rocha, G. M. (2002), 'Neo-Dependency in Brazil', *New Left Review*, No. 16.

Saad-Filho, A. and Lecio Morais (2000), 'Neomonetarist dreams and realities in Brazil', in Paul Davidson (ed.), *A Post Keynesian Perspective on 21st Century Economic Problems*, Cheltenham, UK and Northampton, MA, USA: Edward Elgar.

Taylor, Lance (1999), 'Introduction' in Lance Taylor (ed.), *After Neoliberalism: What Next for Latin America*, Ann Harbor: The University of Michigan Press.

Tingas, N. and P. Miguel (2001), 'Capital Flows and Economic Policy in Brazil', in B. N. Ghosh (ed.), *Global Financial Crises and Reforms*, New York: Routledge.

Vernengo, Matias (2003), 'Late Globalization and Maladjustment: The Brazilian Reforms in Retrospective', Working Paper in IDEAS, www.networkideas.org.

9. A Development Comparative Approach to Capital Flight: the Case of the Middle East and North Africa, 1970–2002

Abdullah Almounsor

INTRODUCTION

Capital flight from developing countries represents lost potential for economic growth and development. In the contemporary literature of development economics, increasing attention has been paid to the notion of capital flight, with many analysts attributing sluggish economic growth and persistent balance of payments deficits in developing countries to capital flight (Onwioduokit 2001). In addition, capital flight has other adverse consequences for developing countries. First, it reduces the ability of the banking system to create money for investment projects. Second, and probably most importantly, the loss of capital affects income distribution by eroding the domestic tax base and by redistributing income from the poor to the rich (Pastor 1990; Ajayi 1997).

The literature also highlights several routes of capital flight from developing countries. Prime among these are external borrowing and trade misinvoicing. Other authors have cited the risk of inflation, taxation, political risk and instability, financial repression, weak institutions, ineffectiveness of macroeconomic policies, business cycles, overvaluation of exchange rates and a poor investment climate as some of the factors that contribute to capital flight (Hermes, Lensink and Murinde 2002; Schneider 2003; Boyce and Ndikumana 2002).

There are several measures of capital flight; these include the hot money measure, the balance of payments measure and the residual measure, which is the most widely used (Schneider 2003; Hermes, Lensink and Murinde 2002). The residual measure, a broad measure based on the discrepancies between sources of foreign exchange (capital inflows) and uses of those funds (capital outflows), is more inclusive and therefore gives a measure of capital flight that takes into account most capital flows between nations including external debt, foreign direct investment, and portfolio investment. Capital flight, according to this approach, comprises the surplus of capital inflows over foreign exchange outflows that are not recorded in government official statistics.

This chapter makes use of the residual approach to estimate capital flight from the Middle East and North Africa (MENA).[1] To the best of my knowledge, this is the first set of estimates of capital flight from the MENA region utilizing the residual approach, focusing exclusively on the region and covering such a wide range of countries in the region.[2]

The rest of the chapter is organized as follows. Section two provides a brief discussion of the economic, political and historical background of the MENA region. Section three presents the methodology used in the estimation of capital flight from the MENA region. The fourth section presents a description of capital flight from the region based on the reported figures. The last section provides policy implications and conclusions.

BACKGROUND ON MENA

The countries of the Middle East and North Africa have a shared heritage, language and culture, as well as similar political structures. However, their factor endowments are substantially different. While some are resource-rich and labor-scarce states (the countries of the Gulf Cooperation Council), others are resource-rich and labor-abundant states (such as Algeria and Iran), and the rest are resource-poor and labor-rich states (such as Egypt, Jordan and Morocco).[3] Standards of living as well as the sizes of economies also differ vastly among the countries of the region (see Table 9.1 for macroeconomic indicators).[4]

The political structures of the MENA region are traditional and persistent. Regardless of the nominal type of regime, the political elites continue to resist political reforms that they perceive as threatening to the status quo. The continuity of the current political organization in the countries of the region is widely regarded as the prime reason behind the marginalization of popular politics and is the product of domestic socioeconomic and political environments – not external manipulation. Ultimately, the monopoly of the state over resources and decision-making activities, outside of the purview of civil society, hinders popular participation in fostering long-term prosperity of the countries of the region (see Abootalebi 1999). In addition, the quality of institutions in the MENA region is low by international standards.[5]

The globalization process has had little success in the MENA region. In terms of economic integration, the MENA Region lags considerably behind the rest of the world.[6] According to a World Bank study, the region's trade has grown at 3 percent in the last decade, compared to 8 percent for the rest of the world. The major Latin American and East Asian countries have made consistent inroads into the region's import markets, while the region's exports have been unable to significantly penetrate the markets of Latin America and

Table 9.1 Macroeconomic indicators, period average 1970–2002

Country	GDP per capita (1995 USD)	Growth rate of GDP (%)	Growth rate of per capita GDP (%)	Inflation (%)	Unemployment (%)	Current account balance (% of GDP)
Algeria	1576	3.9	1.14	11.03	20.4	(2.24)
Bahrain	9,392	3.2	(0.1)	5.15	2.3	0.15
Comoros	499	2	(0.52)	–	–	(7.7)
Djibouti	1,135	(0.65)	(5)	11.03	43.5	(10)
Egypt	822.98	5.5	3.2	5.15	7.8	(4.9)
Iran	1,610.2	1.94	(0.8)	17.57	–	2.9
Iraq	–	(12.25)	(15.07)	–	–	12.8
Jordan	1,593	8	3.9	7.42	14.4	(2.13)
Kuwait	16,717.5	2.3	(2.6)	5.04	–	25
Lebanon	2,286	(18)	(18.4)	–	8.6	(6)
Libya	–	(3.8)	(5.4)	–	–	4
Mauritania	476.7	2.83	0.19	6.7	28.9	(11)
Morocco	1,159.5	4.05	1.86	6.4	16.6	(5.8)
Oman	4,634.5	6.9	2.7	0.22	–	2.81
Saudi Arabia	8,379	4.8	0.33	4.5	–	3.75

Somalia	–	1.74	(2.98)	–	–	–
Sudan	244	4.28	1.6	42	–	–
Syria	670.7	5.6	2.3	12.9	5.7	1.01
Tunisia	1,721	5.2	3.1	6.02	–	(5.6)
UAE	27,237.5	5.8	(3.5)	–	–	–
Yemen	284.66	5.3	1.4	30.6	11.5	0.93

Notes:
[a] Figures represent averages of three period averages calculated from *World Development Indicators*, CD-ROM Edition (2003).
[b] For countries that have data shortages, we compute period averages of available data in each decade starting from 1970.
[c] Negative figures appear in parentheses.
[d] Countries without data are not reported.

Source: World Development Indicators, CD-ROM Edition (2003).

Table 9.2   Models of economic development

	Resource-based industrialization economies (Algeria, Bahrain, Iran, Kuwait, Libya, Oman, Saudi Arabia and UAE)[8]	State-led development economies (Comoros, Djibouti, Egypt, Mauritania, Syria, Somalia, Sudan and Yemen)	Balanced economies (Jordan, Lebanon, Morocco and Tunisia)[9]
Dominant sector(s)[10]	Industry	Agriculture and services[11]	Manufacturing and services
Dominant export categories	Fuels, ores and metals	Food, agricultural raw materials and natural resources	Manufacturing and natural resources
Openness (X+M/GDP)	Open	Least open	Less open
Import duties (% of total tax revenues)	Low	Relatively high	Highest
Capital controls on outflows[12]	Low	Highest	High

Note: * Indices for capital controls are borrowed from Karam (2002).

Source: World Development Indicators, CD-ROM Edition (2003).

East Asia (Page 1998).[7] In addition, the international capital flows of foreign direct investment and portfolio investment have bypassed the MENA region considerably.[13]

The growth performance of the MENA region has been rather disappointing. Several macroeconomic indicators illustrate the poor health of the economies of the region. Mounting external debt, increasing budgetary deficits, falling per capita incomes as well as rising poverty and income inequality characterize most of the economies in the MENA region. The greatest challenge facing the MENA region is to create enough employment opportunities for the large and rapidly growing labor force. According to the World Bank, the region has one of the highest rates of unemployment in the world.

Historically speaking, the dependence on natural resources and the legacy of central planning have shaped the development trajectories pursued by the countries of this region. Over the last three decades, the resource-rich states have adopted resource-based industrialization while the overwhelming majority of capital-scarce states follow state-led development strategies in which the states command productive activities.[14] The third category consists of economies in which sectoral contribution to national output is fairly balanced. For the purposes of this study, we categorize the countries of the region into three groups according to the development models followed by each country: resource-based industrialization states, state-led development economies and balanced economies (Table 9.2).[15]

Resource-based industrialization states are characterized by their heavy reliance on the export of natural resources, along with their capitalist orientation and the monarchial character of most of their political systems. State-led development economies as well as balanced economies rely heavily on external borrowing (see Tables 9.3 and 9.4), citizens' remittances, tourism, foreign aid and grants and share a common heritage of central planning as well as a socialist orientation. The latter is assisted by one-party or military governments and exemplified in their trade and finance policies as well as in the internal management of their economies. Balanced economies, while sharing some characteristics with their state-led development counterparts, have greater economic diversification as well as more rigorous private sectors than state-led development economies.

While the first oil shock contributed to one of the worst global economic downturns, the MENA region benefited enormously from the wealth generated from oil rents. In particular, the resource-based industrialization states experienced an explosion of growth and investment as well as high rates of capacity utilization. Public sector spending, particularly on infrastructure building and construction projects, largely absorbed the growth in oil revenues. The skyrocketing crude oil prices in 1973 provided the conditions for unprecedented high standards of living as these economies tripled their exports of crude oil to exploit the tilt of the terms of trade in their favor.

Many state-led development and balanced economies produced some oil of their own and profited directly from the high prices of the era. In addition, they witnessed an excess demand for their abundant and relatively more skillful labor from the resource-based industrialization states.[16] This resulted in massive inflows of remittances from their citizens working in the Gulf countries, as well as a rise in their trade shares and capital flows. Flows of aid, cheap loans, outright grants, profits earned by their contractors in resource-rich states as well as smaller amounts of investment inflows provided those governments with unprecedented inflows of foreign exchange.

However, reality began to dawn in the mid-1980s when crude oil prices fell sharply as western economies adjusted to the oil shocks of 1973 and 1979 by using oil more efficiently, contracting domestic demand and developing

Table 9.3 Currency composition (%) of long-term debt: weighted averages, 1970–2002

Country	USD	Swiss franc	British pound	SDRs	Multiple currencies	Japanese yen	French franc	Deutsche mark	Other currencies
Algeria	41.05	1.06	2.51	0	6.25	11	15.87	6.87	15.36
Comoros	22.56	0	0	0.56	4.78	0	34.28	0	37.79
Djibouti	8.99	0	0	3.22	8.9	0	45.28	0.23	33.36
Egypt	52.97	2	1.71	0.09	4.45	6.18	9.07	8.02	15.47
Iran	45.97	0.67	0.19	0	5.39	5.25	1.94	8.66	2.85
Jordan	43.97	0.31	10.35	0.49	6.33	7.95	4.01	9.77	16.79
Lebanon	52.18	0.12	0.21	0	9.23	0.17	16.56	2.19	19.3
Mauritania	39.2	0.05	0.34	1.35	3.73	1.29	14.14	1.55	38.27
Morocco	42.25	0.28	0.28	0.11	12.84	2.07	22.98	7.23	11
Oman	50.4	0	12.9	0	1.3	4.6	2.82	1.84	19.4
Syria	69.4	1.35	0.92	0	3.13	1.43	2.83	1.98	18.94
Somalia	43.7	0	0.23	0.68	15.84	1.3	2.31	3.03	32.9
Sudan	46.3	9.49	6.32	0.26	5.28	–	2.29	2.11	26.19
Tunisia	29.61	0.48	0.2	0.12	14.21	6.85	16.6	9.92	21.95
Yemen	31.12	2.28	2.36	1.57	1.97	2.69	0.82	3.69	53.47

Note: *Averages for the period 1970–2002 are weighted by total long-term debt. Countries without data are not reported.

Source: Author's computations from *Global Development Finance 2002* (CD-ROM Edition).

Table 9.4 External debt, annual average (1970–2000), millions of current USD

Country	Long-term debt	Short-term debt	IMF credits	Total external debt stock	Total change in debt adjusted for exchange rate fluctuations	Total external debt adjusted for exchange rate fluctuation (Debt adj.)	Debt adj. (% of GDP)
Algeria	17,542	1,033.5	512	19,086	257.3	18,822.9	36.2
Comoros	110	7.1	0.73	118	(112.3)	117.9	82.77
Djibouti	115	14.3	1.4	130	(11.4)	146.1	53.6
Egypt	20,502	3,523.3	171	24,196	336.3	24,605.7	69.2
Iran	3,733	3,750.8	–	7,484	582	10,170.6	10.49
Jordan	3,779	548.7	108	4,436	121.9	4,457.7	83.04
Lebanon	1,037	742.6	–	1,780	(465)	1,728	41
Mauritania	1,209	123.4	55	1,387	12	1,421.9	158.3
Morocco	12,703	457.2	406	13,566	140.6	13,844.9	64.5
Oman	2,124	436.4	–	2,560	0.5	2,647.9	26.8
Somalia	1,189	207	94	1,490	7.6	1,529	122.9
Sudan	6,002	2,569	575	9,146	80	9,358.4	100.03
Syria	9,100	1,562	2	11,052	428.4	10,983	85.6
Tunisia	5,044	489	108	5,642	116.6	5,693.2	52.06
Yemen	3,072	446	65	3,585	24.9	3,559.7	114.8

Note: * Negative figures appear in parentheses. Countries without data are not reported.

Source: Author's computations from Global Development Finance 2002 (CD-ROM Edition) and World Development Indicators 2003 (CD-ROM Edition).

241

Table 9.5   Sources and uses of funds, annual averages in millions of current US$

Country	Net foreign investment	Change in debt adj.	Current account balance	Changes in net reserves
Algeria	33.67	257.3	(517.28)	82.65
Bahrain	158	NA	(64)	(61)
Comoros	1.01	(112.3)	(12.73)	(2.27)
Djibouti	2.09	(11.4)	(47.72)	7.66
Egypt	569.53	336.3	(897.73)	(201.28)
Iran	61.15	582	741.05	741.44
Jordan	81.70	121.9	(133.75)	(311.03)
Kuwait	5,380	–	108	(400)
Lebanon	1,211.05	(465)	(2,683.23)	(216.77)
Libya	(241)	–	569	(338)
Mauritania	2.97	12	(64.49)	2.78
Morocco	222.79	140.6	(731.68)	(204.01)
Oman	92.15	0.5	159.38	(199.10)
Saudi Arabia	838	–	451	(657)
Somalia	6.60	7.6	(121.43)	6.60
Sudan	42.92	80	(386.35)	(4.93)
Syria	51.83	428.4	68.32	(182.37)
Tunisia	51.83	116.6	(538.21)	(182.37)
Yemen	–	24.9	157.9	(201)

Note: *Negative figures appear in parentheses. Countries without data are not reported.

Source: Author's computations from *Global Development Finance 2002* and *World Development Indicators 2003* (CD-ROM Edition).

alternative sources of energy. Oil rents dropped drastically and the flows of aid and remittances in the region were much reduced. In addition, both investment and savings ratios to GDP decreased. Countries following state-led development strategies as well as balanced economies had to increase their external borrowing and financing to compensate for adverse trade balances following the fall of crude oil prices. Derived from their common heritage of central planning, state intervention theories and socialist legacies, which encouraged limited private sector participation and private business initiatives and advocated the control of the state over much of the economic, political and social aspects of people's lives, this option was preferred by countries under the two models outlined above over trade and financial liberalization advocated by international organizations in the early 1980s (see Owen and Paumuk 1998; Field 1994). Nevertheless, the deterioration of economic conditions and the increasing leverage of the international organizations (the IMF and the World Bank) brought most of the countries of the region under Structural Adjustment Programs (SAPs). Following the implementation of the latter, however, the region's average rate of economic growth in the decade of the 1990s fell short of that in the1960s and 1970s.

Given the huge expansion of crude oil exports and the large external loans disbursed to non-oil states between the early 1970s and the mid-1980s, the question of the appropriate public usage of such funds to finance internal public development projects inevitably arises. For this purpose, this chapter attempts an explanation of the public utilization of those funds and provides policy implications based on the results obtained (see Table 9.5 for annual averages of sources and uses of funds). More specifically, it addresses the problem of capital flight from the Middle East and North Africa utilizing the residual approach to capital flight developed by the World Bank in 1985, and further developed by various authors including Ajayi (1997) and Nkidumana and Boyce (2000). The following section provides details of the use of the residual approach in measuring capital flight from the countries of the MENA region.

METHODOLOGY

Following Boyce and Ndikumana (2000), and according to the residual approach developed by the World Bank, capital flight is defined as the difference between capital inflows and foreign exchange outflows. The rationale behind such characterization lies in the argument that capital inflows are either used to finance current account deficits or else accumulated in the central bank as foreign exchange reserves. Accordingly, flows that do not go to either account are regarded as capital flight. More specifically, a surplus of inflows over reported uses reflects positive capital flight. Such funds are not recorded in the official statistics and therefore, according to the residual approach, are counted as capital flight. In short, our methodology is as follows:

$$KF_{it} = \Delta Debt_{it} + NFI_{it} - (CA_{it} + \Delta Reserves_{it}) \qquad (9.1)$$

where *KF* refers to capital flight in current USD, *ΔDebt* refers to change in total external debt stock, *NFI* refers to the net flows of foreign investment, *CA* refers to the current account balance, and *ΔReserves* refers to the changes in the accumulation of foreign exchange reserves.

The adjustments for exchange rate fluctuations in long-term debt stock are carried out as follows:

since

$$\Delta Debt = Debt_t - Debt_{t-1} \qquad (9.2)$$

then

$$\Delta DebtAdj_t = Debt_t - NEWDebt_{t-1} \qquad (9.3)$$

where $\Delta DebtAdj$ refers to the change in long-term external debt disbursed at the end of the year and adjusted for exchange rate fluctuations and *NEWDebt* is total long-term external debt valued at the beginning of the year. The latter is obtained as follows:

$$NEWDebt_{i,\,t-1} = \sum_{j=1}^{6} [\,(\lambda_{ij,\,t-1} * LTDebt_{i,\,t-1})/(EX_{jt}/EX_{j,\,t-1})\,]$$
$$+ IMFCR_{i,t-1}/(EX_{SDR,\,t}/EX_{SDR,\,t-1}) + LTOther_{i,t-1}$$
$$+ LTMult_{i,t-1} + LTUSD_{i,t-1} + STDebt_{i,t-1} \qquad (9.4)$$

where *LTDebt* is the total long-term debt, λ being the proportion of long-term debt held in currency for each of the non-US currencies; *EX* is the end-of-year exchange rate of the currency of denomination with respect to the USD; *IMFCR* is the use of IMF credit; *LTOther* is long-term debt denominated in other unspecified currencies; *LTMult* is long-term debt denominated in multiple currencies; *LTUSD* is long-term debt denominated in US dollars and finally *STDebt* is short-term debt.[17] Accordingly, we modify the residual Equation (9.1) to be:

$$KF_{it} = \Delta DebtAdj_{it} + NFI_{it} - (CA_{it} + \Delta Reserves_{it}) \qquad (9.5)$$

The adjustments for trade misinvoicing are conducted as follows:

$$DEXP_{it} = PEXP_{it} - (CIF_t * EXP_{it}) \qquad (9.6)$$

$$DIMP_{it} = IMP_{it} - (CIF_t * PIMP_{it}) \qquad (9.7)$$

and

$$MISINV = (DEXP/ICXS) + (DIMP/ICMS) \qquad (9.8)$$

where *DEXP* and *DIMP* refer to export and import discrepancies, *PEXP* and

PIMP refer to exports and imports of a MENA country recorded in industrial countries' official statistics, *EXP* and *IMP* are exports and imports of a MENA country as reported in its own statistics, and *CIF* refers to the cost of freight and insurance.[18] *MISINV* refers to total trade misinvoicing.

Thus, we add misinvoicing to the calculation of capital flight in Equation (9.1) as follows:

$$KF\ Adj_{it} = KF_{it} + MISINV_{it} \qquad (9.9)$$

Finally, we adjust for inflation by transforming capital flight into constant 1995 USD using the Producer Price Index (PPI):

$$Real\ KFAdj_{it} = KF\ Adj_{it}/PPI_t \qquad (9.10)$$

A further adjustment employed concerns interest earnings on capital flight. This step is done as follows:

$$Interest\ KF\ Adj_{it} = Interest\ KF\ Adj_{I,t-1}\ (1+TBILL_{it}) + KF\ Adj_{it}{}^{19} \qquad (9.11)$$

The results of the adopted methodology appear in Tables 9.A1 and 9.A2 and are elaborated on in the following section.

RESULTS AND CAPITAL FLIGHT ACCOUNTING

According to reported estimates, the MENA region as a whole is indeed a net creditor to the rest of the world. Driven overwhelmingly by the resource-based industrialization states, the region registers $57.8 billion (measured in 1995 USD) of capital flight with imputed interest-earning capital flight of $525.6 billion (in current USD). This implies that large amounts of capital generated mainly by oil rents were not used to finance public development projects. Rather, significant amounts of such flows of foreign exchange fled those states in the form of capital flight to finance external private assets.

This study, however, draws attention to the significance of natural resource rents, especially crude oil rents, in contributing to capital flight from resource-rich states. Exporting revenues generated mostly from the early 1970s to the mid-1980s, the era of high crude oil prices, and assisted by the low controls on capital outflows, drive the occurrence of the phenomenon in those states considerably. The minimal implementation of capital controls on outflows in the resource-rich states is reflected in the high reported figures of capital flight from the economies of the model. The estimates of real capital flight provided in Table 9.A1 (see Appendix) indicate an increase of approximately 900 percent in capital flight from Saudi Arabia in 1974, following the first oil shock, an increase of approximately 55 percent in capital flight from Algeria, an increase of more than 48 percent in capital flight from Bahrain, an increase of more than 90 percent in capital flight from Kuwait, an increase of more than 653 percent in capital flight from Oman, an increase of approximately 31 percent in capital flight from Libya and an increase of approximately 865 percent in capital flight from Iran in 1979,[20] in the aftermath of the second oil shock.[21]

The link between capital flight and crude oil prices is further shown by the sharp decline in capital flight figures for resource-based industrialization states in 1986–87 accompanying the fall in oil prices in the same year. The decrease in capital flight in those economies from its value in 1981, prior to the declining trend in oil prices, to its value in 1987, when oil prices approached their pre-1973 values, was $2.09 billion in Algeria, $7.8 billion in Kuwait, $54.4 billion in Saudi Arabia, compared to a $0.6 billion increase in Iran, and a $270 million increase in Bahrain and a $3.5 billion increase in Oman.[22] Figure 9.1 depicts, using pooled data, the positive association between capital flight and oil rents in resource-based industrialization states. The coefficient of the regression is significant even when controlling for outlier countries individually.

On the other hand, both state-led development economies and balanced economies appear to have experienced negative capital flight of $214 billion, a figure driven by large negative trade misinvoicing. This example of large negative misinvoicing characterizing state-led development economies and balanced economies is not a unique one. Boyce and Nkidumana (2000) identify several factors contributing to such phenomenon; namely tax evasion and smuggling activities. Trade in these states is subject to significant trade barriers and restrictions and agents in the international market try to maximize their gains by avoiding import duties. Data from the World Bank's World Development Indicators show that state-led development economies as well as balanced economies have, on average, considerably higher rates of import duty revenues as a percentage of total government tax revenues compared to resource-based industrialization states.[23] In addition, according to Karam (2002), the countries under these two models of development have higher indices of capital controls on outflows than the economies following resource-based industrialization. Figure 9.2 shows the negative association between capital flight in state-led development and balanced economies and import duties in those states. The coefficient of the regression remains negative even when controlling for outlier countries individually. However, it declines the most when controlling for Morocco in the regression.

The estimates of trade misinvoicing in Table 9.6 show that state-led development economies and balanced economies have experienced large negative import misinvoicing. Coupled with poor institutional quality and effectiveness, the import substitution strategy that characterizes the two models of development has paved the way for importers to undermine state revenues through tax evasion and smuggling activities in order to maximize their gains.

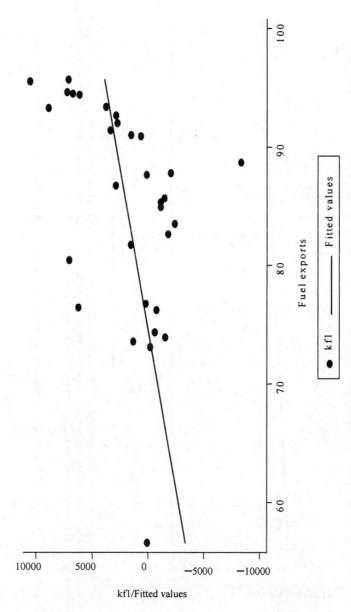

Note: *The dependent variable is average capital flight in resource-based industrialization states whereas the independent variable is the average ratio of fuel exports as a percentage of merchandise exports. The results are robust even when controlling for outlier countries.

Figure 9.1 Capital flight and fuel exports in resource-based industrialization states

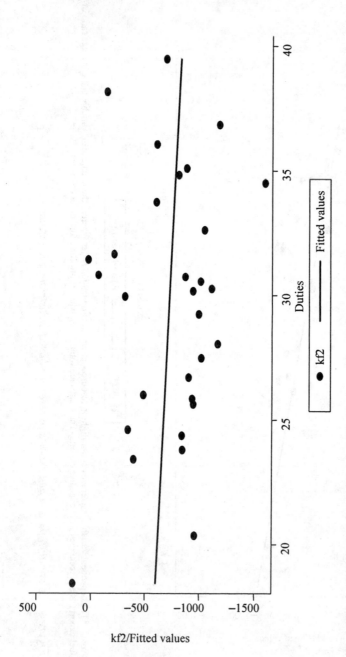

Note: *The dependent variable is average capital flight in state-led development economies and balanced economies whereas the independent variable is the average ratio of import tariffs as a percentage of total government tax revenues. The coefficient remains negative when controlling for outlier countries. However, it declines the most when controlling for Morocco in the regression.

Figure 9.2 Capital flight and tariff revenues (%) of total government taxes in state-led development and balanced economies.

Table 9.6   Total trade misinvoicing, 1980–2002, millions of 1995 US$

Country	Total trade misinvoicing	Total export misinvoicing	Total import misinvoicing	Annual average
Algeria	35,504.2	38,191	(2,686.8)	1,543.7
Bahrain	2,909.7	2,235	674.7	126.5
Comoros	(163.90)	15.28	(179.1)	(7.13)
Djibouti	(748.6)	(1.58)	(747.1)	(32.55)
Egypt	(77,661.6)	58,944.2	(136,605.8)	(3,376.5)
Iran	(4,599.2)	(37,727.5)	30,499.5	(199.9)
Iraq	108.29	371	(262.7)	4.7
Jordan	(7,735.1)	11,918.2	(19,653.3)	(336.3)
Kuwait	(9,837.1)	(2,858.7)	(6,978.3)	(427.7)
Lebanon	2,314.7	1,094.2	1,220.5	100.6
Libya	(6,748.9)	8,697.4	(15,446.4)	(293.4)
Mauritania	(928.5)	830.1	(1,758.6)	(40.3)
Morocco	(16,629.1)	26,480.5	(43,109.6)	(723)
Oman	5,847.9	14,407.8	(8,559.9)	254.2
Qatar	(5,082.1)	16.9	(5,099.1)	(220.9)
Saudi Arabia	(71,578.8)	46,390.3	(117,969.1)	(3,112.1)
Somalia	(742.1)	183.2	(925.4)	(32.2)
Sudan	(4,171.2)	1,148.4	(5,319.6)	(181.3)
Syria	(11,675.8)	(4,699.4)	(6,976.3)	(507.6)
Tunisia	(29,816.5)	(7,809.6)	(22,006.9)	(1,296.3)
UAE	(23,835.6)	25,550.7	(49,386.4)	(1,036.3)
Yemen	(2,701.65)	(131.5)	(2,569.9)	(675.3)

Note: *Negative figures appear in parentheses.

Source: Author's computations from: *Direction of Trade Statistics 2003* and *World Development Indicators, 2003* (CD-ROM Editions).

The under-reporting of import transactions substantially reduces import duties as a percentage of total government tax revenues. According to the World Development Indicators (2003), over a three-period interval, imports constituted on average about 50 percent of total GDP in those states, while import duties as a percentage of total government tax revenues averaged about 32 percent. This implies that negative trade misinvoicing undermined a large proportion of GDP in state-led development economies and balanced economies.

CONCLUSIONS AND POLICY IMPLICATIONS

This is the first attempt to examine and estimate capital flight from the MENA region. The outcomes clearly show a link between capital flight and the development trajectory undertaken. Resource-based industrialization states of the MENA region have experienced $273 billion of capital flight relative to negative $102 billion for state-led development economies and negative $112 billion for balanced economies. It is crucial to highlight the association of each particular model of development with certain political and economic ideologies. The outward-looking orientation of resource-based industrialization economies of the MENA region is supported by the common interests of the political elites of those states with the industrial world. Likewise, the state-led development and balanced economies follow socialist-derived development paths and socio-economic state intervention theories. The inward-looking features of this model reflect the lingering socialist legacies of these states. Finally, balanced economies, while sharing some features of a state-dominated approach to economic development, appear to minimize the role of the government more than their state-led development counterparts by attempting to diversify economic activity and create a balance between the different economic sectors. Nevertheless, the capital flight figures for countries under this model resemble those of the countries following the state-led development approach.

This chapter suggests the need for a reevaluation of the region's international trade and finance policies. More specifically, since resource-based economies, on average, employ less capital controls on outflows than the other two groups, the implementation of higher capital controls might help restrict the occurrence and frequency of the capital flight phenomenon from those states. In contrast, import duties for balanced economies as well as state-led development economies are significantly reduced by those international traders under-reporting their import transactions. Thus, new evaluations of trade duties in those economies should take these consequences into account. Finally, the countries of the region should attempt to diversify economic activities, promote investment opportunities and improve institutional quality to provide the conditions for capital flight reversal and suppress tax evasion and smuggling activities.

APPENDIX

Table 9.A1 Annual capital flight (1970–1981) adjusted for exchange rate fluctuations and trade misinvoicing (millions of 1995 US$)

Country	1970	1971	1972	1973	1974	1975	1976	1977	1978	1979	1980	1981
Algeria	–	–	–	–	–	–	–	(1,312.3)	(2,739.5)	(1,227.7)	(3,925.8)	2,779.4
Bahrain	–	–	–	–	–	(794.4)	(1,034.4)	(752.5)	(618.6)	(318.3)	(854.5)	(469.2)
Comoros	–	–	–	–	–	–	–	–	–	–	(8.3)	(14.0)
Djibouti	–	–	–	–	–	–	–	–	–	–	–	0.1
Egypt	–	–	–	–	(3,176.4)	(3,308.6)	(247.4)	4,262.1	(2,582.6)	75.4	(4,793.6)	(3,900.8)
Iran	–	–	–	–	–	–	10,708.9	1,396.9	1,461.2	14,110	12,430.8	(3,623.8)
Jordan	–	–	28.8	(64.1)	(6.6)	(179.8)	43.3	(327.5)	(838.7)	(419.0)	(663.7)	(1,388.1)
Kuwait	–	–	–	–	–	11,794.8	13,412.9	6,857.6	11,557.0	21,966.6	15,372.8	15,698
Lebanon	–	–	–	–	–	–	–	–	–	–	–	2.34
Libya	–	–	–	–	–	–	–	(51)	1,139.3	1,494	(3,217)	(9,231.2)
Mauritania	–	–	–	–	–	(0.2)	(0.1)	(0.1)	(0.1)	(0.1)	(0.1)	(0.2)
Morocco	–	–	–	–	–	(34.0)	(2,220.4)	(3,193.6)	(1,558.4)	(2,042)	(1,417.7)	(2,341.2)
Oman	–	–	–	–	179.0	336.8	291.6	685.5	87.7	653.7	53.5	(590.6)
S. Arabia	–	613.5	3,345	2,707.5	20,776	15,361	20,890	19,380.1	8,998.7	13,796.1	29,628.0	38,179.9
Somalia	–	–	–	–	–	–	–	(272.3)	(187.9)	(49.8)	(309.3)	(110.9)
Sudan	–	–	–	–	–	–	–	(244.4)	(109.7)	90.8	(183.8)	(1,135)
Syria	–	–	–	–	–	–	–	(522.4)	90.4	1135.9	(701.7)	(1229.7)
Tunisia	–	–	–	–	–	–	–	(867.7)	(356.5)	(484.5)	(1320.2)	(2088.4)

Table 9.A1 Annual capital flight (1982–1992) adjusted for exchange rate fluctuations and trade misinvoicing (millions of 1995 US$)

Country	1982	1983	1984	1985	1986	1987	1988	1989	1990	1991	1992
Algeria	3803.9	617.7	2506.8	4191.3	3126.9	687.1	(38.2)	2108.8	4309.7	2746.9	3006.8
Bahrain	202.1	107.7	132.8	(208.6)	(120.4)	(199.2)	1330.7	501.1	(1131.5)	(460.9)	(91.2)
Comoros	(14.2)	(11.3)	(22.2)	(14.3)	(13.9)	(20.2)	12.2	(27.3)	(6.5)	(7.3)	(16.0)
Djibouti	0.1	(44.2)	(44.5)	0.2	(91.8)	(85.0)	(84.8)	(85.0)	(128.3)	(180.7)	(76.9)
Egypt	(3570.4)	(2987.8)	(3924.3)	(7419.5)	(5577.1)	466.2	(2568.8)	(2048.1)	(154.5)	(1930.2)	(2676.4)
Iran	2740.63	1735.97	4624.9	(1601.1)	(5348.1)	(3070.6)	(5171.1)	(5478.7)	(6070.7)	64.99	619.65
Jordan	(2688.7)	(1737.2)	(67.3)	33.3	(284.4)	(1579.5)	(1261.0)	(268.5)	52.5	(1519.6)	(812.7)
Kuwait	461.4	829.5	5030.8	2634.8	6404.3	7873.5	7833.8	8656.6	5115.4	(30676.9)	(2380.2)
Lebanon	0.3	1.5	0.5	0.1	(0.1)	8.6	(44.1)	436.8	459.2	(1624.5)	(1899.3)
Libya	3549.6	4693.6	3486	3830.3	(2290)	(2911)	(548)	(4785.9)	(1650.6)	(1848)	(134)
Mauritania	(0.3)	(0.3)	(0.2)	(0.1)	(0.2)	(0.6)	(0.1)	(0.1)	(0.1)	(0.7)	(0.1)
Morocco	(1904.4)	(1042.5)	(1121.2)	(1011.4)	(1168.7)	(492.5)	(209.9)	(1451.0)	(2167.3)	(1774)	(1124.3)
Oman	(233.7)	57.7	(182.1)	(541.3)	1617.6	3002.2	2043.1	2500.4	5339.7	(970.9)	(1146.4)
S. Arabia	33076.6	6770.8	(6400.6)	(13625.7)	(2862.9)	(16274.5)	(6914.4)	(7921.7)	4423.4	(27400.9)	(14276.2)
Somalia	(380.3)	35.4	(221.5)	(134.3)	(340.1)	(139.9)	(87.8)	(14.1.5)	(1268.6)	0.8	0.3
Sudan	(1338)	(3.9)	47.6	752.6	(521.6)	(437.6)	(835.8)	(41.6)	(424.2)	(1032.2)	(484.9)
Syria	(1189.8)	366.9	(1016.6)	(433.2)	(804.9)	(361.2)	201.6	997.8	1232.0	778.6	(154.5)
Tunisia	(1895.9)	(118.9)	(2534)	(1322.8)	(1089.3)	(838.5)	(427.3)	(1149.3)	(1933.5)	(1982.4)	(3123.10

Table 9.A1 Annual capital flight (1993-2002) adjusted for exchange rate fluctuations and trade misinvoicing (millions of 1995 USD)

Country	1993	1994	1995	1996	1997	1998	1999	2000	2001	2002	Total KF
Algeria	2740	1,481.6	3,850.8	5,133.2	436.3	474.3	(1,122)	747.7	377.7	597.8	35,359.3
Bahrain	(567.5)	502	1,953.7	3,599.5	142.7	(978.3)	215.81	880.5	(94.7)	–	1,978.8
Comoros	81.6	(27.4)	(17.5)	(116.2)	(122.2)	0.1	0	(0.1)	0	(331)	(696.2)
Djibouti	(27.1)	(56.7)	(25.2)	(168.9)	(1.8)	(1.1)	0.7	0.3	0.1	0	(1,100.7)
Egypt	(5144.6)	(3,788)	(3,929.3)	(4,089.4)	(7,944.4)	(7,077.5)	(4,483.7)	3,062	(6,148)	(223.1)	(85,829.1)
Iran	4484.1	(345.9)	2,616.7	(41.5)	2,571.9	(415.5)	1,548.1	(36.9)	2,0817.7	0	50,728.5
Jordan	(137.9)	(338.9)	(274.9)	(76.4)	264.4	635.2	(336.2)	(82.4)	(414.2)	(1,044.6)	(15,754.1)
Kuwait	3498.6	4,482.4	17,435	4,287.7	8,254.9	3,462.1	4,372.6	11,956.4	4,923.4	–	171,115.9
Lebanon	(1044.8)	(2,635.7)	(2,016.1)	(2,632.1)	(1,024.4)	(2,275.3)	(2,062.5)	(102.2)	0	0	(16,452)
Libya	927.7	(384.3)	(204.9)	(187)	(371.5)	1,472.6	1,008	–	–	–	(6,197)
Mauritania	(0.1)	0.8.	0.1	0.8	0.3	0.14	(1.6)	0	0	0	(4,820.7)
Morocco	(977)	(1,565.9)	(1,053.1)	(383.2)	(261.2)	(276.5)	(1,879.4)	(481.2)	(2,498)	(730.2)	(36,379.9)
Oman	(342.3)	(524.2)	(1,232.2)	(419.2)	(698.6)	(1,999.2)	(1,278.3)	934.8	946.9	0.0	8,571.2

S. Arabia	21,274.4 (17,964)	(13,626)	(20,516)	(9,749.7)	(18,964.)	(12,909.)	2,739.2	15,275.8	–	11,880 (3,616.6)
Somalia	0.1 (4.7)	0.3	0.3	0.5 (0.3)	(5.4)	(0.2)	0.1	0.7		(6,446.5)
Sudan	10.3 (3.1)	0.8 (16.7)	(1.2) (0.0)	(231.3)	(303.6)	0.0	0.1			(308.7)
Syria	201.6 (786.2)	(371.8) (356.5)	221.1 (87.0)	326.3	2,154.4	(0.0)	0.0			(44,145)
Tunisia	(3303.2) (2,443.6)	(3,216.2) (3,272.4)	(1,387.9) (2,071.5)	(566.0)	(2,408.6)	(1,442)	(1,432)			

Note: *Negative figures appear in parentheses. Countries without data are not reported.

Source: Author's computations from *Global Development Finance 2002* (CD-ROM Edition); *World Development Indicators 2003* (CD-ROM Edition); *International Financial Statistics 2003* (CD- ROM Edition); *Direction of Trade Statistics 2003* (CD-ROM Edition).

Table 9.A2 Total capital flight (%) of GDP with imputed interest earnings (millions of 1995 US$)

Country	Total nominal KF adjusted for exchange rate fluctuations & trade misinvoicng (KF adj.)	Total real KF adj.	Total nominal KF adj. with accumulated interest earnings	Annual average real KF adj.	Annual average KF adj. (% GDP)	Annual average per capita real KF adj. (units of US$)
Algeria	34,576.89	35,359.3	52,303.5	1,359.9	2.41	51.4
Bahrain	3,982.5	1,978.8	(5,630.1)	73.29	9.33	–
Comoros	(347.8)	(696.2)	(406.4)	(30.2)	(9)	(47.8)
Djibouti	(1,006.6)	(1,100.7)	(1,844.1)	(50)	(12.1)	(105.8)
Egypt	(73,753)	(85,829.1)	(162,415)	(2,959.6)	(6.8)	(54.8)
Iran	39,355.9	50,728.5	132,068.7	1,878.84	2	43.7
Jordan	(13,007.9)	(15,754.1)	(35,729.6)	(508.2)	(8.5)	(185.3)
Kuwait	130,605	171,115.9	418,085.8	6,338	63	5,595
Lebanon	(16,258.1)	(16,452)	(22,088)	(747.8)	(10.2)	(237.1)
Libya	(5,467)	(6,197)	(12,775)	(269)	–	(71)
Mauritania	(4,000)	(4,820.7)	(10,116)	(172.1)	(18.2)	(90)
Morocco	(29,774.3)	(36,379.9)	(80,388.8)	(1,299.2)	(5.5)	(58.4)

Oman	6,321.1	8,571.2	19,659.5	295.5	4.2	219
Saudi Arabia	(50,133)	11,880.0	332,190.1	383	0.1	389
Somalia	(2,939.7)	(3,616.6)	(8,171.3)	(139.1)	(25.8)	–
Sudan	(5,483.)	(6,446.5)	(11,067.4)	(247.9)	(2.1)	(10.8)
Syria	478.2	(308.7)	(22,990.9)	(11.8)	(0.1)	(5.7)
Tunisia	(40,528.3)	(44,145)	(54,986.2)	(1,697.8)	(200.9)	(208.9)

Note: *In the case of Bahrain, Kuwait, Libya and Saudi Arabia, the adjustment on capital flight entails correcting for trade misinvoicing only since they do not have data on external debt. Negative figures appear in parentheses. Countries without data are not reported.

Source: Author's computations from *Global Development Finance 2002* (CD-ROM Edition); *World Development Indicators 2003* (CD-ROM Edition); *International Financial Statistics 2003* (CD-ROM Edition); *Direction of Trade Statistics 2003* (CD-ROM Edition).

NOTES

I am grateful to professor Gerald Epstein for various discussions and comments on this paper. I also thank Professor James Boyce for commenting on this study and providing suggestions for further developments.

1.   We follow the Arab Monetary Fund definition of the MENA region, which includes Algeria, Bahrain, Comoros, Djibouti, Egypt, Iraq, Jordan, Kuwait, Lebanon, Libya, Mauritania, Morocco, Oman, Qatar, Saudi Arabia, Somalia, Syria, Tunisia, UAE and Yemen. Iran is added to the region since the World Bank classifies it as such and because of its relevance to the main core analysis of this chapter. Data on the West Bank and Gaza are not available. For the purposes of this study, Pakistan, Afghanistan, Israel and Turkey are not covered.

2.   Schneider (2003) has estimated international capital flight using both the broad measure as well as the hot money measure to capital flight. Since her study incorporates countries for which data are available, she presents some estimates of capital flight and trade misinvoicing separately for the following countries under the MENA region: Algeria, Egypt, Iran, Jordan, Morocco, Oman, Syria and Tunisia. In addition to the fact that her study includes only nine countries of the MENA region, Schneider's estimates of capital flight are less inclusive in terms of number of years of analysis. Moreover, our estimates implement various adjustments to reach the final figure of capital flight such as incorporating trade misinvoicing into capital flight estimates.

3.   This classification is consistent with that of the World Bank. Resource abundance is measured by natural resource endowments whereas labor abundance is measured by net inflows of workers' remittances to each country.

4.   According to the World Bank classifications, five countries (Egypt, Mauritania, Somalia, Sudan, and the Republic of Yemen) are low-income countries. Twelve countries (Algeria, Bahrain, Djibouti, Iran, Iraq, Jordan, Lebanon, Libya, Syria, Morocco, Oman, Saudi Arabia and Tunisia) are middle-income countries while Kuwait, Qatar and the United Arab Emirates are classified as high-income countries. However, per capital real GDP growth in the MENA region over the past two decades has faltered compared to other developing countries.

5.   I construct an institutional quality index based on indicators gathered by Kaufman, Kraay and Zoido-Lobaton (1999b). The index comprises six indicators: namely; voice and accountability, political stability and lack of violence, government effectiveness, regulatory framework, rule of law and control of corruption. The index ranges between –2 (low) and 2 (high). According to the index constructed, the overwhelming majority of the MENA countries have negative or low estimates, especially in voice and accountability and control of corruption, reflecting the poor institutional quality characterizing the region. A study by Abed and Davoodi (2003) at the IMF presents an updated version of the same indices (2002) and compares the MENA region to Latin America and the Caribbean, East Asia and OECD countries. The MENA region by far has the lowest institutional quality on a regional comparison. Only when looking at the rule of law do Latin America and the Caribbean score as low as the MENA region.

6.   This is more pronounced for state-led development economies as well as balanced economies. See Table 9.2 for country classification.

7.   This paper was cited in Almounsor (2003).

8.   Note that, unlike the Gulf Cooperation Council states, Iran, Iraq, Libya and Algeria, being resource-based industrialization states, share the common heritage of central planning with the countries of the other two models. In addition, their political regimes differ from other resource-based states in that they are ruled by single-party or military governments as opposed to the monarchies of the Gulf states.

9.   Note that Jordan and Morocco, unlike other countries of the model and the countries following state-led development, are distinguished by their monarchial governments. Such a feature, however, did not preclude the states of the model from adopting protectionist measures as well as nationalist and socialist orientation in managing economic activities.

10.   Exports of fuel as well as orals and metals in Iran had been seriously disrupted, first by the Iranian Revolution in 1979 and second by the Iraq-Iran war which lasted more than seven

years. Accordingly, the industrial sector in Iran accounts for 37.09 percent of total output over the three decades of analysis. The industrial sector in the other countries under the model accounts for the following percentages of total output: Algeria (51.6 percent), Bahrain (44 percent), Kuwait (58 percent), Libya (65 percent), Oman (61 percent), Saudi Arabia (61.6 percent) and UAE (66.4 percent). For state-led development economies, the share of both agriculture as well as services account for more than 69 percent of total output. Finally, balanced economies have more balanced sectoral contribution to output. The shares of both the manufacturing sector as well as the service sector register more than 66 percent of total output. In particular, they account for 80 percent in Jordan, 75 percent in Lebanon, 68 percent in Morocco and 70 percent in Tunisia.

11. The service sector comprises backbone public utilities such as transportation, finance, information as well as communication. The public sector in the MENA region dominates the overwhelming majority of such activities.

12. The indices of capital control on outflows are borrowed from Karam (2002). According to Karam, the IMF publishes such indices for member countries in the 'Annual Report on Exchange Arrangements and Exchange Restrictions'. The indices are as follows: 0.59 for Algeria, 0.15 for Bahrain, 0.18 for Kuwait, 0.11 for Oman, and 0.27 for Saudi Arabia. For state-led development economies, the indices are: 0.60 for Comoros, 0.16 for Djibouti, 0.17 for Egypt, 0.69 for Mauritania, 0.71 for Somalia, 0.67 for Sudan, 0.66 for Syria and 0.01 for Yemen. Balanced economies indices are: 0.05 for Jordan, 0.17 for Lebanon, 0.66 for Morocco and 0.81 for Tunisia. Thus, the average capital controls for the models are: 0.26 for resource-based, 0.46 for state-led and 0.42 for balanced economies.

13. The MENA region, on overage of three period averages, received well below 1 percent of the world's net foreign direct investment inflows over the last three decades. The data are derived from World Bank Indicators 2003, CD-ROM Edition.

14. According to the World Bank estimates, the output of the public sector, when excluding banks and other financial institutions, in developing countries averaged about 10 percent of GDP in 1980. In addition, state-owned enterprises accounted for one-quarter to one-half of total value added in manufacturing. In many of countries of the MENA region, however, the contribution of the public sector was considerably higher than those averages (Roger Owen and Sevket Paumuk, 1998).

15. Note that this classification is not intended to simplify the complexity of the region and does not assume perfection of the suggested models of development. The region has experienced political and economic shocks including country wars, civil wars, revolutions, policy shifts, oil shocks and institutional changes which might cause disruptions to the development process. The classification is then intended to help accounting for the capital flight phenomenon within each model of development for the ease of understanding as well as for model-specific policy implications. The classification in Table 9.2 is based on the average of three period averages of data derived from the *World Development Indicators* (2003), CD-ROM Edition. For alternative development model specifications, see Richards, Alan and John Waterbury (1990).

16. The Gulf Cooperation Council countries of the MENA region (GCC) had been the main actor importing labor during the construction and infrastructure boom in the mid-1970s to the mid-1980s.

17. The adjustment for exchange rate fluctuations excludes IMF credit, short-term debt, debt in other currencies and debt held in multiple currencies. For further details, see Boyce and Ndikumana (2000).

18. We standardize the cost of freight and insurance to 10 percent of the value of exports or imports throughout our computation.

19. See Chapter 3 of this book for details on the methodology.

20. One exception in the case of resource-based industrialization economies is that of Libya registering small negative capital flight. This could be explained within the political structure and ideology of the country. Libya is ruled by military government, which distinguishes the country from other states within the model that are characterized by monarchical systems. In addition, while the other economies within the model are characterized by their capitalist and integrative orientation, Libya shares the influence of socialist ideas with the countries under state-led development and balanced economies. This

feature, however, coupled with United Nations' sanctions on Libya for supporting 'terrorism', which limited if not constrained Libya's ability to export crude oil, provides an illustration of the deviation of Libya's figure of capital flight from most countries adopting the same development strategy.

21. Note that the second oil shock resulted from the Iranian Revolution. Both the Iranian Revolution and the rise in crude oil prices contributed to the sharp rise in capital flight from Iran.

22. Note that capital flight was negative in Iran both in 1981 and 1987. However, the figure of 1987 is $0.6 billion larger than that for 1981. In the latter year, capital flight in Iran was seriously disrupted by the Iraqi invasion of the country in 1980, but picked up again in the second year following the invasion. A plausible explanation of the negative capital flight from Iran in 1981 is the need for increased military spending and purchases of USSR-made artillery, thereby decreasing capital flight.

23. Note the relevance of this argument to the import misinvoicing estimates in Table 9.6. Economies following state-led industrialization strategies as well as balanced economies register, on average, considerably higher import negative misinvoicing than resource-based industrialization economies. Thus, according to conventional wisdom, the high negative magnitude of import misinvoicing is related to the implementation of international trade duties in those economies.

REFERENCES

Abed, George and Hamid R. Davoodi (2003), 'Challenges of Growth and Globalization in the Middle East and North Africa', International Monetary Fund.

Abootalebi, Ali (1999), 'Middle East Economies: A Survey of Current Problems and Issues', *Middle East Review of International Affairs*, **3** (3), available online at www.meria.idc.ac.il/journal/1999/issue 3/jv3n3a6.html.

Ajayi, Ibi (1997), 'An Analysis of External Debt and Capital Flight in the Severely Indebted Low Income Countries in Sub-Saharan Africa', International Monetary Fund.

Almounsor, Abdullah (2003), 'The Economies of the MENA Region: Diagnosis and Prospects', University of Massachusetts, Amherst (unpublished paper).

Boyce, James and Léonce Ndikumana (2000), 'Is Africa a Net Creditor? New Estimates of Capital Flight from Severely Indebted Sub-Saharan African Countries, 1970–1996', *Journal of Development Studies*, **38** (2), 27–56

Boyce, James and Léonce Ndikumana (2002), 'Public Debts and Private Assets: Explaining Capital Flight from Sub-Saharan African Countries', University of Massachusetts, Department of Economics and Political Economy Research Institute, Working Paper No. 32, www.umass.edu/peri/pdfs/WP32.pdf *World Development*, January 2003.

Field, Michael (1994), *Inside the Arab World*, UK: John Murray Publishers Ltd.

Hermes N., R. Lensink and V. Murinde (2002), 'Flight Capital and its Reversal for Development Financing', World Institute for Development Economics Research, United Nations University.

International Monetary Fund (2003), *International Financial Statistics* (CD-ROM Edition).

International Monetary Fund (2003), *Direction of Trade Statistics* (CD-ROM Edition).

Karam, Philippe D. (2002), 'Exchange Rate Policies in Arab Countries: Assessment and Recommendations', Arab Monetary Fund, UAE.

Kaufman, D., A. Kraay and P. Zoido-Lobaton (1999b), 'Governance Matters', World Bank Policy Research Working Paper No. 2196.

Onwioduokit, E. (2001), 'Capital Flight from Nigeria: An Empirical Re-examination', Accra, Ghana: West African Monetary Institute.

Owen, Roger and Sevket Paumuk (1998), *A History of Middle East Economies in the Twentieth Century*, Cambridge, MA: Harvard University Press.

Page, John (2003), 'Structural Reforms in the Middle East and North Africa', Arab World Competitiveness Report: 2002–2003', World Economic Forum 2003.

Pastor, Manuel, Jr. (1990), 'Capital Flight and the Latin American Debt Crisis', Economic Policy Institute, Washington DC.

Richards, Alan and John Waterbury (1990), *A Political Economy of the Middle East: States, Class and Economic Development*, Boulder, Colorado: Westview Press.

Schneider, Benu (2003), 'Measuring Capital Flight: Estimates and Interpretations', Oversees Development Institute, UK.

World Bank (2002), *Global Development Finance*, (CD-ROM Edition).

World Bank (2003a), *World Development Indicators* (CD-ROM Edition).

World Bank (2003b), 'Trade, Investment, and Development in the Middle East and North Africa', World Bank.

10. Capital Flight from China, 1982–2001

Andong Zhu, Chunxiang Li and Gerald Epstein

INTRODUCTION

According to neoclassical theory, the marginal returns to capital are higher in developing countries and, therefore, capital should flow from the industrial countries to the developing ones. At the same time, according to the two-gap approach to aid and development, since the developing countries lack both domestic savings to fund necessary domestic investment and foreign exchange to import necessary capital goods, they should make every effort to attract foreign investment (Chenery and Strout 1966). Since the 1980s, the 'Washington Consensus' has insisted on financial and trade liberalization as the best mechanisms for achieving this foreign investment-led growth.

Many developing countries have tried very hard to follow the prescriptions of these theories by making great effort to attract foreign investment, which they consider to be the main engine of growth. However, only a few countries have succeeded. At the same time, many of these developing countries have experienced significant capital outflows, flows that many economists, journalists and politicians have termed 'capital flight'. This capital flight has sometimes been associated with economic crisis, slow growth and stagflation.

The Chinese case fits none of these patterns. Like many other countries, China has experienced a large amount of capital flight. Yet, China has also attracted huge amounts of foreign investment and has achieved the highest growth rate in the world in the past two decades. At least during the 1990s, one cannot observe the 'two gaps'; domestic savings are comparable to, sometimes even higher than, domestic investment; at the same time, China has experienced trade surpluses in most years during the past 20 years. (See Figure 10.1 for basic data on the Chinese economy from 1980 to 2001.)

Thus, China is a valuable case to study. Despite being an economic success story and attracting large amounts of foreign capital, it has also experienced large amounts of capital flight. At the same time, the negative

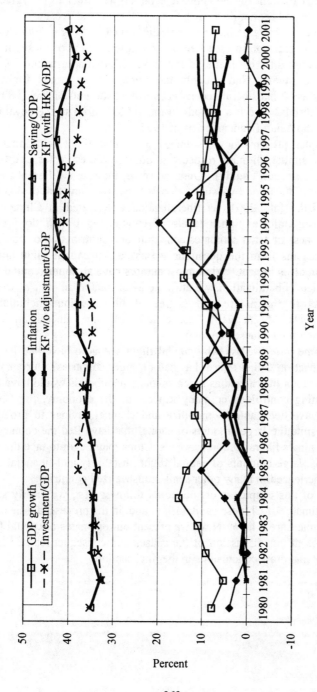

Figure 10.1   Some basic economic indicators and capital flight in China

impact of capital flight on the Chinese economy is harder to see, given the rapid and sustained economic growth over the last several decades.

There have been a large number of studies on capital flight from China in the last fifteen years or so (see below for a brief review of these studies). These studies use different methods and make different adjustments. Still, in the end, most studies find roughly the same trends: capital flight rose substantially as China liberalized its economy at the end of the 1980s and accelerated during two crisis periods in the 1990s – prior to the devaluation of 1994 and the Asian financial crisis of 1997.

This chapter presents new estimates of capital flight for China. Its estimates are similar, in many respects, to other recent estimates (see Gunter 2004 for the best recent study). Ours, however, indicate a different trend in the latter part of the period we study: in particular, we show that capital flight continued rising into 2001, as liberalization accelerated in China. Our estimates also indicate higher levels of capital flight than do previous estimates. These updated estimates constitute one contribution of our study. The second stems from the questions we ask about capital flight and our interpretation of its impact. While most authors have attributed capital flight to 'incomplete' liberalization, we attribute a substantial amount of Chinese capital flight to the nature and degree of liberalization, including the increased levels of inequality associated with the liberalization and privatization of the Chinese economy.

At the same time, we ask why capital flight seems to have had less of a negative impact on China than it has had on other countries? Our answer is that China has not liberalized as much as many neoliberals would have liked. By maintaining controls over many aspects of the economy, the Chinese authorities have been able to mobilize and channel savings to productive purposes despite the large amounts of capital that have fled the country. Of course, as China's liberalization proceeds, China may begin to face the worst of all worlds: large amounts of capital flight, instability and financial crisis, like that experienced in many other semi-industrialized countries.

The rest of this chapter is organized as follows: first, we briefly survey previous estimates of Chinese capital flight and, in the process, define capital flight as we measure it here. Next, we present our estimates of capital flight. We then present our discussion of the causes and consequences of Chinese capital flight and draw conclusions in the final section.

CAPITAL FLIGHT FROM CHINA: DEFINITIONS AND PREVIOUS ESTIMATES

Estimating Capital Flight[1]

There are two general methods of estimating capital flight: the balance of payments method (the direct method) and the residual method (the indirect method) (See Lessard and Williamson 1987; Kant 1996). The first method, developed by Cuddington, incorporates the belief that capital flight is basically the outflow of 'hot' money. This method estimates capital flight as the sum of reported short-term capital exports by the non-bank sector and the errors and omissions entry on the balance of payments. Like the other authors in this volume, we believe that this estimate is too narrow.

The second approach, the so-called residual method, is broader and more widely accepted. It treats capital flight as a residual, the difference between net capital inflows (changes in foreign debt, trade surplus and net foreign direct investment) and the change in foreign reserves (Erbe 1985; World Bank 1985; Bank for International Settlements 1989; Gunter 1991, 1996). It attempts to measure 'unreported' net outflows as an estimate of capital flight.

However, even this method suffers from at least two flaws. First, in the capital account, the recorded foreign debts are often considerably smaller than the corresponding amounts given by the World Bank's *World Debt Tables* and other sources, such as Bank of International Settlements, implying that the country's balance of payments data on debt flows are incomplete. Second, in the current account, widespread trade misinvoicing undermines the accuracy of the official balance of payments data on the value of exports and imports (Boyce and Ndikumana 2000; Gunter 1996). Therefore, the residual method estimates has to be adjusted with these two considerations in mind.

The common remedy for the first problem is to adjust the foreign debt by comparing the data from the balance of payments with World Bank data or with data from the Bank of International Settlements. The second problem can be resolved by comparing the trade data between the importer and exporter countries and adding it to the official trade surplus data[2] to estimate the amount of misinvoicing. Most of the chapters in this book follow this approach, using only data on trade with developed countries and then multiplying up the amount of global misinvoicing by assuming that the rest of the world's misinvoicing represents the same share of total trade as does misinvoicing with developed countries.

These solutions, however, are not without problems. For example, due to the complexity of international trade, it is difficult to identify the exact country of origin of the commodities. This problem is especially acute in the

Table 10. 1 Estimates of capital flight in China by Different Authors (Billions of U.S. Dollars)

Author	Estimate	1982	1983	1984	1985	1986	1987	1988	1989	1990	1991	1992	1993	1994	1995	1996	1997	1998	1999	2000
Yang (2000)	Low est.	—	4.2	-1.0	4.3	4.9	1.4	4.0	7.0	3.7	23.2	23	18.0	25.6	19.6	56.0	70.2	11.5	—	—
	Avg. est.	—	5.5	3.6	8.0	9.0	8.4	13.7	19.7	20.8	41.3	40.1	42.6	51.0	51.6	81.0	103.3	48.6	—	—
	High est.	—	6.7	8.3	11.7	13.0	15.5	23.5	32.5	37.9	59.4	57.2	67.2	76.3	83.5	106.7	136.5	85.6	—	—
Gunter (1996)	Low BOP est.	—	0.99	2.14	1.59	1.72	-0.99	0.43	6.93	-2.33	9.31	1.54	8.0	—	—	—	—	—	—	—
	RES.	—	3.47	0.81	6.06	5.12	-1.18	3.5	2.7	3.48	17.59	9.41	15.0	—	—	—	—	—	—	—
	Avg. est.	—	3.87	3.68	6.26	8.47	7.19	11.3	19.83	17.99	34.62	27.17	38.0	—	—	—	—	—	—	—
	High BOP est.	—	4.27	5.37	6.54	10.17	13.6	20.55	31.24	29.69	48.31	44.65	63.0	—	—	—	—	—	—	—
	Adj. RES.	—	6.74	6.41	10.84	16.87	17.32	20.73	38.43	41.13	63.25	56.17	66.0	—	—	—	—	—	—	—
Wu and Tang (2000) Est. based on data from	PBOC	—	—	—	—	—	—	—	—	20.4	14.2	24.7	24.0	17.5	27.2	24.2	52.3	80.4	—	—
	World Bank	—	—	—	—	—	—	—	—	19.5	11.1	28.0	24.0	22.8	31.1	25.2	54.4	NA	—	—
	IIF	—	—	—	—	—	—	—	—	19.2	20.5	27.8	19.4	23.5	32.8	30.6	52.7	71.5	16.9	—
	Avg. Est.**	—	—	—	—	—	—	—	—	—	15.3	26.8	22.5	21.3	30.4	26.7	53.1	76.0	16.9	—

Song (1999)	Capital Flight	—	—	—	—	—	-0.16	3.94	4.22	4.78	12.93	12.04	21.0	14.43	25.71	18.64	40.75	—	—
Chen (2003)	Errors and Omissions	-0.3	-0.13	0.89	-0.01	0.96	1.52	0.96	-0.12	3.21	6.77	8.21	10.1	9.1	17.82	15.50	22.12	18.9	17.64	11.75
	BOP Method	-0.2	0.15	1.78	0.31	0.47	1.41	1.52	0.87	3.53	6.96	11.7	13.66	12.8	17.33	16.42	40.29	54.73	28.33	15.07
	Residual Method	2.32	1.89	5.49	-3.31	2.09	5.91	5.97	0.08	13.86	10.2	24.38	23.99	17.48	26.78	23.29	57.46	81.42	55.23	41.21
	Res. Method Adjusted 1	2.36	1.87	5.48	-0.79	-1.2	6.13	6.41	-0.51	11.1	10.76	26.82	23.44	17.07	25.56	21.37	47.04	83.11	66.96	35.28
	Res. Method Adjusted 2	1.07	-0.33	2.73	-2.97	-2.91	4.65	4.77	-2.22	8.3	7.57	23.04	20.04	10.78	28.6	23.60	45.97	87.16	67.34	33.72
Beijing University (2000)		—	—	—	—	—	—	—	—	—	—	—	—	—	—	36.4	38.6	23.8	—
Official Estimates		—	—	—	—	—	—	—	—	—	—	—	—	—	—	16.95	16.5	—	—

case of China and Hong Kong. Hong Kong is a very important entrepôt. For example, many goods are sent to Hong Kong and then shipped on to other destinations, such as the USA. China records these as exports to Hong Kong and the USA records these as imports from China, not Hong Kong. So, the discrepancy between the Chinese numbers and the USA numbers will show up as underinvoicing of exports from China to the USA and will therefore be recorded by us as capital flight. However, this is not capital flight but a data-recording idiosyncrasy. To solve this problem, we could treat Hong Kong as a developed country and use its trade data to correct the invoicing data from China. In this example, Hong Kong records the imports from China as imports and this would balance off the exports recorded from China and therefore eliminate the discrepancy. Another possible problem is that certain discrepancies may also reflect the profit or value-added of the Hong Kong company that processes exports from China before they are re-exported. One way to solve this problem is to treat China and Hong Kong as one entity (Gunter 1996). Another way is to subtract the value-added of Hong Kong companies from the discrepancy (Song 1999). After making these adjustments, one can obtain estimates of the total capital outflow.[3]

Previous Studies of Capital Flight from China

In recent years, the issue of capital flight from China has attracted a lot of attention both in the mass media and among economists. Using a variety of methods, a number of authors have made different estimates of the scale of China's capital flight. Table 10.1 lists 20 series of estimates, 18 of which were taken from 5 papers (Yang 2000; Gunter 1996; Wu and Tang 2000; Song 1999; Chen 2003). The other two were obtained from the mass media.[4]

As can be seen in Table 10.1 and Figure 10.1, it is apparent that the estimates vary. The differences result from the different methods adopted, and for those estimates based on the same method, the differences come from the different data sources used in the estimations.

Most of these estimates are based on the residual method. Gunter's (1996) residual method can be used as a baseline to evaluate the other estimates. The basic residual method estimate is the sum of the current account surplus, net foreign direct investment and the increase in foreign debt minus the increase in foreign exchange reserves. Gunter made three adjustments to this basic residual figure. The first one takes out the legitimate resident foreign capital, that is, the non-reserve foreign assets of China's banking system. The second adds the misinvoicing of exports and imports (after adjusting for price discrepancies between c.i.f. and f.o.b.). Gunter's low estimates take the special role of Hong Kong into consideration, while the higher estimates do not.[5] The third one adjusts the foreign debt figures by comparing the data from China, the World Bank and the Bank for International Settlements.

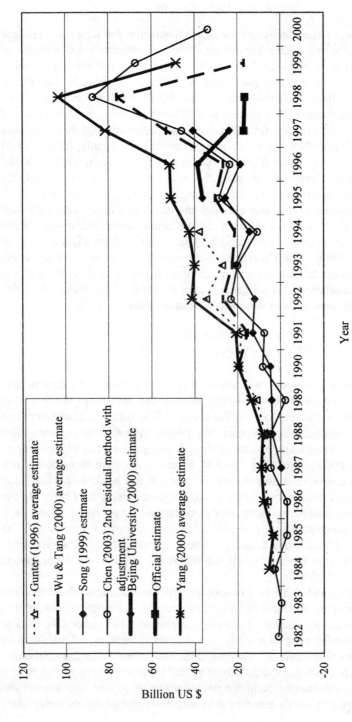

Figure 10.2 Estimates of China's capital flight by different authors

Legend:
- Gunter (1996) average estimate
- Wu & Tang (2000) average estimate
- Song (1999) estimate
- Chen (2003) 2nd residual method with adjustment
- Bejing University (2000) estimate
- Official estimate
- Yang (2000) average estimate

Yang's low estimate does not include adjustments for legitimate resident foreign capital and trade misinvoicing. Her high estimate is quite similar to that of Gunter.[6] Wu and Tang (2000) utilize the basic residual method. What is special is that they use three sets of China's external debt data from the People's Bank of China (PBOC), the World Bank and the Institute of International Finance (IIF), respectively. Therefore, they obtain three sets of estimates. Because they did not include trade misinvoicing, their estimates are much lower than those of Gunter and Yang. Finally, Chen (2003) estimates China's capital flight for the longest period, from 1982 to 2000.[7] Overall, since Chen did not make the trade misinvoicing adjustment, his estimates are much lower than those taking misinvoicing into account.

It is important to note that although the levels of capital flight estimated by these authors are very different, all the computations show very similar patterns in the movement of capital. It is apparent from Figure 10.2 that during the 1980s, China's capital flight was relatively low. Since 1990, capital flight has taken place on a much larger scale. In 1992, 1997 and 1998, China suffered enormous increases in capital flight. After peaking in 1998, the figure dropped back to the level of the mid-1990s.

OUR ESTIMATES OF CAPITAL FLIGHT

In this section we present our estimates of capital flight. We first present estimates based on the basic residual method and then make the following adjustments: exchange rate adjustments, misinvoicing calculations and sanctioned bank accounts overseas. We present the misinvoicing adjustment calculations in two ways: excluding Hong Kong and including Hong Kong as a trading partner. Excluding Hong Kong means we treat Hong Kong as a developing country and, like the other chapters in this book, do not use Hong Kong's export and import data to calculate misinvoicing by China. In the second case, including Hong Kong means we treat Hong Kong as a developed country and use Hong Kong's import and export data with China to calculate China's misinvoicing. These adjustments make a substantial difference both in terms of levels and trends in capital flows. These points are discussed further below.

Figure 10.3 and Table 10.2 present the different estimates of capital flight with and without adjustments.[8] Our basic residual calculation without any adjustments is very close to the analogous estimates by Gunter (2004). The trend suggests two big jumps: the first in 1992, preceding a devaluation of the yuan, and then again in 1997 around the time of the Asian financial crisis. Capital flight peaks in 1998 and drops by half by 2001.

Then we incorporate exchange rate adjustments to take into account the composition of China's external debt and how changes in exchange rates

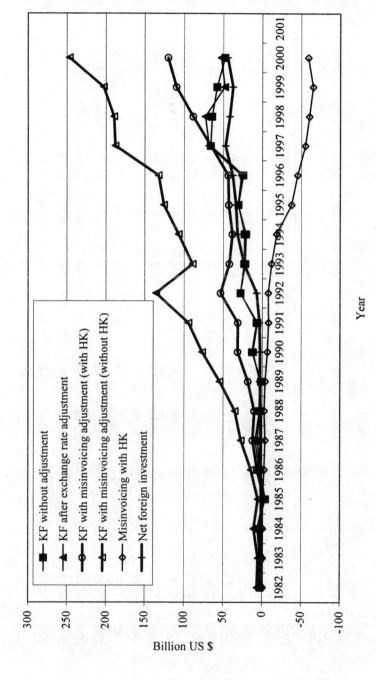

Figure 10.3   Capital flight estimates, misinvoicing with Hong Kong and net foreign investment

Table 10.2 Our Estimates of capital flight in China (Billions of U.S. Dollars)

Year	No adj.	With exchange rate adj.	After misinvoicing adj.		After bank assets adj.		After inflation adj.		After interest earning adj.		Net foreign invest-ment	Diff-erence due to Hong Kong
			With Hong Kong	W/out Hong Kong	With Hong Kong	W/out Hong Kong	With Hong Kong	W/out Hong Kong	With Hong Kong	W/out Hong Kong		
1982	2.32	2.49	3.88	6.35	3.88	6.35	4.84	7.93	3.88	6.35	0.39	−0.8
1983	1.89	1.99	2.11	5.03	2.11	5.03	2.6	6.2	2.46	5.59	0.54	−0.92
1984	5.49	5.77	5.15	10.48	5.15	10.48	6.2	12.61	5.39	11.02	1.12	−0.82
1985	−3.33	−4.22	−3.1	5.11	−3.1	5.11	−3.75	6.18	−2.69	5.96	1.03	−1.03
1986	3.46	1.95	6.33	14.18	7.16	15.01	7.88	17.67	6.16	14.55	1.43	−2.7
1987	8.81	5.93	12.18	27.28	8.3	23.4	14.78	33.1	12.54	28.14	1.67	−3.88
1988	3.27	3.72	9.97	35.05	8.11	33.18	11.63	40.89	10.83	36.98	2.34	−2.73
1989	1.27	2.88	18.24	54.46	20.94	57.16	20.27	60.53	19.15	57.56	2.61	−3.98
1990	12.98	11.85	31.33	76.89	25.3	70.86	33.62	82.53	32.81	81.35	2.66	−6.73
1991	7.15	6.16	31.25	94.36	27.79	90.9	33.47	101.05	33.07	98.86	3.45	−8.16
1992	27.79	27.89	53.43	135.51	48.82	130.91	56.88	144.26	54.59	138.98	7.16	−7.8
1993	23.24	21.79	42.28	89.08	17.01	63.81	44.36	93.46	43.95	93.33	23.12	−11.9
1994	22.77	20.85	38.32	106.94	37.03	105.65	39.69	110.76	40.23	111	31.79	−18.4
1995	30.63	31.06	43.08	125.61	48.27	130.8	43.08	125.61	45.36	131.88	33.85	−37.6

Year												
1996	24.33	26.71	43.76	132.49	39.05	127.78	42.76	129.45	46.09	139.27	38.07	-45.2
1997	66.32	68.32	65.97	187.87	53.38	175.27	64.5	183.68	68.37	195.11	47.33	-55.1
1998	64.42	73.2	88.48	189.54	80.15	181.21	88.71	190.03	91.83	199.1	41.88	-60.3
1999	58.13	48.2	109.83	202.87	104.32	197.35	109.21	201.71	114.21	212.37	37.59	-65.1
2000	47.84	52.65	120.35	246.61	89.31	215.57	113.12	231.81	127.2	259.35	44.4	-59.2
2001	32.59										38.24	

Table 10. 3 Capital flight in China as a percentage of GDP

Year	Without adjustment	After exchange rate adjustment	After all adjustments	
			With Hong Kong	Without Hong Kong
1982	0.81	0.87	1.36	2.22
1983	0.62	0.65	0.8	1.82
1984	2.15	2.25	2.11	4.31
1985	−1.21	−1.54	−0.98	2.17
1986	1.27	0.72	2.26	5.34
1987	2.78	1.87	3.96	8.88
1988	0.83	0.94	2.74	9.36
1989	0.36	0.83	5.49	16.5
1990	3.7	3.38	9.35	23.18
1991	1.82	1.57	8.44	25.23
1992	6.18	6.2	12.14	30.9
1993	3.91	3.66	7.39	15.69
1994	4.12	3.77	7.28	20.09
1995	4.36	4.42	6.45	18.75

1996	2.96	3.24	5.6	16.92
1997	7.33	7.55	7.56	21.57
1998	6.75	7.67	9.62	20.87
1999	5.82	4.83	11.44	21.27
2000	4.43	4.88	11.79	24.03

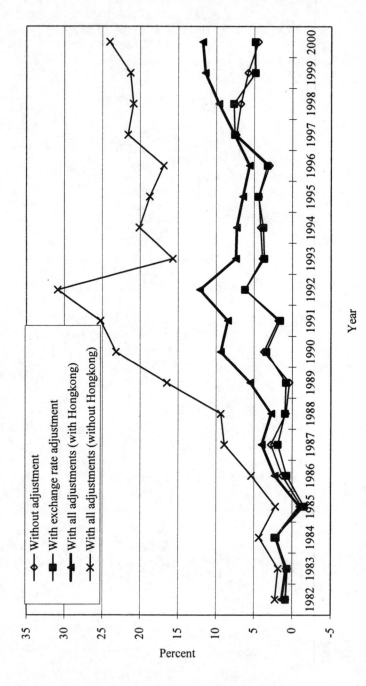

Figure 10.4   Different estimates of capital flight as a percentage of GDP

affect the value of its debt inflows (Boyce and Ndikumana 2001; Beja, Chapter 3). As one can see, including the estimates with exchange rate adjustments seems to make little difference except at the very end of the period.

Including misinvoicing does make a substantial difference to the estimates of capital flight. First, for the estimates without Hong Kong, it raises the estimates of capital flight threefold. If Hong Kong is treated as a developed country (with Hong Kong), capital flight estimates are much lower. Both of these estimates also differ in another respect from the basic residual calculations: capital flight continues to increase in the latter part of the period, rather than peaking in 1998 in the unadjusted figures.

One reason why capital flight estimates are smaller when Hong Kong data are included is because there is a substantial amount of smuggling that occurs from Hong Kong to China. Smuggling of imports would involve underinvoicing of imports of China from Hong Kong. Underinvoicing of imports reduces estimates of capital flight.[9] Figure 10.6, using Hong Kong data on trade with China, indicates the sizeable amount of smuggling that has occurred over the period (the negative sign for import discrepancies indicates underinvoicing of imports, most of which presumably represents smuggling).

Figure 10.4 and Table 10.3 present data on capital flight as a share of GDP. The figure shows that capital flight without any adjustment peaks at below 8 percent of GDP, while the estimate derived by treating Hong Kong as a developing country for misinvoicing calculations (without Hong Kong) is extremely large, peaking at over 30 percent of GDP in 1991 and remaining above 20 percent in the late 1990s. On the other hand, the calculation that utilizes Hong Kong data shows capital flight peaking at 11 percent of GDP in 1991 and rising back up to over 10 percent of GDP by 2001.

Figure 10.3 and Table 10.2 also compare capital flight with foreign direct investment. In all cases capital flight represents a substantial portion of foreign direct investment and by some measures, *exceeds* foreign direct investment. Since FDI is seen as one of the most important signs of China's economic success, this large amount of capital flight in relation to the very large amount of FDI is a stark indicator of the vast amount of capital flight from China.

EXPLANATIONS FOR CAPITAL FLIGHT

Explanations in the Literature

The factors that have been widely used to explain capital flight include the anticipation of higher rates of return abroad, accumulation of foreign debt, increases in budget deficits, relatively high domestic inflation, overvalued local currency, domestic financial repression, domestic economic recession and political and financial risks (Cuddington 1986, 1987; Conesa 1987; Pastor 1990; Mikkelsen 1991; Lensink et. al. 2000). In the case of China, all the above factors have been cited as relevant, with the exception of recessions. However, we think it is important to place China's capital flight in a broader perspective.

Our Explanation for China's Capital Flight

We argue that corruption, privatization and liberalization are the most important factors that provide the sources and channels of capital flight in China. It is no secret that public corruption in China is extensive. In 1992, the 14th Congress of the Chinese Communist Party (CCP) set the establishment of a 'Socialist Market Economy System' as its goal. This destroyed the belief of many officials in socialism and convinced many that the direction of reform would not be reversed. These developments hastened the spread of corruption and may help to explain, at least in part, the upward trend in capital flight and the doubling of the scale of capital flight in 1992. A related factor was the wave of privatization that began in 1995 and which offered much opportunity for corruption.

The liberalization of the economy, especially the foreign sector, offered both opportunities for corruption and also channels for capital flight. In fact, the liberalization of the current account, together with the privatization wave and the Asian crisis, may account for another doubling of the capital flight after 1996.

The Impact of Capital Flight on China's Economy

One of the biggest puzzles about China's capital flight is reconciling the great success of the country's economic growth with the large amount of capital flight reported above. The puzzle has several components. First, why would there have been so much capital flight if the economy was performing so well? Second, how could the economy continue to grow so rapidly despite the large amounts of capital flight? We have addressed the first question above. There we argue that liberalization, privatization and associated corruption, as well as the desire of wealthy elites to protect their assets from social control, help to explain capital flight. Here we would like to focus on the second question.

The reason why capital flight had a smaller negative impact on the Chinese economy than it did in other countries is that the government retained a high degree of control over the economy during much of this period. As discussed above, despite liberalization, the government retained significant controls over the capital account. Public investment continues to be a significant part of total investment in China. Many sectors of the Chinese economy, including the financial sector, continue to be tightly controlled. Performance requirements and other state regulations continue to be imposed on foreign direct investment. The slow trend of financial liberalization has allowed the government to retain control over the exchange rate to promote exports. These financial and macroeconomic policies have allowed the Chinese government to take advantage of its huge pool of cheap and productive labor and thereby run an enormous trade surplus. More rapid liberalization of financial markets and policy would have brought about significant economic instability and, in that context, capital flight would most likely have had a much more negative impact on the economy.

Still, capital flight has had some severe consequences. Perhaps most importantly, it has facilitated public corruption in China. Apart from the enormous problems created by such corruption, capital flight has also contributed to the worsening of income and wealth distribution that has characterized recent Chinese economic development.

Solutions to the Problem of Capital Flight

Most authors argue that Chinese capital flight stems primarily from insufficient liberalization. We argue, on the contrary, that limited liberalization has greatly reduced the costs of the capital flight that has occurred. Thus, the solution to costly capital flight does not lie in more rapid liberalization, but a continuation and improvement of government management of the economy. This is not the place to develop a complete economic plan for China. Nonetheless, continuing along this path of liberalization and unequal economic growth can only lead to more capital flight. Indeed, our main statistical finding is that, contrary to other estimates, capital flight has continued to increase beyond the period of the Asian financial crisis and into the period of accelerating privatization and economic liberalization.

SUMMARY AND CONCLUSIONS

This chapter presents new estimates of Chinese capital flight. Like other estimates, our calculations indicate that, as China liberalized its economy and financial markets, starting in the late 1980s, capital flight has been substantial, at times running as high as 10 percent of GDP. Moreover, like others, our estimates indicate that capital flight accelerated during the two crisis periods of the 1990s: prior to the devaluation of the yuan in 1994 and then again during the Asian financial crisis of 1997, despite the tightening up of capital controls in the latter period. Unlike previous estimates, however, most of our calculations suggest that Chinese capital flight has continued growing into the twenty-first century, during the period of accelerating economic liberalization. Moreover, our measures indicate that the volume of capital flight has matched or even been greater than the large volume of foreign direct investment flowing into China in the last several decades.

A solution to Chinese capital flight and the problems associated with it is likely to require a reinvigoration of Chinese government economic management, not an acceleration of economic liberalization, as many of the authors in this field have suggested.

APPENDIX

Data Notes on Misinvoicing Calculations[10]

The trade misinvoicing adjustment for China raises special problems due to the fact that a number of its top trading partners are developing countries. The rationale for using industrialized countries in computing discrepancies (Boyce and Ndikumana 2001) is that we believe their data to be of generally higher quality. This is partly because of better data collection systems, but also partly because as hard-currency countries their data are not expected to be systematically biased by export underinvoicing and import overinvoicing for capital flight and because their customs services are better at minimizing smuggling (both pure smuggling, that is, outright evasion, and technical smuggling, that is, import underinvoicing).

Based on the statistics reported by China, the top 10 export partners for China are the USA, Japan, Germany, Hong Kong, Korea, Taiwan, Singapore, Netherlands, UK and Italy and the top 10 import partners are the USA, Japan, Germany, Hong Kong, Korea, Malaysia, Singapore, Thailand, Taiwan and Russia. Malaysia, Singapore and Thailand are dropped out of our misinvoicing calculations for the reasons noted above. Russia, Korea and Taiwan are dropped due to data availability problems.

The inclusion of Hong Kong is difficult to justify for a different reason: some of the trade may be simply passing through it to or from a third country. Actually, the Direction of Trade data published by the IMF specifically noted: 'Discrepancies in bilateral trade statistics as reported by China and its trading partners exist, particularly with industrial countries. Trade with these countries is classified by China as trade with Hong Kong Special Administrative Region (HKSAR) if it passes through HKSAR ports'. However, Hong Kong does not record these transit trade transactions as imports to or exports from Hong Kong. Our calculation shows the anomaly of export 'overinvoicing' – that is, Hong Kong recording lower imports from China than China's recorded exports to Hong Kong. Still, leaving out Hong Kong completely carries the risk of over-estimating capital flight because it fails to capture the smuggling that comes into China from Hong Kong (underinvoicing of imports by China from Hong Kong). Hence, we chose to present estimates both ways: including misinvoicing calculations based on data from Hong Kong and excluding these data.

Finally, in all cases we included nine industrialized countries in our misinvoicing calculations: USA, UK, Australia, France, Germany, Italy, Netherlands, Canada and Japan.

NOTES

The authors thank James Boyce, Leonce Ndikumana and the members of the capital flight group of the Economics Department, University of Massachusetts, Amherst, for assistance and Mehrene Larudee and Christian Weller for helpful comments and suggestions. Of course, all errors are ours alone.

1. See Beja, Chapter 3, this book, for an extensive discussion of the meaning and measurement of capital flight.
2. The discrepancies between the trade data of importer and exporter countries need further adjustments because the import data include costs of insurance and freight (c.i.f.) but the export data exclude them (f.o.b.).
3. However, by some definitions, not all of this outflow is capital flight. Changes in legitimate resident foreign capital, such as reported non-reserve foreign assets of the banking system, authorized direct and portfolio investment in foreign countries, net authorized lending to foreigners and net deferred earnings from exports might not constitute 'capital flight' (Gunter 1996; Song 1999).
4. The first was cited in the *China Daily* 2002 and the second comes from the China News website. Figure 10.1 also shows some of these estimates.
5. The special role of Hong Kong is discussed further later in the chapter.
6. She did not adjust for the price difference between c.i.f and f.o.b. She also did not adjust the foreign debt data. We find that the differences between their high estimates are relatively small.
7. His first three series of estimates are quite straightforward; the fourth is more complicated. It takes out the net short-term lending by the banking system of China, which is similar to the legitimate resident foreign capital adjustment made by Gunter. Based on this, Chen's fifth estimate excludes tourism income and other capital earnings. Song's (1999) method is the most complex one among those listed in the table above, though he basically follows Gunter's approach.
8. For data sources for the graphs, please see the data Appendix.
9. Capital flight increases through underinvoicing of exports and overinvoicing of imports. Both of these leave unreported funds abroad and can be used as a mechanism for capital flight. Overinvoicing of exports and underinvoicing of imports have the opposite effect. These two forms of misinvoicing reduce estimates of capital flight, because they use up more foreign exchange than is reported. Underinvoicing of imports, for example, is used to smuggle in goods to avoid paying taxes and fees or avoid quotas.
10. We thank James Boyce and Leonce Ndikumana for helping us to clarify these points.

REFERENCES

Bank for International Settlements (1989), 59th Annual Report, Basle: BIS.

Boyce, James and Léonce Ndikumana, (2001), 'Is Africa a Net Creditor? New Estimates of Capital Flight from Severely Indebted Sub-Saharan African Countries, 1970–1996', *Journal of Development Studies*, **38** (2), 27–56.

Braunstein, Elissa and Gerald Epstein (2002), 'Bargaining power and Foreign Direct Investment in China: Can 1.3 Billion Consumers Tame the Multinationals?', University of Massachusetts, Amherst: Political Economy Research Institute Working Paper No. 45.

Chen, Guihong (2003), 'The Scale and Reasons of China's Capital Flight', Working Paper No. C2003004, China Center for Economic Research.

Chenery, Hollis B. and Alan M. Strout (1966), 'Foreign Aid and Economic Development', *American Economic Review*, **56** (4), 679–733.

China Daily (2002), 'China plans crackdown on capital flight', August 21, Beijing.

Camdessus, M. (1998), 'Capital Account Liberalization and the Role of the Fund', Speech: March 9, www.imf.org/external/np/speeches/1998/030998.

Conesa, E. R. (1987), 'The Flight of Capital From Latin America', Washington: Inter-American Bank, mimeo.

Cuddington, John T. (1986), 'Capital Flight: Estimates, Issues and Explanations', *Princeton Studies in International Finance*, No. 58, Princeton, NJ: Princeton University, International Finance Section, Princeton, New Jersey.

Cuddington, John T. (1987), 'Macroeconomic Determinants of Capital Flight: An Econometric Investigation', in Donald R. Lessard and John Williamson (eds), *Capital Flight and Third World Debt*, Washington, DC: Institute for International Economics.

Dooley, M. (1986), 'Country Specific Risk Premiums, Capital Flight and Net Investment Income Payments in Selected Developing Countries', IMF Department Memorandum 86/17.

Epstein, Gerald, Ilene Grabel and K. S. Jomo (2003), 'Capital Management Techniques In Developing Countries: An Assessment of Experiences from the 1990s and Lessons For the Future', University of Massachusetts, Amherst: Political Economy Research Institute, Working Paper No. 56.

Erbe, S. (1985), 'The Flight of Capital from Developing Countries', *Intereconomics*, **20** (6), 268–275.

Fitzgerald, Valpy and Alex Cobham (2000), 'Capital Flight: Causes, Effects, Magnitude and Implications', Background paper for the White Paper 2000 of the UK government, www.globalization.gov.uk/BackgroundWord/TransNational CorporationsAmarInamdar.doc.

Groombridge, Mark A. (2001), 'Capital Account Liberalization in China: Prospects, Prerequisites and Pitfalls', *Cato Journal*, **21** (1), 119-131.

Gunter, Frank (1991), Colombian Capital Flight, *Journal of Interamerican Studies and World Affairs*, **33**, 123–147.

Gunter, Frank (1994), 'Determinants of Capital Flight and Repatriation: A Transaction Costs Approach', Working Paper, Inter-American Development Bank.

Gunter, Frank (1996), 'Capital Flight from the People's Republic of China: 1984–1994', *China Economic Review*, **7**, 77–96.

Gunter, Frank (2004), 'Capital flight from China: 1984–2001', *China Economic Review* **15**, 63–85.

International Monetary Fund (1998), 'Seminar Discusses the Orderly Path to Capital Account Liberalization', *IMF Survey*, 27 (March).

Kant, Chander (1996), Foreign Direct Investment and Capital Flight, (Princeton Studies in International Finance, No. 80). Princeton, New Jersey: Princeton University International Finance.

Khan, M. S. and N. Haque (1987), 'Capital Flight from Developing Countries', *Finance and Development*, March.

Kim,Tacho (1993), *International Money and Banking*, London: Routledge.

Kindleberger,C. (1937), '*International Short-term Capital Movement*', Columbia University Press.

Lessard, Donald R. and John Williamson (eds) (1987), *Capital Flight and Third World Debt*, Washington, DC: Institute for International Economics.

Lensink, R., N. Hermes and V. Murinde (2000), 'Capital Flight and Political Risk', *Journal of International Money and Finance*, **19** (1), 73-92.

Mikkelsen, J. G. (1991), 'An Econometric Investigation of Capital Flight', *Applied Economics*, **23**, 73–85.

Pastor, M. (1990), 'Capital Flight from Latin America', *World Development*, **18** (1), 1–18.

Shaw, Edward S. (1973), *Financial Deepening in Economic Development*, New York: Oxford University Press.

Song, Wenbing (1999), 'A Study on China's Capital Flight: 1987–1997', *Economic Research*, May (*Zhongguo Ziben Waitao Wenti De Yanjiu: 1987–1997, Jingji Yanjiu*).

Tornell, A. (1992),'The Tragedy of Commons and Economic Growth: Why Does Capital Flow from Poor ·to Rich Countries?' *Journal of Political Economy*, **100** (6).

Walter Ingo (1985), *Secret Money*, London: George Allen & Unwin.

World Bank (1985), *World Development Report*, New York: Oxford University Press.

Wu, Friedrich and Leslie Tang (2000), 'China's Capital Flight, 1990–1999: Estimates and Implications', *Review of Pacific Basin Financial Markets and Policies*, **3** (1) 59–75.

Yang, Haizhen and Shidi Zhang (2000), *China's Capital Flight: An Analysis of the Effects on Investments*, unpublished manuscript.

Yang, Haizhen (2000), An Econometric Analysis of the Factors Influencing China's Capital Flight, Mimeo, (Zhongguo Ziben Waitao Yingxiang Yinshu De Jiliang Fenxi.)

Yao, Zhizhong (2000), 'The Change of China's Capital Account and its Macroeconomic Effects', Working Paper No. 11, 2000, National Economy Institute, Chinese Economic Reform Research Fund, (Ziben Xiangmu De Bianhua Ji Hongguan Yingxiang, Zhongguo Jingji Gaige Yanjiu Jijinhui Guomin Jingji Yanjiusuo).

PART THREE

Policy Issues

11. Regulating Capital Flight

Eric Helleiner

INTRODUCTION

In the last few years, the regulation of global finance has emerged centrally on the global policy agenda. One issue, however, has been strikingly absent from the public debates: the regulation of the flow of private flight capital from poorer to richer countries. Considerable discussion has been focused on the management of the enormous private flows of money from rich to poor countries. But financial globalization has been a two-way street. At the same time that investors from rich countries have poured money into 'emerging markets', citizens from many poorer countries have been sending their money in the other direction. The absence of interest in regulating this capital flight is puzzling, given its economic importance.

During the international debt crisis of the 1980s, the private assets of citizens of some Latin American and African countries held abroad were equal to, or even greater than, the size of the country's external official debt. These countries were, in other words, creditors to the world economy at the very moment they were experiencing 'debt crises'. If capital flight could have been prevented, or if the foreign private assets of their citizens could have been mobilized to help pay off the public liabilities of the country, there would have been no debt crisis. More recently, despite all the attention on the volatile role of foreign investors, domestic citizens exporting their money largely triggered the 1994 Mexican crisis and the 1997 East Asian crisis. Massive capital flight from Russia during the 1990s was a major cause of that country's ongoing financial difficulties. The size of flight capital held abroad by Russian citizens was estimated to be roughly the size of the country's external debt and the annual outflows in the late 1990s were more than four times the country's annual external debt servicing costs.[1]

The neglect of capital flight in current debates is also striking given the attention it received at the 1944 Bretton Woods conference. This conference is often said to have laid the foundations for today's financial order and many reformers today talk of the need for a 'renewed Bretton Woods' vision. Usually overlooked, however, is the fact that the Bretton Woods architects saw the regulation of capital flight as a key pillar of the international financial order they hoped to construct. In their minds, capital flight from poorer countries needed to be regulated in order to reduce the scale of international financial crises, enhance the policy autonomy of poorer countries and preserve a stable exchange rate and international trading system. The Bretton Woods architects also outlined innovative ideas about the role that international cooperation could play in making the regulation of capital flight more effective. Although these ideas were implemented only rarely in the post-1945 years, I argue in this chapter that the time may have finally come to consider them more seriously.

THE BRETTON WOODS VISION: REGULATING CAPITAL FLIGHT THROUGH INTERNATIONAL COOPERATION

'Capital flight' is a notoriously difficult term to define precisely, but it refers generally to an outflow of capital that is not part of normal commercial transactions from a country where capital is relatively scarce. Some argue that it can only be stopped by changing the afflicted countries' economic policies that are said to have caused the exodus of 'hot money', such as overvalued exchange rates or inflationary monetary policies. This view, however, ignores the extent to which capital flight – especially in a context such as that of contemporary Russia – is also related to factors more difficult to correct by economic reforms, such as political instability or corruption. Furthermore, deflationary stabilization programs may encourage further flight of money that is escaping the low returns on capital in the country's depressed economy. Finally, some analysts critique the focus on economic stabilization on more political grounds that it does not call into question whether domestic elites should have the right to take their money abroad in the face of domestic difficulties. In Manuel Pastor's (1990: 14) words, 'What is essentially being said is that wealthy individuals...be allowed veto power over the direction of national policy.'

For these reasons, many analysts argue that capital controls have a role to play – usually alongside various economic stabilization measures – in stemming capital flight. This too was the view of the principal Bretton Woods architects, John Maynard Keynes from Britain and Harry Dexter White from the USA (Helleiner 1994). At that time, their fear was of large-scale capital flight from war-devastated Europe to the USA in the post-war period. This fear was a key reason for their insistence that all countries have the right to introduce capital controls under Article 6 of the IMF's Articles of Agreement. They worried that, without such controls, European countries' policy autonomy would be undermined, stable exchange rates and international trading patterns would be disrupted, and that the meager resources of the IMF would be exhausted trying to finance payments imbalances caused by the flight capital.

But Keynes and White also recognized the difficulties that countries would have making their controls on capital outflows fully effective because of the fungibility and mobility of money. Indeed, it is these very difficulties that have led some analysts today to be skeptical of the role that controls on capital outflows could play in the new international financial architecture. What is often forgotten, however, is that Keynes and White addressed this issue directly with a further proposal. They argued that controls on capital flight would be much more effective if the countries receiving that flight capital assisted in their enforcement.

In their initial drafts of the Bretton Woods agreement, both Keynes and White required the governments of receiving countries to share information with the governments of countries using capital controls about foreign holdings of the latter's citizens. White went further in his draft to suggest also that receiving countries should refuse to accept capital flight altogether without the agreement of the sending country's government. As he wrote in 1942:

> It would seem to be an important step in the direction of world stability if a member government could obtain the full cooperation of other member governments in the control of capital flows. For example, after the war a number of countries could request the US not to permit increases in the deposits or holdings of their nationals, or to do so only with a license granted by the government making the request. Or, some governments greatly in need of capital might request the US to supplement their efforts to attract capital back to the native country by providing information or imposing special regulations or even special taxes on the holdings of the nationals of the foreign countries (quoted in Helleiner 1995: 83–4).

Both of these proposals were strongly opposed by the US financial community which had profited from the handling of flight capital during the 1930s and which feared that the proposals would affect New York's reputation as an international financial center. In the face of this opposition, the final IMF Articles of Agreement contained watered-down versions of Keynes' and White's initial proposals. Cooperation between countries to control capital movements was now simply permitted, rather than required (Article 8–2b). The only requirement in this area was a limited one in that IMF members had to ensure that all exchange contracts which contravened other members' exchange controls were 'unenforceable' in their territory (Article 8–2b).

POST-WAR INTEREST IN CAPITAL CONTROLS

Keynes and White's proposals to use international cooperation to strengthen national efforts to control capital flight were innovative and interesting ones, but they were rarely implemented during the post-1945 period. The only exception came during the 1947–48 economic crisis in Western Europe which produced the Marshall aid program. As Keynes and White had predicted at Bretton Woods, there was enormous capital flight from European countries to the USA immediately after World War Two, and it contributed greatly to the 1947–48 crisis. When they encountered difficulties controlling this flight capital unilaterally, many European governments turned to the USA for assistance. Some governments requested that the US government share information it might have about the holdings of their citizens in the USA. The French government went further, asking the US government to force US financial institutions to hold assets of French citizens subject to instructions from the French government.

The issue of whether to provide such assistance became a prominent one politically in the USA during this period because it coincided with the debate on Marshall Aid. Many conservative and often isolationist members of Congress seized on the idea of assisting European efforts to track flight capital as a way of reducing the cost of the aid program to US taxpayers. As Republican Senator Henry Cabot Lodge argued at the time, 'It seems to me that you cannot defend either before an American audience or a foreign audience, for that matter, a proposition whereby the people of moderate means in this country are being taxed to support a foreign aid program which the well-to-do people abroad are not helping to support.' He continued, 'In a lot of these countries it is a well-known fact that there is small, bloated, selfish class of people whose assets have been spread all over the place and that that is a very bad thing for the morale of those countries and it is a bad thing for the morale over here.' Former US president Herbert Hoover also defended the proposal to mobilize European flight capital saying, 'If there is protest that taking over these privately held resources is a hardship to the owners, it may be pointed out that the alternative is a far greater hardship for the American taxpayer.'[2] As at Bretton Woods, however, strong opposition to the initiative came from members of the US financial community. They argued that initiatives to share information and repatriate assets would violate the property rights of foreigners and undermine the private relationship between bankers and their clients. Government officials also argued that obtaining information about all the assets of foreign citizens held in the USA would be very time-consuming and costly. In the end, the government found a compromise. It chose not to collect information on the flight capital that had entered the USA since the end of the war – this was seen as too burdensome a task and was strongly opposed by US financiers. However, it did agree to share information with European governments about European private assets that the government had seized during wartime (which represented flight capital from the 1930s and early war years) that had not yet been claimed by European citizens. A clause requiring any government receiving aid to take measures 'available to it' to 'locate and identify and put into appropriate use' the foreign assets of its citizens was also included in the Congressional act that approved Marshall Aid. Although the initiative fell short of what many were calling for, it represented an example of the kind of idea that Keynes and White had floated.

Interest in curtailing capital flight through international cooperation then faded away for most of the post-1945 period, with the exception of some discussions in the USA during the 1980s Latin American debt crisis. Because of the size of Latin American flight capital held abroad, a number of observers suggested that the US government might use regulatory initiatives to try to reduce capital flight as part of their effort to help Latin American governments solve the debt crisis. One of the more prominent proposals was put forward in late 1985 by the economist David Felix (1985). He argued that US banks should be prompted to share information about the assets of Latin America citizens with Latin American governments in order to assist them to repatriate the assets. In 1986, some interesting proposals were also put forward at a conference hosted by the Institute for International Economics and attended by representatives from the international financial institutions, banks, and creditor and debtor governments (Williamson and Lessard 1987). These included measures to discourage US banks from aggressively soliciting flight capital from Latin America as well as proposals to tax the interest income earned on Latin American deposits in the USA and to give the proceeds to the Inter-American Development Bank (IADB).

Little came of these proposals. Again, many in the financial community argued against the proposals and US policymakers feared that any US move would simply encourage Latin American asset-holders to move their funds to Switzerland or other offshore locations which offered bank secrecy. More generally, Reagan administration officials argued that the better solution to capital flight was not a regulatory one but rather one involving the implementation of anti-inflationary, liberalizing policies in Latin American countries (Helleiner 1995).

AN IDEA WORTH RECONSIDERING

Although the proposal to use international cooperation to regulate flight capital has rarely been implemented, it is an idea whose time may finally have come for several reasons. To begin with, the USA and many other Western governments appear to be more sympathetic to the role that capital controls might play in stemming capital flight since the 1997–98 international financial crises. In February 1999, for example, US President Clinton (1999) expressed his concern about the difficulties Russia was having in trying to 'control the flow of its money...across its borders'. At their report to the G-8 Summit meeting in Cologne in June 1999, the G-7 Finance Ministers (1999) also noted that controls on capital outflows 'may be necessary in certain exceptional circumstances'. As they explained: 'In exceptional circumstances, countries may impose capital or exchange controls as part of payments suspensions or standstills, in conjunction with IMF support for their policies and programmes, to provide time for an orderly debt restructuring.' One of the key supporters of such an internationally legitimated standstill arrangement has been Canada's Finance Minister Paul Martin (1999: 6) who recently argued: 'The point is that we need to stop condoning capital flight – by either international or domestic investors'.

Perhaps more important is a growing interest in drawing connections between the regulation of money laundering and that of capital flight. The importance of this connection is that international cooperation with respect to the control of money laundering has become very sophisticated over the last decade. Led by the US, the G-7 countries launched a major initiative in the late 1980s to target international money laundering. They have pressed countries around the world to criminalize money laundering and to force financial institutions to report all 'suspicious' transactions to domestic authorities and refuse to engage in transactions where the identity of the customers involved is unknown. Particularly important, they have also created extensive arrangements for international information sharing and legal cooperation between governments with respect to the pursuit and prosecution of money laundering cases. A key aspect of these arrangements has been a commitment that participating governments have made not to allow bank secrecy provisions to interfere with these forms of international cooperation. Even countries traditionally strict about bank secrecy, such as Switzerland, have agreed to this provision.

This international initiative is still very much in progress: laws are still being implemented, regulatory techniques are being refined, and some financial centers have not yet agreed to participate. In the wake of September 11, 2001, the effort to stop terrorism-related financial flows has also given new impetus to efforts to combat illicit international movements of funds. As this emerging international regime of financial control becomes increasingly sophisticated, its potential importance for the regulation of capital flight is being recognized. With the creation of complex information-collecting and sharing procedures, the international community is putting in place structures that could be used to operationalize the kind of cooperation proposed at Bretton Woods and attempted in a limited way during the

Marshall Plan. Among the first to make this point prominently was Karin Lissakers, former US Executive Director to the IMF, in her important 1991 book *Banks, Borrowers and the Establishment*. After lamenting the fact that the USA did nothing during the 1980s to discourage inflows of flight capital from Latin America (and indeed actually encouraged them with some regulatory changes), she suggested briefly that the new anti-money laundering regulations might help to enable future US governments to take a different approach. As she pointed out, 'The potential of the new record-keeping and client-identification requirements as a tool for tracking flight capital is obvious' (Lissakers 1991: 158).

The importance of the international fight against money laundering does not lie just in its creation of international cooperative structures that might be useful for tracking flight capital. Equally significant is the fact that policymakers are increasingly linking certain kinds of capital flight with the crime of money laundering. This link has been made, for example, in the Russian context. At their June 1999 summit, the G-8 countries made an important commitment in speaking of their support Russia's reform: 'We agreed to deepen our cooperation on law enforcement, fighting organized crime and money laundering, *including as they relate to capital flight*' (emphasis added). This last statement seemed to indicate that the G-7 governments have now formally agreed to cooperate with the Russian government in curtailing capital flight and that they may also be prepared to draw on the anti-money laundering regime as part of this initiative.

The possibility of using the anti-money laundering regulations to curtail flight capital has also begun to appear in the context of growing US interest in cracking down on government corruption in poorer countries. In September 1999, both the US Senate and House of Representatives introduced bills that aimed to widen the definition of unlawful money laundering activities to include fraud committed against a foreign government and misuse of funds of international institutions such as the IMF. The early Congressional committee hearings on the bills made clear that this initially was driven by allegations of improper use of IMF loans to Russia as well as dramatic cases of corruption-related capital flight involving Third World leaders. Although the bills addressed only these specific elements of the phenomenon of 'capital flight', its provisions were important because they went beyond simply sharing information as a way of curtailing capital flight. Had these bills passed (and they reportedly had the support of the Clinton administration), they would have prevented US banks from handling money involved in these activities altogether. Interestingly, the idea is attracting support beyond the USA as well. In October 1999, a G-8 ministerial conference on combating transnational organized crime agreed 'on the importance of extending predicate offenses of money laundering beyond drug-related offenses to other serious crimes, such as bribery or corruption' (Ministerial Conference 1999; see also Baker 1999).

EMBEDDING THE REGULATION OF CAPITAL FLIGHT IN 'THE NEW FINANCIAL ARCHITECTURE'

With this growing interest, now may be a useful moment to consider more generally whether some kind of international cooperation relating to capital flight could be embedded within the new international financial architecture, as the Bretton Woods architects initially intended. One approach would be to widen the definition of money laundering activities used by the international community to include capital flight. Some key policymakers have in fact suggested this idea in the past. In 1993, the then president of the Financial Action Task Force – the international body leading the fight against money laundering – wrote that he thought it necessary to recognize that 'money laundering' could be associated with 'in the case of developing countries, offenses relating to capital flight' (Sherman 1993: 13). By speaking of 'offenses' relating to capital flight, he highlights that this kind of initiative would only target capital flight that broke exchange control regulations in poor countries. Other kinds of capital flight might be targeted by a different approach that widened the definition of money laundering to include crimes related to fraud and government corruption, as suggested by the recent US Congressional bills.

A less ambitious initiative might involve only the use of information-sharing from the money-laundering regime to pursue flight capital. Here, I am not thinking of the kind of far-reaching proposal that Keynes and White had in mind in which countries should be required to share all information about foreign private holdings with any foreign government that requested it. Instead, what may make more sense today is a more limited proposal in which information-sharing could be provided only in instances where countries are introducing capital controls as a way of coping with a severe financial crisis.

Like the proposals for the activation of standstill clauses on cross-border contracts, the IMF could be empowered to declare when such a crisis moment exists. When the declaration is made, the information-collecting and sharing mechanisms developed to fight money laundering could be mobilized to track capital flight from the crisis-struck country and to share the relevant information with that country's government. The information-collecting and sharing obligations, in other words, would not be considered part of the normal functioning of the global financial system (as Keynes and White had imagined) but rather simply part of its crisis-management procedures.

This proposal might have several advantages in helping the resolution of financial crises. First, it might help to reduce the costs of financial bailouts to Western taxpayers and international organizations. This is not just because capital flight might be slowed; existing flight capital abroad might also be mobilized either by the country experiencing the crisis or by the international community. During the discussions in the late 1940s, members of Congress raised this issue. The US government at the time also considered a number of other interesting proposals of this kind, including one IBRD proposal that would have seen a portion of the European flight capital invested in either US or IBRD bonds with the proceeds used for aid or loans to European governments. We have also seen in the 1980s that some proposals were made to tax foreign deposits and use the revenue for international public financial support.

Second, this proposal might help spread the distribution of the adjustment burden within the country experiencing a financial crisis in a more equitable fashion. During the international debt crisis of the 1980s and also during more recent crises, there has been pressure from international creditors for debtor governments to assume the private foreign debt of their citizens as part of their crisis-management procedures. There are important reasons why this has been seen as necessary, but it has had the side-effect of shifting the burden of adjustment for private borrowing behavior – usually that of more wealthy citizens – onto the nation as a whole. By mobilizing flight capital in crisis moments to help service the external debt of the country, the international community would ensure that it was not just the foreign debts of wealthier citizens in these countries that were 'nationalized' but also their foreign assets.

Third, the existence of this kind of procedure at the international level might discourage flight capital in the future. At the moment, the prospect of financial crises creates a strong incentive for wealthy domestic asset holders in poorer countries to engage in capital flight. Not only do they protect their money from a potential devaluation or from the imposition of capital controls this way, but they also have the prospect of 'round-tripping' the money after a devaluation to buy up domestic assets at bargain prices. If domestic asset holders were aware that their foreign assets might be mobilized for public purposes as part of a financial rescue plan, they might be less inclined to flee at the first sign of a possible crisis. In this way, the existence of this kind of procedure might help to discourage speculative flows and contribute to a more stable international financial order.

CAN IT BE DONE?

What are the prospects for these kinds of reforms to bolster international cooperation in curtailing capital flight? In a legal sense, they would require little change to IMF rules, since several parts of its Articles of Agreement – the legacies of Keynes' and White's original proposal – allow international cooperation of this kind. With respect to money-laundering regulations and procedures, it might be necessary simply to expand the definition of 'money laundering' in the ways discussed above.

In a more political sense, opposition can be expected from groups in poorer countries whose involvement in capital flight is the target of the initiative. If past experiences are any guide, opposition will also come in Northern countries from the financial community and those who oppose capital controls more generally – what one prominent economist has called the 'Wall Street-Treasury complex' in the US context (Bhagwati 1998). Then Treasury Secretary Robert Rubin provided an interesting example of the importance with which the principle of free capital movements is sometimes defended in the context of capital flight in March 1999. After telling a Congressional panel that he suspected much of the $4.8 billion IMF loan to Russia last year 'may have been siphoned off improperly', he later qualified his testimony saying 'it may have been careless to use the word "improper" because there is nothing improper about moving money out of Russia or any other country' (quoted in Sanger 1999: 8).

On the other hand, the proposal may attract support from some important quarters. In many poorer countries, the issue of capital flight is a highly politicized one and governments in these countries may see this reform as a popular one for them to back. In Russia, for example, Vladimir Tikhomirov (1997: 595, 599, 595) notes that the issue is 'socially explosive' and 'one of the most hotly debated in Russian politics', with capital flight being 'seen by the majority of the Russian people as a gross economic crime being committed in the process of redistribution of the national property inherited by all of the population from the Soviet era.'

Support may also come from people in the North who are concerned about development issues in poorer countries. Northern 'civil society' groups, for example, have recently displayed their growing interest and influence in global financial debates. To date, the more influential of these groups have focused their attention primarily on proposals such as the Tobin tax, debt relief, and changes to IMF and World Bank lending practices; the cause of regulating capital flight would seem equally deserving of their support.

If they were to politicize the issue, they may also find support from more conservative and isolationist quarters. As we saw in 1947–48, the greatest support for the proposal to help European governments track down flight capital in the USA came from Republican congressmen who were wary of extending aid to western Europe. They saw the regulation of European flight capital as a way to bolster the political and economic stability of western Europe without taxing US citizens. Among US politicians today, there is also a wariness of providing more funds for international aid and financial rescue packages. Even in the Russian context where the political stakes are high, there is little desire to provide enormous assistance packages of the Marshall Plan kind. Much cheaper than providing more loans or aid might be to help poorer countries experiencing economic crises track down the flight capital of their citizens. In this way, the regulation of capital flight may be one of the few causes in which US isolationist sentiments can be mobilized to support stronger international regulatory cooperation. In so doing, they would also revive ideas from that great era in US foreign economic policymaking: the days of Bretton Woods and the Marshall Plan.

NOTES

1. This article originally appeared in 'Challenge: The Magazine of Economic Affairs' (January 2001) and is reprinted here with permission from the editors.
2. For the 1980s experience, see for example Karin Lissakers, *Banks, Borrowers and the Establishment* (Basic Books, 1991: ch. 6). For Russia, see A. Abalkin and John Whalley (1999) 'The Problem of Capital Flight from Russia' *The World Economy* **22** (3), 421–44.
3. Quotes from Helleiner, 'Handling', p. 87.

REFERENCES

Baker, Raymond (1999), 'The Biggest Loophole in the Free-Market System', *The Washington Quarterly*, **22** (4), 29–46.

Bhagwati, Jagdish (1998), 'The Capital Myth', *Foreign Affairs*, **77** (3), 7–12.

Felix, David (1985), 'How to Resolve Latin America's Debt Crisis', *Challenge*, **28**, 44–51.

G-7 Finance Ministers (1999), 'Strengthening the International Financial Architecture', Report to the Cologne Economic Summit, June 18–20.

G-8 Press Communique (1999), Cologne Summit, June 18–20.

Helleiner, Eric (1994), *States and the Reemergence of Global Finance: From Bretton Woods to the 1990s*, Ithaca: Cornell University Press.

Helleiner, Eric (1995), 'Handling 'Hot Money': US Policy Toward Latin American Capital Flight in Historical Perspective', *Alternatives*, **20** (1), 81–115.

Lissakers, Karin (1991), *Banks, Borrowers and the Establishment*, US: Basic Books.

Martin, Paul (1999), 'International Financial Architecture Reform: Completing Bretton Woods', Statement by the Honorable Paul Martin, Minister of Finance for Canada to the Chicago Council on Foreign Relations, June 7, 1999', Ottawa: Department of Finance, p. 6.

Ministerial Conference of the G-8 Countries on Combatting Transnational Organized Crime (1999). *Communique Moscow*, October 19–20.

Pastor, Manuel (1990), 'Capital Flight from Latin America', *World Development*, **18** (1), 1–18.

President Clinton (1999), 'Remarks by President Clinton on Foreign Policy, Grand
    Hyatt Hotel, San Francisco, February 26, 1999', Office of the Press Secretary,
    White House, February 26.
Sanger, David (1999), 'US Official Questions How Russia Used Loan', *The New
    York Times*, March 19.
Sherman, Tom (1993), 'International Efforts to Combat Money Laundering: The Role
    of the Financial Action Task Force', in David Hume Institute, *Money Laundering*,
    Edinburgh: Edinburgh University Press.
Tikhomirov, Vladimir (1997), 'Capital Flight from Post-Soviet Russia', *Europe-Asia
    Studies*, **49** (591–615).
Williamson, J. and D. Lessard (eds) (1987), *Capital Flight and Third World Debt*,
    Washington: Institute for International Economics.

12. Capital Management Techniques in Developing Countries

Gerald Epstein, Ilene Grabel and Sundaram Kwame Jomo.

CAPITAL MANAGEMENT TECHNIQUES

We use the term capital management techniques (CMTs) to refer to two complementary (and often overlapping) types of financial policies: policies that govern international private capital flows, called capital controls, and those that enforce prudential management of domestic financial institutions. A strict bifurcation between capital controls and prudential regulations often cannot be maintained in practice (as Ocampo 2002 and Schneider 2001 observe). Policymakers frequently implement multi-faceted regimes of capital management since no single measure can achieve diverse objectives (as we will see later in this chapter).

Moreover, the effectiveness of any single management technique magnifies the effectiveness of other techniques and enhances the efficacy of the entire regime of capital management. For example, certain prudential financial regulations magnify the effectiveness of capital controls (and vice versa). In this case, the stabilizing aspect of prudential regulation reduces the need for the most stringent form of capital control. Thus, a program of complementary CMTs reduces the necessary severity of any one technique and magnifies the effectiveness of the regime of financial control.

There are a number of characteristics of capital management techniques that are worth noting. CMTs can be static or dynamic. Static management techniques are those that authorities do not modify in response to changes in circumstances. Examples of static management techniques include restrictions on the convertibility of the currency or maintenance of minimum-stay requirements on foreign investment. By contrast, dynamic CMTs can be activated or adjusted as circumstances warrant. Several types of circumstances trigger implementation of management techniques or lead authorities to strengthen or adjust existing regulations: CMTs are typically activated in response to changes in the economic environment or to prevent identified vulnerabilities from culminating in a financial crisis or to reduce the severity of a crisis[1]; they are strengthened or modified as authorities attempt to close loopholes in existing measures.

Policymakers use CMTs to achieve some or all of the following objectives: promote financial stability, encourage desirable investment and financing arrangements, enhance policy autonomy and strengthen democracy.[2] CMTs can promote financial stability through their ability to reduce currency flight, fragility and contagion risks, thereby reducing the potential for financial crisis and attendant economic and social devastation. They can also influence the composition of the economy's aggregate investment portfolio and can influence the financing arrangements that underpin these investments. Moreover, CMTs can promote desirable types of investment and financing strategies by rewarding investors and borrowers for engaging in them. Desirable types of investment are those that create employment, improve living standards, promote greater income equality, technology transfer, learning by doing and long-term growth; desirable types of financing are those that are long-term, stable and sustainable. Capital management can discourage less socially useful types of investment and financing strategies by increasing their cost or precluding them altogether.

CMTs can enhance policy autonomy in a number of ways: they can reduce the severity of currency risk and can thereby allow authorities to protect a currency peg; they can create space for the government and the central bank to pursue growth-promoting and reflationary macroeconomic policies by neutralizing the threat of capital flight; by reducing the risk of financial crisis in the first place, CMTs can reduce the likelihood that governments may be compelled to use contractionary macro- and microeconomic and social policy to attract foreign investment back to the country or as a precondition for IMF assistance; finally, CMTs can reduce the specter of foreign control or ownership of domestic resources.

It follows from the above that capital management can enhance democracy by reducing the potential for speculators and external actors to exercise undue influence over domestic decision-making directly or indirectly (via the threat of capital flight). CMTs can reduce the veto power of the financial community and the IMF and create space for the interests of other groups (such as advocates for the poor) to play a role in the design of policy. They can thus be said to enhance democracy because they create the opportunity for pluralism in policy design.

CASE STUDIES

Objectives and Case Selection

In this section of the chapter we present five case studies that analyze the CMTs employed during the 1990s in Chile, Colombia, Malaysia, Singapore and Taiwan Province of China (POC).[3] The presentation of the case studies is guided by five principal goals. First, to provide a detailed institutional guide to the CMTs pursued in diverse areas of the world from the 1990s to the present. Second, to examine the extent to which these management techniques achieved the objectives of their architects. Third, to elaborate the underlying structural factors that explain the success or failure of the techniques employed. Fourth, to examine the costs associated with these measures, and fifth, to draw general conclusions about the desirability and feasibility of replicating or adapting particular techniques to developing countries outside of our sample.

We have limited our examination to the 1990s because this period is distinguished by the combination of high levels of financial integration, a global norm of financial and economic liberalization, an increase in the power and autonomy of the global financial community and by significant advances in telecommunications technology. It is commonly held that any one of these factors (let alone their combined presence) frustrates the possibility for successful capital management. We have selected these five cases because policymakers employed diverse CMTs (in line with levels of state capacity and sovereignty) with different objectives and disparate degrees of success. Table 12.1 presents a summary of the major CMTs and their objectives for each of our cases.

CMTs in Chile and Colombia[4]

In the aftermath of the Asian crisis, heterodox and even prominent mainstream economists (for example, Eichengreen 1999) focused a great deal of attention on the 'Chilean model', a term that has been used to refer to a policy regime that Chilean and Colombian authorities began to implement in June 1991 and September 1993, respectively.

Context in Chile and Colombia

During the 1990s, policymakers in Chile and Colombia sought to improve investor confidence and to promote stable, sustainable economic and export growth. The CMTs of the 1990s were an integral component of the overall economic plan in both countries. CMTs in Chile and Colombia can perhaps be best understood in the context of the economic challenges that confronted the region's economies during the 1970s and 1980s. These problems

Table 12.1 Types and Objectives of CMTs Employed during the 1990s

Country	Types of CMTs	Objectives of CMTs
Chile	**Inflows:** FDI and PI: One year Residence Requirement 30% URR Tax on foreign loans: 1.2% per year **Outflows:** No significant restrictions **Domestic financial Regulations:** Strong regulatory measures	Lengthen maturity structures and stabilize inflows Help manage exchange rates to maintain export competitiveness Protect economy from financial instability
Colombia Taiwan	Similar to Chile Inflows *(non-residents)*: Bank accounts can only be used for domestic spending, not financial speculation Foreign participation in stock market regulated FDI tightly regulated Inflows *(residents)*: Regulation of foreign borrowing Outflows: Exchange controls **Domestic Financial Regulations:** Restrictions on lending for real estate and other speculative purposes	Similar to Chile Promote industrialization Help manage exchange rate for export competitiveness Maintain financial stability and insulated from foreign financial crises.

Singapore	Inflows: 'Non-Internationalization' of Singapore dollar (S$)	To prevent speculation against S$
		To support 'soft peg' of S$
	Outflows: *(non-residents)* Financial institutions can not extend S$ credit to non-residents if they are likely to use the facility for speculation Non-residents who borrow for use abroad must swap first into foreign currency	To help maintain export competitiveness
		To help insulate Singapore from foreign financial crises
	Domestic Financial Regulations: Restrictions on creation of swaps and other derivatives that could be used for speculation against S$	
Malaysia (1998)	Inflows: Restrictions on foreign borrowing	To maintain political and economic sovereignty
	Outflows *(non-residents)*: 12 month repatriation waiting period Graduated exit levies inversely proportional to length of stay	To kill the offshore ringgit market
	Outflows *(residents)*: Exchange controls	To shut down offshore share market
	Domestic financial regulations *(non-residents)*: Restrict access to ringgit	To help reflate the economy
	Domestic financial regulations *(residents)*: Encourage to borrow domestically and invest	To help create financial stability and insulate the economy from contagion

included high inflation, severe currency and banking instability, financial crises, high levels of external debt and capital flight and low levels of investor confidence.

Chilean context

Chile experienced a 'boom-bust cycle' in the two decades that preceded the CMTs of the 1990s. During the neo-liberal experiment of the 1970s, surges in foreign capital inflows led to a consumption boom and created significant pressure for currency appreciation. Experience with the 'Dutch disease' in the 1970s reinforced policymakers' commitment to preventing the fallout from surges in private capital inflows in the 1990s. The financial implosion, reduction in international capital flows and the deep recession of the early to mid-1980s also played a powerful role in the design of CMTs in the 1990s. Thus, the experiences of the 1970s and 1980s created a consensus around the idea that it was necessary to insulate the economy from volatile international capital flows.

Preventing the Dutch disease was of paramount importance in the 1990s because of the government's commitment to an export-led economic model. Chilean economic policy in the 1990s is difficult to characterize. In some senses, it was rather strongly neo-liberal. For instance, the country's status as a pioneer in the area of pension fund privatization earned it much respect in the international investment community. The government also pursued a vigorous program of trade liberalization and privatization of state-owned enterprises. But at the same time, the government also provided education and income support to the poor and unemployed and maintained a stringent regime of CMTs. It should also be noted that the health of the country's banking system improved significantly during the 1990s, thanks to a number of prudential banking and regulatory reforms.

Colombian context

As in Chile, the architects of Colombia's CMTs in the 1990s were influenced by the economic problems of the previous two decades. The promotion of investor confidence was a far more daunting task in Colombia than in Chile because of the country's political and civil uncertainties. Inflation was also a severe problem in Colombia in the 1970s and 1980s (and indeed, remained a problem during the 1990s as well). The 1990s was a time of far-reaching economic reform in Colombia. Authorities sought to attract international capital flows and promote trade and price stability through a number of structural reforms. These reforms included trade liberalization, increased exchange rate flexibility, tax reductions, labor market liberalization, partial privatization of social security and state-owned enterprises and central bank independence. Most of the economic reforms in the 1990s were in the direction of neo-liberalism; however, the CMTs and the increases in public expenditure were important exceptions in this regard.

Objectives

Though there were national differences in policy design, Chilean and Colombian policies shared the same objectives. The policy regime sought to balance the challenges and opportunities of financial integration, stabilize capital inflows and lengthen their maturity structure, mitigate the effect of large volumes of inflows on the currency and exports and protect the economy from the instability associated with speculative excess and the sudden withdrawal of external finance.

CMTs in Chile, 1991– 99

Financial integration in Chile was regulated through a number of complementary, dynamic measures, the most important of which are described here. During the lifetime of the Chilean model, authorities widened and revalued the crawling exchange rate band that was initially adopted in the early 1980s. The monetary effects of the rapid accumulation of international reserves were also largely sterilized.

Central to the success of the Chilean model was a multi-faceted program of inflows management. Foreign loans faced a tax of 1.2 percent per year. FDI and PI faced a one-year residence requirement, and from May 1992 to October 1998, Chilean authorities imposed a non-interest-bearing reserve requirement of 30 percent on all types of external credits and all foreign financial investments in the country. Note that the level and scope of the reserve requirement ratio was, in fact, changed several times during the lifespan of this policy regime in response to changes in the economic environment and to identified channels of evasion. The required reserves were held at the Central Bank for one year, regardless of the maturity of the obligation.

The Central Bank eliminated the management of inflows (and other controls over international capital flows) in several steps, beginning in September 1998. This decision was taken because the country confronted a radical reduction in inflows in the post-Asian/Russian/Brazilian crisis environment (rendering flight risk not immediately relevant). Chilean authorities determined that the attraction of international private capital flows was a regrettable necessity in light of declining copper prices and a rising current account deficit. Critics of the Chilean model heralded its demise as proof of its failure.

But others viewed the dismantling of the model as evidence of its success insofar as the economy had outgrown the need for protections. For example, Eichengreen (1999: 53) notes that by the summer of 1998 it was no longer necessary to provide disincentives to foreign funding because the Chilean banking system was on such strong footing following a number of improvements in bank regulation.[5] In our view, the decision to terminate inflow and other controls over international capital flows was imprudent given the substantial risks of a future surge in capital inflows to the country and the risk that the country could experience contagion from financial instability in Argentina, Brazil, Paraguay and Uruguay. It would have been far more desirable to maintain the controls at a low level while addressing the current account deficit and the need to attract inflows through other means. Indeed, flexible deployment of the inflows policy was a hallmark of the Chilean model (consistent with the dynamic approach to capital management described above) and it is regrettable that authorities have moved away from this strategy at the present juncture.

CMTs in Colombia, 1993– 99
Colombia's inflows management policies relating to foreign borrowing were similar to (though blunter than) those in Chile. This difference is perhaps attributable to limitations on state capacity in Colombia. Beginning in September 1993, the Central Bank required that non-interest-bearing reserves of 47 percent should be held for one year against foreign loans with maturities of 18 months or less (this was extended to loans with a maturity of up to five years in August 1994). Foreign borrowing related to real estate was prohibited. Moreover, foreigners were simply precluded from purchasing debt instruments and corporate equity (there were no comparable restrictions on FDI). Colombian policy also sought to discourage the accretion of external obligations in the form of import payments by increasing the cost of import financing. Authorities experimented with a variety of measures to protect exports from currency appreciation induced by inflows. These measures ranged from a limited sterilization of inflows, to maintenance of a managed float, to a crawling peg. As in Chile, regulations on international capital flows were gradually eliminated following the reduction in flows after the Asian crisis.

Assessment
The array of CMTs that constitute the Chilean model represents a highly effective means of achieving the economic objectives identified by the architects of these policies. The CMTs achieved these objectives via their effects on currency, flight, fragility and contagion risks.

Chilean authorities managed currency risk via adjustments to the crawling peg, sterilization and inflows management. Taken together, these measures greatly reduced the likelihood that the currency would appreciate to such a degree as to jeopardize the current account and made it difficult for investor flight to induce a currency collapse. Indeed, the appreciation of the Chilean currency and the current account deficit (as a share of GDP) were smaller than in other Latin American countries that were also recipients of large capital inflows (Agosin 1998). Moreover, the currency never came under attack following the Mexican and Asian crises.

Colombian efforts to manage currency risk were less successful than those in Chile. This is the case for three reasons. There was a lack of consistency in the exchange rate regime in Colombia as a consequence of the frequent changes in the exchange rate strategy employed (managed float, crawling peg, and so on). Inflow sterilization was rather limited in scope when compared to sterilization in Chile. Furthermore, inflation continued to be a problem in Colombia during the 1990s. Nonetheless, currency and inflows management offered some protection to exports in Colombia when the country was receiving relatively large capital inflows. The currency also held up fairly well following the Mexican crisis.

Chilean and Colombian policies reduced the likelihood of a sudden exit of foreign investors by discouraging those inflows that introduce the highest degree of flight risk. The reserve requirement tax in Chile was designed to discourage such flows by raising the cost of these investments. The Chilean minimum-stay policy governing FDI reinforced the strategy of encouraging longer-term investments while also preventing short-term flows disguised as FDI. Colombian policy precluded the possibility of an exit of foreign investors from liquid investment by prohibiting their participation in debt and equity markets (while maintaining their access to FDI). The reduction in flight risk in both countries complemented efforts to reduce currency risk, particularly in Chile where policy effectively targeted currency risk.

Chilean and Colombian inflows management also mitigated fragility risk. The regime reduced the opportunity for maturity mismatch by demonstrating an effective bias against short-term, unstable capital inflows. In Chile, taxes on foreign borrowing were designed precisely to discourage the financing strategies that introduced so much fragility risk to Asian economies and Mexico. In Colombia, the rather large reserve requirement tax on foreign borrowing and the prohibition on foreign borrowing for real estate played this role as well.

Numerous empirical studies find that inflows management in Chile and Colombia played a constructive role in changing the composition and maturity structure (though not the volume) of net capital inflows, particularly after the controls were strengthened in 1994–95 (for example, Ffrench-Davis and Reisen 1998; Le Fort and Budnevich 1997; Ocampo and Tovar 1998; Palma 2000). These studies also find that leakages from these regulations had no macroeconomic significance. Following implementation of these policies in both countries, the maturity structure of foreign debt lengthened and external financing in general moved from debt to FDI. Moreover, Chile received a larger supply of external finance (relative to GDP) than other countries in the region and FDI became a much larger proportion of inflows than in many other developing economies. Colombia's prohibition on foreign equity and bond market participation dramatically reduced the relative importance of short-term, liquid forms of finance. More strikingly, FDI became a major source of finance in the country despite political turbulence and blunt financial controls.

The move toward FDI and away from short-term, highly liquid debt and PI flows is a clear achievement of the Chilean model. However, it is important to note that FDI is not without its problems. It can and has introduced sovereignty risk in some important cases (such as Chile's earlier experience with ITT) and can introduce other problems to developing countries (see Chang and Grabel, 2004, Chapter 10; Singh 2002).

The Chilean model also reduced the vulnerability to contagion by fostering macroeconomic stability. It is noteworthy that the transmission effects of the Asian crisis in Chile and Colombia were quite mild compared to those in other Latin countries (such as Brazil), let alone elsewhere. The decline in capital flows in Chile and Colombia following the Mexican and Asian crises was rather orderly and did not trigger currency, asset and investment collapse. Unlike the experience in East Asia, the decision to float the currency in Chile and Colombia (in the post-Asian crisis environment) did not induce instability.

Some analysts challenge the generally sanguine assessment of the Chilean model. Edwards (1999), for example, argues that the effectiveness of the model has been exaggerated. However, in a paper published a year later, De Gregorio, Edwards and Valdés (2000) conclude that Chilean controls affected the composition and maturity of inflows, though not their volume. The De Gregorio et al. (2000) result is confirmed for Chile in other studies that claim to demonstrate the failure of the model, even though their reported results show just the opposite (Ariyoshi et al. 2000; Valdés-Prieto and Soto 1998). As Eichengreen aptly remarks, the controls affected only the composition and maturity and not the volume of inflows is 'hardly a devastating critique' (1999: 53), since this was precisely their purpose.

Supporting factors

CMTs in both Chile and Colombia were able to achieve the economic objectives of their architects for several reasons. The policies were well designed, consistent and reasonably transparent throughout their life. Policymakers in both countries were 'nimble' in the sense that they dynamically modified CMTs as the economic environment changed[6] and as loopholes in the policies were revealed (see Massad 1998: 44, for a discussion of the Chilean case).[7] Both countries offered investors attractive opportuni- ties and growing markets, such that investors were willing to commit funds despite the constraints imposed by the capital management regime.

Chile certainly had advantages over Colombia. The greater degree of state capacity in Chile may well explain why its policies (particularly with regard to exchange rate management) were more successful. Moreover, Chile's status as a large developing economy certainly rendered it more attractive to foreign investors and may have granted the country a greater degree of policy autonomy than was available to Colombia. The general soundness of its banking system and macroeconomic policy, the maintenance of price stability and the high level of official reserves were important sources of investor confidence in Chile. Finally, international support for the neo-liberal aspects of Chile's economic reforms provided the government with the political space to experiment with CMTs.

Costs

At this point, compelling evidence on the costs of CMTs in Chile and Colombia is not available. Indeed, the two most comprehensive studies of this issue deal only with Chile (and in an unsatisfactory manner).

Forbes (2002) is the most extensive study available on the micro-economic costs of Chilean CMTs. Using a variety of empirical tests (and sensitivity analyses thereof), Forbes shows that CMTs in Chile resulted in an increase in capital costs to small-sized enterprises.[8] Forbes is careful to note that the results themselves must be treated cautiously because of limitations on data availability.

In a broad study of the macro-economic effects of the Chilean CMTs, Edwards (1999) notes in passing that CMTs increased capital costs for the SMEs that had difficulty evading controls on capital inflows. He reports that the cost of funds to smaller enterprises in Chile was more than 21 percent and 19 percent per year in dollar terms in 1996 and 1997, respectively. Edwards does not, however, place these data into the necessary comparative context, rendering them entirely unpersuasive as an indictment of the Chilean CMTs.

Both Forbes and Edwards conclude their studies with the argument that the cost to smaller firms of Chilean CMTs is far from a trivial matter because these enterprises play an important role in investment, growth and employment creation in developing countries. Neither study provides empirical support for the argument that these firms do, in fact, play a significant role in macro-economic performance, and neither study provides unambiguous evidence that the macro-economic benefits of Chilean CMTs fail to outweigh even the modest evidence of their microeconomic costs (and much the same could be said of Colombian experience).

On the issue of costs versus benefits, it should be noted that Forbes (2002) remains agnostic on the relative importance of micro-economic costs versus macro-economic benefits. Edwards (1999), by contrast, is entirely clear on this matter. He argues that proponents of Chilean CMTs vastly overstate their macroeconomic benefits and fail to acknowledge their microeconomic costs. On this basis, he argues that the Chilean CMTs should not serve as a model for other developing countries. We find the empirical basis for this conclusion entirely unconvincing.

Other achievements

As discussed above, the CMTs associated with the Chilean model achieved the most important goals of its architects (though to a greater extent in Chile than in Colombia). Additionally, the CMTs in both countries can be credited with enhancing the sovereignty of economic and social policy. The importance of this achievement warrants discussion.

The CMTs of the Chilean model afforded policymakers insulation from potential challenges to economic and social policy sovereignty through the reduction in various types of risks (particularly, through reduction in flight and fragility risks). Both countries were able to maintain relatively autonomous, somewhat restrictive monetary policies because of the protections afforded by the CMTs (Le Fort and Budnevich 1997).[9] Moreover, the protection from flight risk afforded by the CMTs made it possible for policymakers to implement some growth-oriented fiscal policies (Le Fort and Budnevich, 1997). Finally, as Le Fort and Budnevich (1997) argue, the protections and advantages conferred on both countries by their CMTs were essential to the success of the entire regime of economic policy.[10] For instance, the attraction of certain types of international capital flows promoted economic growth in both countries, while the protection from currency appreciation (to a large extent in Chile and to a modest extent in Colombia) contributed to success in current account performance.

The insulation afforded to both countries by the CMTs also meant that monetary authorities were able to navigate the transition to a floating exchange rate far more smoothly. In many other countries (such as in East Asia), the transition to a floating rate involved significant currency depreciations and financial instability.

The CMTs employed in both countries also reduced the risk of financial crisis and thereby buttressed the sovereignty of economic and social policies in both countries. CMTs reduced the potential for IMF involvement in both countries. Policymakers were therefore never pressed to change the direction of economic or social policy to satisfy the demands of the IMF or to calm investors.

Taiwan Province of China (POC)

Context

The CMTs employed in Taiwan POC can only be understood in the context of a 'developmentalist state' and an extended notion of national security that includes economic and financial stability.[11] That is, CMTs are an integral component of the macroeconomic and security objectives of Taiwan POC (see below for a discussion of these objectives). These economic and security objectives were and largely still are the guiding forces behind extensive regulation of domestic financial institutions and credit flows, monetary and exchange rate policy and controls over international capital flows. Taiwan POC built its industrial base on the basis of restrictive policies toward FDI in 'strategic sectors' (for details, see Chang and Grabel 2004). CMTs played a critical role in promoting industrialization and export performance.

Objectives
Prior to the mid-1980s, Taiwan POC's policymakers employed a multi-faceted set of CMTs in the pursuit of three goals: the promotion of industrialization and export supremacy, economic growth and economic stability. Since the goal of industrialization had been achieved by the mid-1980s, CMTs are directed toward growth and stability objectives. CMTs that restrict investment in unproductive assets are critical in this regard.

Extensive CMTs are still in use, though policymakers began to liberalize aspects of the financial sector and loosen some controls over international capital flows in 1995 as part of the Asia Pacific Regional Operations Center Plan (APROC) and the goal of joining the WTO. The APROC aimed at making Taiwan POC a regional center for high value-added manufacturing, transportation, finance, telecommunications and several other areas. However, as Chin and Nordhaug (2002: 82) make clear, financial liberalization in Taiwan POC in the 1990s in no way weakened prudential financial regulation in the country.

CMTs in Taiwan POC
As discussed above, Taiwan POC maintains an extensive set of CMTs that are tied to economic and security objectives.[12]

Policymakers maintain a rather tight rein on the domestic currency, the New Taiwan dollar (NT dollar), and on currency risk more generally. Most important among the CMTs that relate to currency risk is the lack of convertibility of the NT dollar. There are a number of other ways that the Central Bank of China (the CBC) manages the NT dollar. Prior to September 1994, foreign nationals without residency visas were prohibited from opening NT dollar accounts. But as of September 1994, the CBC has permitted non-resident foreign nationals and corporations to hold savings accounts denominated in NT dollars, although the use of these is limited to domestic spending or to the purchase of imports. These accounts may not be used to purchase foreign exchange or for securities trading. The CBC also adjusts the reserve ratios that must be held against foreign currency deposits in order to prevent inflows of foreign investment from leading to an appreciation of the NT dollar.

The domestic banking system is highly regulated by the state. Indeed, domestic banks in Taiwan POC were primarily owned by the state until the early 1990s. In 1995 71.9 percent of Taiwan POC 's total banking assets were housed in banks that were controlled fully or partly by the government; in the same year, government-controlled credit and financial institutions provided 62.2 percent of overall credit (Chin and Nordhaug 2002: 81). Authorities maintain restrictions on bank participation in speculative activities. Bank involvement in securities holdings remains limited. In 1989, the Central Bank imposed a 20 percent ceiling on bank lending to the real estate sector for six years following problems associated with a real estate bubble in the 1980s (Chin and Nordhaug 2002).

Authorities also regulate foreign borrowing. Foreign-owned companies must apply to the CBC and the Investment Commission of the Ministry of Economic Affairs to secure government approval for borrowing from abroad. Control over foreign borrowing aims to concentrate most private foreign borrowing from international banks in Taiwan POC 's banks rather than in the hands of individuals. In fact, at the end of June 1997, 62 percent of all private foreign borrowing in the country went to its banks (Chin and Nordhaug 2002: 93).

Foreign investment in Taiwan POC remains tightly regulated. During the 1990s certain strategic sectors were off-limits to foreign investors. These restrictions have been loosened considerably beginning in March 1996. However, authorities retain the ability to manage foreign investment: at present what are termed 'qualified foreign institutional investors' are subject to a ceiling on maximum investment; foreign individual investors are also subject to a ceiling on maximum investment and must receive approval from the CBC.

The stock market and PI are closely regulated as well. Chin and Nordhaug (2002: 89) point out that Taiwan POC 's stock bubble in the 1980s exposed some regulatory weaknesses, leading authorities to improve the quality of capital market regulation and to increase control over PI inflows. They also note that a number of events in the 1990s reinforced the CBC's regulatory caution toward the stock market and PI inflows. These events also encouraged the CBC to develop new strategies for discouraging speculation and channeling capital toward developmentally productive uses. The CBC's power to regulate the stock market and PI inflows increased following the country's stock market crash in 1990 and following its interventions to support the currency and the stock market in the aftermath of the cross-strait tensions and the ensuing missile crisis from August 1995 to March 1996. The CBC also monitored evasion of its regulations and had the political will to enforce penalties when malfeasance was uncovered. For example, in 1995 the CBC closed Taiwan POC's foreign exchange market for one year when it was discovered that a major share of the foreign inflows that it had approved for equity investment had been used to speculate against the currency (Chin and Nordhaug 2002:88). During the Asian financial crisis, Taiwan POC's authorities also took steps to prevent illegal trading of funds by financier George Soros (because these funds were blamed for causing the stock market to plummet).

Taiwan POC's stock market was not very 'internationalized' during the 1990s as a direct result of its policies toward PI. In 1997, foreign investors held only 4 percent of stocks on the domestic exchange (Chin and Nordhaug 2002: 94). Moreover, authorities maintained firm entry and exit barriers and high withholding taxes on dividends (in 1996 the tax rate on dividends was 35 percent) (Chin and Nordhaug 2002: 87). Currently, buying stocks on margin and short selling are still prohibited.

Assessment
It is clear that Taiwan POC's CMTs have achieved the objectives of its architects. The regime of capital management clearly plays an essential role in Taiwan POC's industrialization, export performance, economic growth and economic and financial stability. The strategic stance toward FDI was critical to industrialization.

CMTs are central to Taiwan POC's financial stability. The restrictions on currency convertibility mean that it is difficult for Taiwan POC to experience a currency collapse (and related currency-induced fragility risk). Investors have little reason to fear a collapse of currency values and they behave accordingly (as was evident during the regional crisis of 1997–98). Thus, even a decline in asset values (for example, stocks) is unlikely to translate into a currency crash.

Taiwan POC's exposure to currency, fragility and flight risks is reduced by the restrictions on foreign investors' ability to use the currency for speculation. The regulation of the stock market (for example, prohibitions on buying on margin and short-selling) and the cautious stance toward PI curtail the fragility and flight risks to which Taiwan POC is exposed. It is notable that regulatory authorities have responded to the evasion of financial controls and the appearance of regulatory gaps by dynamically refashioning their CMTs.

The regulations that govern banks and foreign lending support the objective of promoting financial and economic stability. Banks in Taiwan POC do not have a high exposure to securities and real estate transactions. As a consequence, banks do not hold a large portfolio of non-performing or under-collateralized loans. Curbs on foreign lending also reduce fragility in the economy and render the risk of lender flight not terribly important.

Taiwan POC's resilience during the Asian financial crisis is in no small part due to the economic and financial stability fostered by its CMTs. It was simply not vulnerable to the currency, flight or fragility risks that proved so devastating to many countries in the region.

Supporting factors

The achievements of Taiwan POC's CMTs were facilitated by a number of structural and geopolitical factors.[13] Critical among these were the high degree of regulatory capacity and the independence of the CBC from political bodies. This independence allowed the CBC to exercise its authority to curb speculation, close loopholes in policy and to resist international and external pressures to liberalize the financial system imprudently. The policy independence of the CBC stemmed from its Presidential backing and the government's historic commitment to financial stability. National security concerns and geopolitical uncertainties reinforced the commitment to financial stability, as stability is seen as essential to the task of withstanding diplomatic, military and economic shocks. The reaction of the CBC to several events in the 1990s 'served as an unplanned rehearsal for the subsequent 1997–98 regional financial crisis' (Chin and Nordhaug 2002: 91).

As part of its national development vision, the Taiwan POC channeled rents to promote exports and upgrade industry. These efforts were accompanied by strict performance criteria and disciplinary measures. In this context, stringent and dynamic CMTs were essential to the promotion of productive investment and industrial dynamism.

Costs

There is scant evidence available on the costs of Taiwan POC's CMTs. A report by the Institute for International Economics (1998), for instance, reports that CMTs in Taiwan POC have created a concentration of credit in large firms and an illiquid financial system, provided incentives for a rather large informal financial sector to flourish and reinforced conservatism on the part of its banks. Chin and Nordhaug (2002: 83) report that this conservatism leads banks to favor short-term lending backed by tangible collateral, such as real estate. This study also reports that banks are limited in their ability to engage in project, company and credit assessments and do not have reliable accounting and auditing systems.

Clearly, the evidence on costs reviewed here is limited and anecdotal. Even if one were to accept this evidence fully, these costs in no way outweigh the macroeconomic benefits afforded to Taiwan POC by its CMTs.

Other achievements

CMTs afforded Taiwan POC insulation from the Asian financial crisis. This insulation from crisis, coupled with its vast resources, meant that Taiwan POC did not confront challenges to the sovereignty of economic and social policy associated with IMF involvement or with the need to regain investor confidence.

Singapore[14]

Singapore is widely believed to have a completely free and open capital account, a 'fact' that is often cited as an essential component of Singapore's outward-oriented economic policy and its rapid post-war economic growth.[15] It is true that Singapore eliminated its exchange controls in 1978 and since that time, both residents and non-residents have been free to engage in a broad range of international financial market activities. However, it less well known that the 'Monetary Authority of Singapore (MAS) has a long-standing policy of not encouraging the internationalization of the Singapore Dollar (S$)' (MAS 2002:1). The S$ 'non-internationalization policy' limits the borrowing of S$ by residents and non-residents for 'currency speculation' (MAS 2002: 13, fn. 9). This policy is clearly a type of CMT and evidently has been successful in the sense that it has contributed to Singapore's macroeconomic and industrial policy and economic stability.

Context

By virtually any measure, Singapore's economy has been a major success story of post-war economic development. To cite just one statistic, the per capita income in Singapore has more than quadrupled in less than 20 years, growing from US$5,200 in 1981 to US$23,000 in 1999. Moreover, Singapore's economy has been relatively stable for the last twenty years, notably escaping the worst ravages of the Asian financial crisis of the late 1990s (see MAS 2001). The government of Singapore has used a creative mix of macroeconomic tools and other government policies to achieve these outcomes. Macroeconomic policy has been rather conservative in a number of ways. The government has sought to maintain fiscal surpluses and low rates of inflation and has sought to attract large amounts of foreign direct investment. Few would deny the success of these policies. To take just one example, between 1981 and 1999, Singapore attracted FDI in an amount of over 9 percent of its GDP, far higher than any of its neighbors (MAS 2001: 11).

At the same time, the government of Singapore has projected an image of greater adherence to economic orthodoxy than is actually the case. For example, Singapore has pursued a very successful industrial policy, huge infrastructure investments and large investment in public housing for its population, all of which have contributed to a rapid growth of living standards. Most important for our purposes, the government has pursued a managed exchange rate policy designed to stabilize the exchange rate and maintain the competitiveness of Singapore's industry. It turns out that Singapore's CMTs have played an important, but little understood, role in the success of many of these policies.[16]

Objectives

According to the MAS, the aim of the policy of non-internationalization of the S$ 'is to prevent the exchange rate from being de-stabilized and to ensure the effective conduct of our monetary policy' (ibid.) The policy is also designed to help Singapore maintain the 'soft peg' that has been crucial for its export-led strategy of development. Singapore's successful maintenance of its soft peg defies the conventional wisdom that soft-pegs are not viable (Eichengreen 1999).

CMTs in Singapore

Singapore progressively dismantled exchange controls in the 1970's until virtually all restrictions were removed in 1978. In 1981, the MAS moved to an exchange rate-centered monetary policy. As the MAS put it: 'the absence of exchange or capital controls, coupled with the small size and openness of our economy, made the conduct of monetary policy that much more difficult when Singapore shifted to an exchange rate-centered monetary policy in 1981.' (MAS 2002: 2).

To support this policy, the MAS instituted an explicit policy of discouraging the internationalization of the S$ by discouraging 'the use of the S$ outside Singapore for activities unrelated to its real economy'. In 1983, when the policy was first codified, financial institutions located in Singapore were forbidden to lend S$ to any residents or non-residents that planned to take the S$ outside of the country. Moreover, there were restrictions on equities and foreign bond listings by foreign companies in S$ to limit the development of an internationally connected domestic capital market denominated in the S$. After nine years, in 1992, the policy was loosened somewhat, when it was amended to allow the extension of S$ credit facilities of any amount to non-residents provided that the S$ funds were used for real activities in Singapore. (MAS 2002: 4). Under that amendment, non-residents can only borrow S$ to finance their activities outside Singapore provided the S$ proceeds are exchanged for foreign currency. (MAS 2001: 13, fn. 9). In addition, some restrictions were placed on inter-bank S$ derivatives, such as foreign exchange, currency and interest rate swaps and options, which could facilitate the leveraging or hedging of S$ positions. (MAS, 2002: 2). As the SMA puts it, 'These restrictions made it harder for potential speculators to short the S$ and signaled unambiguously our disapproval of such speculation' (ibid.).

In response to pressures from the domestic and foreign financial sectors for more liberalization, the MAS has reviewed the non-internationalization policy four times since 1998 and has liberalized it to some extent during these years. In August 1998, the MAS issued a new directive, MAS 757, reaffirming the basic thrust of the non-internationalization policy, but establishing clearer and more explicit provisions than previously. These more explicit regulations reduced the need for banks to consult MAS and then, to some extent, reduced the ability of MAS to implement 'moral suasion' and 'supervision'. Moreover, some activities, specifically in relation to the arrangement of S$ equities listings and bond issues of foreign companies were relaxed to foster the development of the capital market in Singapore (MAS 2002: 4).

In late 1999, there was further liberalization of S$ interest rate derivatives. Moreover, foreign companies were allowed to list S$ equity, provided the proceeds are converted into foreign currency before being used outside Singapore. In late 2000, key changes were made to MAS 757 to allow banks to lend S$ to non-residents for investment purposes in Singapore. These changes to MAS 757 were intended to allow non-residents to obtain S$ funding for investment in S$ equities, bonds and real estate and broaden the investor base for S$ assets and to extend S$ credit facilities to non-residents to fund offshore activities, as long as the S$ proceeds were first swapped into foreign currency before being used outside Singapore. Finally, in March of 2002, the policy was further liberalized, exempting individuals and non-financial entities from the S$ lending restrictions, 'recognizing...that such entities were not usually the prime drivers of destabilizing currency speculation' (MAS 2002: 5). Moreover, the amendments significantly loosened up restrictions on non-resident financial entities to transact freely in asset swaps, cross-currency swaps and cross-currency repos; lend any amount of S$-denominated securities in exchange for both S$ or foreign currency-denominated collateral (previously, lending of S$ securities exceeding $5 million had to be fully collateralized by S$ collateral) and transact freely in S$ foreign exchange options with non-resident entities. Previously, such transactions had been allowed only if they were supported by underlying economic and financial activities in Singapore (MAS 2002).

Thus, following the revisions of March 2002, only two core requirements of the policy remain. First, financial institutions may not extend S$ credit facilities in excess of S$5 million to non-resident financial entities, where 'they have reason to believe that the proceeds may be used for speculation against the S$'. This continues to be necessary to prevent offshore speculators from accessing the liquidity in Singapore's onshore foreign exchange swaps and money markets. (MAS 2002: 5). Second, for a S$ loan to a non-resident financial entity exceeding S$5 million or for a S$ equity or bond issue by a non-resident entity that is used to fund overseas activities, the S$ proceeds must be swapped or converted into foreign currency before use outside Singapore.

Assessment

Observers attribute at least part of the success of Singapore's macroeconomic policy to the significant CMTs that have hindered speculation against the S$ and allowed authorities to pursue a managed exchange rate. The MAS itself finds its CMTs extremely useful. A recent report states that: 'The S$ has served Singapore well. The strength and stability of the S$ have instilled confidence and kept inflation low. These have in turn provided the foundation for sustained economic growth as well as continued strengthening of the S$' (ibid.).

According to the MAS, interest rates in S$ instruments have generally been lower than corresponding US$ rates. This has helped to keep the cost of capital low in Singapore. Moreover, as a result, domestic banks and corporations did not suffer from the currency and maturity mismatches that existed in other emerging-market economies (MAS 2001: 13). Part of the reason that it was able to maintain low interest rates was the expectation of an exchange rate appreciation. It is important to note that Singapore avoided the familiar problems associated with expectations of appreciation: namely massive capital inflows, overvaluation and then crash (see, for example, Taylor 2002). It seems likely that Singapore's CMTs, which discouraged speculation against the currency, helped the country avoid that all too familiar malady. It also helped to support Singapore's export-led model by keeping the exchange rate from becoming excessively overvalued.

Supporting factors

The success of this policy is partly due to the ability of the MAS to use 'moral suasion' to discourage banks and other financial institutions from using the S$ for purposes of speculating against (or in favor) of the local currency. Close, ongoing interaction between the MAS and international and domestic financial institutions has allowed the MAS to shape and monitor implementation of what appear to be deliberately vague formal regulations. Moral suasion allows the MAS to make sure that loans are 'tied to economic activities in Singapore.' Singapore's 'strong fundamentals' are often cited as the key to its policy success. These include low inflation, fiscal surpluses, stable unit labor costs and current account surpluses – factors that are undoubtedly important.[17] Often ignored, however, is the role of CMTs in enhancing these fundamentals. In short, Singapore's experience demonstrates that there is a two-way causation between CMTs and fundamentals.

Costs

There has been no systematic analysis of the costs of Singapore's CMTs; hence only qualitative guesses exist. Some have argued that the restrictions have hindered the development of Singapore's capital markets, especially the bond markets, and may have also reduced the inflow of foreign investment, though there is little hard evidence to support these assertions (MAS, 2001). Another possible cost is that the government of Singapore forgoes the opportunity to earn seignorage from the international use of the S$; but there have been no quantitative estimates of these costs to date.

Other achievements
Singapore has been able to maintain a high level of foreign direct investmentand political stability. Singapore's CMTs have contributed to this success by allowing the MAS to maintain a stable exchange rate and avoid the financial crises that have generated so much instability elsewhere in the region.

Malaysia[18]

Context
In the first two-thirds of the 1990s, Malaysia experienced rapid economic growth due to growth in spending on infrastructure, FDI and exports. During this period, the Malaysian capital account was so liberalized that there was an offshore market in ringgit, perhaps the only case of an offshore market in an emerging-market currency (Rajaraman 2001). Rapid economic growth in Malaysia came to a halt with the Asian financial crisis of 1997. The Malaysian government bucked trends in the region and, rather than implement an IMF stabilization program, implemented capital controls and adopted an expansionary monetary policy 14 months after September 1998. Malaysia's introduction of capital controls was widely seen as a major departure from its long reputation for maintaining a liberal capital account.

Objectives
The goals of the 1998 controls were to facilitate expansionary macroeconomic policy while defending the exchange rate, reduce capital flight, preserve foreign exchange reserves and avoid an IMF stabilization program (Kaplan and Rodrik 2002).

CMTs in Malaysia in September 1998
The policy package is generally recognized as comprehensive and well designed to limit foreign exchange outflows and ringgit speculation by non-residents as well as residents, while not adversely affecting foreign direct investors. The offshore ringgit market had facilitated exchange rate turbulence in 1997–98. Thus, the measures were designed to eliminate this source of disturbance.
The measures introduced on 1 September 1998 were designed to achieve the following objectives (Rajaraman 2001; BNM; Mohamad 2001; Jomo 2001):

- eliminate the offshore ringgit market, by prohibiting the transfer of funds into the country from externally held ringgit accounts except for investment in Malaysia (excluding credit to residents) or for purchase of goods in Malaysia;
- eliminate access by non-residents to domestic ringgit sources by prohibiting ringgit credit facilities to them. All trade transactions now had to be settled in foreign currencies and only authorized depository institutions were allowed to handle transactions in ringgit financial assets;
- shut down the offshore market in Malaysian shares conducted through the Central Limit Order Book (CLOB) in Singapore;
- obstruct speculative outward capital flows by requiring prior approval for Malaysian residents to invest abroad in any form and limiting exports of foreign currency by residents for other than valid current account purposes;
- protect the ringgit's value and raise foreign exchange reserves by requiring repatriation of export proceeds within six months from the time of export;
- further insulate monetary policy from the foreign exchange market by imposing a 12-month ban on the outflow of external portfolio capital (only on the principal; interest and dividend payments could be freely repatriated).

The September 1998 measures imposed a 12-month waiting period for repatriation of investment proceeds from the liquidation of external portfolio investments. To pre-empt a large-scale outflow at the end of the twelve-month period in September 1999 and to try to attract new portfolio investments from abroad, a system of graduated exit levies was introduced from February 15, 1999, with different rules for capital already in the country and for capital brought in after that date. For capital already in the country, there was an exit tax inversely proportional to the duration of stay within the earlier stipulated period of twelve months. Capital that had entered the country before February 15, 1998 was free to leave without paying any exit tax. For new capital yet to come in, the levy would only be imposed on profits, defined to exclude dividends and interest, also graduated by length of stay. In effect, profits were being defined by the new rules as realized capital gains.

Credit facilities for share as well as property purchases were actually increased as part of the package. The government has even encouraged its employees to take second mortgages for additional property purchases at its heavily discounted interest rate. The exchange controls, still in place, limit access to ringgit for non-residents, preventing the re-emergence of an offshore ringgit market. Free movement from ringgit to dollars for residents is possible, but dollars must be held in foreign exchange accounts in Malaysia, for example, at the officially approved foreign currency offshore banking center on Labuan.

Assessment

Did Malaysia's September 1998 selective capital control measures succeed? They clearly succeeded in meeting some of the government's objectives. The offshore ringgit market was eliminated by the September 1998 measures. By late 1999, international rating agencies had begun restoring Malaysia's credit rating; for example, the Malaysian market was re-inserted on the Morgan Stanley Capital International Indices in May 2000.

But did these controls succeed in the sense of allowing more rapid recovery of the Malaysian economy? The merits and demerits of the Malaysian government's regime of capital controls to deal with the regional currency and financial crises will continue to be debated for a long time to come. Proponents claim that the economic and stock market decline came to a stop soon after the controls were implemented (Kaplan and Rodrik 2002; Jomo 2001; Palma 2000; Dornbusch 2002). On the other hand, opponents argue that such reversals have been more pronounced in the rest of the region. Kaplan and Rodrik present strong evidence that the controls did have a significant positive effect on the ability of Malaysia to weather the 1997 crisis and reflate its economy. While this debate is likely to go on for some time, our reading of the evidence suggests that Kaplan and Rodrik are correct: controls segmented financial markets and provided breathing room for domestic monetary and financial policies and allowed for a speedier recovery than would have been possible via the orthodox IMF route.

Supporting factors

In the other cases we discuss above, prior experience with CMTs has been important to the success of capital management in the 1990s. However, the case of Malaysia seems quite different: the country had a highly liberalized capital account prior to the 1990s. Nonetheless, the government was able to implement numerous CMTs, all under rather difficult circumstances. This suggests that a history of capital management is not a necessary prerequisite for policy success.

Costs

The most important cost of the 1998 controls was the political favoritism associated with their implementation. It is difficult, however, to estimate the economic costs of political favoritism (Jomo 2001; Kaplan and Rodrik 2002; Johnson and Mitton 2003). Moreover, these costs (if quantified) must be weighed against the significant evidence of the macroeconomic benefits of the 1998 controls.

Other achievements

The Malaysian experience enriches debate on the policy options available to developing countries. It demonstrates that it is possible for outflow controls to achieve their objectives.

OPPORTUNITIES FOR CAPITAL MANAGEMENT IN DEVELOPING COUNTRIES

What policy lessons can be derived from these case studies? Before turning to positive lessons, we consider four commonly held but mistaken claims about CMTs.

The first common view of capital management is that it can only work in the 'short run' but not in the 'long run.' However, with the exception of Malaysia, which did not attempt long-term controls, all of our cases show that management can achieve important objectives over a significant number of years. Singapore, for example, employed CMTs for more than a decade in the service of important policy objectives.

A second common view is that for capital management to work for a long period of time, measures have to be consistently strengthened. In fact, the reality is much more complex than this. As the cases of Malaysia and Chile show, at times of stress, it may be necessary to strengthen controls to address leakages that are exploited by the private sector. However, as these same cases demonstrate, controls can be loosened when a crisis subsides or when the international environment changes and then reinstated or strengthened as necessary. More generally, looking at a broad cross-section of country experiences, one finds that dynamic capital management evolves endogenously according to the economic environment and the evolution of government goals.

We see that in Chile, for example, CMTs were adjusted several times (and ultimately abandoned) during the 1990s in response to changes in the economic environment. During its 2003 bilateral trade negotiations with the USA, Chilean policymakers sought and won the right to reinstate these controls during financial crises. In Malaysia, capital management was strengthened to address evasion during the Asian financial crisis and then was eventually loosened. In Singapore, the government strengthened enforcement and moral suasion during times of stress and then stepped away from this strategy when the situation changed.

Third, many have recently suggested that controls on capital inflows work, but those on outflows do not. However, our cases reveal that this is not always true. For example, Chile and Colombia maintained controls on inflows, while Malaysia maintained controls on outflows. In addition, Singapore and Taiwan POC maintain controls on the ability of residents and non-residents to use domestic currency offshore for purposes of speculating against the home currency. This is a control on outflows that has successfully insulated these countries from crises and has helped governments to manage their exchange rates.

Fourth, a common view is that CMTs impose significant costs by leading to higher costs of capital, especially for small firms. As we have seen, in some cases there may be some merit to these arguments. But much more evidence needs to be presented before this is established as a widespread cost.[19]

The positive lessons are as follows (see Table 12.A2 in the Appendix for a summary). First and most generally, we find that CMTs can contribute to currency and financial stability, macro- and microeconomic policy autonomy, stable long-term investment and sound current account performance. CMTs also impart some costs. Specifically, there is evidence that in some countries the cost of capital to small firms is increased and capital management can create space for corruption.

Second, successful implementation of controls over a significant period of time depends on the presence of a sound policy environment and strong fundamentals. These include a relatively low debt ratio, moderate rates of inflation, sustainable current account and fiscal balances, consistent exchange rate policies, a public sector that functions well enough to be able to implement coherent policies (that is, administrative capacity) and governments that are sufficiently independent of narrow political interests so that they can maintain some degree of control over the financial sector (that is, state capacity).

Third, our cases show that causation works both ways: from good fundamentals to successful CMTs and from successful CMTs to good fundamentals. Good fundamentals are important to the long-run success of CMTs because they reduce the stress on these controls and thereby enhance their chance of success. On the other hand, these techniques also improve fundamentals. Thus, there is a synergy between CMTs and fundamentals.

Fourth, the dynamic aspects of CMTs are perhaps their most important feature. Policymakers need to retain the ability to implement a variety of management techniques and alter them as circumstances warrant. Nimble and flexible capital management is very desirable. The experience of Chile and Taiwan POC with these techniques is a good example of this type of flexibility. Countries that have had successful experience with controls must maintain the option to continue using them as circumstances warrant.

Fifth, CMTs work best when they are coherent and consistent with the overall aims of the economic policy regime or even better, when they are an integral part of a national economic vision. To be clear, this vision does not have to be one of widespread state control over economic activity. Singapore is a good example of an economy that is highly liberalized in some ways, but one where CMTs are an integral part of an overall vision of economic policy and development.[20]

Sixth, prudential regulations are often an important complement to capital controls, traditionally defined, and vice versa. In Singapore, for example, government moral suasion aimed at discouraging banks from lending to firms or individuals intending to speculate against the currency is an example of an effective prudential regulation. In Chile, taxes on short-term inflows that prevent maturity mismatches are an example of a capital control that also serves as a prudential regulation. Our case studies present many such examples.

Seventh, there is not one type of CMT that works best for all countries: in other words, there is no one 'best practice' when it comes to CMTs. We have found a variety of strategies that work in countries with very different levels of state and administrative capacities, with financial systems that differ according to their depth and degree of liberalization, with different mixes of dynamic and static controls and different combinations of prudential financial regulations and capital controls.

Many countries that have had extensive controls in the past are now liberalizing them. Do our case studies offer any insight as to whether countries that employ extensive CMTs should begin to abandon them? Our research suggests that, in many cases, it is not in the interests of developing countries to seek full capital account liberalization. The lesson of dynamic capital management is that countries need to have the flexibility to both tighten and loosen controls.

However, if countries completely liberalize their capital accounts, they might find it very difficult to re-establish any degree of control when the situation warrants or even demands it. This is because market actors might see the attempt to re-establish capital management as abandonment of a liberalized capital account and then might react rather radically to this perceived change. By contrast, if investors understand that a country is maintaining a system of dynamic capital management they will expect management to tighten and loosen over time. It is therefore less likely that investors will over-react if management techniques are tightened.

To sum up, we have shown that the CMTs employed in five developing countries during the 1990's have achieved many important objectives. The achievements of these CMTs therefore warrant close examination by policymakers in developing countries.

APPENDIX

Table 12.A1 Assessment of the CMTs employed during the 1990s

Country	Achievements	Supporting Factors	Costs
Chile	Altered composition and maturity of inflows	Well-designed policies and sound fundamentals	Limited evidence of higher capital costs for SMEs
	Currency stability	Neoliberal economic policy in many domains	
	Reduced vulnerability to contagion	Offered good returns to foreign investors	
		State and administrative capacity	
		Dynamic capital management	
Colombia	Similar to Chile, but less successful in several respects	Less state and administrative capacity than in Chile meant that blunter policies were employed	No evidence available
		Economic reforms in the direction of neoliberalism	

Taiwan POC	Debt burdens and financial fragility are insignificant	High levels of state and administrative capacity	Limited evidence of concentration of lending to large firms, conservatism of banks, inadequate auditing and risk and project assessment capabilities
	Competitive exchange rate and stable currency	Policy independence of the CBC	
	Insulated from financial crises	Dynamic capital management	Large informal financial sector
	Enhanced economic sovereignty		Limited evidence of inadequate liquidity in financial system
Singapore	Insulated from disruptive speculation	Strong state capacity and ability to use moral suasion	Possibly undermined financial sector development
	Protection of soft peg	Strong economic fundamentals	Loss of seignorage
	Financial stability		
Malaysia 1998	Facilitated macroeconomic reflation	Public support for policies	Possibly contributed to cronyism and corruption
	Helped to maintain domestic economic sovereignty	Strong state and administrative capacity	
		Dynamic capital management	

NOTES

This chapter was originally published in Ariel Buira (ed.) (2003), *'Challenges to the World Bank and IMF: Developing Country Perspectives'*, London: Anthem Press.

1.   Grabel (1999, 2003a) proposes 'trip wires and speed bumps' as a framework for dynamic capital management.
2.   Discussion of objectives and costs draws on Chang and Grabel (2004, Chapter 10) and Grabel (2003b); discussion of the means by which CMTs attain their objectives draws on Grabel (2003a).
3.   Epstein, Grabel and Jomo (2003) also include case studies of China and India, omitted here because of space constraints.
4.   This case study draws heavily on Grabel (2003a). Details and assessment of Chilean and Colombian CMTs are drawn from Agosin (1998); Eichengreen (1999); Ffrench-Davis and Reisen (1998); Le Fort and Budnevich (1997); Ocampo (2002); Palma (2000).
5.   Nevertheless Eichengreen (1999) makes it clear that authorities erred in terminating inflows management.
6.   For example, Chile's reserve requirement was adjusted several times because of changes in the volume of capital flows.
7.   Ocampo (2002: 7) points out that the frequency with which authorities changed the rules pertaining to exchange rates in Chile and reserve requirements in Colombia were not without cost, however.
8.   To date, Forbes' (2002) findings have not been challenged in the literature. This, however, is not surprising given that the draft paper only became available in November 2002.
9.   Even Edwards (1999: 77), a prominent critic of CMTs in Chile, shows that they increased the autonomy of monetary policy in the country. However, he argues that the extent of increased autonomy was trivial insofar as the small benefit accruing from increased monetary policy autonomy was outweighed by the increase in capital costs that were associated with the CMTs.
10. Note that CMTs and macroeconomic policy did not succeed in promoting price stability in Colombia (Le Fort and Budnevich 1997).
11. See Chin and Nordhaug (2002) on the extended notion of security in Taiwan POC and, more generally, for a rich discussion of the broader context of its economic and financial policies.
12. The description of CMTs draws heavily on Chin and Nordhaug (2002). Details are also drawn from the EIU (2002) and the US Commercial Service (2002).
13. This discussion draws heavily on Chin and Nordhaug (2002). See this work for an in-depth historical examination of relevant structural considerations.
14. This section draws heavily on MAS (2001, 2002); Errico and Musalem (1999); IMF (1999, 2001); McCauley (2001) and Ishi et al. (2001).
15. See IMF (1999, 2001) for useful surveys of the Singapore economy during this period.
16. Since 1981, monetary policy in Singapore has been centered on exchange rate management. First, the exchange rate is managed against a basket of currencies of Singapore's major trading partners. The composition of the basket is revised periodically to take account of Singapore's trade patterns. Second, the MAS operates a managed float. The trade-weighted exchange rate is allowed to fluctuate within an undisclosed policy band. If the exchange rate moves outside the band, the MAS will step in, buying or selling foreign exchange to steer the exchange rate back within the band. In conducting this policy, the MAS has generally given up control over domestic interest rates in order to maintain its exchange rate within its target band. McCauley (2001) argues that the main target of this policy is inflation.
17. IMF (2001) emphasizes the role of fundamentals and discounts the importance of capital management.
18. This section draws mainly on Jomo (2001); BNM, various years; Kaplan and Rodrik (2002); Rajamaran (2001); Mohamad (2001).

19. In any case, this observation says nothing about the balance of costs and benefits. As economists are fond of pointing out, there are always tradeoffs. Our cases demonstrate that CMTs can have important macroeconomic or prudential benefits. Of course, these benefits must be weighed against the micro costs. But as James Tobin was fond of remarking, 'It takes a lot of Harberger Triangles to fill an Okun Gap'.
20. See Nembhard 1992, for an excellent discussion of these issues.

REFERENCES

Agosin, Manuel and Ricardo Ffrench-Davis (1996), 'Managing Capital Inflows in Latin America', in Mahbub ul Haq et al., (eds) *The Tobin Tax*, New York: Oxford University Press.

Agosin, Manuel R. (1998), 'Capital Inflows and Investment Performance In the 1990s', in Ffrench Davis, et al., *'Capital Flows and Investment Performance: Lessons from Latin America in the 1990's*, America, Santiago: ECLAC.

Ariyoshi, Akira, Karl Habermeier, Bernard Laurens et al. (2000), 'Capital Controls: Country Experiences with their Use and Liberalization,' IMF Occasional Paper No. 190.

Bank Negara Malaysia, (various years), Annual Reports, Kuala Lampur: Bank Negara Malaysia.

Carlson, Mark and Leonardo Hernandez (2002), 'Determinants and Repercussions of the Composition of Capital Inflows', IMF Working Paper No. WP/02/86.

Chang, Ha-Joon and Ilene Grabel (2004), *Reclaiming Development*, London: Zed Press.

Chin, Kok Fay and Kristen Nordhaug (2002), 'Why are there Differences in the Resilience of Malaysia and Taiwan to Financial Crisis?', *European Journal of Development Research*, **14** (1), 77–100.

De Gregorio J., S. Edwards and R. O. Valdes (2000), 'Controls On Capital Inflows: Do they Work?', NBER Working Paper No. 7645.

De Gregorio J. and R. O. Valdes (2000), 'Crisis Transmission: Evidence from the Debt, Tequila and Asian Flu Crises', *World Bank Economic Review*, **15** (2), 289–314.

Dornbusch, R. (2002), 'Malaysia's Crisis: Was it Different?', in Sebastian Edwards and Jeffrey A. Frankel (eds), *Preventing Currency Crises in Emerging Markets*, Chicago: The University of Chicago Press, pp. 441–460.

Economist Intelligence Unit (EIU) (2002), Country Report: Taiwan, www.biz.yahoo.com/ifc/tw/forex.html.

Edwards, S. (1999), 'How effective are capital controls?', *Journal of Economic Perspectives*, **13** (4).

Edwards, S. (2001), 'Capital Mobility and Economic Performance: Are Emerging Economies Different?', NBER Working Paper No. 8076.

Eichengreen Barry (1999), *Toward a New International Financial Architecture*, Washington DC: Institute for International Economics.

Epstein, Gerald, Ilene Grabel and Sundaram Kwame Jomo (2003), 'Capital Management Techniques for Developing Countries in the 1990s: An Assessment of Experiences From the 1990s and Lessons for the Future', G-24, www.g24.org

Errico, Luca and Alberto Musalem (1999), 'Offshore Banking: An Analysis of Micro- and Macro Prudential Issues', IMF Working Paper No. WP/99/5.

Ffrench-Davis, R. and Reisen, H. (eds) (1998) *Capital Flows and Investment Performance*, Paris, UN/ECLAC Development Center of the OECD.

Forbes, Kristin (2002), 'One Cost of the Chilean Capital Controls: Increased Financial Constraints for Small Firms', MIT Sloan School of Management and NBER, unpublished paper, November.

Grabel, Ilene (1999), 'Rejecting Exceptionalism: Reinterpreting the Asian Financial Crises', in J. Michie and J. G. Smith, (eds), *Global Instability: The Political Economy of World Economic Governance*, London: Routledge, pp. 37–67.

Grabel, Ilene (2003a), 'Averting Crisis: Assessing Measures to Manage Financial Integration in Emerging Economies', *Cambridge Journal of Economics*, **27** (3), 317–36.

Grabel, Ilene 2003b), 'International Private Capital Flows and Developing Countries', in Ha-Joon Chang (ed), *Papers from the Cambridge Advanced Program on Rethinking Development Economics*, London: Anthem Press.

Gregorio, Edwards and Valdes (2000), 'Controls on Capital Inflows: Do They Work?', NBER Working Paper No. 7645.

Institute for International Economics (IIE) (1998), *Financial Services Liberalization in the WTO: Taiwan*, Washington, DC, www.iee.com/CATALOG/CaseStudies/DOBSON?dobtaiwa.html.

International Monetary Fund (1999), 'Singapore: Selected Issues', *IMF Country Report* No. 99/35.

International Monetary Fund (2000), *Annual Report on Exchange Arrangements and Exchange Restrictions*, Washington, DC: IMF.

International Monetary Fund (2001), 'Singapore: Selected Issues', *IMF Country Report* No. 01/177.

Ishi, Shogo, Inci Otker-Robe and Li Cui (2001), 'Measures to Limit the Offshore Use of Currencies: Pros and Cons', IMF Working Paper No. WP/01/43.

Johnson, Simon and Todd Mitton, (2003), 'Cronyism and Capital Controls: Evidence from Malaysia', *Journal of Financial Economics*, **67**, 351–382.

Johnston, R. Barry, Mark Swinburne, Alexander Kyei, Bernard Laurens et al. (1999), *Exchange Rate Arrangements and Currency Convertibility: Developments and Issues*, Washington, DC: International Monetary Fund.

Jomo, K. S. (ed) (2001), *Malaysian Eclipse*, London: Zed Press.

Kaplan, E. and Rodrik, D (2002), 'Did the Malaysian Capital Controls Work?', in Sebastian Edwards and Jeffrey A. Frankel (eds), *Preventing Currency Crises in Emerging Markets*, Chicago: The University of Chicago Press, pp. 393–441.

Krugman, P. (1998), 'Open letter to Mr. Mahathir', *Fortune*, September 28.

Le Fort, V.G. and C. Budnevich (1997), 'Capital Account Regulations and Macroeconomic Policy: Two Latin American Experiences', International Monetary and Financial Issues for the 1990s, *Research Papers from the Group of 24*, **VIII**.

Massad, Carlos (1998), 'The Liberalization of the Capital Account: Chile in the 1990s', in 'Should the IMF Pursue Capital-Account Convertibility?', *Princeton Essays in International Finance*, No. 207, pp. 34–46.

McCauley, Robert N. (2001), *Setting Monetary Policy in East Asia: Goals, Developments and Polices*, Basel: Bank for International Settlements.

Mohamad, Mahathir (2001), *The Malaysian Currency Crisis: How and Why it Happened*, Kuala Lumpur: Pelanduk Publications.

Monetary Authority of Singapore (MAS) (2001), 'Singapore's Exchange Rate Policy', February.

Monetary Authority of Singapore, (MAS), (2002), 'Singapore: Policy of Non-internationalization of the S$ and the Asian Dollar Market', paper presented to the BIS/SAFE Seminar on Capital Account Liberalization, September 12–13, Beijing.

Nembhard, J. G. (1996), *Capital Control, Financial Policy and Industrial Policy in South Korea and Brazil*, New York: Praeger Press.

Ocampo, J. A. (2002), 'Capital-account and Counter-cyclical Prudential Regulations in Developing Countries', UNU/WIDER Discussion Paper, August.

Ocampo, J. A. and Camilo Tovar (1998), 'Capital Flows, Savings and Investment in Colombia, 1990–1996', in R. Ffrench-Davis and H. Reisen (eds), *Capital Flows and Investment Performance: Lessons from Latin and America*, Paris and Santiago: OECD Development Center/ECLAC.

Palma, Gabriel (2000), 'The Three Routes to Financial Crises: The Need for Capital Controls', CEPA Working Paper, Series III, No. 18.

Rajamaran, Indira (2001), 'Management of the Capital Account: A study of India and Malaysia', Mimeo, New Delhi: National Institute of Public Finance and Policy, March.

Schneider, Benu (2000), 'Conference Report: Conference on Capital Account Liberalization; A Developing Country Perspective', London: Overseas Development Institute.

Schneider, Benu (2001), 'Issues in Capital Account Convertibility in Developing Countries', *Development Policy Review*, **19** (1), pp. 31-84.

Singh, Ajit (2002), 'Capital Account Liberalization, Free Long-Term Capital Flows, Financial Crises and Economic Development', paper presented to IDEAS Conference, Chennai, India, November 3–5.

US Commercial Service (2002), Taiwan Country Commercial Guide FY2002, Washington,D.C.,
www.usatrade.gov/Website/CCG.nsf/CCGurl/CCGTAIWAN2002-CH-7:-00443.

Valdes-Prieto, S. and Soto, M. (1998), 'The Effectiveness of Capital Controls: Theory and Evidence from Chile', *Empirica*, **25** (2) pp. 133–164.

13. Africa's Debt: Who Owes Whom?

James K. Boyce and Léonce Ndikumana

SUB-SAHARAN AFRICA'S DEBT BURDEN

Sub-Saharan Africa includes 34 of the 42 countries classified as 'Heavily Indebted Poor Countries' by the World Bank. The debt burden forces these countries to divert scarce resources from basic necessities, such as health and education, into debt service. Despite bearing these heavy social costs, African countries cannot keep up with the payments and so they become ever more indebted.

The total debt of sub-Saharan African countries reached a staggering $209 billion in 2001. In that year, the sub-continent borrowed $11.4 billion, but paid $14.5 billion in debt service – $9.8 billion as principal repayment and $4.7 billion as interest. As a result, the region recorded a negative 'net transfer' (new borrowing minus debt service) of –$3.1 billion. This continued a trend of negative net transfers in the previous decade (see Figure 13.1).

In Sub-Saharan Africa (SSA) as a whole, debt service amounted to 3.8 percent of gross domestic product (GDP) in 2000. By comparison, SSA countries spent 2.4 percent of GDP on health care. The World Bank estimates that only 55 percent of the people in SSA have access to clean drinking water, compared to an average of 76 percent for low-income countries worldwide (*World Development Indicators 2002*). Illiteracy rates and infant mortality rates in SSA are among the highest in the world.

The inability of many SSA countries to meet their social needs and escape from debt is, to a large extent, a result of the fact that the borrowed funds have not been used productively. In theory, borrowing decisions are motivated by expectations of positive returns to investment financed by loans and by expectations of higher future income to repay loans that financed consumption. In the case of most African countries, however, it appears that past borrowing was not justified by either the investment motive or the consumption-smoothing rationale. Where, then, did the borrowed money go?

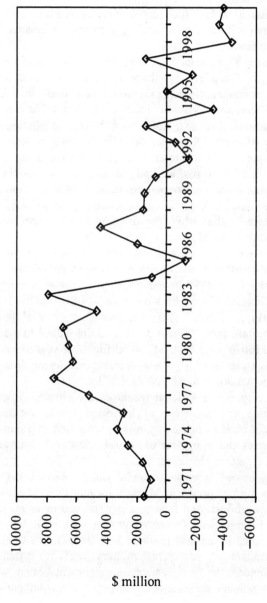

$ million

Source: Authors' computations using data from World Bank (2002), *Global Development Finance.*

Figure 13.1 Total net transfers on debt for 41 SSA countries, 1971–2000 (million $)

DEBT AND CAPITAL FLIGHT: AFRICA'S REVOLVING DOOR

Instead of financing domestic investment or consumption, a substantial fraction of the borrowed funds was captured by African political elites and channeled abroad in the form of capital flight. Through this 'revolving door', public external debts (contracted via borrowing by African governments or by private firms with government guarantees) were transformed into private external assets.

Estimates of capital flight from SSA indicate that the sub-continent has experienced a dramatic financial hemorrhage over the past three decades. In a study of 30 SSA countries, we estimate total capital flight for the period 1970–1996 to have been about $187 billion in 1996 dollars (Ndikumana and Boyce 2003; see also Boyce and Ndikumana 2001). Including interest earnings, the stock of capital flight for the sample stood at $274 billion, equivalent to 145 percent of the total debt owed by the same group of countries in 1996. In other words, we find that SSA is a net creditor to the rest of the world in the sense that external assets, as measured by the stock of capital flight, exceed external liabilities, as measured by the stock of external debt. The difference is that while the assets are in private hands, the liabilities are the public debts of African governments.

Statistical evidence reveals that external borrowing was the single most important determinant of both the timing and magnitude of capital flight from SSA. Over the 1970–1996 period, roughly 80 cents on every dollar borrowed by SSA countries flowed back out as capital flight in the same year (Ndikumana and Boyce 2003). This suggests that external borrowing directly financed capital flight. Moreover, every dollar added to a country's total debt generated roughly 3.5 cents of capital flight per year in subsequent years, suggesting that capital flight was also a response to the deteriorating economic environment associated with rising debt burdens.

The mechanisms by which national resources are channeled abroad as capital flight include embezzlement of borrowed funds, kickbacks on government contracts, trade misinvoicing, misappropriation of revenues from state-owned enterprises and smuggling of natural resources. Countries with rich endowments of natural resources, especially when headed by corrupt regimes, have experienced large-scale capital flight. During his 32-year reign in the Congo, former president Mobutu accumulated massive wealth through the diversion of borrowed funds, foreign aid and revenues from the state-owned mineral companies (Ndikumana and Boyce 1998). His personal assets reportedly peaked in the mid-1980s at $4 billion (Burns et al. 1997). In Nigeria, the leaders of successive military regimes systematically embezzled oil revenues for their personal enrichment, often with the complicity of multinational corporations. In April 2002, an out-of-court settlement in Switzerland ordered the return to Nigeria of more than $1 billion in frozen assets of former dictator Sani Abacha and his family (*International Herald Tribune* 2002). A recent IMF investigation reveals that in the past five years, up to $4 billion is unaccounted for in government finances in Angola (Pearce 2002).

Responsibility for the diversion of borrowed funds falls not only on past African governments, but also on their creditors, including private bankers as well as bilateral and multilateral institutions. Knowingly or unknowingly, these creditors financed the accumulation of private assets with their loans. In many cases, creditors continued to pour loans into the hands of corrupt regimes, despite ample evidence that these funds were not being used for legitimate purposes. Sound banking practice would have dictated a moratorium on lending to such governments. Failure to halt lending suggests either that creditors were shielded from losses or that they were pursuing other objectives. On the one hand, private lenders were shielded from risk by guarantees provided by governments and international institutions. All too often, these guarantees encouraged irresponsible lending. On the other hand, official creditors continued to lend to client regimes for political and strategic reasons. The Mobutu regime and the military regimes in Nigeria are examples of instances where lending supported dictatorships in the region.

WHAT IS TO BE DONE?

African countries must not only overcome the debt payment crisis, but also design strategies to prevent borrowed funds from being squandered in the future.

Since the early 1980s, a series of strategies have been proposed to alleviate the external debt burden in developing countries. Traditional mechanisms of rescheduling debt payments have failed, as these only amount to postponing the debt burden and actually result in an increase in future debt stocks. The debt forgiveness initiatives that were initiated in 1988 at the G-7 meetings in Toronto, which provided for various arrangements aimed at reducing the present value of debt outstanding, also failed to resolve the debt problem. The external position of African countries continued to deteriorate as indicated by the decline in net transfers on debt depicted in Figure 13.1. The Highly-Indebted Poor Countries (HIPC) debt-relief initiative launched in 1996 by the World Bank and other donors is a step in the right direction, in that it provides for larger reductions in the present value of debt. Yet, this strategy too has proven to be insufficient for reducing the debt burden, due to the slow pace of delivery of relief by donors and the slow progress of debtor countries in meeting the often-stringent conditions for qualification. The volume of debt relief remains low compared to total liabilities of African countries and their development needs.

One effective strategy for ending the debt crisis in African countries would be the complete cancellation of all debts. This would release resources now drained by debt service for reallocation to socially productive investment programs. While debt cancellation has been advocated by a number of non-governmental organizations, it seems unlikely to happen in the foreseeable future. Creditors are unwilling to set a precedent for across-the-board write-offs and SSA governments are unwilling to risk the reprisals that might follow from outright repudiation of debt. Moreover, even if the debt slate could be wiped clean at a single stroke and lending were then to resume, in the absence of systematic changes in the practices of borrowers and lenders this would simply clear the way for another spin of the revolving door, setting the stage for a new debt crisis in years to come.

An alternative strategy is for African countries to selectively repudiate past loans, invoking the doctrine of 'odious debt' in international law as well as historical precedents. At the end of the 19th century, the US government repudiated the external debt owed by Cuba after seizing the island in the Spanish-American war. The US authorities did this on the grounds that Cuba's debt had not been incurred for the benefit of the Cuban people, that it had been contracted without their consent and that the loans had helped to finance their oppression by the Spanish colonial government. For similar reasons, much of the debt of SSA can today be termed 'odious'. Well-functioning credit markets require that creditors bear the consequences of imprudent lending. The notion that creditors should always be repaid, regardless of how and to whom they lend, is indefensible. The logic of sound banking suggests that current and future African governments should accept liability for only those portions of public debts incurred by past regimes that were used to finance *bona fide* domestic investment or public consumption. By invoking the doctrine of odious debt, they could selectively repudiate liability for those portions of the debt for which no such uses can be demonstrated.

Application of this strategy of selective repudiation faces two potential practical problems. The first problem is to determine who should bear the burden of proof in identifying which portions of past debts are 'odious'. The second is the risk of credit rationing against African countries that choose to repudiate debt, even if they do so selectively. Given the evidence of widespread capital flight fueled by external borrowing, African governments can insist that creditors have the responsibility of establishing that their loans were used for *bona fide* purposes. Following this logic, SSA governments could inform their creditors that outstanding debts will be treated as legitimate if, and only if, the real counterparts of the borrowing can be identified. If the creditors can document where the money went and show that it benefited the citizens of the borrowing country via investment or consumption, then the debt will be accepted as a *bona fide* external obligation of the government. If, however, the fate of the borrowed money cannot be traced, then the present African governments must infer that it was diverted into private pockets and quite possibly into capital flight. In such cases, the liability for the debt should lie not with the government, but with the private individuals whose personal fortunes are the real counterpart of the debt.

Some may worry that even selective repudiation is risky, because 'Africa can ill afford to incur the wrath of the hand that feeds it' (Donnelly 2002). But the question today is: Whose hand is feeding whom? In recent years, resources flowed from Africa to Western countries, rather than the reverse, as indicated by the negative net transfers and massive capital flight. Africa has been 'feeding' its creditors. In the short run, the savings from halting service payments on odious debts therefore are likely to outweigh any losses from credit rationing. And in the long run, selective debt repudiation will benefit lenders as well as African countries. By inducing more responsible lending practices, the threat of selective repudiation ultimately will result in fewer losses due to default and greater efficiency in the allocation of resources by the international financial system. Indeed, if lenders apply stricter criteria with respect to the uses to which their loans are put, this will be a desirable change from the standpoint of most citizens in the borrower countries. Whatever the short-run costs of selective repudiation, it is a win-win solution for both lenders and borrowers in the long run.

In addition to greater accountability on the creditor side, it is equally important that debtor countries establish mechanisms of transparency and accountability in their own decision-making processes with regard to foreign borrowing and the management of borrowed funds. In the absence of debt cancellation or repudiation, the burden of debt repayment ultimately lies with the population of the debtor countries. It is appropriate, therefore, to require debtor governments to provide full information to the public as well as to their creditors and to ensure public representation in the management of public debt. In future years, greater accountability on the part of both borrowers and creditors will be needed to prevent repeated cycles of external borrowing, capital flight and financial distress.

NOTES

This paper was first published in German under the title, 'Afrika: Schuldenlast und Schuldenlust', in *Der Uberblick* (March 2003).

REFERENCES

Boyce, James K. (1992), 'The revolving door? External debt and capital flight: A Philippine case study', *World Development*, **20** (3), 335–345.

Boyce, James K. and Léonce Ndikumana (2001), 'Is Africa a net creditor? New estimates of capital flight from severely indebted Sub-Saharan African countries, 1970–1996', *Journal of Development Studies*, **38** (2), 27–56.

Burns, Jimmy, Michael Homan and Mark Huband (1997), 'How Mobutu built up to $4 billion fortune: Zaire's dictator plundered IMF loans', *Financial Times*, 12 May 1997, p. 1.

Donnelly, John (2002), 'A bold proposal for poor African nations: Forget the debt', *Boston Globe*, 4 August 2002, p. D1.

International Herald Tribune (2002), 'Ex-dicator's family to pay back Nigeria', 18 April 2002, p. 3.

Ndikumana, Léonce and James K. Boyce (1998), 'Congo's odious debt: External borrowing and capital flight in Zaire', *Development and Change*, **29** (2), 195–217.

Ndikumana, Léonce and James K. Boyce (2003), 'Public debts and private assets: explaining capital flight from sub-Saharan African Countries', *World Development*, **31** (1), 107–130.

Pearce, Justin (2002), 'Angola's 'missing millions',' BBC News, 18 October 2002.

World Bank (2002), *Global Development Finance*, CDROM edition.

World Bank (2002), *World Development Indicators*, CDROM edition.

Index